Quantitative Studies in Green and Conservation Criminology

AF766424

During the early development and throughout the short history of green/conservation criminology, limited attention has been directed toward quantitative analyses of relevant environmental crime, law, and justice concerns. While recognizing the importance of establishing a theory and terminology in the early stages of development, this book redresses this imbalance. The work features contributions that undertake empirical quantitative studies of green/conservation crime and justice issues by both conservation and green criminologists. The collection highlights the shared concerns of these groups within important forms of ecological crime and victimization, and illustrates the ways in which these approaches can be undertaken quantitatively. It includes quantitative conservation/green criminological studies that represent the work of well-established scholars in these fields along with studies by scholars whose works are less well-known but who are also contributing to shaping this area of research.

The book presents a valuable contribution to the areas of Green and Conservation Criminology. It will appeal to academics and students working in these areas.

Michael J. Lynch is a Professor in the Department of Criminology, University of South Florida. He has examined green crime, law, and justice issues for over 30 years, and he published the first discussion of green criminology. His recent publications have appeared in *Capitalism, Nature, Socialism; Ecological Economics; Global Ecology and Conservation; Society and Natural Resources; Journal of Quantitative Criminology; Theoretical Criminology; Deviant Behavior*; and *Sociological Spectrum*, among others. He is recipient of Lifetime Achievement Awards from the American Society of Criminology Division on Critical Criminology & Social Justice, and the Division on White Collar and Corporate Crime.

Stephen F. Pires, Ph.D., is an Associate Professor in the Department of Criminology and Criminal Justice at Florida International University. He is an expert on the illegal wildlife trade with a particular focus on commonly poached species (i.e., hot products), illicit markets, and the organization of the illegal trade. His work has appeared in the *Journal of Research in Crime & Delinquency, British Journal of Criminology, Bird Conservational International*, and *Forest Policy & Economics*, and he has co-authored the book *Wildlife Crime: An Environmental Criminology and Crime Science Perspective* (2018).

Green Criminology

Series Editors: Michael J. Lynch
University of South Florida, USA
and
Paul B. Stretesky
University of Northumbria, UK

Now two decades old, green criminology – the study of environmental harm, crime, law, regulation, victimization, and justice – has increasing relevance to contemporary problems at local, national, and international levels. This series comes at a time when societies and governments worldwide seek new ways to alleviate and deal with the consequences of various environmental harms as they relate to humans, non-human animals, plant species, and the ecosystem and its components. Green criminology offers a unique theoretical perspective on how human behavior causes and exacerbates environmental conditions that threaten the planet's viability. Volumes in the series consider such topics and controversies as corporate environmental crime, the complicity of international financial institutions, state-sponsored environmental destruction, and the role of non-governmental organizations in addressing environmental harms. Titles also examine the intersections between green criminology and other branches of criminology and other areas of law, such as human rights and national security. The series is international in scope, investigating environmental crime in specific countries as well as comparatively and globally. In sum, by bringing together a diverse body of research on all aspects of this subject, the series makes a significant contribution to our understanding of the dynamics between the natural world and the quite imperfect human world, and sets the stage for the future study in this growing area of concern.

Other titles in this series

The Crimes of Wildlife Trafficking
Issues of Justice, Legality and Morality
Ragnhild Aslaug Sollund

Quantitative Studies in Green and Conservation Criminology
The Measurement of Environmental Harm and Crime
Edited by Michael J. Lynch and Stephen F. Pires

For more information about this series, please visit: www.routledge.com/Green-Criminology/book-series/GREENCRIM

Quantitative Studies in Green and Conservation Criminology

The Measurement of Environmental Harm and Crime

Edited by Michael J. Lynch and Stephen F. Pires

Routledge
Taylor & Francis Group
LONDON AND NEW YORK

First published 2019
by Routledge
2 Park Square, Milton Park, Abingdon, Oxon OX14 4RN

and by Routledge
605 Third Avenue, New York, NY 10017

First issued in paperback 2020

Routledge is an imprint of the Taylor & Francis Group, an informa business

© 2020 selection and editorial matter, Michael J. Lynch and Stephen F. Pires; individual chapters, the contributors

The right of Michael J. Lynch and Stephen F. Pires to be identified as the authors of the editorial material, and of the authors for their individual chapters, has been asserted in accordance with sections 77 and 78 of the Copyright, Designs and Patents Act 1988.

All rights reserved. No part of this book may be reprinted or reproduced or utilised in any form or by any electronic, mechanical, or other means, now known or hereafter invented, including photocopying and recording, or in any information storage or retrieval system, without permission in writing from the publishers.

Trademark notice: Product or corporate names may be trademarks or registered trademarks, and are used only for identification and explanation without intent to infringe.

British Library Cataloguing-in-Publication Data
A catalogue record for this book is available from the British Library

Library of Congress Cataloging-in-Publication Data
Names: Lynch, Michael J., editor. | Pires, Stephen F., editor.
Title: Quantitative studies in green and conservation criminology : the measurement of environmental harm and crime / Michael J Lynch and Stephen Pires.
Description: Abingdon, Oxon ; New York, NY : Routledge, 2020. | Series: Green criminology | Includes bibliographical references and index.
Identifiers: LCCN 2019007291 | ISBN 9781138319424 (hardback) | ISBN 9780429453946 (ebook)
Subjects: LCSH: Offenses against the environment.
Classification: LCC HV6401 .Q36 2020 | DDC 364.1/45—dc23
LC record available at https://lccn.loc.gov/2019007291

ISBN 13: 978-0-367-72712-3 (pbk)
ISBN 13: 978-1-138-31942-4 (hbk)
ISBN 13: 978-0-429-45394-6 (ebk)

Typeset in Galliard
by Apex CoVantage, LLC

Contents

Contributors

Daniela Andreatta is a Ph.D. candidate in Criminology at Università Cattolica del Sacro Cuore in Milan (Italy) and researcher at eCrime-ICT Law & Criminology Research Group at the Faculty of Law of the University of Trento (Italy). Her research interests focus on environmental crime (especially illegal waste management), organized crime, and crime spatial analysis. As junior researcher at Transcrime–Joint Research Centre on Trasnational Crime of Università Cattolica (2015–2018), she contributed to research projects on these topics, such as "Blockwaste – Blocking the loopholes for illicit waste trafficking" and "MORE – Mapping the risk of serious and organised crime infiltration in European businesses."

Kimberly L. Barrett is an Associate Professor in the Department of Sociology, Anthropology and Criminology, Eastern Michigan University. Her research interests include green criminology, environmental crime and justice, and corporate crime.

Kwan-Lamar Blount-Hill, J.D., is a doctoral candidate in criminal justice at the City University of New York (CUNY) Graduate Center/John Jay College of Criminal Justice. He is also currently a research manager for the New York City Mayor's Office of Criminal Justice (MOCJ). He received his Juris Doctor from Emory University, where he concentrated his legal studies on environmental law and regulation, and his Bachelor of Science in Natural Resource Management from Tuskegee University, focusing on water management. His current research includes environmental justice and the application of sociological theory to natural resource management.

Rachel Boratto is a doctoral student in the School of Criminal Justice at Michigan State University. She holds an M.Sc. from University College Dublin, Ireland in Natural World Heritage Management and a B.Sc. in Biological Sciences and Zoology from the University of Guelph, Canada. Her research interests include anti-poaching strategies, illegal wildlife trade, and transnational environmental crime. Rachel has collaborated directly with governmental and non-profit organizations on numerous interdisciplinary wildlife trade research projects.

Leo J. Genco is a doctoral candidate at the University of South Florida. His research focuses on structural factors associated with a wide range of animal cruelty such as animal abuse and wildlife crime, typologies of animal abusers, structural explanations of court convictions of animal abusers, and wildlife trade. Genco is also assistant managing editor for Justice Quarterly, and past managing editor of The Journal of Crime and Justice.

Liam Downs is an undergraduate student in both the Sociology and Criminology & Law Department, and the Psychology Department at the University of Florida.

Meredith Gore is an Associate Professor in the Department of Fisheries & Wildlife at Michigan State University and a National Academies of Sciences Jefferson Science Fellow with the US Department of State. She is a conservation social scientist with expertise in levering principles of risk to understand human-environment relationships. She has published over 70 journal articles and reports on this topic in journals such as *Conservation Letters, PLoS ONE*, and *British Journal of Criminology*. She edited *Conservation Criminology*, the first book exploring disciplinary convergence between criminology, conservation, and decision science.

Melissa Jarrell is currently Professor of Criminal Justice and Dean of University College at Texas A&M University–Corpus Christi. She earned a B.A. in Anthropology from Eckerd College and an M.A. and Ph.D. in Criminology from the University of South Florida. Her research interests include green criminology, environmental justice, and white collar/corporate crime, and she has published in such journals as *Crime, Law and Social Change; Environmental Politics*; and *Environmental Justice*. She works with local communities to address issues of poverty, pollution, and injustice.

Jessica S. Kahler is an Assistant Professor in the Department of Sociology and Criminology & Law at the University of Florida. Her research focuses on community-based wildlife crime prevention, human-wildlife conflicts, the application of situational crime prevention to wildlife crime, and wildlife guardianship. She has conducted applied conservation criminology research and consulting on wildlife crimes such as poaching, and has facilitated trainings related to wildlife crime prevention in Cambodia, Cameroon, Indonesia, Madagascar, and Namibia. Her research has been published in *Biological Conservation, Conservation Biology, Human Dimensions of Wildlife, International Journal of Comparative and Applied Criminal Justice*, and *PLoS ONE*.

Justin Kurland is a Senior Lecturer in Security and Crime Science at the University of Waikato. He received his bachelor's degree from Rutgers University, his masters from Boston University, and his Ph.D. from University College London (UCL). He is interested in the spatiotemporal analysis of crime in and around large-scale sport and event venues, crowd control, wildlife and conservation crimes, and how methods from other disciplines can inform our understanding of crime and security issues as well as prevention.

Michael A. Long is an Associate Professor of Sociology at Oklahoma State University. His research focuses on green criminology, environmental sociology, political economy, food insecurity, and quantitative research methods. He has co-authored three books and over 60 journal articles and book chapters. Some of his recent research has appeared in *Capitalism, Nature, Socialism; Ecological Economics; European Journal of Criminology; Local Environment; Risk Analysis; Society and Natural Resources; Theoretical Criminology*; and *ANNALS of the American Academy of Political and Social Science.*

Michael J. Lynch is a Professor in the Department of Criminology, University of South Florida. He has examined green crime, law, and justice issues for over 30 years, and he published the first discussion of green criminology. His recent publications have appeared in *Capitalism, Nature, Socialism; Ecological Economics; Global Ecology and Conservation; Society and Natural Resources; Journal of Quantitative Criminology; Theoretical Criminology; Deviant Behavior*; and *Sociological Spectrum*, among others. He is recipient of Lifetime Achievement Awards from the American Society of Criminology's Division on Critical Criminology & Social Justice, and the Division on White Collar and Corporate Crime.

Mangai Natarajan, Ph.D., is a Professor in the Department of Criminal Justice at John Jay College of Criminal Justice. She is an active policy-oriented researcher with wider academic interests around crime theories that promote crime reduction and problem solving. Her research with Ronald V. Clarke and Kevin Chetty was published in 2014, titled "Eyes on the Forest: CCTV and Ecotourism in Indian Tiger Reserves," in Andrew M. Lemieux's (Ed.) *Understanding and Preventing Poaching: An International Perspective* (London: Routledge). In addition, she is currently working on a research project on human-elephant conflict in India.

Joshua Ozymy is Professor of Political Science and Director of the University Honors Program at Texas A&M University–Corpus Christi. His primary research agenda focuses on the institutional dynamics of why environmental policies fail to meet intended policy goals in the United States and subsequently, the health and policy effects of those failures. His research has appeared in such journals as *Environmental Politics, Global Environmental Politics, Review of Policy Research*, and *Political Behavior.* He received his Ph.D. in Political Science from Texas Tech University.

Gohar A. Petrossian is Assistant Professor at John Jay College of Criminal Justice, Department of Criminal Justice. Her research focuses on applying environmental criminology theories to study crimes against wildlife, with a particular focus on illegal fishing. She is the author of the book *The Last Fish*

Swimming: The Global Crime of Illegal Fishing (Global Crime and Justice Series, ABC-CLIO, LLC, Praeger Imprint), which is due to be published in May 2019. She holds a Master's Degree in Criminal Justice from John Jay College and a Doctorate in Criminal Justice from Rutgers University–Newark, School of Criminal Justice.

Stephen F. Pires, Ph.D., is an Associate Professor in the Department of Criminology and Criminal Justice at Florida International University. He is an expert on the illegal wildlife trade with a particular focus on commonly poached species (i.e., hot products), illicit markets, and the organization of the illegal trade. His work has appeared in the *Journal of Research in Crime & Delinquency, British Journal of Criminology, Bird Conservational International*, and *Forest Policy & Economics*, and he has co-authored the book *Wildlife Crime: An Environmental Criminology and Crime Science Perspective* (2018).

Tameka Samuels-Jones is a doctoral candidate and Instructor in the Department of Sociology and Criminology & Law at the University of Florida. Her research interests include environmental crime, regulatory law, and state-corporate crime. She is currently conducting research on the role of legal pluralism on environmental compliance among local and indigenous groups. Tameka is a founding member of the University of Florida's Environmental Crime & Justice Working Group and has published in *Environmental Sociology* and *Social Sciences Quarterly*. Tameka is the recipient of the American Society of Criminology's 2018 Ruth D. Peterson Fellowship for Racial & Ethnic Diversity.

Monique Sosnowski is a doctoral student at the John Jay College of Criminal Justice in New York. She specializes in global wildlife conservation and wildlife crime, with particular interests in illegal wildlife trade, poaching, and security. She holds an MSc in Global Wildlife Health and Conservation from the University of Bristol.

Paul B. Stretesky is Professor of Criminology and Research Lead, Department of Social Sciences, Northumbria University, Senior Fellow of the UK Higher Education Academy, and Member of the ESRC and NERC Peer Review Colleges. His research has three major emphases: (1) environmental injustice, the unequal distribution of environmental burdens and benefits, the unequal enforcement of environmental laws, policies, and regulations; (2) natural resource–related development; (3) food justice; and (4) the impact of social and economic inequality on crime rates. His recent publications appear in *Global Ecology and Conservation, Ecological Economics, European Journal of Criminology*, and *Society and Natural Resources*.

Ryan Thomson is a doctoral candidate and Research Fellow in the Department of Sociology and Criminology & Law at the University of Florida. His research focuses on environmental injustice with an emphasis on GIS, social network analysis, and community mobilization. Ryan is a founding member of the University of Florida's Environmental Crime & Justice Working Group and has published in *Social Sciences Quarterly* and *Environmental Sociology*. Ryan is the board chair of NC Warn, a member of the Gullah-Geechee Think Tank, and an active organizer with the Civic Media Center.

Daan P. van Uhm is Assistant Professor in Criminology at Utrecht University. He conducted research on various forms of environmental crime such as illegal wildlife trafficking, deforestation, illegal mining, and the illegal trade in dogs. He attained his Ph.D. in Criminology in 2016 (*The Illegal Wildlife Trade*, Springer). In 2018 he received the prestigious Veni-grant of the Dutch Organisation for Scientific Research for his research project: "The Diversification of Organized Crime into the Illegal Trade in Natural Resources." He primarily focuses on research in the context of green crimes and harms.

Liliana Vanegas is a Forestry Engineer with a Master's Degree in Sustainable Development, Biodiversity and Land Management from Paris Saclay University. She is interested in researching processes related to the generation of sustainable strategies for adaptive wildlife management, and the impact of bushmeat on the food security of communities that rely on forest resources for their subsistence. After working in Colombia, Guyana, Peru, Brazil, and Gabon in the sustainable management of hunting at different scales of urbanism, she is now working in the reduction of urban bushmeat demand as the WCS Project Leader of the Urban Bushmeat Project in Pointe Noire, Republic of Congo.

Michelle Wieland is a former Fulbright fellow with a Ph.D. in Conservation Biology, minoring in Development and Social Change in the University of Minnesota's MacArthur Program. She has been a conservation practitioner in Africa working on the human-conservation interface for the past 20 years. For the past 5 years she has focused on tackling systemic challenges that transcend individual protected areas of Central Africa. This includes capacity building of field staff on monitoring/evaluation, governance, and theories of change; mining in and around protected areas; and the bushmeat trade, which is emptying the forests of the region and leaving rural families protein-deficient. As WCS-Africa's socioeconomic advisor, she is working towards better political engagement, behavior change, and rural livelihood diversification approaches to address intractable problems in African conservation.

Lauren Wilson is a doctoral student at the Rutgers School of Criminal Justice and a Research Associate at the Center for Conservation Criminology and Ecology. Her previous work includes sustainable population management with the Association of Zoos and Aquariums, molecular genetics research for her Master of Science in Environmental Science and Policy from George Mason University, and ecological monitoring.

Foreword

This book, edited by Michael J. Lynch and Stephen F. Pires, is unusual although it is based on the familiar premise that, in seeking to influence some new or foreign group, one must use the language customarily used by that group. As the grandson (on my mother's side) of Christian missionaries in East Africa, this premise seems to me obvious and indeed common sense. How else could missionaries communicate their religious views?

While not a work of theology, this book is also bent on conversion. It seeks to broaden the focus and scope of the discipline of criminology through communicating the lessons of green and conservation criminology. The editors recognize that if they are to succeed in this objective, then they must employ the predominantly quantitative/empirical discourse of criminology. As they say, green and conservation criminology "cannot fully develop and be more broadly integrated into the quantitatively oriented field of criminology without quantitative studies."

This may be common sense, but why is the book unusual? One reason is that while the editors describe themselves as green/conservation criminologists, their backgrounds are quite different. Michael J. Lynch's intellectual origins are in radical-Marxist criminology, while Stephen F. Pires is more rooted in mainstream criminology. Individuals from these two different backgrounds would normally view each other with suspicion, if not hostility. However, it is clear from their introductory chapter that whatever their differences of approach, they have put these aside in pursuit of their shared ambition to influence the parent discipline. (Incidentally, their introduction does not describe, though this would have made interesting reading, how two such different criminologists from two different universities came to collaborate.) Michael J. Lynch, in particular, seems to have been influenced by the failure of radical-Marxist criminologists from the late 1960s through the early 1980s to change criminological orthodoxy. He thinks this was because Marxist scholars did not seek change by undertaking empirical/quantitative studies that would be appreciated by mainstream criminology – a mistake that green/conservation criminologists must not repeat.

Unlike missionaries, intellectuals often conceal their imperial ambitions for fear of alienating those they seek to convert. Lynch and Pires have no such inhibitions. While willing to communicate with mainstream criminology in the latter's preferred language, they make no secret of their ultimate ambition to change, and in their view enlarge the vision of mainstream criminologists by making them aware of the findings of green/conservation criminology. Given that mainstream criminology is much larger and of much higher status than green/ conservation criminology, this runs the risk of rejection – "Who do these green/conservation criminologists think they are?" – and it constitutes a second reason that makes this book unusual.

A third reason is that the empirical chapters it collects are diverse and original and constitute a credible down payment on the editors' promise of bringing new insights to criminology. While all the chapters are interesting, several deal with subjects that are rarely, if ever, addressed in the parent discipline, at least not in its core journals. Not surprisingly, a number of these are drawn from the rapidly expanding field of wildlife crimes, including the part played by hunting for bushmeat and the pet trade in the worldwide decline of primates; the illegal trafficking of bushmeat in the Republic of Congo; the relationship between the decline of mammalian species and increased human activity and water scarcity; similarities in wildlife contraband seizures in the US and the EU; and wildlife killings by the US Fish and Wildlife Service. Two empirical chapters on hazardous waste violations in the United States and in Italy provide examples from a completely different category of environmental crimes.

Even if, as Aristotle cautions, "one swallow doth not a summer make," the empirical contributions made by this one book do support the editors' claim that the findings of green/conservation criminology could materially enrich the parent discipline. For this reason alone, the book will be of interest to all criminologists.

Ronald V. Clarke
Rutgers School of Criminal Justice
December 2018

1 Introduction to quantitative and empirical studies in green and conservation criminology

Michael J. Lynch and Stephen F. Pires

This book contains examples of quantitative/empirical studies useful for further development of green and conservation criminology. Here, we shall use the abbreviation GCC to refer to green/conservation criminology. There are two issues we need to address before elaborating on the subject of this book further.

The first issue is: *why an edited book specifically addressing quantitative and empirical studies in GCC*? We provide some extensive discussion of these reasons below. For now, however, it is important to note that *any* field of research which hopes to advance and to generate useful (i.e., applicable, policy relevant) knowledge requires the collection and analysis of data. Researchers often pose hypotheses about the relationship between things or what philosophers call "stuff" in the world around them. These hypotheses and explanations may be simple or elaborate. To know whether those hypotheses make sense and are useful, data that allows those hypotheses to be tested are required. Useful hypotheses – those that are not rejected by data – can then be employed to construct theories that help explain the world around us.

Historically, this view is linked to the emergence of what are now called the British Empiricists, who extended the perspective taken by Sir Francis Bacon, the father of empiricism, in the late 1500s and early 1600s. This view is based on collecting and observing data through the use of inductive reasoning, which later was more specifically broadened into the scientific method.

In short, then, empirical studies are useful because they add to the GCC knowledge base by testing relevant GCC hypotheses through an exploration of interesting and important research questions. The ability to address research questions empirically also provides the kind of information and knowledge that can be useful to policy makers interested in constraining green harms and injustice. For example, Petrossian, Marteache, and Viollaz (2015) examined factors associated with unloading illegal, unreported, and unregulated (IUU) fishing vessel catches. One of their findings was that IUU vessels were more likely to visit large ports with high volumes of vessel traffic. They suggest that by doing so, IUU vessels may be better able to conceal their illegal activity. This finding suggests that improving inspection protocols at those kinds of ports could reduce IUU fishing activities.

Second, some might object to the fact that we appear to use the terms quantitative and empirical interchangeably. To be sure, in some cases this is true to the extent that empirical data – that is information that is collected about the world in specific ways that allow those observations to be analyzed – and quantitative analysis can be the same thing. That is, you cannot have a quantitative analysis without first having empirical data. Empirical data, of course, need not be quantitative alone, and some forms of empirical data can be subject to certain types of qualitative analysis. In short, in using these terms, what we are referring to are studies that offer observations about the world around us based upon the purposeful, methodologically sound (i.e., scientific) collection of data. This approach excludes, therefore, general discussions about concepts such as harm, which are certainly important to defining the boundaries of GCC but which are, as a result of the absence of data, subjective and continually open for debate.

Empirical research and perceptions/evaluations by others

It has also been argued that empirical research by conservation and green criminologists is important for enhancing the perception of GCC by traditional criminologists. This argument suggests that by engaging in empirical and quantitative research, GCC demonstrates a willingness to engage with mainstream criminology (Lynch et al., 2017a). This is, in our view, no small issue. It can be argued that within criminology, several important areas of research have been marginalized because those research areas tend to emphasize descriptive analyses, while the majority of the criminological literature is empirical in orientation (see below for further discussion). GCC research focuses on one of the most important concerns in the contemporary period – *ecological harms* – and how those harms impact ecological stability and, some would argue, the survival of different species. In our view, given the importance of ecologically related research, it is unfortunate that GCC should be overlooked within criminology due to a lack of empirical research. Moreover, this is a situation that can, as the chapters in this book illustrate, be addressed and remedied. With those observations in mind, the empirical studies in this book serve as important examples of the kinds of empirical work criminologists in this field can pursue to expand criminological knowledge concerning environmental issues and problems, enhance the policy relevance of GCC, and perhaps promote greater attention to this area of research and greater acceptance of this work within (as well as outside of) criminology.

In taking that position, it is not our intention to imply that the existing GCC literature suffers from any particular kinds of flaws other than a deficiency in the volume of empirically oriented research. More specifically, it is within the green criminology literature in particular where this empirically oriented deficiency is the greatest, and our observations about empirical research apply less so to the conservation criminology literature.

Intersections of green *and* conservation criminology

As editors of this collection, each of us has been more closely associated with one of the two forms of criminology addressed here. Sometimes, it seems, conservation and green criminologists travel in different circles, and there is often not significant overlap between these views even though they address the same set of issues, and researchers from both approaches are committed to exposing, researching, and addressing the significant ecological problems of our times from a criminological perspective. To be sure, there are some theoretical differences between conservation and green criminology, and as noted, conservation criminologists are much more likely to engage in empirical research than green criminologists. Despite those differences, however, and in the spirit of promoting enhanced collaboration between these approaches, we offer the chapters in this volume as an example of how both approaches can address environmental crime and justice concerns, and how a collaboration between green and conservation criminologists can promote studies focused on ecological issues.

As background for this collection, in the following sections, we build upon the comments made above. We begin with some background information concerning GCC that addresses the use of empirical and qualitative data. The sections that follow examine the use of quantitative data in general terms, obstacles to generalization, and the extent to which various kinds of data are generalizable. This is followed by a discussion of the extent to which empirical data is employed in the social sciences, conservation sciences, within criminology and within GCC. That discussion illustrates that the literature in each of these fields relies heavily on empirical data, and that in conservation science there has been growing awareness of the need for additional empirical research. We then discuss some limitations that might be associated with the neglect of empirical research by green/conservation criminologists. The chapter ends with some discussion of the chapters found in this collection.

Generating "knowledge": the general state of green criminology's methods

As Lynch et al. (2017a) have argued, the vast majority of *criminological research – approximately 90%* – is empirical. However, when examining the GCC literature, a much smaller percentage of studies are empirical in nature (see Chapter 3). For example, about half of all criminology and criminal justice peer-reviewed journal articles on the topic of wildlife crime – a branch of GCC – have been empirically driven, and only one-fifth are quantitatively focused (McFann and Pires, 2019). Within the green criminological literature, at most 10% of the published research is empirical (Lynch et al., 2017a). From these facts, one might conclude that GCC, like some critical criminological approaches, harbors an anti-empirical bias. We do not believe that such conclusions are warranted about GCC. Rather, we suggest that as in any newer field of research, a great deal of attention has been paid to defining the scope of this area of research and its key terms, and to identifying the various types of behaviors that can be considered or counted as environmental, green, or conservation crimes. It is, however, we suggest, time to move a larger portion of GCC research beyond these kinds of questions as they cannot make up the bulk of the GCC literature.

Certainly, studies that identify the core subject matter of GCC are necessary and relevant, and no area of research can develop if there are inconsistent definitions of relevant concepts and disagreements about the scope of that area of research. After all, what we wish to avoid is a situation such as the one that surrounds research on white collar crime, where a definitional quandary concerning that areas' core concept can still be said to exist after nearly 80 years of study (Podgor and Dervan, 2016). But once researchers in an area demarcate, explore, and hopefully settle, at least in part, these boundary and definitional issues, the time comes to move beyond those concerns and to assess and apply those arguments. While academically, one might find it interesting to debate definitions endlessly, doing so fails to move a useful research agenda or to produce research results that could be employed in ways that can generate real-world changes that might, in the case of GCC, reduce harms to ecosystems and species.

Definitional studies may also provide a variety of typologies of green/conservation crimes and behaviors, and in doing so, again have utility for conceptualizing those crimes and laying the groundwork for research on these subjects. It should be noted, however, that typologies, like theories, *can be* empirically tested, and it is important to know how the real distribution of environmental and conservation crimes fits into those typologies, and whether the typologies fit reality and enhance their utility (see the example in Podgor and Dervan, 2016 on white collar crime).

A number of GCC studies add to the above arguments by examining specific examples of related offenses and offenders, and sometimes those studies describe those offenses and offenders using empirical data. More often than not, in green criminology, that empirical data has been subjected to qualitative interpretations (and often not qualitative analysis) rather than quantitative assessments. When collected and analyzed appropriately, qualitative data has many important uses and can certainly contribute to an understanding of green crime. The use of qualitative data can, however, have several important limitations, which have been discussed relative to the empirical literature found within green criminology (Lynch et al., 2017a). Some of those limitations relate specifically to the kinds of methods of analysis and data and sampling methods employed in green criminological research. As Lynch et al. (2017a: 191) note,

> Case studies . . . are not chosen on the basis of random sampling (i.e., they contain selection bias), but are specifically selected to illustrate a particular type of problem – or the emergence of a particular problem in a particular place – thereby limiting their broader applicability and utility.

This case selection method limits the ability to generalize. As Lynch et al. argue, the *N* of a case study is often 1, and lacking other important methodological considerations, statistically speaking, cannot produce generalizable knowledge. This is an important concern. To be sure, there are ways to address this concern. If there were, for instance, a substantial number of case studies on a well-identified, specific topic, research could later collect data from those case studies and perform a meta-analysis, an issue that has been addressed in the broader environmental literature (Matarazzo and Nijkamp, 1997; Rudel, 2008). In this case, quantitative assessment of qualitative (empirical) results can be employed to aggregate research findings from individual case studies, enhancing the ability to generalize from those results when presented as meta-analysis results. On their own, however, single case studies often fail to generate the kinds of knowledge that allow the building of a large base of knowledge that is, at the same time, generalizable. Case studies thus can limit the acceptance and appeal of such research results in disciplines that largely build knowledge from empirical studies and also limit the utility of such research for building policy responses that address ecological harms or conservation/green crimes and injustices.

The extant GCC literature also contains some excellent historical studies of green crimes that contain rich descriptive content needed to understand how these behaviors change and emerge over time, and how those behaviors are conceptualized and treated within societies as societies evolve. Some excellent examples of these kinds of studies are found in the work of Piers Beirne (1995, 1997, 2004; Yates, Powell and Beirne, 2001). Some studies also use qualitative data to address the processing of conservation crimes, using interviews with enforcement personnel or legal documents as data, and these studies, too, have a place in the GCC literature (Moreto, Brunson and Braga, 2016; Moreto and Matusiak, 2017). To be sure, these are all important studies that address issues and forms of information relevant to developing GCC, and, moreover, GCC *cannot fully* develop without them. But these cannot be the only types of studies GCC generates. More to the point, GCC cannot fully develop and be more broadly integrated into the quantitatively oriented field of criminology without quantitative studies. Here, we also limit our comments because these issues are also explored in Chapter 3 in this collection by Lynch, Stretesky, Long, and Barrett.

Quantitative analysis and criminology in general

In brief, most criminologists value quantitative studies and research that tests hypotheses related to the study, distribution, causes, control, and punishment of crime (for more on this point, see below), and these kinds of studies, as we shall show below, make up the vast majority of the published content in criminological journals. It is difficult to pinpoint any particular reason the criminological literature is so heavily empirical. One reason this occurs, however, is because historically, criminologists have placed great value on empirical studies, and the earliest studies of crime attached to the history of criminology (e.g., Quetelet in 1831, and later Lombroso in 1876) were empirical in orientation.

Quantitative studies have long been employed to gain knowledge about the world around us and processes that occur in that context. Quantitative studies, when approached correctly, provide important information about relevant hypotheses and are useful for assessing whether a given theory or hypothesis is empirically sustainable and worth retaining and developing. Certainly, one could, depending on how they evaluate empirical criminological knowledge, claim that the use of quantitative assessments has worked rather poorly, leading to very few cases where a hypothesis, but more importantly, a theory has been rejected. In part this has to do with the fact that there is no agreed-upon criteria for rejection of a hypothesis or theory within criminology, resulting in the use of criteria where weak relationships are accepted as definitive evidence of an effect by individual researchers using perhaps subjectively identified criteria. As a result, criminology tends to be rather theoretically "stocked" – by which we mean that there are many theories that attempt to explain crime. Empirical evidence does not, however, dramatically favor any particular theory of crime, and though many theories have some level of empirical support, those theories are also often in conflict with another, meaning that they point to opposing or contradictory claims about the causes of crime. There are, one could argue, quantitative ways to settle these conflicts – but those methods have not been widely employed within criminology (e.g., rival hypothesis testing). In contrast to the situation in criminology generally, conservation and green criminology contain less debate about the causes of ecological harms but offer less empirically relevant, generalizable material and findings to build upon. Thus, the situation within green/conservation criminology with respect to the use of empirical methods and data is different than the situation within the field of criminology more generally. In this sense, conservation/green criminology is at a different phase of development than criminology and needs to attend to a different set of issues.

One of the advantages of quantitative and empirical studies is that when they are carried out correctly, they can be generalized and applied. That is, they can help us understand a range of similar cases and may also be able to be used to predict and control outcomes. These are not unusual observations but rather are the hallmarks of the scientific method. Being able to perform this kind of analysis requires paying careful consideration to how studies are carried out methodologically. Research experts suggest that it is much more difficult to meet generalization criteria when employing qualitative, as opposed to quantitative, research methods. This observation about the relationship between qualitative research and generalization is recognized in a variety of different fields of research (Firestone, 1993; Höijer, 2008; Leininger, 1994; Payne and Williams, 2005; Polit and Hungler, 1991). One can suggest that it is therefore extremely important to pay attention and adhere to scientific methods of research when conducting qualitative research in order to ensure the study is designed well enough to facilitate generalization. In short, any particular field that has an overreliance on qualitative data can be criticized because that kind of data makes it more difficult to develop explanations with wider, generalizable applications. Other researchers note that those engaged in qualitative research are not absolved from meeting other standard research requirements, and that they must also pay special attention to ensuring the reliability and validity of qualitative research (Kirk and Miller, 1986). These are well-known problems in relation to qualitative research. These concerns require additional attention in the conservation/green criminological literature, but especially in the portions of that literature that are more strongly identified as green criminology.

When applied appropriately, quantitative studies help us know whether we can be relatively certain about something or some relationship using mathematical probabilities, and whether particular relationships we are studying are weak, especially in the context in which they have been assessed. Knowing whether we can be somewhat certain about the empirical results generated from quantitative studies is useful – though as scientists often note, even quantitative studies are never certain in many cases. Even if there is some uncertainty, quantitative studies can be extremely useful (as in the law of gravity – that is, you have never dropped a rock on earth under normal conditions and seen it float around you). To create that condition of certainty requires repeating the quantitative studies numerous times to see if the result is consistent, and even changing the study conditions to see what happens when one of the relational parameters is changed (i.e., in this case, changing one of the conditions constitutes a kind of quasi-experiment). What we can learn from these studies is how an outcome changes when an initial condition is different than in other qualitative or quantitative studies. Again, this is an extremely important methodological issue, and researchers must remain aware of the fact that when qualitative studies are not carried out correctly, and the methodological issues are not well spelled out, those results can be challenged on numerous grounds.

The above observations do not, however, mean that quantitative data are somehow "magical," or better than qualitative data, or that quantitative data *necessarily* generates appropriate or useful knowledge. To be sure, when undertaken inappropriately quantitative studies can certainly generate useless results. But just because the latter could happen, that doesn't mean that it will, or that quantitative studies should be avoided because such a possibility exists – recall also that the same possibility is associated with the use of qualitative data and analysis. To ensure that green/conservation criminologists *do not* generate useless knowledge, it is the responsibility of researchers in these areas to use proper methods of research, to adequately specify how the data was collected, to provide evidence that the sample of data is appropriate, and to meet all the conditions for performing sound research, whether the research project uses qualitative or quantitative data.

In theory, a series of quantitative studies addressing a similar issue can tell us whether or not research or hypotheses on that subject are fruitful enough to continue, or whether we should look elsewhere for insight and inspiration. As we noted above, that condition might also be produced from a meta-analysis of qualitative research outcomes. In the next section, we address some of the obstacles to performing such studies adequately, including paying attention to small samples and skewed distributions, and how to overcome those problems to attain generalizability of results.

Obstacles to generalizability and overcoming them

Questions of generalizability plague even well-crafted quantitative studies. As it relates to wildlife crime research, much publicly accessible wildlife crime data comes with numerous limitations beyond undercounting. Small samples are often one of those limitations. One way of overcoming this obstacle is to conduct a number of studies on the same subject matter in different contexts (i.e., replication) or to examine different aspects of a larger problem to corroborate earlier findings. To illustrate how this has been accomplished in the GCC field, we turn to recent studies on illegal, unreported, and unregulated (IUU) fishing at the global level and the illegal parrot trade in the neotropics. As it relates to the latter, little was known about the illegal parrot trade until a Mexican comprehensive report was published in 2007, which surveyed parrot trappers to estimate the extent of poaching at the national level. Cantu and associates (2007) found that much of the parrot poaching problem was concentrated in just a small number of species and that the large majority of the trade was for the domestic market in pet parrot ownership, not for international markets as many had originally thought. Using this report as a basis for further inquiry, Pires and Clarke (2012) applied the CRAVED model (Clarke, 1999; CRAVED stands for concealable, removable, available, valuable, enjoyable, and disposable) to explain variation in poaching among Mexican parrot species and how it might shed light on offender behavior. They found that much of the poaching variation could be explained by CRAVED concepts. More specifically, the opportunity-based concepts such as removability, accessibility, and availability, as opposed to demand-based concepts such as value and enjoyability, were more likely to explain poaching variation. This suggested that much of parrot poaching *is opportunistic* and that peasants, not professional trappers or organized criminals, may account for an ample portion of this problem. Yet, generalizing these findings to other neotropical countries would be problematic for two major reasons. First, the statistical analysis was limited to non-parametric univariate analyses given several limitations with the data. Second, how parrot poaching operates in Mexico may not be true in other contexts with different species, people, and settings. Consequently, this study was replicated several times in different contexts using a variety of illicit wildlife market survey data. Follow-up studies in Bolivia (Pires and Clarke, 2011; Pires et al., 2016) and Peru (Pires, 2015a; Pires, 2015b) consistently found that opportunity-based concepts were able to explain poaching variation better than demand-based concepts, although some opportunity-based concepts mattered more in different contexts. Altogether, results from these CRAVED-based quantitative studies in three neotropical countries, along with qualitative research on the organization of the illegal trade in parrots (Pires et al., 2016), confirmed the initial findings that parrot poaching can be explained in part by the opportunity structures in the environment and that much of the trade is conducted by peasants who supplement their income. Still, three specific CRAVED concepts sometimes vary across the locations studied, and at this point, given the few studies that have been conducted, it is inappropriate to create broad generalizations about the applicability of CRAVED models within GCC. Part of the issue of generalizability can be addressed by examining results from a similar (i.e., CRAVED) analysis for other kinds of species. One related example comes from the study of illegal, unreported, and unregulated (IUU) fishing.

With regard to IUU fishing, a number of criminological studies on the topic have begun to understand why certain species of marine life are overharvested, and the role that criminogenic ports play in influencing IUU fishing. In the first study of its kind, Petrossian and Clarke (2014) applied the revised CRAAVED model (Pires and Clarke, 2012) to commercial species of fish to explain why some fish are illicitly taken more often than others. Using a matched case-control design, this study *found that all CRAAVED concepts were significantly related to poaching variation*, although a skewed distribution and a small sample precluded a multivariate analysis in identifying the most important concepts while controlling for other effects. This study was later replicated at the global level for lobsters and crabs that are commercially overfished. In this second study, Petrossian and associates (2015) found that only some of the CRAAVED concepts could explain variation in overharvesting of crabs and lobsters, but again, the proxy measure for abundance – a measure of opportunity – was significantly related to poaching along with demand-side measures.

These IUU fishing studies implicate rationality on the part of the offender, at least with respect to targeted species of marine life. That is, fishermen are targeting the most attractive and valuable species that are often easier to obtain. Yet, many other decisions are made when deciding to partake in IUU fishing relating to risk, effort, and reward, which are key concepts in rational choice theory (Cornish and Clarke, 1986) and situational crime prevention (Clarke, 1980). To further corroborate previous research on the rationality of IUU fishers, Petrossian (2015) examined which situational factors, if any, could predict the degree of illegal fishing in the exclusive economic zones (EEZs; i.e., the 200-nautical-mile sea zone in the control of a nation as defined by the United Nations) of 53 countries. She found various measures of risk, effort, and reward were able to significantly predict the degree of IUU fishing in EEZs, and this was further corroborated by port-focused studies that collectively found certain criminogenic ports – also known as ports of convenience – attracted IUU fishers because of ease and convenience of disposing cargo, reduced risk of detection, and providing concealability (Petrossian et al., 2014; Marteache et al., 2015).

CRAAVED-based studies, particularly in the wildlife sphere, are often limited to univariate analyses, and sometimes non-parametric assessment. However, the consistent finding that most concepts of CRAAVED, particularly the measures of opportunity, are significantly related to theft variation suggests that hot products, whether inanimate or animate ones, can be explained, in part, by opportunistic factors. Therefore, this small collection of studies as a whole suggests that hot products are CRAAVED regardless of the product or the context, and this line of research informs us of offender behavior as it relates to decision-making. These kinds of studies and the addition of new studies to this literature is important for creating a knowledge base about environmental crimes which can lead to the ability to generalize those findings.

Empirical research in the social and conservation sciences

Essentially, to know what is going on in the world around us, we need quantitative information – and though not everyone might agree with that statement, certainly the things we know about the world around us and important information we use routinely to create great discoveries that allow all types of ordinary technology to be implemented require quantitative studies and understanding. Much could be – and has been – written about this issue, and here it is not our intention to review this debate and try to reconcile the two sides of the arguments about empirical/quantitative studies (for a relevant criminological discussion, see DiCristina, 1997, 2000; Worrall, 2000).

To be sure, both quantitative and qualitative data – as well as theorizing and hypothesizing about what is going on in the world around us – are needed to "know" something. The problem is that within GCC, at this point in time, there are relatively few empirical/quantitative studies, and the vast majority of what we know about GCC remains speculative because most assumptions, theories, hypotheses, and explanations posed in the green criminological literature have not been empirically assessed, while others have only been assessed in limited fashion. Certainly, there are some good quantitative GCC studies available, but relative to the entire GCC literature, these studies are few (see Chapter 3).

The fact that quantitative studies are underrepresented in the GCC literature is problematic particularly because the social science fields, as well as conservation sciences, are predominantly quantitative fields. For example, a study conducted by Hunter and Leahey (2008) assessed the percentage of articles in top sociology journals from 1935 through 2005 that used empirical/quantitative methods. About two-thirds of the 1,274 articles examined *employed empirical/quantitative data and methods*. Extant research on this issue in criminology and criminal justice shows that the majority of published studies in those disciplines are also empirical/quantitative (Kleck, Tark and Bellows, 2006; Tewksbury, DeMichele and Miller, 2005). Buckler (2008) examined the contents of five upper-tier and three lower-tier criminology and criminal justice journals from 2003 through 2007 to determine the extent to which empirical/quantitative results were published in 948 articles. He reports that 90.7% of published studies in those journals used quantitative data and empirical methods. Buckler also found that qualitative studies were more likely to be found in lower-tier journals. From a recent work that addresses a related question (Lynch et al, 2017b), we generously estimate that only about 10% of GCC studies are empirical/quantitative. In comparison to publications in top sociology and criminology and criminal justice journals – as well as in lower-tier criminology journals – it is evident that GCC studies are far less likely to rely upon empirical/quantitative evidence and analysis. More specifically, the prevalence of empirically oriented studies in the GCC literature when excluding conservation criminology studies is closer to 3% or 4%. And that's an important observation in our view.

Moreover, quantitative data is heavily employed in conservation and biodiversity research outside of criminology (Drury, Homewood and Randall, 2011). Indeed, in conservation sciences, Newing (2010) reports an increasing tendency for studies to take a quantitative as opposed to a qualitative approach. Arguments favoring quantitative assessment of eco-regions have also been posited in the biological conservation literature (Hargrove and Hoffman, 2004), and researchers in this field have also noted growing reliance on quantitative methods (see examples in various chapters in Ferson and Burgman, 2006) in wildlife ecological research (McGarigal, Cushman and Stafford, 2013). One conclusion that can be drawn from these observations is that these scientific areas of research overlap with issues GCC addresses. Thus, if this sub-field of criminology wishes to be relevant to conservation biology and wildlife ecological research – and certainly, some conservation criminologists have contributed to crossover research in these areas (Petrossian, 2018, 2015; Pires et al., 2016) – it seems to us that this will require additional attention to empirical studies, which as noted above have received increased attention in those areas of research in recent years.

The relevance of the above discussion is important in the following ways. First, we can say that what is "known" in a much more general sense (i.e., published and postulated, described theoretically, or inferred qualitatively) in GCC often is not the result of empirical studies, and this may mean, depending on the content of that literature, that it contains unsubstantiated speculation and untested hypotheses which are shaping the literature even though we don't have the type of evidence needed to generalize from those arguments. Second, that observation is important because it means there are likely important questions that can be addressed empirically/quantitatively that are slipping through the research cracks, and that there is insufficient information in the GCC literature on those issues. Third, this means potentially important hypotheses contained in GCC research are not being addressed empirically/quantitatively, and as a result, there is a gap in knowledge as important things remain unknown. Fourth, one also has to consider these results with respect to the effort of GC criminologists to penetrate criminology and criminal justice journals (and as noted already, the scientific literature) and change what criminologists are willing to recognize and study as belonging to the study of crime and justice. This effort must also be evaluated relative to the kind of content criminology and criminal justice journals publish. As noted above, that content is overwhelmingly empirical/quantitative while the GCC literature is not. That difference limits the ability of GCC to penetrate those journals (Lynch et al., 2017a). As a result, the neglect of empirical/quantitative studies is also limiting the ability of GCC to change the nature of criminology and the knowledge base that constitutes the field of criminology. In effect, we suggest that the avoidance of empirical/quantitative studies within GCC limits the appeal and impact of that kind of research and allows traditional criminology to continue without sufficient opposition. This also means that the criminological image of crime will also not be challenged, and is less likely to change, limiting the space allowed for the further and broader development of GCC, at least in mainstream journals. Such a situation can lead, if not addressed, to the permanent marginalization of green/conservation research, despite its importance and its expansion in literatures in other disciplines (see further discussion and example below).

Again, like it or not, as disciplines, criminology and criminal justice research *is* empirically oriented. And that means that to get green/conservation research into top-tier criminology journals, and to have the potential to change the nature of criminology, GC criminologists should be relying on quantitative methods more often than they do currently. The examples in this collection illustrate how that can be done.

Implications related to underutilization of empirical research in GCC

Quantitative data and methods add to our understanding of things around us, and building an appropriately broad and sound GCC knowledge base cannot happen when quantitative studies are neglected. So there are, in our view, five important problems. Because GC criminologists pay less attention than (we argue) they should to empirical/quantitative research, those researchers are typically going to (1) encounter difficulties placing green/conservation studies in top-tier criminology journals, given that most of those journals are quantitatively oriented; (2) that due to #1, GC criminologists are going to have less impact on the fields of criminology and criminal justice than they might otherwise have; (3) the lack of a substantial volume of GCC empirical/quantitative studies becomes a justification for quantitatively oriented criminologists to dismiss GCC; (4) due to the lack of empirical/quantitative studies, GC criminologists are not building the best possible knowledge base and are failing to assess relevant hypotheses about green crime and justice, limiting not only the refinement of knowledge, but the direction of green/conservation studies; and (5) there is a potential for this problem to become intergenerational and long-lasting. That is, the efforts of GC criminologists to change the criminological literature will move quite slowly and affect future generations of green criminologists.

These are not small problems in our view, and the issue before us is whether empirical/quantitative GCC studies are sufficient to challenge criminological orthodoxy concerning the definition of crimes and forms of justice that criminologists ought to study. Criminology has a long history of incorporating class and racially biased approaches within the boundaries of criminological theorizing, and commentary addressing the causes of crime or injustice in the criminal justice system (for discussion on this issue related to radical-Marxist criminology, see Lynch, 2015). That long history, challenged by radical-Marxist criminologists beginning in the late 1960s and through the early 1980s, did little to change criminological orthodoxy. One reason that has been suggested for the failure of this radical challenge to mainstream criminology centers on the absence of empirical/quantitative studies by radical-Marxist criminologists (Lynch, 1987, 2013, 2015). Essentially, the failure of radical-Marxist criminologists to perceive that undertaking empirical/quantitative studies was not only useful but necessary for attempting to penetrate mainstream criminology is similar to the situation faced by GCC: it is history repeating itself. And this time, as criminologists, we should understand the outcome if we correctly assess what happened to radical-Marxist criminology. In response to the failure of radical-Marxist criminology to remake criminology, the reaction was a further withdrawal from mainstream criminology and empirical analysis rather than the alternative – an effort to confront mainstream criminology on its own terms: empirically (Lynch, 2015, 2013, 1987). This interpretation may not be the most popular view of the failure of radical-Marxist criminology and the turn to critical, postmodern, and cultural forms of criminology which supplanted radical-Marxist analysis, but this argument also has not been critiqued, suggesting it potentially contains some relevant points. Nevertheless, much of GCC finds itself in the same place as radical-Marxists did in the 1980s, lacking sufficient empirical evidence to be taken seriously in the mainstream of criminology.

Being empirically oriented does not always instantly translate into success. In part and with respect to GCC, the success or failure of empirical GCC is also affected by whether GC criminologists, as the first potential audience for such work, refers to those studies and reinforces the need for empirical work. If GC criminologists ignore relevant empirical studies, why would mainstream criminologists care about them? Fortunately, on this front, GC criminologists, while they tend not to undertake empirical studies, they do indeed appear to refer to relevant empirical studies by other GC criminologists. Such studies, however, have not appeared to motivate a larger proportion of GC criminologists to have undertaken additional empirical studies. So, perhaps our suggestions above are misdirected. However, it is also true that GC criminologists are currently relying on a small group of researchers to produce the empirical evidence needed to stimulate broader acceptance of GC criminology within criminology more generally. There are only a limited number of studies those researchers can produce, and without broader support, the dearth of empirical GCC will fail to persuade mainstream criminologists that the study of green/conservation crime and justice is important.

The contents of this book

This book constitutes an effort to increase exposure to empirical/quantitative green and conservation criminology. It contains chapters that have varying degrees of empirical sophistication and different types of empirical evidence to illustrate that important empirical GC articles need not always be highly sophisticated to make appropriate use of data. These chapters also illustrate that there is a wide range of data available that can serve as the basis for empirical/quantitative GCC.

In Chapter 2, Thomson, Samuels-Jones, and Downs provide a citation analysis using bibliographic methods to analyze and visualize the keywords, journals, and references used by green criminologists. Using a network of 5,524 publications based on shared references, this empirical study identifies four unique branches of research, consisting of (1) green criminology, (2) conservation criminology, (3) eco-global and green cultural criminology, and (4) environmental justice and green victimology. In addition, many sub-lateral branches are identified, particularly within the conservation criminology branch that is growing at the fastest pace. Finally, several criminology journals are identified as producing the most work in the field while several other journals outside the field are also identified as receptive to this type of work.

Related to the chapter above, Lynch, Stretesky, Long, and Barrett provide a literature review on quantitative studies in green and conservation criminology (Chapter 3). Classified by the topic of focus, this chapter provides an in-depth review of studies conducted in the field that include environmental justice, the distribution of and consequences of pollution, the social control of environmental crime, environmental social movement research, and harms against animals. Such quantitatively based studies add important information about a subject area that can shape the kinds of knowledge generated about topical areas. Importantly, Lynch and associates identify gaps in the literature for the purposes of future research.

The following four chapters of this book focus attention on studies in conservation criminology. In Chapter 4, Wilson and Kurland examine the decline of primate populations at the global level. More specifically, they compare conservation threats across all primate species in an effort to detect whether criminal acts, such as the bushmeat and pet trades, have led to population decline and species endangerment compared to other threats. Using a logistic regression model, Wilson and Kurland found that habitat loss, fragmentation, and the bushmeat and pet trades significantly contributed to primate population declines and endangerment risk while other threats were not significantly related. Consequently, both criminologists and conservationists should focus their efforts on these identified threats to improve the conservation of primates worldwide.

Related to the previous chapter on primate poaching, bushmeat trafficking in the Republic of Congo is the focus of Chapter 5. The illegal trafficking of bushmeat is a growing problem in urban areas that are exacerbating wildlife population declines. To understand the trafficking networks and structural conditions supporting this trade, Kahler, Boratto, Vanegas, Wieland, and Gore set out to characterize these networks from a structural and geographic perspective using routine activities theory. Using interviews, observations, and market surveys, the authors found the role of key points of entry into the city of Pointe Noire and transportation hubs in the trade. A number of opportunities in the trade were identified that can inform prevention and enforcement strategies, as outlined by Kahler and associates.

In Chapter 6, Blount-Hill and Natarajan of John Jay College of Criminal Justice provide a global analysis of whether and how humans impact mammalian species loss. Blount-Hill and Natarajan argue that human-based activities are associated with wildlife decline at the local level. This association manifests itself as human-animal conflict which can take various forms, from habitat loss to water diversion, climate change, or pollution, among other factors. If such activities are related to wildlife decline at the local level, this relationship should hold at the national level and specifically for one taxonomic group: mammalian species. This study tests measures of "direct human activities and ecological environmental mediators to explaining the number of [mammalian] species under existential threat worldwide" for 142 countries where data have been systematically collected. Using a multivariate regression model, they found a significant relationship between increased human economic activities and water scarcity with an increase in mammalian species threatened. They provide a number of different interpretations for this exploratory analysis that can be the foundation for more future work in this field.

In Chapter 7, van Uhm, Pires, Sosnowski, and Petrossian focus their attention on wildlife trafficking being brought into two of the largest demand markets for illegal wildlife worldwide: the United States and the European Union. This study analyzes wildlife contraband seizures made at US ports of entry with those made in the EU between 2003 and 2010 in order to identify concentrations of illegal wildlife imports with regard to products, genera, and export nations. Using the EU-TWIX and the USFWS LEMIS datasets, findings show that the majority of seizures involve non-live wildlife products and are reptile- and mammal-based. Similarly, the top 25 genera seized in both markets resemble each other and are disproportionately exported from countries in Southeast Asia and China, among other problematic nations. Some differences exist regarding seizure patterns between both markets, and this may be due to sociocultural demand differences. The authors argue that sociocultural demand along with factors of opportunity may help explain why certain wildlife is commonly seized more often in both markets and what the implications of this means for enforcement strategies.

In Chapter 8, Genco explores whether political and economic indicators at the state level in the United States are associated with wildlife killings by the US Fish and Wildlife Service (USFWS). Few studies have examined state killing of wildlife, and even fewer examine this issue quantitatively. Using data from various sources, Genco fills this research gap by measuring political-economic variables such as farming, hunting, political party membership, and animal interest group resources for each state. The study found that certain features of the US economic and political power structure affect the frequency of wildlife killings, although at times not in the expected direction.

Going in a different direction, the next two chapters focus on hazardous waste violations and crimes in two different contexts. Few criminological studies have examined the extent of environmental crime and punishment, and little is known about how widespread environmental crimes are in society or the kinds of punishments environmental crimes receive. To fill this gap, in Chapter 9, Lynch analyzes hazardous waste violations and punishments in the United States between 1999 and 2008 using Resource Conservation and Recovery Act data. In this study, Lynch focuses on the volume and formal responses at the state level to violations of hazardous waste. The results indicate that the number of reported hazardous waste crime varies significantly across states and that rates of punishments for these crimes are relatively low and consist of relatively small fines. The violation rate data also seems to suggest that hazardous waste environmental violations may be significantly underreported in official data. Conversely, in Chapter 10, Andreatta examines the spatial distribution of waste crime in the context of Italy and the possible underlying reasons for these patterns. More specifically, Andreatta explores whether the human population, the presence of organized crime, the number of businesses, and production of urban waste and special waste at both the regional and provincial administrative units are associated with waste crimes.

In the spirit of this edited collection on empirical contributions to the field, Long, Stretesky, and Barrett provide an overview of how to execute an analysis of longitudinal data using various statistical models (Chapter 11). Specifically, they cover fixed-effects, random-effects, and multilevel models for change, and the use of diagnostic tests and model fit measures. To provide examples of these models, Long and associates use CITES wildlife trade data on annual exports of Accipitridae for each country for a ten-year period to identify variables that can predict export totals over time. Using Stata (v.15), the authors provide an easy to understand, step-by-step approach to analyzing longitudinal data.

Finally, in the last chapter, Ozymy and Jarrell use the *United States v. CITGO* trial as a means to explore victim impact statements and how green victims interpret their victimization. The Citgo case is important because it was the first Clean Air Act case whereby an oil refinery was convicted on criminal grounds, and it was the "first criminal case to use victim impact statements to legally recognize how individuals interpret their victimization by a corporation." By examining the victim impact statements, Ozymy and Jarrell were able to identify primary and sub-themes of how individuals felt victimized by Citgo.

Concluding comments

In sum, this collection of chapters covers a wide range of topics, contexts, theoretical perspectives, and methods of understanding crimes and harms against the environment and wildlife. While these chapters have elucidated much about the nature of environmental and wildlife crime, there is still much to know and a criminological perspective has much to offer. Many of these chapters have a macro-level focus, either at the national or global level, which lends well to understanding the larger forces at play. However, such studies come with a trade-off: they neglect the local context in which these harms occur. As a result, the opportunity structures at the ground level that facilitate such harms are not taken into account or understood. For example, Kahler et al.'s study on the nature of bushmeat trafficking uses various methods at the micro-level to understand how bushmeat is trafficked from source points to markets. As a result, this local-level analysis was able to identify opportunity structures in this context that can inform enforcement and prevention strategies tailored to the problem. Examples like this are but one example of the importance of studying harms and crimes at the micro-level.

When we decided to create this edited collection on quantitative and empirical studies in green and conservation criminology, we had three goals in mind. First, we sought to draw together both green and conservation criminologists and illustrate a commitment among both groups to collaborating in ways that help promote access to, knowledge of, and greater acceptance of conservation and green criminological research. Second, we aimed to draw attention to the fact that these forms of criminology appreciate and promote empirical research, and that these areas – green criminology in particular – do not simply comprise qualitative, theoretical, and definitional research. By doing so, we believe this work can help counteract some of the assumptions many criminologists have about green/conservation criminology and its content. Finally, our last goal was to collect a sample of high-quality empirical studies representing the work of conservation/green criminologists into one edition to serve as a kind of sourcebook for such studies. We believe we have met these objectives by providing a wide array of high-quality empirical and quantitative chapters that significantly add to the scientific body of work in the fields of green and conservation criminology, and we hope the reader feels the same, too.

References

Beirne, Piers. 2004. From animal abuse to interhuman violence? A critical review of the progression thesis. *Society & Animals*, 12 (1): 39–65.

Beirne, Piers. 1997. Rethinking bestiality: Towards a concept of interspecies sexual assault. *Theoretical Criminology*, 1 (3): 317–340.

Beirne, Piers. 1995. The use and abuse of animals in criminology: A brief history and current review. *Social Justice*, 22 (1): 5–31.

Buckler, Kevin. 2008. The quantitative/qualitative divide revisited: A study of published research, doctoral program curricula, and journal editor perceptions. *Journal of Criminal Justice Education*, 19 (3): 383–403.

Cantu, J. C., M.E.S. Saldana, M. Grosselet, and J. S. Gamez. 2007. *The illegal parrot trade in Mexico: A comprehensive assessment.* Washington, DC: Defenders of Wildlife.

Clarke, Ronald V. 1980. Situational crime prevention: Theory and practice. *The British Journal of Criminology*, 20 (2): 136–147.

Clarke, Ronald V., and B. Webb. 1999. *Hot products: Understanding, anticipating and reducing demand for stolen goods* (Vol. 112). Home Office, Policing and Reducing Crime Unit, Research, Development and Statistics Directorate.

Cornish, D. B., and Ronald V. Clarke (eds.). 1986. *Reasoning criminal-rational choice perspectives on offending.* New York: Springer-Verlag.

DiCristina, Bruce. 2000. Prediction, policy, and quantitative inquiry: A reply to Worrall. *Journal of Criminal Justice Education*, 11: 363–369.

DiCristina, Bruce. 1997. The quantitative emphasis in criminal justice education. *Journal of Criminal Justice Education*, 8: 181–199.

Drury, Rebecca, K. Homewood, and S. Randall. 2011. Less is more: The potential of qualitative approaches in conservation research. *Animal Conservation*, 14 (1): 18–24.

Ferson, Scott, and Mark Burgman (eds.). 2006. *Quantitative methods for conservation biology*. New York: Springer Science & Business Media.

Firestone, William A. 1993. Alternative arguments for generalizing from data as applied to qualitative research. *Educational Researcher*, 22 (4): 16–23.

Hargrove, William W., and Forrest M. Hoffman. 2004. Potential of multivariate quantitative methods for delineation and visualization of ecoregions. *Environmental Management*, 34 (1): S39–S60.

Höijer, Birgitta. 2008. Ontological assumptions and generalizations in qualitative (audience) research. *European Journal of Communication*, 23 (3): 275–294.

Hunter, Laura, and Erin Leahey. 2008. Collaborative research in sociology: Trends and contributing factors. *The American Sociologist*, 39 (4): 290–306.

Kirk, Jerome, and Marc L. Miller. 1986. *Reliability and validity in qualitative research*. Beverly Hills, CA: Sage.

Kleck, Gary, J. Tark, and J. J. Bellows. 2006. What methods are most frequently used in research in criminology and criminal justice. *Journal of Criminal Justice*, 34 (2): 147–152.

Leininger, Madeleine. 1994. Evaluation criteria and critique of qualitative research studies. Pp. 95–115 in J. M. Morse (ed), *Critical issues in qualitative research methods*. Thousand Oaks, CA: Sage.

Lynch, Michael J. 2015. The classless state of criminology and why criminology without class is rather meaningless. *Crime, Law and Social Change*, 63 (1): 65–90.

Lynch, Michael J. 2013. Political economy and crime: An overview. *Journal of Crime and Justice*, 36 (2): 138–140.

Lynch, Michael J. 1987. Quantitative analysis and Marxist criminology: Old answers to a dilemma in Marxist criminology. *Crime and Social Justice*, 29: 110-127.

Lynch, Michael J., Kimberly L. Barrett, Paul B. Stretesky, and Michael A. Long. 2017a. The neglect of empirical research in green criminology and its consequences. *Critical Criminology*, 25 (2): 183–198.

Lynch, Michael J., Michael A. Long, Paul B. Stretesky, and Kimberly A. Barrett. 2017b. *Green criminology: Crime, justice and the environment*. Berkeley: University of California Press.

Marteache, N., J. Viollaz, and Gohar A. Petrossian. 2015. Factors influencing the choice of a safe haven for offloading illegally caught fish: A comparative analysis of developed and developing economies. *Crime Science*, 4 (1): 32.

Matarazzo, Benedetto, and Peter Nijkamp. 1997. Meta-analysis for comparative environmental case studies: Methodological issues. *International Journal of Social Economics*, 24 (7–9): 799–811.

McFann, Sara, and Stephen F. Pires. 2019. Taking stock in wildlife crime research: Trends & implications for future research. *Deviant Behavior*, DOI: 10.1080/01639625.2018.1556851

McGarigal, Kevin, Samuel A. Cushman, and Susan Stafford. 2013. *Multivariate statistics for wildlife and ecology research*. New York: Springer Science & Business Media.

Moreto, William D., Rod K. Brunson, and Anthony A. Braga. 2016. "Anything we do, we have to include the communities": Law enforcement rangers' attitudes towards and experiences of community – ranger relations in wildlife protected areas in Uganda. *British Journal of Criminology*, 57 (4): 924–944.

Moreto, William D., and Matthew C. Matusiak. 2017. "We fight against wrong doers": Law enforcement rangers' roles, responsibilities, and patrol operations in Uganda. *Deviant Behaviour*, 38 (4): 426–447.

Newing, Helen. 2010. *Conducting research in conservation: Social science methods and practice*. London: Routledge.

Payne, Geoff, and Malcolm Williams. 2005. Generalization in qualitative research. *Sociology*, 39 (2): 295–314.

Petrossian, Gohar A. 2018. A micro-spatial analysis of opportunities for IUU fishing in 23 Western African countries. *Biological Conservation*, 225: 31–41.

Petrossian, Gohar A. 2015. Preventing illegal, unreported and unregulated (IUU) fishing: A situational approach. *Biological Conservation*, 189: 39–48.

Petrossian, Gohar A., and Ronald R. V. Clarke. 2014. Explaining and controlling illegal commercial fishing an application of the CRAVED theft model. *British Journal of Criminology*, 54 (1): 73–90.

Petrossian, Gohar A., N. Marteache, and J. Viollaz. 2015. Where do "undocumented" fish land? An empirical assessment of port characteristics for IUU fishing. *European Journal on Criminal Policy and Research*, 21 (3): 337–351.

Petrossian, Gohar A., J. S. Weis, and Stephen F. Pires. 2015. Factors affecting crab and lobster species subject to IUU fishing. *Ocean & Coastal Management*, 106: 29–34.

Pires, Stephen F. 2015a. A CRAVED analysis of multiple illicit parrot markets in Peru and Bolivia. *European Journal on Criminal Policy and Research*, 21 (3): 321–336.

Pires, Stephen F. 2015b. The heterogeneity of illicit parrot markets: An analysis of seven Neo-tropical open-air markets. *European Journal on Criminal Policy and Research*, 21 (1): 151–166.

Pires, Stephen F., and Ronald R. V. Clarke. 2012. Are parrots CRAVED? An analysis of parrot poaching in Mexico. *Journal of Research in Crime and Delinquency*, 49: 122–146.

Pires, Stephen F., and Ronald V. Clarke. 2011. Sequential foraging, itinerant fences and parrot poaching in Bolivia. *The British Journal of Criminology*, 51 (2): 314–335.

Pires, Stephen F., J. L. Schneider, and M. Herrera. 2016. Organized crime or crime that is organized? The parrot trade in the neotropics. *Trends in Organized Crime*, 19 (1): 4–20.

Pires, Stephen F., J. L. Schneider, M. Herrera, and J. L. Tella. 2016. Spatial, temporal and age sources of variation in parrot poaching in Bolivia. *Bird Conservation International*, 26 (3): 293–306.

Podgor, Ellen S., and Lucian E. Dervan. 2016. "White collar crime": Still hazy after all these years. *Georgia Law Review*, 50 (3): 711–767.

Polit, D., and B. Hungler. 1991. *Nursing research: Principles and methods*. New York: JB Lippincott.

Rudel, Thomas K. 2008. Meta-analysis of case studies: A method for studying regional and global environmental change. *Global Environmental Change*, 18 (1): 18–25.

Tewksbury, R., M. T. DeMichele, and J. M. Miller. 2005. Methodological orientations of articles appearing in criminal justice's top journals: Who publishes what and where? *Journal of Criminal Justice Education*, 16 (2): 265–279.

Worrall, John L. 2000. In defense of the "Quantoids": More on the reasons for the quantitative emphasis in criminal justice education and research. *Journal of Criminal Justice Education*, 11: 353–361.

Yates, Roger, Chris Powell, and Piers Beirne. 2001. Horse maiming in the English countryside: Moral panic, human deviance, and the social construction of victimhood. *Society & Animals*, 9 (1): 1–23.

2 The branches of green criminology

A bibliometric citation analysis 2000–2017

Ryan Thomson, Tameka Samuels-Jones, and Liam Downs

The subdiscipline of green criminology has come a long way since its inception as a scholastic sprout in 1990. Unfortunately, the tree of green crime research has been subject to non-ideal growing conditions given a relatively tenuous relation to the broader criminology field. Consequently, green criminology grew slowly throughout its first decade. It was not until the early 2000s that growth conditions became more favorable. This period was significant, especially among certain branches of green criminology, but a neglect of quantitative research persisted (Lynch et al., 2017). In sync with the larger effort of this book, the following study offers a quantitative bibliometric network analysis aimed at moving the field forward. Furthermore, we summarize the subdiscipline's growth following this first decade. In doing so, we have organized our analysis of green criminology with each publication serving as a node connected to other referenced works.

We recognize that these types of citation studies have in some instances been viewed as divisive (e.g., Cohn & Farrington, 2011). In order to acknowledge and appreciate the smaller branches, we seek to avoid the creation of an unnecessary hierarchy. In doing so, we have employed a network ecology approach for understanding green criminology as an ecological science. "Network ecology lies at the intersection of ecological science and network concepts, tools, and techniques" (Borrett, Moody, & Edelmann, 2014, p. 2). Accordingly, network ecologists explore the structure, function and evolution of ecological systems using network analysis. This strategy appreciates the numerous branches and supporting root structures of green criminology. With a total sample of 118 green criminology peer-reviewed studies published between 2000 and 2017 and their corresponding 5,576 references, we employ bibliometric methods to explore both books and articles that have established the subdiscipline over the last 17 years.

While the impacts of environmental harms have been discussed in the academic literature since the 1970s, there has not yet been a comprehensive attempt to characterize the origins and evolution of green criminology. Perhaps this has been because, as noted by Hall et al. (2016, p. 13), that green criminology research has

> tended towards the piecemeal publication of papers by some dedicated researchers, along with the odd special edition or edited collection, the

occasional panel at generalist criminological conferences, and a few specialist under- and post-graduate courses taught at a select few institutions in Europe and the United States.

Accordingly, there are numerous widely cited edited books, such as South and Brisman's (2013) handbook, which have led to substantial scholastic growth. And yet, with the renewed interest in environmental issues in the past decade, green criminology has experienced greater acceptance both within and outside the discipline. The evolution of green criminology has also grown beyond its historical roots to reflect a creative integration of transdisciplinary perspectives bearing new scholastic and empirical fruit.

The roots of green criminology

The term "green criminology" was first introduced by Lynch in 1990, however criminological work on the natural environment preceded this work (Goyes & South, 2017). For example, Janez Pecar (1981) advanced an early position about new, environmentally damaging forms of criminality in Slovenia and the role of criminology (Eman, Meško, & Fields, 2009). Without an English-language translation of this article, however, Pecar's work failed to make an impact (Hall et al., 2016). Other scholars also embarked on green scholarship during the 1980s and 1990s which would well be defined as "green criminology" today based on the application of the term. These include works by Jean-Denis André (1980), who reviewed the conceptual and definitional issues surrounding ecological crime (Goyes & South, 2017). Nevertheless, within the field of criminology, Lynch's application of the "green criminology" label set the stage for its development, although the term did not receive much publicity at the time. Lynch acknowledged that his green perspective was not entirely new, and capitalized on the environmental awakening of the 1990s. DiMento's (1993) article on enforcement issues pertaining to environmental law was another early work. Within the broader scholastic framework, this environmental movement was influenced by Veblen's (1899) work on conspicuous consumption and O'Connor's (1986) perspectives on individualism. Marx's (1909) views on exploitation were also a significant influence that provided historical context for the green crime framework (Lynch, 1990).

The radical roots of green crime

From the outset, green criminology reflected principles from the radical/critical school of criminology. This school can be traced to Taylor, Walton, and Young's (1973) groundbreaking book, *The New Criminology*, which provided at that time the best exemplification of a critique of inequities within criminological research (Mol, 2017). Today, critical criminology remains primarily concerned with the process by which some acts are criminalized (while others are not) and therefore emphasizes the political and social factors that impact criminal justice processes to address specific crimes (Hall, 2015).

Marx's (1909) writings played a significant role in the development of critical criminology, with its emphasis on how the wealthy capitalist class (the bourgeoisie) controlled the means of production. This means of disempowering the working class (the proletariat) set the stage for further evaluations of how the status quo created division. From the perspective of criminologists, this hierarchy was especially relevant to studies on the creation of laws. The green movement during the 1990s, which largely reflected an extension of Marxist criminological thought, emphasized environmentally destructive behavior as a result of capitalism. Neo-Marxism within the green crime perspective extended this thought by emphasizing how powerful corporations abuse their power through environmentally damaging activities (Foster, 2000; Hall, 2015). Important historical works demonstrating these Marxist and Neo-Marxist perspectives within criminology include Shifferd's (1972) work on pollution and Leff's (1993) writings which drew on Marx's work to explain environmental harms. These politico-economic Marxist and Neo-Marxist foundations resulted in much debate with mainstream criminology concerning the legal definition of crime, which later allowed for debates concerning expanding criminology to include the concept of green crime.

The debate over criminology's core focus – whether it should incorporate harm into definitions of crime – can be traced back to Edwin Sutherland's 1939 presidential address to the American Sociological Society, which directed attention to the social harms caused by white collar offenders. This was undertaken during a period in which criminology defined crime specifically as legal violations and the notion of blurring concepts of harm and crime was not particularly palatable. This debate has also impacted green criminology's evolution. Sutherland's pioneering work explained how the criminal activities of corporations became learned behaviors over time which became accepted ways of conducting business. This notion of corporate offenders provided the foundation for the legality vs. harm debate which has influenced green criminology today. In the words of Lynch and Stretesky "As a discipline, criminology has neglected the crimes of the powerful and the laws and regulations that define, sanction and control these offences" (2003, p. 248) Notably, green criminology's branch of "green collar crime" reflects the evolution of Sutherland's (1949) work in which he incorporated crimes of the powerful into mainstream criminology through the concept of "white collar crime." Sutherland's *White-Collar Crime* (1949) is the oldest shared citation contained within our study. These interests have been at the forefront of the subdiscipline and are reflected by the numerous co-citations of Frank and Lynch's *Corporate Crime, Corporate Violence* (1992). References to these roots have become commonplace within the field; "dirty collar crime" within justice studies (Ruggiero & South, 2010) and "camo-collar crime" among wildlife analysis (Crow, Shelley, & Stretesky, 2013). Wolf (2011) returned to the concept of green collar crime illustrating its links and numerous applications throughout the subdisciplines various branches.

Despite the critical beginnings of green criminology, the field's development over the past 20 years is characterized by a diverging root structure depending on the definition of green criminology being employed. Clifford's (1998) expanded review of criminal activities built on the white collar mold to include harm and changes within environmental laws, but it did little to slow a broader philosophical debate. The continued harm vs. legal debate emphasized by Lynch and Stretesky (2003) prompted a timely dispute that warranted an entire issue of *Theoretical Criminology* devoted to contesting concepts of green criminology. Yet, while the methodological and theoretical issues have been noted, the definitional debate has failed to offer a concrete and substantive definition for "green crime." This highlights the fact that the concept of green criminology remains heavily disputed, a dispute which centers predominantly on whether green criminologists adopt a traditional or radical approach. Situ and Emmons (2000), for example, offer a strict legalistic approach in their definition of an environmental crime as "an unauthorized act or omission that violates the law and is therefore subject to criminal prosecution and sanctions" (p. 19). Yet for radical/critical criminologists, an emphasis on the structural inequalities and harms form important tenets of the green criminology framework. This framework challenges many commonly adopted notions of crime to incorporate harms within a wider societal context and addresses the resulting negative consequences for the environment and human relations (Beirne & South, 2007).

Traditional criminologists consider the linkages between environmental crime and more traditional crimes as overlapping violations of the penal code. More radical or critical criminologists also consider harms to the environment, many of which are not defined as crimes in the traditional sense. Therefore, their research is inclusive of less traditional crimes, such as the illegal wildlife trade and the transnational movement of hazardous wastes. For radical/critical criminologists, the green criminology framework challenges strict legalistic notions of crime by incorporating broader notions of harm and inequality to better understand the distribution and effect of its negative impacts. Bibliographical methods are equipped to account for a range of analytical approaches which speaks to the variety of different works found throughout the subdiscipline.

Bibliometric methods and citation data

Bibliometric analysis is the "statistical analysis of written publications, such as books or articles" (OECD, 2002, p. 203). Broadly considered, bibliometrics is an analytical approach used to quantitatively analyze academic literature as networks. With academic publications as data sources, bibliometrics uses citation and reference data to address questions about who cites who. This generates a refined understanding of how research is produced, organized, and exerts influence on later scholarship. Historically, this approach has been employed as a quantitative exercise tracing the relationships within scientific disciplines to gauge the impact of individual publications (De Bellis, 2009). Some institutions of higher learning have gone so far as to conduct bibliometric assessments as part of their tenure and promotion review processes (Kolowich, 2009). Given the nature of the academy, it is easy to see how such methods could lend themselves to a prestige-based "publish or perish" mentality. Other real-world examples include Hamilton, Vacca, and Stacciarini's (2017) study of team-based adoption research and Ziegler's (2009) examination of renewable energy initiatives among engineers.

Citation analysis

Key to bibliometric analysis is citation analysis, a specialized application of social network analysis. Citation analysis focuses on the examination of the frequency, patterns, and visualization of citation ties contained within a body of published literature. In citation analysis, journals or individual publications typically constitute network "nodes." Those nodes, in turn, contain keywords and references that can be used to identify network "edges" as links to other journals or individual publications. Citation analysis allows for the evaluation of patterning of citations to reveal network properties among a group of publications. A typical aim of citation analysis is to assess the underlying network structure of a body of work, or to identify the seminal works in a literature.

Via citation analysis, one can conduct bibliographic coupling. This occurs when two academic works reference a common third work. Thus, each publication constitutes a node, and a link represents a shared reference (Weinberg, 1974). Bibliographic coupling is an indication that two works address a related subject (Martyn, 1964). The idea of bibliographic coupling was first introduced by Kessler (1963). This early citation analysis laid the groundwork for computational approaches to documenting similarities and linkages among published works. In the wake of numerous methodological developments and offshoots in techniques, the bibliometric approach featuring bibliographic coupling is often used to analyze network ties among scholarly works that reference previous publications.

Co-citation is the inverse relation of bibliographic coupling. Co-citing occurs when a third publication cites two other publications. This measurement approach, as articulated by White and Griffith (1981), offers insights into the structure and influence of ideas in a network of publications. There seems to be consensus among network analysts that bibliographic coupling is more accurate for smaller amounts of data, while co-citing is a better technique for larger amounts of data (Waltman & Van Eck, 2013).

Citation data

The data for the study were obtained from the Thomson Reuters Institute for Scientific Information's Web of Science using the Core Collection citation indexes. We identified publications in the primary Social Science Citation Index and Emerging Sources Citation Index for the 1990 to 2017 period. This time frame represents the subdiscipline from its formal origins to the present. Pertinent publications were identified by conducting independent title and keyword searches for each subdiscipline, specifically "green criminology," "conservation criminology," "green cultural criminology," "transnational green criminology," and "green collar criminology." Each search contained all known variations of these terms which could indicate an association with one of the subdisciplines various branches (the green criminology search contained "green crime" + "green criminology," etc.). Works which did not contain some variation of these words have been omitted from the analysis.

The primary search yielded 124 articles with a total of 5,576 references. The full records for these publications and their references were downloaded. Given the huge number of references considered, all the references could not be cited here. Bibliographic coupling was employed to identify links among the publications selected, whether in terms of shared keywords or references cited. Only the connected publications (n = 118) were included within the analysis – six fewer than what we originally started with – given that the aim of bibliometric analysis is to evaluate the relational structure of linkages among publications. We dropped these six studies because they were isolated from the central component and shared no common references to (or with) any other studies. Given that our sample is not considered large (n < 300), we pursued a full counting technique. The links among the publications in our sample indicated relations between pairs of publications that share either one or more keywords or common references, or which directly cite one another.

We used visualization techniques to better observe the structure of shared keywords and citations among the works in the sample (in the bibliographic coupling method) and their shared citations (using the co-citation method). The bibliometric analyses were performed with VOSviewer, a software package developed for constructing and visualizing bibliometric networks at the University of Leiden, the Netherlands (Van Eck & Waltman, 2010, 2014). VOSviewer has a "smart local moving algorithm" code to detect the presence of clusters and network centrality as specified by Waltman and Van Eck (2013).

Limitations

A primary limitation of our study is that we cannot entirely appreciate and detail the immense variety of work in the area. To discuss every leaf and twig of green criminology's budding tree would require an entire volume, let alone a sizeable book, perhaps something along the lines of a dense annotated bibliography. We instead have opted to summarize these areas through different types of network visualizations. A second limitation is more technical. The Web of Science Core Collection only includes peer-reviewed journal articles and omits published books, conference presentations, and other non-peer-reviewed sources from its central search. This prevents us from including these works within our bibliometric coupling analysis which would otherwise be of immediate interest. That said, we remedy this by including a co-citation analysis which enables the assessment of what might be considered classical green criminology works cited by two or more publications. The numerous texts referenced here are contained within the expanded co-citation sample. Together, bibliometric and co-citation analyses enable the identification of network structure based on recent shared references between 118 publications, as well as the examination of the seminal texts published before the year 2000.

Results

Consistent topical clustering patterns emerged within our citation networks with an occasional exception. Networks revealed that the subdiscipline is rooted in the common "trunk" of green criminology, which then splits into three broad "branches," which include (1) conservation criminology, (2) environmental justice/green victimology, and (3) eco-global/cultural green criminology. Each branch is further characterized by distinct features and smaller offshoots. Many seminal works straddle two different branches and bring them closer in doing so. We begin with an overview of common themes in green criminology before exploring the various publication and journal networks which detail the subdiscipline of green criminology.

Key themes in green criminology

A network representation of green crime keywords presents a scholastic summation of discourse concepts and terms used to express different environmental harms (see Figure 2.1). Notions ranging from climate conflict, to conservation enforcement, to disaster vulnerability issues, to illicit markets, to explicit reference of criminal locales (such as Colombia and Florida, USA) and specific chemical toxins present (e.g., lead, dibenzo-p-dioxins, and nitric oxide). The most central terms in order of occurrence are: green criminology (N = 48), criminology (33), crime (27), and environmental crime (18). A second tier of popular terms include conservation, environmental justice, green, and conservation criminology. Biodiversity is immediately linked to studies of Africa (specifically Uganda, Namibia, and South Africa) as well as poaching, game wardens, policing, corruption, and other issues pertaining to environmental enforcement. Furthermore, the broad concept of harm is linked with several terms such as vulnerability, risk, impacts, pollution, and inequality. Such connections suggest that the distinct research approaches express these ideas in different ways.

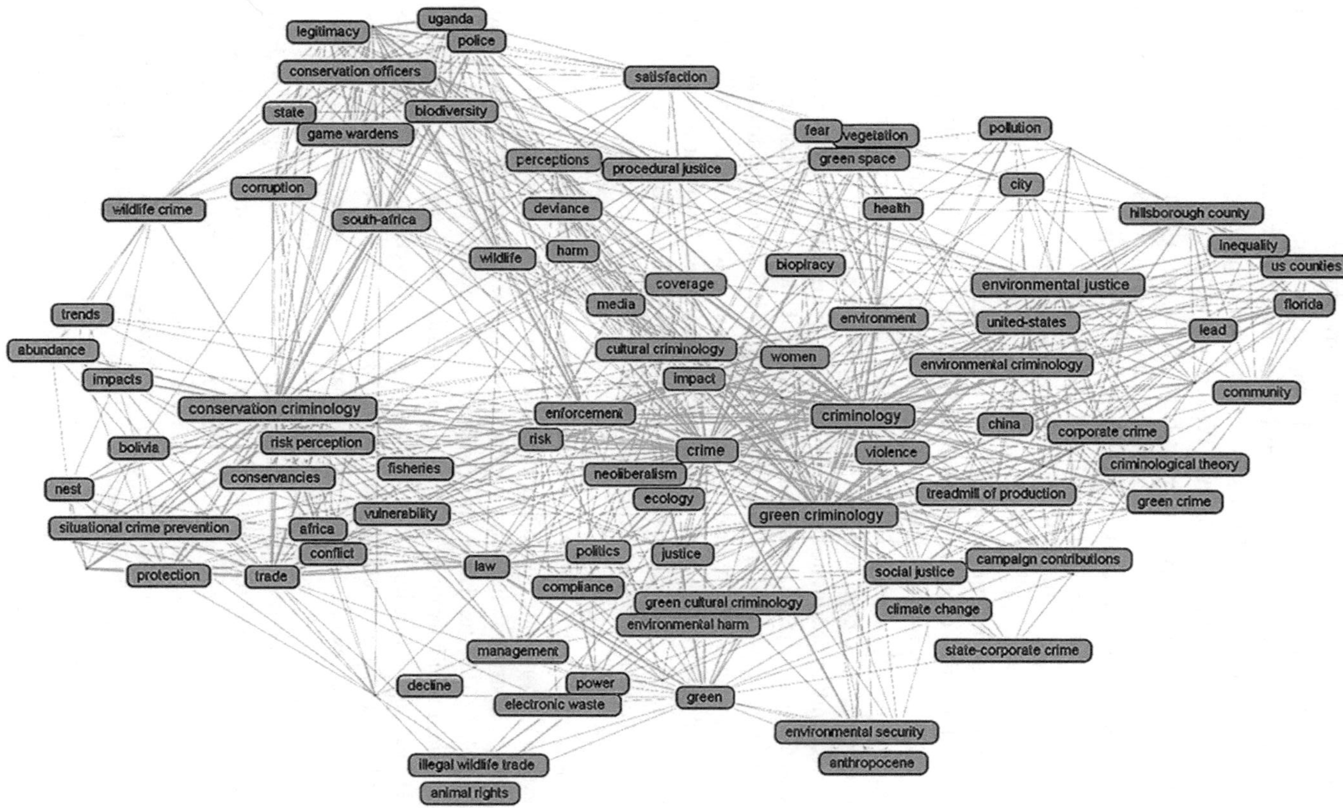

Figure 2.1 Keyword co-occurrence network in green criminology 2000–2017

Green criminology

The trunk of the subdiscipline is a conceptual body of work often described as macro-oriented in scale (see Figure 2.2). This dense cluster of co-cited works draws upon the roots of political economy and white collar crime. Since environmental harm cannot be separated from the global economic context within which it occurs and the corresponding state legal structures, green criminological research stems from this common conceptual trunk (Westerhuis, Walters, & Wyatt, 2013). This common stem is invoked by numerous branches of green criminology and found to be heavily influenced by theories of state and economic relations. In terms of the larger bibliometric network, the trunk holds a central position as a work referenced by a variety of areas. The trunk is relatively diverse. For example, within this cluster is Shover and Routhe's (2005) legalist environmental review of US regulatory framework, changes in precedents, and different compliance strategies. The trunk of green criminology is firmly rooted in critical research as expressed by its immediate concern with political economy. We also find Ruggiero and South's (2013a, 2013b) review of the economic foundations of environmental harm through an illustrative case study of the oil industry. They conclude by advocating for green criminological praxis to seriously engage with post-growth economics.

The treadmill of production theory (ToP), as developed in 1980 by Schnaiberg, provided an influential analysis detailing the role of the political economy in environmental problems and how this is structured within modern industrial society. The ToP represents a constant need for the economic system to produce and expand. Ecological withdrawals (raw materials extracted from nature) and additions (pollution) from ongoing industrialization destabilizes ecosystems. However, the process continues because the ToP profits capitalists and investors (Gould & Lewis, 2016). The validity of a theory such as ToP in advancing environmental harm research is that it offers a macro perspective through which to explain the motivation for corporate interests and the state to facilitate environmental harm. In this context, environmental harm is viewed as a necessary byproduct of production. Long et al. (2012) used the ToP perspective to advance green criminology in their evaluation of harm caused by the coal industry. Stretesky, Long, and Lynch (2013a) examined the impact of environmental enforcement on toxic releases and ToP as a cause of ecological disorganization. They found that the most punished companies in 2006 and 2007 expanded their rate of toxin production. Stretesky, Long, and Lynch's (2013b) timely book expanded this body of work regarding the treadmill of crime (ToC) and explored how ecological additions and withdrawals are central causes of ecological disorganization. By standing on the shoulders of ToP, green crime evolved to integrate a firm historical materialist perspective previously considered well outside the formal discipline. Specifically, ToP's role in furthering the green crime framework centers on its proposition that class conflict can help explain the distribution of environmental problems (Long et al., 2012). Similar works in political economy include Lynch, Stretesky, and Long's (2016) study of the Alberta Tar Sands, Lynch's (2016) examination of green-state power structures, and Bond's (2016) analysis of climate violence research. The ToP perspective is present within many of the branches. Johnson,

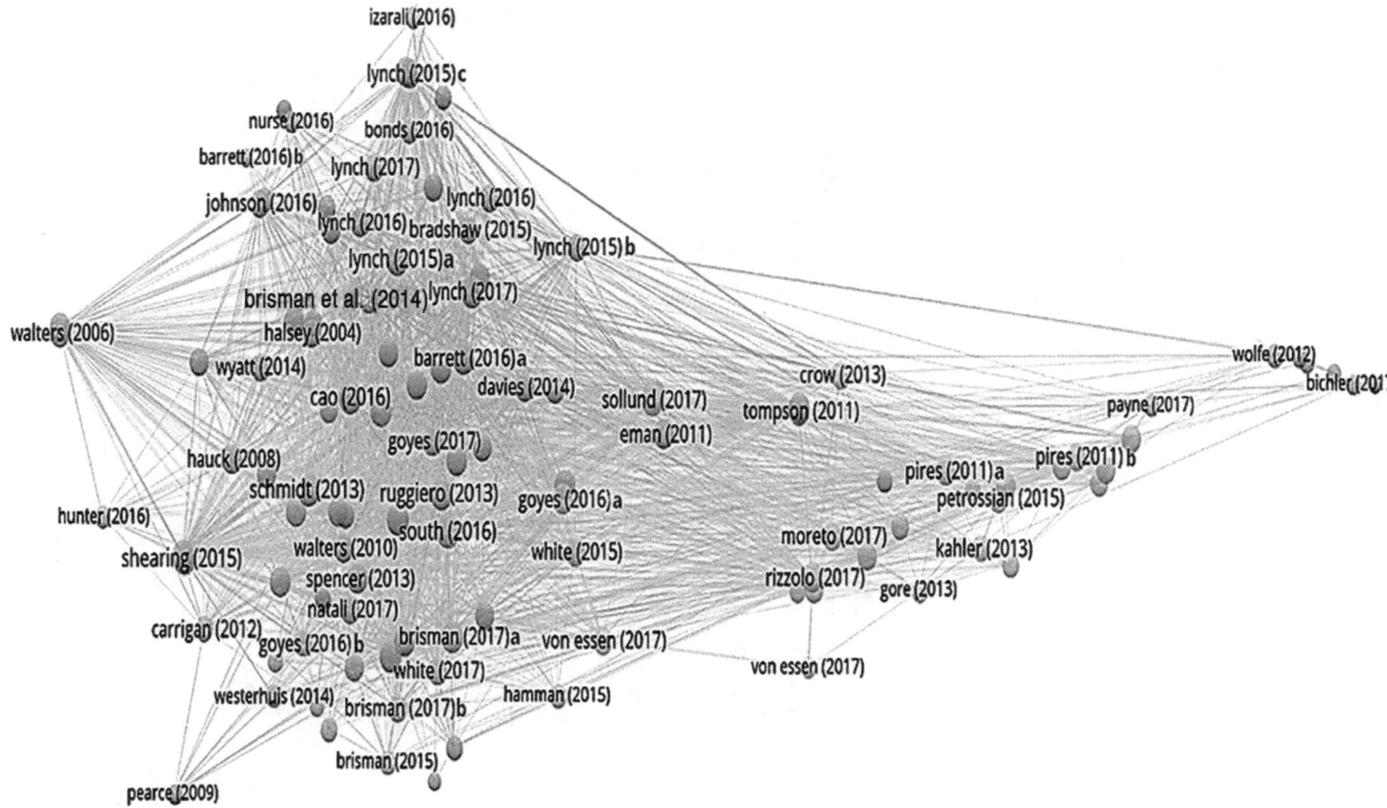

Figure 2.2 Bibliometric citation network in green criminology 2000–2017

South, and Walters (2016) (which falls within the conservation criminology cluster) detailed how state and corporate entities construct laws that enable the commodification of fresh water and corresponding scarcities.

Like the ToC theorization, green criminology has benefited from similar adoptions of ideas from other disciplines. Many of these works are shown to cluster with the trunk. These range of perspectives and methodologies spanning from the disposal of e-waste (South, 2016) and the imposition of genetically modified crops (Walters, 2005; Walters & Westerhuis, 2013) to the rights of non-human species (Beirne, 2007). Other works that laid the conceptual groundwork necessary for analytical synthesis include Lynch and Boggess's (2015) study of ecocities and Nurse's (2016b) review of animal welfare beyond the property debate.

Conservation criminology

Perhaps the most significant fork emerged with Gibbs, Gore, McGarrell, and River's publication "Introducing Conservation Criminology" (2009) in the *British Journal of Criminology*. This interdisciplinary group comprised scholars from the Fisheries & Wildlife, Criminal Justice, and Environmental Science & Policy Departments at Michigan State. Whereas green criminology took a decade to emerge, this branch of conservation criminology grew rapidly with a clear applied focus and strong emphasis on guiding policy reforms. Gore (2011) further outlined how conservation science was the key for "community groups to collaborate with law enforcement personnel in policing and enforcing civil, regulatory, legal, or normative rules" (p. 660). The interdisciplinary branch is primarily comprised of case studies guided by the common theme of conservation science within a criminological perspective (Hall et al., 2016). In terms of network clustering, the conservation branch was the only branch to comprise smaller topical clusters. The crown of the branch ranges from studies of illegal poaching/fishing, ranger issues, wildlife tracking, and offender characteristics.

Conservation criminologists have incorporated notions of risk management in studies of environmental issues by referring to the work of Giddens (1990), who accounted for the fact that risks in modernity were typically manufactured by man rather than nature, and Ulrich Beck (1992), a German sociologist who developed the theoretical notion of "risk society," and hypothesized that Western societies were organized around risk avoidance (White, 1999; Hall, 2015). This appreciation for environmental risks has been present in conservation criminology's foundation since its inception (Gibbs et al., 2009). From an environmental standpoint, Beck's risk society perspective proposes that technology and science intersect to inform collective decision-making and posits that when individuals lack knowledge about institutions of modernization (e.g., technical scientific Toxic Release Inventory reports on nearby pollutant discharges) or do not trust them (because of technological hazards), they begin to rely on their own individual concepts of risk (Gould & Lewis, 2016). The ideas of risk society were illustrated by Newburn's (2013) examination of the 2011 earthquake in Japan and resulting tsunami as a contemporary example of how green criminology incorporates natural and manufactured risk in its examination of environmental disasters.

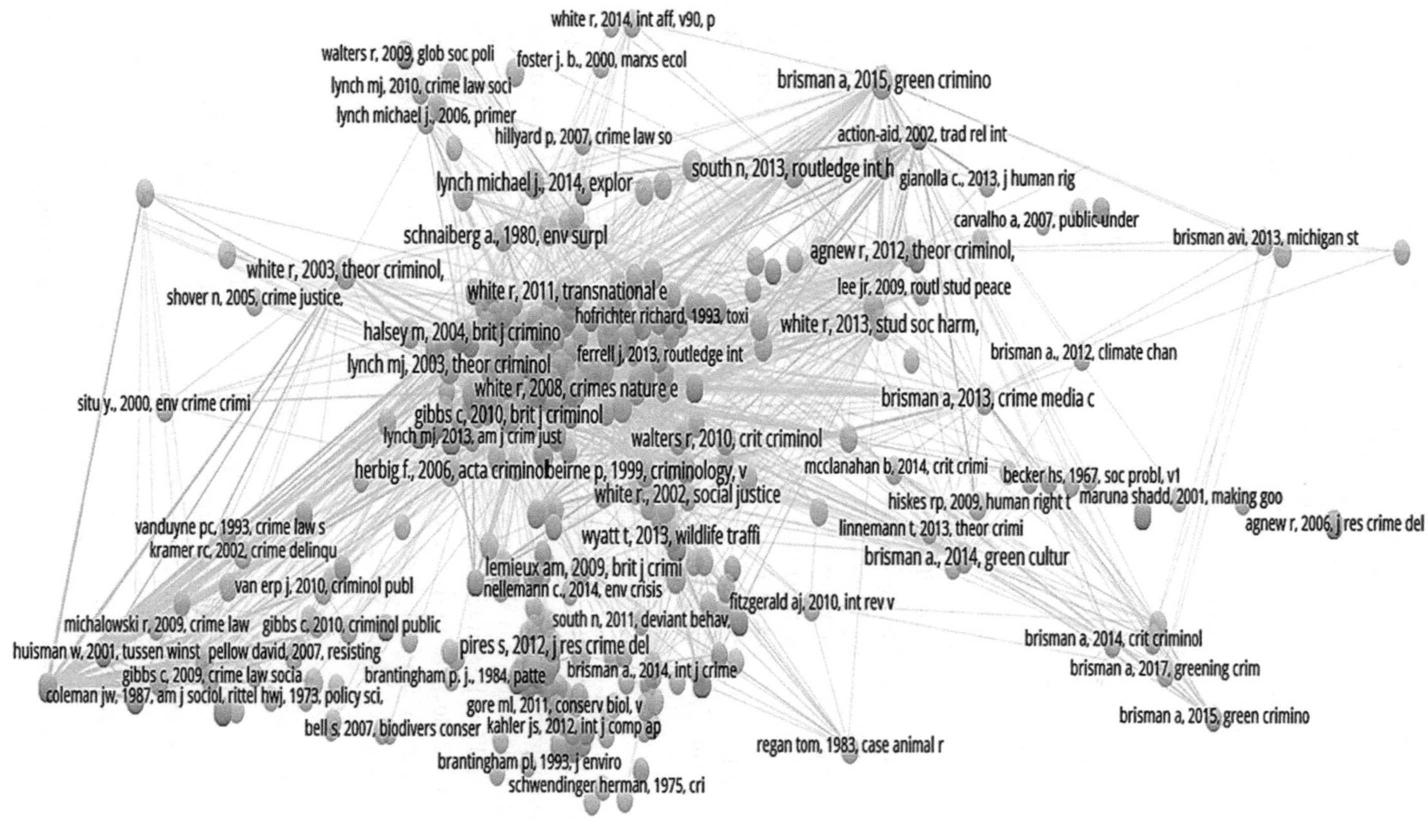

Figure 2.3 Shared co-citation network of green criminology references 2000–2017

Poaching/illegal fishing

Poaching and fishing is one issue at the forefront of conservation criminology. This area engages a variety of harms including studies of parrot poaching, bushmeat trade, unregulated fishing, trophy hunting, and retaliatory killings. While this area appears broad, it is united by criminological emphasis on compliance as it pertains to conservation issues. This common theme has also been applied to address a range of theoretical understandings. Take, for example, Kahler, Roloff, and Gore's (2013) study, like many in this sub-lateral branch, which situates poaching risk squarely in the natural resource management framework.

This is closely related to Hardin's "tragedy of the commons" framing used to describe shared-resource systems and the various situational crime prevention efforts seeking to conserve them. Some of these studies, such as Pires and Moreto's (2011), have been more theoretical in orientation. Others such as Moreto, Brunson, and Braga (2014) take a qualitative approach to study corruption among Ugandan rangers, while Petrossian (2015) presents a theoretical and quantitative study of illegal fishing. The range of methodological approaches contained within this budding area of research share in a common practical effort to limit crimes hindering conservation.

This methodological and scalar diversity is also a theme beyond management and poaching theorizations. The micro-descriptive approach has also been utilized in research characterized by an emphasis on local contexts. Pires and Clark (2012), for example, explored poaching opportunities throughout Mexico and found that the more accessible parrot nests were most frequently targeted. Similar criminal patterns were found among protected crab and lobster species (Petrossian, Weis, & Pires, 2015). Conversely, other works retain a macro-orientation with a structural emphasis. One of the more popular examples is Eliason's (2012) critical historical study which outlined the emergence of poaching laws alongside the increasing commercial value associated with trophy hunting. This area has also greatly benefited from geospatial analysis (e.g., Pires, 2015) and has begun to forge a direct bridge to human geography scholarship with works such as Potter, Nurse, and Hall (2016). This citation sub-cluster also has a few curious exceptions, such as Hauck's (2008) study of fisheries compliance, which fell within the victimology cluster.

Ranger issues

While deeply intertwined with illegal poaching and fishing practices and the conservation criminology literature, ranger issues are an emerging focus which emphasizes enforcement and prevention responses. Wellsmith's (2011) work outlined a variety of enforcement issues such as underresourcing and marginalization, the large "dark figure" of wildlife crime, corruption, lack of seriousness with which such crimes are viewed, lack of deterrent effect, and a few potential solutions. Gore, Ratsimbazafy, and Lute's (2013) study of corruption throughout

Madagascar is in this body of work. They addressed the definitional dilemma by distinguishing between a strict criminal justice perspective and the rules in use perspective. Such an approach enables them to engage the local context and real-world effects of corruption on biodiversity hot spots. Similarly, Kahler and Gore (2015) conducted a study of local risk perceptions and their effect on human-wildlife conflicts throughout the Zambezi region of Namibia. They found that species perceived to pose high risk to local livelihoods were moderately correlated with increased perceived poaching vulnerability and retaliation poaching. As noted in Nurse's (2015) important *Policing Wildlife* book, wildlife crime is rapidly growing and demands a serious effort to curb these grave environmental harms.

Wildlife trafficking

The wildlife trafficking sub-area integrates the study of animal rights with that of deviant human behaviors. These criminal acts can occur for a variety of reasons and take many forms. A strict legalist definition of wildlife trade, as defined by INTERPOL, "is the taking, trading, exploiting or possessing of the world's wild flora and fauna in contravention of natural and international laws" (Interpol, 2010) Goyes and Sollund's (2016) review of the enactment of the Convention on International Trade in Endangered Species (CITES) legislation aimed at regulating endangered species, including 5,600 species threatened by wildlife trafficking, also falls in this group of work. Their four-part motivation typology helps inform trafficking induced harm for the 181 signatories. CITES legislation is frequently cited within many of these studies as the legal framework for combating wildlife trafficking. Numerous studies regarding organized crime and trade of a multitude of illegal wildlife commodities have taken off in recent years. The illegal trade of flora have also been incorporated within the study of wildlife trafficking, including studies of timber trafficking (Wyatt, 2014b; Cao, 2018). Crimes pertaining to fauna include the harvesting and trade of ivory (Lemieux & Clarke, 2009), tiger bones (Wong, 2015), and black caviar (van Uhm & Siegel, 2016), among others.

Beginning with Beirne (1999), the issue of animal abuse as a crime quickly blossomed into a rich area of research exploring the cruelty or exploitation of animals (see also Beirne, 2002, 2009). Non-speciesist criminology partially falls in this vein of work, given a shared emphasis on animal rights, welfare, and interspecies violence (Beirne, 1999, 2007, 2013). These types of studies, loosely tied with Critical Animal Studies, are also found in the trunk (Nurse, 2016a) along with green victimization studies (Nurse, 2016b). Beirne's *Murdering Animals* (2018) engages animal rights scholarship such as Tom Regan (1983) to expand notions of harm beyond the endangered species list. Wyatt (2011, 2014a) expanded the effects of green crime to non-human animals via case studies on the illegal trading of birds of prey in the Russian Federation and the harm done by fur and falcon trades. Von Essen and Allen (2017) also focused on exploring wildlife victimhood and more conventional property arguments.

Offender characteristics and green profiling

Crow, Shelley, and Stretesky's (2013) multivariate examination of offender characteristics throughout Florida found that black and Hispanic individuals are more likely to be cited for improper permitting and illegal fishing methods compared to whites. Rizzolo et al. (2017) assessed cultural attitudes regarding poaching practices throughout Analamazaotra Special Reserve in Madagascar. This work is well-situated between the contextual dynamics of offender perceptions, Malagasy laws, and localized motivations. Conservation efforts have been shown to be significantly affected by gendered risk perceptions that, in turn, alter the process of cooperative management activities (Gore & Kahler, 2012). Eliason's (2008) study of Kentucky rangers' perceptions found a variety of different types of poachers driven by different intentions. Wyatt's (2013) book draws upon several conservation criminology's sub-lateral branches in her deconstruction of wildlife trafficking's victims and offenders. Issues associated with criminogenic effects have also begun to emerge from this area (Potter, 2016). Lastly, while profiling efforts have primarily taken place within conservation criminology, some works such as Tompson and Chainey (2011) have begun to explore illegal dumping offenders.

Eco-global and green cultural criminology

Green cultural criminology also serves as an important branch within green crime and is primarily concerned with the study of environmental harm and crime from the perspective of constructivist criminology (Westerhuis, 2013). Pioneered by Berger and Luckmann (1967), the social constructivist perspective argued that individuals' reality is objectively and externally created by others. Lynch and Stretesky (2003) argue that green crimes, as is the case with other crimes, are social constructions which are influenced by social locations and power relations in society. Since these social constructions do not adequately reflect the harm caused by environmental degradation, they point to the attention which critical green criminologists place on corporate actors, environmental justice activists, and movements based on gender, race, and class-based inequalities. More recently, Brisman and South (2013) built on these constructivist approaches to argue for a green cultural criminology that examines the social and political constructions of labels and terminology employed within green crime. Brisman and South (2014) further demonstrated the importance of constructivist approaches for understanding harm and resistance actions. Epistemological differences across space is also a primary concern within this branch; both between rural and urban settings and global North/South relations (Goyes, 2016). McClanahan (2014) integrated environmental justice (originating in Stretesky & Lynch, 1998; see section on environmental justice below) concerns into the green cultural framework in his study of opposition to water privatization and oppressive neoliberal regulations. Brisman (2017) further built on this body of work by examining how narratives and stories can sustain environmental harm and suffering. Conversely, he also notes that narratives and stories can shape future action with respect to the natural world.

Another extension of the constructivist perspective is eco-global criminology, which is in many ways associated with green cultural criminology. Eco-global criminology acknowledges that social constructions are socially patterned, and therefore our interpretations of environmental harm are shaped by the contexts within which environmental harm are presented by those in positions of power and authority (White, 2017). Accordingly, eco-global work calls for an assessment of how we ascribe meaning to environmental issues, particularly in relation to transnational and global harm. This branch calls for an examination of the ontological and subjective nature of environmental crime.

In addition to its constructivist alignment, eco-global criminology also embraces criminology's more mainstream place-based or "environmental criminology" associated with early works in the Chicago School of sociology (Burgess, McKenzie, & Wirth, 1925). This root has contributed to the development of green criminology by offering a space for the geospatial analysis of green crime (ranging in types of criminal activities from Kurland, Pires, and Marteache, 2018; Lynch, 2016; Thomson, Espin, and Samuels-Jones, forthcoming). Such studies have proven valuable in providing data for the prevention of illegal wildlife trade and endangered species protection. On a more global level, it has also influenced green crime through distinct areas of inquiry such as eco-global criminology, which is particularly concerned with the transnational nature of environmental crime. This type of work emphasizes the impact of climate change, ecological justice, and transnational crimes on the environment (White, 2011). White's (2008, 2017) work in this area argued for the inclusion of scale to incorporate local and internal dimensions in the examination of environmental harm.

The intersection of green cultural and eco-global criminology is illustrated by works such as White's (2015) examination of incarceration among indigenous Australian youth. In addition, White's (2017) argument that green criminologists must take the constructions of meaning into their consideration to adequately understand what nature means to various groups, how interpretations of the experiences on non-indigenous groups impact Indigenous peoples, and how non-human species may be also understood as environmental victims. This area contains two notable works that sought to expand work within the sub-discipline. Through their ethnographic studies of Huelva Spain and Central Appalachia, Natali and McClanahan (2017) promoted an integration of photographic images, visual perceptions, and communication into green cultural criminology. Similarly, Sollund (2017) explored the legal and illegal wildlife trafficking through interviews with enforcement agencies in Brazil, Colombia, and Norway. In doing so, her comparative study demonstrated the value of an auto-ethnographic and feminist analytical approach.

Environmental justice and green victimology

Environmental justice (EJ) has also provided a fertile soil for green crime. EJ advocates for the fair treatment and meaningful involvement of all with respect to the access to and use of natural resources. Within green criminology, EJ has been viewed as an extension of human rights issues as influenced by the work of scholars such as Bullard (1990, 1994), Schlosberg (1999, 2009), Pellow (2000), and Clapp and Dauvergne (2011), among numerous others, and was first pursued in green criminology by Stretesky and Lynch (1998, 1999, 2002). This heavily influential current brought awareness to environmental racism through a combination of grassroots resistance and critical scholarship. Brisman (2008) and Lynch, Stretesky, and Long (2015) offer reviews of the diverse work within this branch. We also find Gerrard's (1999) edited book, in collaboration with the American Bar Association, as another notable work that provided a strict legalist review. Gerrard incorporated the theories and procedures from EJ to address issues of disproportionate risk. Similar legalistic reviews of regulatory policies and processes include Lavelle and Coyle (1992), Zilney, McGurrin, and Zahran (2006), Lynch, Burns, and Stretesky (2008), and Rechtschaffen, Gauna, and O'Neill (2009). Green criminology's interests, grounded within EJ research, are largely concerned with the empirical links between environmental harm (such as toxicity) and poor and marginalized groups (Westerhuis, 2013). The bridge from EJ to green victimology can be found in the work of Stretesky and Lynch (1998), Barrett (2013), and Hall (2014). White, Kluin, and Spapens's (2014) edited book also offered 17 chapters which significantly reinforced the injustice/victimology branch. In addition, Cao and Wyatt (2016) advocated for a human security perspective in their study of timber trafficking as a means for green victimization.

Within green criminology and the broader criminological discourse, there has historically been a dearth of studies on the victims of environmental crime (Hall, 2014). Lynch and Stretesky (2014) argue this exclusion has omitted "those who most need to be empowered and to have their rights protected" (p. 81). The relatively small collection of studies that have been undertaken in this area have consistently reflected a critical and interdisciplinary approach. Given that environmental harm and notions of green victimization are invoked ranging from an individual animal to entire territories, we observe a broad range of work across different geographic scales. Walters (2005) for example, discussed the aggressive worldwide pressure to shift towards genetically modified foods, and emphasized the pressure exerted by Western countries upon underdeveloped countries, such as Zambia, to accept these modified foods. This argument is incorporated into an "eco-crimes" state and corporate crime framework which highlights the fact that environmental harms are often the byproduct of *legal* state and corporate activities (Walters, 2005). Hauck's (2008) publication on small-scale fisheries expanded on Walters's work using the illustration of small-scale fisheries and argues for a revision of the definition of compliance when environmental laws are based on power dynamics rather than conservation science. One surprising study which falls in this branch is by Carrigan (2012), who examined Indra Sinha's novel on post-disaster life in Bhopal to explore the criminal implications of lasting violence (for an earlier study, see Lynch, Nalla, & Miller, 1989). Barrett, Lynch, and Stretesky's (2016b) study of school violence also falls within this category. As with most branches of green crime, work on green victimology has grown and is beginning to incorporate more non-human species, as well as a stronger context within the Anthropocene. Despite the significant amount of growth throughout the subdiscipline, acceptance among the larger discipline is yet to be seen.

Journals

Of the journals which have begun to publish green criminology research, five journals have begun publishing this type of work (impact factor in parentheses): *Critical Criminology* (0.607); *British Journal of Criminology* (2.464); *Crime, Law, and Social Change* (0.662); *Theoretical Criminology* (1.873); and *Social Justice Research* (0.826) have been the first to publish green crime scholarship (Clarivate Analytics JCR, 2018). A few notable non-criminology journals have also been welcoming scholarship, such as *Society and Animals* (0.475); *Critical Sociology* (1.295); *Biological Conservation* (4.660); *Social Science Quarterly* (0.874); *Social Problems* (2.071); and *Society and Natural Resources* (1.823) (Clarivate Analytics JCR, 2018). Many of these studies published outside the discipline have proven to be widely cited and, in many instances, benefited from these venues (see Figure 2.4).

And while the field of green criminology is far more accepted today than ten years ago, it is still struggling to gain access to certain key disciplinary venues. Green criminological work remains absent from the discipline's top-tier journals. This suggests that, while parts of the discipline have begun to appreciate the value of environmental concerns, many of green criminology's seminal works have been published as book chapters rather than peer-reviewed journals (Lynch et al., 2017).

Discussions and conclusions

Our bibliometric citation network analyses of green criminology identified many established research areas and various undercurrents. Throughout the tree of research, harm is expressed differently depending upon the scholastic approach being employed. At the core of the subdiscipline, we find a common and frequently referenced trunk grounded within criminology, political economy, and environmental studies. The rate of peer-reviewed journal articles appears to be increasing throughout the subdiscipline. Many of these publications have found venues outside criminology. Branches exhibiting rapid growth such as conservation criminology have quickly sprouted new sub-lateral branches examining issues such as poaching/illegal fishing, ranger issues, wildlife trafficking, and offender characteristics. Green victimology appears to still be budding as it continues to establish itself and overcome the scarcity of research in this area. We also find that the perceptions and profiles of environmental offenders appears understudied. Many green criminological works defy easy classification. Non-speciesist criminology can be found within multiple clusters (most notably green victimology and wildlife trafficking).

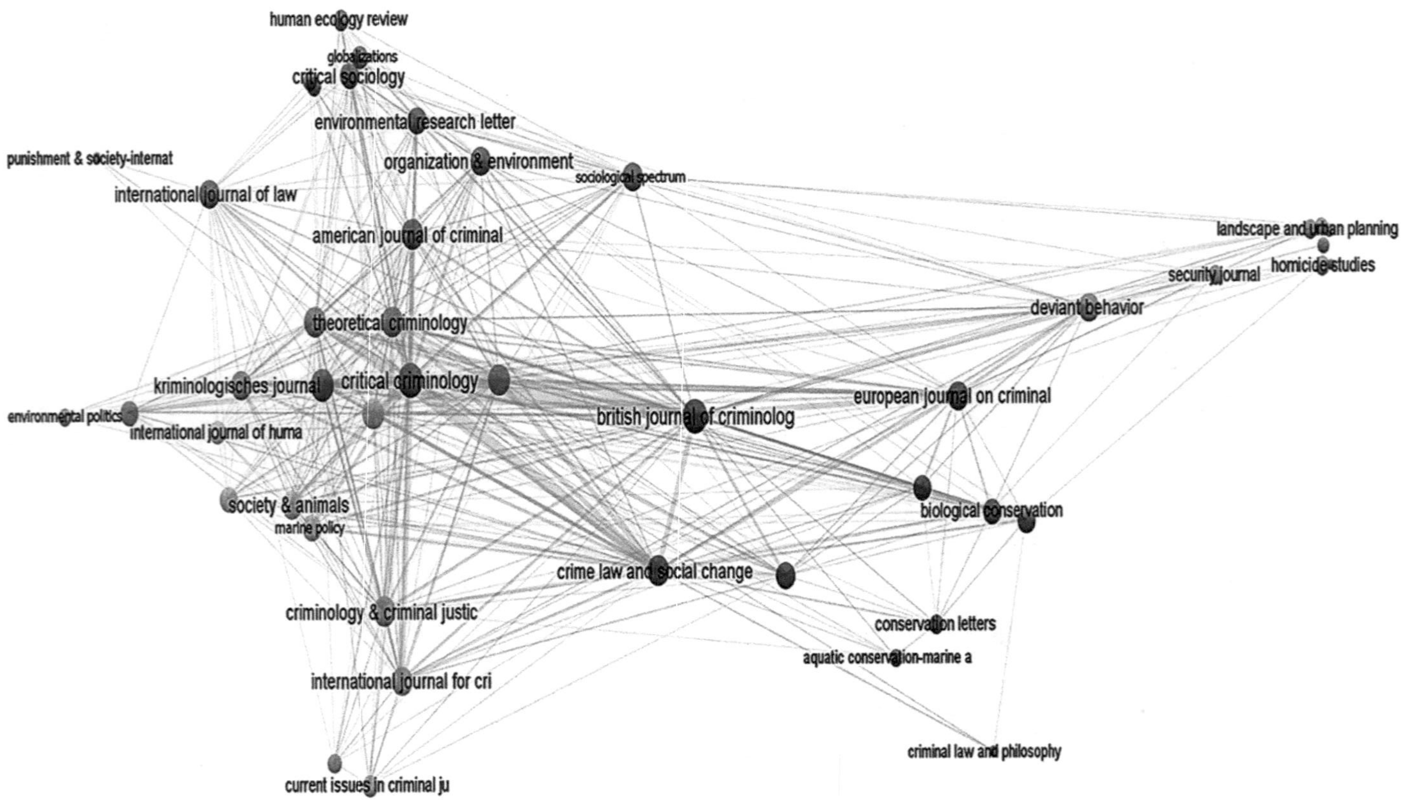

Figure 2.4 Journals in green criminology 2000–2017

The analyses contained within this book do not belong to any single branch, but each strives to grow the tree of green criminology and its numerous sub-lateral branches. We hope this network review of the subdiscipline informs the following chapters. Moreover, network analysis has been helpful in analyzing and describing the present state of the subdiscipline. We contend that network analysis could prove even more fruitful in the study of environmental harm. These techniques remain an underutilized method which can be used to explore the social ties associated with offender networks, enforcement embeddedness within local communities, and regulatory capture and corruption, as well as transdisciplinary research collaborations.

As green criminology continues to grow, it builds new annual rings and produces new lateral branches. These branches reinforce the earlier conceptual groundwork, roots, and trunk necessary for supporting the next generation of scholarship to come. The effort to expand quantitative research presents new opportunities for criminological and environmental synthesis. Clusters and citation patterns will undoubtedly change. The subdisciplinary tree of today will surely become the tree of tomorrow. Environmental concerns are slowly being accepted within mainstream criminology, albeit at a slow rate. So, while the discipline has been subject to less than ideal growing conditions, its perseverance and growth over the past two decades gives us grounds for optimism. As the effects of the Anthropocene and sixth great extinction become increasingly dire (IPCC, 2018), we contend that green criminology is poised to become a central area of research within the discipline.

References

André, J. D. (1980). Délinquance écologique: De l'artificiel au transactionnel. *Déviance et société*, *4*(4), 399–412.

Barrett, K. L. (2013). Bethlehem steel at Lackawanna: The state-corporate crimes that continue to victimize the residents and environment of Western New York. *Journal of Crime and Justice*, *36*(2), 263–282.

Barrett, K. L., Lynch, M. J., & Stretesky, P. B. (2016b). Green criminology and the reconceptualization of school violence: Comparing green school violence and traditional forms of school violence for school children. *Critical Criminology*, *24*(1), 19–37.

Beck, U. (1992). *Risk society: Towards a new modernity*. Newbury Park, CA; London: Sage Publications.

Beirne, P. (2018). *Murdering animals*. London: Palgrave Macmillan.

Beirne, P. (2013). Animal rights, animal abuse and green criminology. In *Issues in green criminology* (pp. 77–106). Milton Park, UK: Willan.

Beirne, P. (2009). *Confronting animal abuse: Law, criminology, and human-animal relationships*. Totowa, NJ: Rowman & Littlefield Publishers.

Beirne, P. (2007). Animal rights, animal abuse and green criminology. In P. Beirne & N. South (Eds.), *Issues in green criminology: Confronting harms against environments, humanity and other animals*. Devon: Willan Publishing.

Beirne, P. (2002). Criminology and animal studies: A sociological view. *Society & Animals*, *10*(4), 381–386.

Beirne, P. (1999). For a nonspeciesist criminology: Animal abuse as an object of study. *Criminology, 37*(1), 117–148.

Beirne, P., & South, N. (Eds.). (2007). *Issues in green criminology: Confronting harms against environments, other animals and humanity.* Portland, OR: Willan.

Berger, P. L., & Luckmann, T. (1967). *The social construction of reality: A treatise in the sociology of knowledge.* Garden City, NY: Anchor.

Bonds, E. (2016). Upending climate violence research: Fossil fuel corporations and the structural violence of climate change. *Human Ecology Review, 22*(2), 3–24.

Borrett, S. R., Moody, J., & Edelmann, A. (2014). The rise of network ecology: Maps of the topic diversity and scientific collaboration. *Ecological Modelling, 293*, 111–127.

Brisman, A. (2017). On narrative and green cultural criminology. *International Journal For Crime, Justice And Social Democracy, 6*(2), 64–77.

Brisman, A. (2008). Crime-environment relationships and environmental justice. *Seattle Journal of Social Justice, 6*, 727–907.

Brisman, A., McClanahan, B., & South, N. (2014). Toward a green-cultural criminology of "the rural." *Critical Criminology, 22*(4), 479–494.

Brisman, A., & South, N. (2014). *Green cultural criminology: Constructions of environmental harm, consumerism, and resistance to ecocide.* Abingdon, UK: Routledge.

Brisman, A., & South, N. (2013). A green-cultural criminology: An exploratory outline. *Crime, Media, Culture, 9*(2), 115–135.

Bullard, R. D. (1994). *Unequal protection: Environmental justice and communities of color.* San Francisco: Sierra Club Books.

Bullard, R. D. (1990). *Dumping in Dixie: Race, class and environmental quality.* Boulder, CO: Westview.

Burgess, E. W., McKenzie, R. D., & Wirth, L. (1925). *The city.* Chicago: University of Chicago Press.

Cao, A. N. (2018). *Timber trafficking in Vietnam: Crime, security and the environment.* London: Palgrave Macmillan.

Cao, A. N., & Wyatt, T. (2016). The conceptual compatibility between green criminology and human security: A proposed interdisciplinary framework for examinations into green victimisation. *Critical Criminology, 24*(3), 413–430.

Carrigan, A. (2012). "Justice is on our side"? Animal's People, generic hybridity, and eco-crime. *The Journal of Commonwealth Literature, 47*(2), 159–174.

Clapp, J., & Dauvergne, P. (2011). *Paths to a green world: The political economy of the global environment.* Cambridge, MA: MIT Press.

Clarivate Analytics. (2018). *Journal Citation Report.* Retrieved from https://clarivate.com/essays/impact-factor/

Clifford, M. (1998). *Environmental crime: Enforcement, policy, and social responsibility.* Burlington, MA: Jones & Bartlett Learning.

Cohn, E. G., & Farrington, D. P. (2011). Scholarly influence and prestige in criminology and criminal justice. *Journal of Criminal Justice Education, 22*(1), 5–11.

Crow, M. S., Shelley, T.O.C., & Stretesky, P. B. (2013). Camouflage-collar crime: An examination of wildlife crime and characteristics of offenders in Florida. *Deviant Behavior, 34*(8), 635–652.

De Bellis, N. (2009). *Bibliometrics and citation analysis from Science citation index to cybermetrics.* Landham, MD: Scarecrow Press.

DiMento, J. F. (1993). Criminal enforcement of environmental law. *The Annals of the American Academy of Political and Social Science, 525*(1), 134–146.

Eliason, S. L. (2012). From the King's deer to a capitalist commodity: A social historical analysis of the poaching law. *International Journal of Comparative and Applied Criminal Justice*, *36*(2), 133–148.

Eliason, S. L. (2008). Wildlife crime: Conservation officers' perceptions of elusive poachers. *Deviant Behavior*, *29*(2), 111–128.

Eman, K., Meško, G., & Fields, C. B. (2009). Crimes against the environment: Green criminology and research challenges in Slovenia. *Varstvoslovje*, *11*(4), 574–592.

Foster, J. B. (2000). *Marx's ecology: Materialism and nature*. New York: NYU Press.

Frank, N. K., & Lynch, M. J. (1992). *Corporate crime, corporate violence: A primer*. New York: Harrow and Heston.

Gerrard, M. (1999). *The law of environmental justice: Theories and procedures to address disproportionate risks*. Chicago: American Bar Association.

Gibbs, C., Gore, M. L., McGarrell, E. F., & Rivers III, L. (2009). Introducing conservation criminology: Towards interdisciplinary scholarship on environmental crimes and risks. *The British Journal of Criminology*, *50*(1), 124–144.

Giddens, A. (1990). The consequences of modemity. *Polity Press, Cambridge, UK*, *99*, 184–197.

Gore, M. L. (2011). The science of conservation crime. *Conservation. Biology*, *25*, 659–661.

Gore, M. L., & Kahler, J. S. (2012). Gendered risk perceptions associated with human wildlife conflict: Implications for participatory conservation. *PLoS ONE*, *7*, e32901.

Gore, M. L., Ratsimbazafy, J., & Lute, M. L. (2013). Rethinking corruption in conservation crime: Insights from Madagascar. *Conservation Letters*, *6*(6), 430–438.

Gould, K. A., & Lewis, T. L. (2016). Making urban greening sustainable. In *Green gentrification* (pp. 161–186). Abingdon, UK: Routledge.

Goyes, D. R. (2016). Green activist criminology and the epistemologies of the South. *Critical Criminology*, *24*(4), 503–518.

Goyes, D. R., & Sollund, R. (2016). Contesting and contextualising CITES: Wildlife trafficking in Colombia and Brazil. *International Journal for Crime, Justice and Social Democracy*, *5*(4), 87–102. doi:10.5204/ijcjsd.v5i4.331

Goyes, D. R., & South, N. (2017). Green criminology before "green criminology": Amnesia and absences. *Critical Criminology*, *25*(2), 165–181.

Hall, M. (2015). *Exploring green crime: Introducing the legal, social and criminological contexts of environmental harm*. New York: Palgrave Macmillan.

Hall, M. (2014). Environmental harm and environmental victims: Scoping out a "green victimology." *International Review of Victimology*, *20*(1), 129–143.

Hall, M., Nurse, A., Wyatt, T., South, N., Maher, J., & Potter, G. (Eds.). (2016). *Greening criminology in the 21st century: Contemporary debates and future directions in the study of environmental harm*. Boca Raton, FL: Taylor & Francis.

Hamilton, Catherine A., Raffaele Vacca, & Jeanne-Marie R. Stacciarini. (2017). The emergence of team science: Understanding the state of adoption research through social network analysis. *Adoption & Fostering* *41*(4), 369–390.

Hauck, M. (2008). Rethinking small-scale fisheries compliance. *Marine Policy*, *32*(4), 635–642.

Intergovernmental Panel on Climate Change. (2018). "Global warming of 1.5°C." Retrieved from www.ipcc.ch/report/sr15/

Interpol. (2010). *Wildlife Crime*. Retrieved from www.interpol.int/public/Environmental Crime/Wildlife/Default.asp

Johnson, H., South, N., & Walters, R. (2016). The commodification and exploitation of fresh water: Property, human rights and green criminology. *International Journal of Law, Crime and Justice*, *44*, 146–162.

Kahler, J. S., & Gore, M. L. (2015). Local perceptions of risk associated with poaching of wildlife implicated in human-wildlife conflicts in Namibia. *Biological Conservation*, *189*, 49–58.

Kahler, J. S., Roloff, G. J., & Gore, M. L. (2013). Poaching risks in community-based natural resource management. *Conservation Biology*, *27*(1), 177–186.

Kessler, M. M. (1963). Bibliographic coupling between scientific papers. *American Documentation*, *14*(1), 10–25. doi:10.1002/asi.5090140103

Kolowich, S. (2009). Tenure-o-Meter. *Inside Higher Education*. Retrieved from www.insidehighered.com/news/2009/12/15/tenure

Kurland, J., Pires, S. F., & Marteache, N. (2018). The spatial pattern of redwood burl poaching and implications for prevention. *Forest Policy and Economics*, *94*, 46–54.

Lavelle, M., & Coyle, M. (1992). Unequal protection. *National Law Journal*, *15*, S1–S12.

Leff, E. (1993). Marxism and the environmental question: From the critical theory of production to an environmental rationality for sustainable development. *Capitalism Nature Socialism*, *4*(1), 44–66.

Lemieux, A. M., & Clarke, R. V. (2009). The international ban on ivory sales and its effects on elephant poaching in Africa. *The British Journal of Criminology*, *49*(4), 451–471.

Long, M. A., Stretesky, P. B., Lynch, M. J., & Fenwick, E. (2012). Crime in the coal industry: Implications for green criminology and treadmill of production. *Organization & Environment*, *25*(3), 328–346.

Lynch, M. J. (2017). Conceptualizing green victimization, green criminology and political economy: A reply. *Critical Sociology*, *43*(3), 473–478.

Lynch, M. J. (2016). The ecological distribution of community advantage and disadvantage: Power structures, political economy, communities, and green-state crime and justice. *Critical Criminology*, *24*(2), 247–262.

Lynch, M. J. (1990/2006). The greening of criminology: A perspective for the 1990s. Reprinted in N. South & P. Beirne (Eds.), *Green criminology*. Hampshire: Aldershot.

Lynch, M. J., Barrett, K. L., Stretesky, P. B., & Long, M. A. (2017). The neglect of quantitative research in green criminology and its consequences. *Critical Criminology*, *25*(2), 183–198.

Lynch, M. J., & Boggess, L. N. (2015). Ecocities, crime, and justice: Ecocity theory, social disorganization, and green criminology. *Sociological Spectrum*, *35*(4), 309–328.

Lynch, M. J., Burns, R., & Stretesky, P. (2008). *Environmental crime, law and justice: An introduction*. New York: LFB Scholarly.

Lynch, M. J., Long, M. A., Barrett, K. L., & Stretesky, P. B. (2013). Is it a crime to produce ecological disorganization? Why green criminology and political economy matter in the analysis of global ecological harms. *British Journal of Criminology*, *53*(6), 997–1016.

Lynch, M. J., Nalla, M., & Miller, K. (1989). Cross cultural perceptions of deviance: The case of Bhopal. *Journal of Research in Crime and Delinquency*, *26*(1), 7–35.

Lynch, M. J., & Stretesky, P. B. (2014). *Exploring green criminology: Toward a green revolution in criminology*. Surrey: Ashgate.

Lynch, M. J., & Stretesky, P. B. (2003). The meaning of green: Contrasting criminological perspectives. *Theoretical Criminology*, *7*(2), 217–238.

Lynch, M. J., Stretesky, P. B., & Long, M. A. (2016). A proposal for the political economy of green criminology: Capitalism and the case of the Alberta Tar Sands. *Canadian Journal of Criminology and Criminal Justice*, *58*(2), 137–160.

Lynch, M. J., Stretesky, P. B., & Long, M. A. (2015). Environmental justice: A criminological perspective. *Environmental Research Letters*, *10*(8), 085008.

Martyn, J. (1964). Bibliographic coupling. *Journal of Documentation*, *20*(4), 236. doi:10.1108/eb026352

Marx, K. (1909). *Capital, Volume I*. Chicago: Charles H. Kerr.

McClanahan, B. (2014). Green and grey: Water justice, criminalization, and resistance. *Critical Criminology*, *22*(3), 403–418.

Mol, H. (2017). Introduction. In *The politics of palm oil harm* (pp. 1–32). Cham: Palgrave Macmillan.

Moreto, W. D. (2017). Avoiding the tragedy of (un) common knowledge: Reflections on conducting qualitative criminological research in conservation science. *Qualitative Research*, *17*(4), 440–456.

Moreto, W. D., Brunson, R. K., and Braga, A. A. (2014). 'Such misconducts don't make a good ranger': Examining law enforcement ranger wrongdoing in Uganda. *British Journal of Criminology*, 55 (2): 359-380.

Natali, L., & McClanahan, B. (2017). Perceiving and communicating environmental contamination and change: Towards a green cultural criminology with images. *Critical Criminology*, *25*(2), 199–214.

Newburn, T. (2013). *Criminology* (2nd ed.). Abingdon, UK: Routledge.

Nurse, A. (2016a). Beyond the property debate: Animal welfare as a public good. *Contemporary Justice Review*, *19*(2), 174–187.

Nurse, A. (2016b). *Animal harm: Perspectives on why people harm and kill animals*. Abingdon, UK: Routledge.

Nurse, A. (2015). *Policing wildlife: Perspectives on the enforcement of wildlife legislation*. New York: Springer.

O'Connor, J. (1986). *Accumulation crisis*. New York: Basil Blackwell.

OECD Frascati Manual, & Oxford Dictionary. (2002). (6th ed.) Annex 7: page 203, paras. 20–22.

Pečar, Janez. 1981. "Ekološka kriminaliteta in kriminologija." Revija za kriminalistiko in kriminologijo 34 (1): 33–45.

Pellow, D. N. (2000). Environmental inequality formation: Toward a theory of environmental injustice. *American Behavioral Scientist*, *43*(4), 581–601.

Petrossian, G. A. (2015). Preventing illegal, unreported and unregulated (IUU) fishing: A situational approach. *Biological Conservation*, *189*, 39–48.

Petrossian, G. A., Weis, J. S., & Pires, S. F. (2015). Factors affecting crab and lobster species subject to IUU fishing. *Ocean & Coastal Management*, *106*, 29–34.

Pires, S. F. (2015). A CRAVED analysis of multiple illicit parrot markets in Peru and Bolivia. *European Journal on Criminal Policy and Research*, *21*(3), 321–336.

Pires, S. F., & Clarke, R. V. (2012). Are parrots CRAVED? An analysis of parrot poaching in Mexico. *Journal of Research in Crime and Delinquency*, *49*(1), 122–146.

Pires, S. F., & Clarke, R. V. (2011). Sequential foraging, itinerant fences and parrot poaching in Bolivia. *The British Journal of Criminology*, *51*(2), 314–335.

Pires, S. F., & Moreto, W. D. (2011). Preventing wildlife crimes: Solutions that can overcome the "tragedy of the commons." *European Journal on Criminal Policy and Research*, *17*(2), 101–123.

Potter, G. R. (2016). The criminogenic effects of environmental harm: Bringing a "green" perspective to mainstream criminology. In *Environmental crime and its victims* (pp. 25–40). Abingdon, UK: Routledge.

Potter, G. R., Nurse, A., & Hall, M. (Eds.). (2016). *The geography of environmental crime: Conservation, wildlife crime and environmental activism*. New York: Springer.

Rechtschaffen, C., Gauna, E., & O'Neill, C. (2009). *Environmental justice: Law, policy & regulation*. Alphen aan den Rijn, Netherlands: Wolters Kluwer.

Regan, T. (1983). *The case for animal rights*. Berkeley: University of California Press.

Rizzolo, J. B., Gore, M. L., Ratsimbazafy, J. H., & Rajaonson, A. (2017). Cultural influences on attitudes about the causes and consequences of wildlife poaching. *Crime, Law and Social Change*, *67*(4), 415–437.

Ruggiero, V., & South, N. (2013a). Green criminology and crimes of the economy: Theory, research and praxis. *Critical Criminology*, *21*(3), 359–373.

Ruggiero, V., & South, N. (2013b). Toxic state-corporate crimes, neo-liberalism and green criminology: The hazards and legacies of the oil, chemical and mineral industries. *International Journal for Crime, Justice and Social Democracy*, *2*(2), 12–26.

Ruggiero, V., & South, N. (2010). Green criminology and dirty collar crime. *Critical Criminology*, *18*(4), 251–262.

Schnaiberg, A. (1980). *The environment: From surplus to scarcity*. New York, NY: Oxford University Press.

Schlosberg, D. (2009). *Defining environmental justice: Theories, movements, and nature*. Oxford: Oxford University Press.

Schlosberg, D. (1999). *Environmental justice and the new pluralism: The challenge of difference for environmentalism*. Oxford: Oxford University Press.

Shifferd, K. D. (1972). Karl Marx and the environment. *The Journal of Environmental Education*, *3*(4), 39–42.

Shover, N., & Routhe, A. S. (2005). Environmental crime. *Crime and Justice*, *32*, 321–371.

Situ, Y., & Emmons, D. (2000). *Environmental crime: The criminal justice system's role in protecting the environment*. Thousand Oaks, CA: Sage Publications.

Sollund, R. (2017). Doing green, critical criminology with an auto-ethnographic, feminist approach. *Critical Criminology*, *25*(2), 245–260.

South, N. (2016). Green criminology and brown crime: Despoliation, disposal and de-manufacturing in global resource industries. In *Hazardous waste and pollution* (pp. 11–25). New York: Springer.

South, N. (2008). Nature, difference, and the rejection of harm: Expanding the agenda for green criminology. In R. Sollund (Ed.), *Global harms: Ecological crime and speciesism* (pp. 187–200). New York: Nova Science Publishers.

South, N., & Brisman, A. (Eds.). (2013). *Routledge international handbook of green criminology*. Abingdon, UK: Routledge.

Stretesky, P. B., Long, M. A., & Lynch, M. J. (2013a). Does environmental enforcement slow the treadmill of production? The relationship between large monetary penalties, ecological disorganization and toxic releases within offending corporations. *Journal of Crime and Justice*, *36*(2), 233–247.

Stretesky, P. B., Long, M. A., & Lynch, M. J. (2013b). *The treadmill of crime: Political economy and green criminology*. Abingdon, UK: Routledge.

Stretesky, P. B., & Lynch, M. J. (2002). Environmental hazards and school segregation in Hillsborough County, Florida, 1987–1999. *The Sociological Quarterly, 43*(4), 553–573.

Stretesky, P. B., & Lynch, M. J. (1999). Environmental justice and the prediction of distance to accidental chemical releases in Hillsborough County, Florida. *Social Science Quarterly, 80*(4), 830–846.

Stretesky, P. B., & Lynch, M. J. (1998). Corporate environmental violence and racism. *Crime, Law and Social Change, 30*(2), 163–184.

Sutherland, E. H. (1949/1961). *White collar crime.* New York: Holt, Reinehart and Winston.

Taylor, I., Walton, P., & Young, J. (1973). *The new criminology: For a theory of social deviance.* London: Routledge.

Tompson, L., & Chainey, S. (2011). Profiling illegal waste activity: Using crime scripts as a data collection and analytical strategy. *European Journal on Criminal Policy and Research, 17*(3), 179.

Thomson, R., Espin, J., & Samuels-Jones, T. (Forthcoming). Green crime havens: A spatial cluster of environmental crime in the U.S. *Social Science Quarterly.*

Van Eck, N. J., & Waltman, L. (2014). Visualizing bibliometric networks. In Y. Ding, R. Rousseau, & D. Wolfram (Eds.), *Measuring scholarly impact: Methods and practice* (pp. 285–320). New York: Springer.

Van Eck, N. J., & Waltman, L. (2010). Software survey: VOSviewer, a computer program for bibliometric mapping. *Scientometrics, 84*(2), 523–538.

van Uhm, D., & Siegel, D. (2016). The illegal trade in black caviar. *Trends in Organized Crime, 19*(1), 67–87.

Veblen, T. (1899). *The theory of the leisure class: An economic study in the evolution of institutions.* London: Palgrave Macmillan.

Von Essen, E., & Allen, M. (2017). Interspecies violence and crimes of dissent: Communication ethics and legitimacy in message crimes involving wildlife. *Critical Criminology, 25*(2), 261–274.

Walters, R. (2005). Crime, bio-agriculture and the exploitation of hunger. *British Journal of Criminology, 46*(1), 26–45.

Walters, R., & Westerhuis, D. S. (2013). Green crime and the role of environmental courts. *Crime, Law and Social Change, 59*(3), 279–290.

Waltman, L., & Van Eck, N. J. (2013). A smart local moving algorithm for large-scale modularity-based community detection. *European Physical Journal B, 86*(11), 471.

Weinberg, B. H. (1974). Bibliographic coupling: A review. *Information Storage and Retrieval, 10*(5), 189–196.

Wellsmith, M. (2011). Wildlife crime: The problems of enforcement. *European Journal on Criminal Policy and Research, 17*(2), 125–148.

Westerhuis, D. S. (2013). A harm analysis of environmental crime. In *Emerging issues in green criminology* (pp. 197–217). London: Palgrave Macmillan.

Westerhuis, D. S., Walters, R., & Wyatt, T. (Eds.). (2013). *Emerging issues in green criminology: Exploring power, justice and harm.* New York: Springer.

White, H. D., & Griffith, B. C. (1981). Author cocitation: A literature measure of intellectual structure. *Journal of the American Society for Information Science, 32*(3), 163–171. doi:10.1002/asi.4630320302

White, R. (2017). The four ways of eco-global criminology. *International Journal for Crime, Justice and Social Democracy, 6*(1), 8–22.

White, R. (2015). Indigenous young people and hyperincarceration in Australia. *Youth Justice, 15*(3), 256–270.
White, R. (2013). *Environmental harm: An eco-justice perspective.* Bristol: Policy Press.
White, R. (2011). *Transnational environmental crime: Toward an eco-global criminology.* London: Routledge.
White, R. (2008). *Crimes against nature: Environmental criminology and ecological justice.* Devon: Willan Publishing.
White, R. (1999). Criminality, risk and environmental harm. *Griffith Law Review, 8*, 235.
White, R., Kluin, M., & Spapens, T. (Eds.). (2014). *Environmental crime and its victims: Perspectives within green criminology.* Farnham, UK: Ashgate Publishing.
Wolf, B. (2011). "Green-collar crime": Environmental crime and justice in the sociological perspective. *Sociology Compass, 5*(7), 499–511.
Wong, R. W. (2015). The organization of the illegal tiger parts trade in China. *British Journal of Criminology, 56*(5), 995–1013.
Wyatt, T. (2014a). Non-human animal abuse and wildlife trade: Harm in the fur and falcon trades. *Society & Animals, 22*(2), 194–210.
Wyatt, T. (2014b). The Russian Far East's illegal timber trade: An organized crime? *Crime, Law and Social Change, 61*(1), 15–35.
Wyatt, T. (2013). *Wildlife trafficking: A deconstruction of the crime, the victims, and the offenders.* New York: Springer.
Wyatt, T. (2011). The illegal trade of raptors in the Russian Federation. *Contemporary Justice Review, 14*(2), 103–123.
Ziegler, B. (2009). *Methods for bibliometric analysis of research: Renewable energy case study.* M.I.T. Working Paper.
Zilney, L. A., McGurrin, D., & Zahran, S. (2006). Environmental justice and the role of criminology: An analytical review of 33 years of environmental justice research. *Criminal Justice Review, 31*(1), 47–62.

3 What we "know"

A review of quantitative studies in green/conservation criminology

Michael J. Lynch, Paul B. Stretesky, Michael A. Long, and Kimberly L. Barrett

This chapter "takes stock" (e.g., Cullen, Wright and Blevins 2006) of quantitative studies in green and conservation criminology. Consistent with arguments concerning the need for quantitative conservation/green criminological research in the introduction (see also Lynch et al. 2017), we limit this review to quantitative studies. Reviewing that research makes it more accessible and enhances its appeal to a larger criminological audience by illustrating its relevance to the study of crime, law, justice, and social control.

By "quantitative," we mean studies that employ various kinds of data and social science research methodologies to assess hypotheses, expectations, and outcomes generated by green/conservation criminological theories and environmental policies. Such studies include, but are not limited to, descriptive and inferential statistics, multivariate statistical modeling, and the analysis of survey and secondary data. There are a limited number of such studies within green/conservation criminology. Using various methods,[1] we identified 117 quantitative studies published since 1998 – a rather small body of literature over two decades, especially in a quantitatively oriented discipline such as criminology. Reviewing these works reveals what conservation/green criminologists know empirically.

We present this research in five areas: (1) environmental justice; (2) the distribution and consequences of pollution; (3) the social control of environmental crime; (4) environmental social movement research; and (5) harms against (nonhuman) animals.[2] These categories are not exclusive, and research described in these area sometimes overlaps.

Environmental justice

Environmental justice (EJ) involves the study of race, ethnic, gender, and class bias in environmental decision-making, including the creation and enforcement of environmental laws/regulations or the siting, geographic distribution, and proximity to environmental hazards (e.g., waste sites, polluting facilities) and benefits (e.g., parks, urban tree coverage). EJ studies examine issues with criminological relevance, such as how extra-legal factors (e.g., race) affect the application of environmental penalties designed to protect victims of environmental crimes. There is a large empirical literature on EJ outside criminology (e.g., Chakraborty and Green 2014; Nelson and Grubesic 2018). Bullard (1983) published the first EJ study. Early studies used rudimentary statistics to examine the proximity of landfills and waste stations to African American neighborhoods. Today, a wide range of issues are explored in the EJ literature, and many employ geographic information systems data.

Environmental injustice has much broader social implications and consequences than racial/ethnic bias in criminal justice processes. Injustice in environmental exposure effects a much larger segment of the population (including children) than criminal justice processing biases, and there are far more green victimizations associated with toxic exposure than there are street crime victimizations (Lynch and Stretesky 2014; Lynch 2013; Jarrell, Lynch and Stretesky 2013). These observations became rationales for the study of EJ by green criminologists.

Three types of biases are relevant in EJ research. First, whether the placement of hazards by corporations and governments creates inequality in exposure to environmental hazards due to their location/proximity to poor and minority communities. Second, whether government responses to EJ claims and the distribution of penalties are affected by community race, ethnic and class characteristics. Third, the analysis of equity in law and regulations. Of these three approaches, the first two have been examined empirically by green criminologists.

In general, EJ literature indicates the existence of racial, ethnic, and class biases. Some studies suggest these biases are more likely to be racially related rather than class related (Ash et al. 2013), though class (Molitor et al. 2011; Lee and Mohai 2011) and ethnicity effects (Gilbert and Chakraborty 2011; Pastor, Saad and Morello-Frosch 2004) have also been discovered. Not all studies discover inequality effects, and outcomes depend on the laws examined and the level of analysis (national, regional, community, census tract, zip code) employed. These points are illustrated by Lynch, Stretesky and Burns (2004a, 2004b), who show that EJ results vary depending on whether census tract or zip code data are employed as the unit of analysis (see also Greife et al. 2015).

Stretesky and Hogan (1998) examined EJ effects related to proximity to Superfund sites in Florida using census tract data from 1970, 1980, and 1990. They found significant effects for African American and Hispanic communities, but no income or poverty associations. They discovered that over time, environmental injustice increased, indicating the influence of indirect forms of bias. In a related study in Hillsborough County, Florida, Stretesky and Lynch (1998) found evidence of injustice related to proximity to accidental chemical releases (ACRs). Their data indicated that ACRs were more likely to occur in or near African American and Hispanic communities. They describe this form of injustice as an example of corporate environmental violence produced by the routine activities of corporations (see also Lynch, Stretesky and Hammond 2000). Environmental injustice results for Hillsborough County, Florida, were also discovered by Stretesky and Lynch (2002) in their analysis of the proximity of schools to hazardous waste sites (1987–1999). Using data on the racial, income, and ethnic composition of Hillsborough County's 84 public schools and geographic areas, Stretesky and Lynch found that schools closer to toxic hazards were disproportionately African American and Hispanic.

Kosmicki and Long (2016) examined EJ related to the locations of coal-fired and nuclear power plants across US census tracts (on coal-fired power plant victimization, see Lynch and Barrett 2015). Linking the treadmill of production (ToP) and EJ literatures, and using multinomial regression analyses, they examined whether community characteristics affected the presence of a power plant in a census tract. They found that areas with higher percentages of minorities and lower median incomes were more likely to have coal-fired power plants compared to census tracts containing nuclear plants or no power plant. These findings support the environmental injustice and treadmill of crime perspectives.

EJ extends beyond urban areas into rural communities. Stretesky, Johnston and Arney (2003) examined this issue in relation to the distribution of hog farms across 17 US states where these farms are concentrated. Hog farms create a significant quantity of pollution, especially water pollution, and therefore if these facilities are unequally distributed, this may indicate an unequal distribution of harms associated with hog farming. This study indicated a positive association between hog farm siting and race in states where hogs farms are being more rapidly added (e.g., North Carolina, Iowa, Minnesota). The study found no evidence of ethnic or class bias.

While most studies find evidence of environmental injustice, Greife et al. (2015) did not, in their study of community demographics and monetary penalties against corporations for 121 US federal criminal cases concluded between 2005 and 2010. However, these results should be viewed with caution. As Greife et al. (2015:339) suggest, despite their best attempts to measure crime severity, "more severe crimes occur in communities that are primarily composed of disadvantaged residents." Thus, it may not be surprising that penalties may be higher in these communities.

The distribution of pollution and adverse consequences

Environmental injustice is one adverse consequence of environmental hazards. Other adverse consequences include the effects of environmental hazards on criminal behavior, health, and the environment.

To examine the relationship between environmental hazards and crime, green criminologists built on medical and public health research indicating that some pollutants play a role in the etiology of crime (Stretesky and Lynch 2001). Of particular concern is the effect of lead (Pb) pollution (Needleman et al. 1990), which at the individual level is hypothesized to impact crime through its effects on aggression, learning disruption, and adverse IQ impacts (Stretesky and Lynch 2001). At the macro level, criminological literature has drawn attention to the relationship between the distribution of lead exposure and crime (Barrett 2017; see also Winter and Sampson 2017). Geographically, these studies suggest that communities with higher lead concentrations also have higher levels of crime, and that the production of crime is, therefore, a product of the economic and social organization of the production and distribution of lead (Sampson and Winter 2016; Stretesky 2003). In this sense the production of lead-induced crime is a macro-social rather than an individual-level problem, even though the effects are evident at the individual level.

Related to this argument, Stretesky (2003) discovered that lead pollution in the US was unequally distributed, and related to population characteristics. He found significant evidence that lead pollution was more likely to be located in minority and low income communities, indicating widespread evidence of an environmental justice effect concerning lead.

In two studies, Stretesky and Lynch (2001, 2004) examined the relationship between homicide rates and air lead pollution (2001) and violent and property crime rates and air lead pollution (2004) across all US counties. Controlling for the effects of a wide variety of other pollutants and for factors that macro-level analyses of crime generally suggest are associated with crime, they found a statistically significant relationship between air lead pollution, homicide, and violent and property crime rates. Their 2001 study indicated that the intensity of air lead pollution and the rate of homicides were also related, so that homicides rates were significantly higher in the most polluted counties. Their 2004 study also found that resource deprivation affected the distribution of crime at the county level, reinforcing arguments in the public health literature linking resource deprivation and lead poisoning/exposure (Chandramouli et al. 2013; Richardson 2002).

Barrett (2017) confirmed the lead-crime relationship in her study of the geographic dispersion of youth crime across Chicago's 77 community areas, which have been well studied in the criminological literature since the 1930s. Her study examined whether youth crime hot spots and lead pollution hot spots co-occur, exploring the relationships between these two forms of violence at the community level. Employing ordinary least squares and geographically weighted regression, Barrett found a statistically significant relationship between lead pollution and youth violence controlling for concentrated disadvantage, racial and ethnic heterogeneity, and residential mobility (see also Sampson and Winter's 2017 findings for Chicago on blood lead levels and the distribution of crime).

As noted, the distribution of environmental pollutants is a concern because of the related adverse consequences they produce, and the possibility that the distribution of those hazards also affects outcomes such as environmental justice. Lynch, Stretesky and Hammond (2000) examined these issues by comparing newspaper reports and official data on the distribution of accidental chemical releases (ACRs). They found that news reporting of ACRs were biased, and that only a handful (10%) were reported in the news over a ten-year time period. The limited availability of news reports indicates the powerful role the news media plays in shaping public knowledge about these events. Illustrating that point, they also compared media ACRs to media homicide reports in the same news sources. In contrast to ACRs, homicides were overreported relative to their occurrence in the study area (by a factor of 87). In a related study in the same location, Stretesky and Lynch (1999) examined whether the distribution of ACRs were random or affected by community racial, ethnic, and class composition. If the ACR pattern was non-random, then these events, which are labeled as accidents, have a structure. Results showed that ACRs were patterned, occurred near manufacturing sites and industrial transportation routes, and occurred most often in locations that adversely impacted minorities and low-income groups. This was the first study of its kind, and additional studies support these observations (Derezinski, Lacy and Stretesky 2003; Elliott et al. 2004; Margai 2001; Pine, Marx and Lakshmanan 2002).

Green criminologists also found an empirical link between resource extraction and crime. Stretesky et al. (2018) found that the prevalence and location of oil and gas extraction wells in the UK impacted the level of violent and property crime rates, supporting treadmill of production (ToP) and ecological disorganization arguments. Among locations with the most well sites, each additional well increased both violent and property crime by almost 5%. Drawing on the concept of the "natural resource curse" – the idea that countries with large quantities of exploited natural resources suffer from reduced economic growth – Stretesky, Long and Lynch (2017a) examined the relationship between natural resource rents and homicide rates across 173 nations (2000–2012). Multilevel growth models indicated that resource rents were related to homicide rates within but not across nations. That finding means that within a nation, increased resource extraction increases the level of homicide, but that across nations, the level of resource extraction is unrelated to cross-national differences in homicide. In a related study, Long, Stretesky and Lynch (2017) found that among a sample of 125 lesser developed countries (LDCs; 2005–2013), foreign direct investment (FDI) increased rates of ecological withdrawal. That finding suggests that the global structure of resource extraction investment produces ecological disorganization in LDCs. Coupled with the prior study, these results suggest that global ToP investment and extraction patterns influence resource extraction in LDCs, and also other adverse outcomes such as crime rates. Those findings illustrate the numerous influences of the ToP. Addressing that issue, Long, Lynch and Stretesky (2018) assessed a ten-year (2005–2014) trend in toxic emissions in the US, which illustrated that the Great Recession of 2008–2009 had, as one would predict from a ToP perspective, a greater negative influence on toxic releases than environmental enforcement.

Carbon dioxide pollution is a significant social concern because of its link to climate change (Solomon et al. 2009). Numerous studies of the effects of CO_2 pollution on environmental health exist. Scientific research, however, overlooks how CO_2 pollution is driven by economic expansion and the behavior of industry. McKie, Stretesky and Long (2015) found that both criminal and noncriminal firms in the voluntary carbon market employ the same advertising messages designed to promote economic development, sustainability, and technological innovation.

Environmental sociologists have undertaken numerous empirical studies of the adverse effects and economic predictors of CO_2 pollution across nations (e.g., Jorgenson 2012; Jorgenson and Clark 2011). Those studies have generally been limited to direct CO_2 emissions, and they show that the US plays the most significant role in generating CO_2 pollution. Stretesky and Lynch (2009b) performed the first study examining the indirect effect of international trade/consumption on CO_2 pollution across nations. Using international trade data linked to carbon emissions, results indicated an enhanced US effect on CO_2 emissions that was significantly higher than prior studies, which only examined direct CO_2 pollution, had estimated. This occurs because the US trade deficit, which measures the balance of imports and exports, increases US pressure on production and CO_2 pollution generation in other nations.

Water pollution, often mentioned as an example of green crimes, has received little empirical attention from green criminologists. Using US EPA Discharge Monitoring Report data, Lynch, Stretesky and Long (2017) describe the extent of ecological disorganization associated with publicly owned treatment works (POTW) discharges. In the US, POTWs legally emit billions of pounds of pollutants into waterways annually after treatment, facilitating ecological disorganization of waterways. They argue that these emissions are also an example of green-state crimes, and that these outcomes are facilitated by the treadmill of law and the treadmill of production.

Ozymy and Jarrell (2011, 2012) examined what are called "upset air events," or unforeseen, accidental air pollution emissions from facilities that are not counted in air pollution measures. Studying 18 oil refineries in Texas, they found that upset emissions were large (75 million pounds over six years), and that in some cases emissions from an upset event exceeded a facility's air pollution permit.

Social control of environmental crime

Both conservation and green criminologists have examined factors that impact the enforcement and effectiveness of environmental regulations. Some studies also address environmental justice concerns by examining whether community race, ethnic and class composition affect the type and level of social control in communities when environmental harms are discovered and prosecuted.

Long et al. (2012) examined enforcement practices in the coal industry to assess whether corporate political donations affected the enforcement of violations against coal companies. Consistent with ToP arguments concerning the role politics plays in maintaining the treadmill, they found that coal companies increased political donations prior to the conclusion of an environmental enforcement action against them. This finding suggests that coal companies endeavor to impact enforcement through political contributions, and in so doing also maintain expansion of the ToP process. In a related study, Stretesky, Long and Lynch (2013) examined whether penalties meted out for environmental violations slowed the expansion of the ToP by decreasing toxic emissions across and within companies. The researchers found a weak effect for large penalties on toxic emissions, indicating that environmental penalties are an inefficient mechanism for reducing toxic emissions or for reducing pollution emitted by the ToP.

Green criminologists have undertaken several studies examining the utility of self-audit or self-policing policies for controlling environmental crime (Stretesky 2006; Stretesky and Gabriel 2005; Stretesky and Lynch 2009a, 2011b). The focus of these studies is on the US Environmental Protection Agency's (EPA) self-audit program. That program waives or eliminates penalties against offending corporations when companies enrolled in the self-audit program voluntarily report violations to US EPA. This research has found that the self-audit policy does not work as expected and is an ineffective tool for correcting serious environmental violations. Corporations that self-report tend to be larger and frequently report smaller rather than large environmental violations. This increases the number of small violations known to the EPA.

Like self-policing/auditing, it is often argued that modernization of enforcement mechanisms through end-of-pipeline regulations encourage corporations to reduce pollution, and hence are effective social control strategies. Testing these propositions, Stretesky et al. (2017) examined whether self-policing and criminal prosecutions deter/reduce toxic emissions, or whether by contrast emissions were driven by expansion of the ToP. Using enforcement data for the US from 1988 through 2014, multivariate models showed no effect for enforcement or self-auditing behavior but indicated a relationship between gross domestic product and pollution over time, confirming ToP arguments. Related outcomes were also found by Barrett et al. (2018) in their study of the effect of monetary penalties on firms' compliance with environmental regulations. It is widely argued that monetary penalties effectively deter environmental violators. In their longitudinal study of environmental violations in Michigan, Barrett et al.'s multivariate analysis found that fines had a small effect on noncompliance in the short term and no effect on long-term environmental compliance. In fact, over the long term, total fines levied against a firm were related to an increase in noncompliance, indicating that over time, the deterrent effect of fines decays – an outcome consistent with ToP arguments.

Lynch and Stretesky (2013) combined research on environmental justice, informal community responses to environmental hazards, and research on community policing to examine factors impacting the distribution of US EPA facilitated community water monitoring programs across the US. They noted that community water monitoring programs are a form of community policing that augments formal environmental enforcement mechanisms. The EPA uses community water monitoring data to identify areas experiencing high or increasing levels of water pollution to step up formal enforcement. The analysis, conducted across US counties, indicated that community water monitoring programs were less likely to be found in African American and Hispanic communities and more likely to be found in communities with high levels of economic resources. Both results indicate the existence of environmental injustice in the formation of community water monitoring programs. This result is important because the US EPA expends financial resources to encourage forming community water monitoring programs to aid EPA enforcement of water pollution violations. Since the outcomes suggests bias in the distribution of these programs, it appears that

US EPA efforts that encourage community water monitoring program formation play a role in producing biases in EPA enforcement of water pollution regulations.

The environmental justice literature also suggests that community poverty impacts the type and quantity of enforcement of violations in low-income as opposed to high-income communities. Stretesky and Lynch (2011a) found evidence of this effect when examining the relationship between poverty and the enforcement of environmental laws at 110 US coal strip mining sites (2002 through 2008). The results suggest that corporations involved in strip mining were more likely to violate the law in and around communities where poverty is elevated, providing evidence of an environmental injustice enforcement effect.

Ozymy and Jarrell (2015) employed data on 972 US EPA environmental cases to examine differences in environmental prosecutions during the G. W. Bush and Obama administrations. Theoretically, the argument is based on the effects "principle agents" can have on organizational behavior. In the case of EPA behavior, the president's guidance can affect the use of sanctioning behavior. They found some minor difference between EPA enforcement during the Bush and Obama administrations, but note "the data do not show that the Bush EPA was extremely friendly towards companies or that the EPA under Obama was relatively punitive" (p. 50). During the Obama administration, fines and months sentenced to probation were slightly higher than during the Bush administration. These data suggest that the effect of presidential administration on EPA enforcement is minimal.

Using the same data, Ozymy and Jarrell (2017) examined geographic variability in US federal environmental crime prosecutions across US states (2001–2011). Their study provided evidence that "green states" (i.e., states where the density of environmental groups is high) had more environmental prosecutions, but that political ideology/liberalism was unrelated to the level of environmental prosecutions across states. They also found that in environmental crime cases, convictions were often for charges related to conspiracy, false statements, document tampering, and obstruction of justice (US Code Title 18 charges) rather than for an environmental crime charge. Finally, states with a higher number of polluting facilities had more criminal environmental prosecutions. In an additional study employing the same data, Jarrell and Ozymy (2014) examined how federal prosecutors describe the kinds of human victimization involved in environmental crime cases they prosecuted. They found that despite the severity of some cases, and the kinds of human harm generated by exposure to environmental hazards and pollution, prosecutors only identified victims as suffering from acute or even identifiable victimization in 3% of cases. These results suggest that unless there is evidence of immediate human harm presented by prosecutors, depictions of environmental crime victims plays no real role in the prosecution of environmental crimes and limits the attention these victims receive from the government and the public. With respect to the latter observation, Opsal and Shelley (2014) used content analysis of citizen complaints ($N =$ 2,444) and interviews with citizens who filed complaints ($N = 65$) regarding oil and gas exploration. An important finding in this study was that the state's response to citizen complaints often denied the complaint's validity, and argued that oil and gas exploration were not the source of the environmental problem citizens reported. This strategy, Opsal and Shelly argue, is one of the ways in which the state's enforcement mechanism is employed to protect the treadmill of production.

Despite the emergence of green and conservation criminology, few empirical studies address evidence of the extent of environmental crime, and studies that do tend to be from the early 1990s. Addressing that issue, Lynch (2017) examined the punishment of green offenders in the US using US EPA data for the years 2000–2013. Across the US over this 14-year period, only 161 corporations (11.5 per year) and 420 individuals (30 per year) were convicted of federal environmental crimes. Mean punishments were rather small for individuals ($211,517) compared to corporations ($39 million). The corporate mean, however, is deceiving and significantly influenced by a handful of outlying fines. For example, BP and Transocean were fined $4 billion and $1.4 billion, respectively, in the Gulf oil spill case, and the four largest fines handed out to corporations during this time period accounted for more than 95% of fines to corporations during the entire 14-year period. Once those fines were removed, the mean corporate fine for the remaining cases was $1.77 million.

The above study indicates that in the US, criminal prosecutions of environmental crimes are relatively rare, and punishments are relatively small compared to the harms generated (for a study of factors influencing environmental prosecutions, see Ozymy and Jarrell 2016). However, many argue that despite these observations (i.e., the Harrington paradox), criminal punishments deter environmental offenders. To determine whether this argument appears feasible, Lynch et al. (2016) examined the probability that a corporation would be charged with an environmental offense in the US using criminal cases from 1983–2013, and examined conviction probabilities for 19 environmental statutes. Five of those statues were never enforced during the time period examined, and 11 others were enforced fewer than once per year on average. Consistent with Ozymy and Jarrell's (2017) study, Lynch et al. found that 31% of environmental cases involved Title 18 (US Criminal Code) convictions rather than environmental crime convictions. While the probability of a criminal conviction increased over time, the mean probability of a corporation being convicted was 8 in 1 million. In another US study employing conviction data from Florida over 15 years (Cochran et al. 2018), researchers found evidence of what they called the "green gap" in punishment. Employing propensity score matching that takes seriousness of offense, prior record, age, race, ethnicity, and gender into account, ecological crimes and crimes against wildlife and animals were matched to samples of street crimes. The findings indicated that only a small percentage of felony convictions in Florida involved green crimes and that punishments for ecological crimes, such as pollution, were less severe than punishments for the matched sample of street crimes. It was also discovered that punishments for some types of wildlife or animal crimes were more serious than those given to street offenders.

In their study of environmental enforcement, Kurland and Pires (2017) examined 40,133 cases involving seizures of wildlife and wildlife products in the US over a ten-year time span. They note that responsibility for policing wildlife trafficking at the 72 international airports and seaports in the United States falls upon 330 agents from the US Fish and Wildlife Service. They employed the data to create profiles and risk assessments of wildlife import crimes to suggest more efficient control strategies.

Much less in known about environmental enforcement effects in countries other than the United States (e.g., Almer and Goeschl [2010] on Germany; Billiet and Rousseau [2014] on Flanders; Telle [2013] on Norway). Green/conservation criminologists, however, have contributed to empirical knowledge about environmental enforcement in several nations. Bisschop (2014) employed document analysis to examine the e-waste trade in EU nations. Sahramäki, Korsell and Kankaanranta (2015) have used analyses of legislation, official documents, and statistical data to compare the prosecution and control of environmental crime in Finland and Sweden. Faulkner et al. (2018) employed data on illegal hunting and wildlife deaths from an eight-year study of the Savé Valley Conservancy, Zimbabwe, to generate geographic profiles of areas where poaching was most likely to occur to created targeted antipoaching social control strategies. Moreto and associates (Moreto, Brunson and Braga 2014; Moreto and Matusiak 2017) have employed data from interviews with wildlife enforcement rangers in Uganda to examine officers' perceptions of their roles and responsibilities and illegal behaviors by those officers. These studies, however, are few in number, and there are statistical databases in many other nations that require empirical examinations to gain a greater understanding of how different nations respond to green crimes.

Environmental movement organization research

The environmental literature suggests that the formation of social movements against environmental disorganization plays a role in influencing formal responses to environmental pollution. Green criminologists have addressed this issue by examining the development and dispersion of environmental movements.

In the first of these studies, Stretesky et al. (2011) examined the formation of environmental social movements (ESM) across US states during two time periods: 1990–1999 and 2000–2008. They found that in the earlier period, ESMs were more likely to form in areas with successful civil rights organizations, indicating that environmental groups build on the success of civil rights groups. In the later period, however, ESMs compete with one another for resources, slowing their formation (see also Stretesky, Huss and Lynch 2012; Huss, Stretesky and Lynch 2012). Stretesky, Long and Lynch (2017b) extended these assessments to the formation of environmental non-governmental organizations (NGOs) across nations for the period 1950–2010. They found that over time, NGO formation slowed due to competition for economic resources (it had an inverted U-shape), which they argued benefits expansion of the treadmill of production.

An issue these studies do not address is whether the location of an environmental group in an area affects the enforcement of law. That question was addressed by Stretesky, Shelley and Crow (2010). Using data from Florida's 67 counties, they found that the concentration of environmental organizations was associated with natural resource enforcement controlling for other factors. They did not find a similar effect for animal rights groups or hunting and fishing organizations, however. This study indicates that citizens can influence the enforcement of environmental laws by organizing.

Harms against animals

Conservation and green criminologists pay significant attention to harms/crimes against animals. Much of the green criminological literature on animal harm is theoretical and qualitative (e.g., Beirne 1999). Conservation and green criminologists also examine enforcement-wildlife crime prevention associations.

In an early study, Lemieux and Clarke (2009) examined the effect of international poaching regulations/treaties on elephant poaching and herd size to address whether they disrupted illegal trade markets. Study data were drawn from the 37 African nations with elephant herds and from the Convention on International Trades in Endangered Species of Wild Fauna and Flora (CITES) database. Lemieux and Clarke noted that studies conducted during the 1970s suggested a significant decline in African elephant herds. During that time it appears elephant poaching was driven by the price of ivory, which increased by a factor of 360. Because long-term elephant poaching had eliminated older animals with larger tusks, there was a concern that continued poaching would expand to meet ivory trade demands. In response, the CITES treaty was amended to increase protection for African elephants by making it illegal to transport elephant ivory internationally. As Lemieux and Clarke note (p. 455), within a day of these revisions, the price of ivory declined from $100 to $5 per pound, raising hope that the new amendments would better protect elephants. However, CITES does not regulate national ivory markets, leaving that to individual nations and potentially undermining CITES' intentions. In fact, poaching of African elephants has increased since 2008.

To determine the impact of the new regulations, Lemieux and Clarke used a pre-ban/post-ban comparison method. The pre-ban data indicated a decline in elephant herds in 20 of the 37 nations examined. The post-ban data, in contrast, indicated a rise in elephant herds for several nations, indicating that the law had some effect on protecting elephants (for other examples of pre-post test methods, see Triezenberg, Riley and Gore 2016; Triezenberg et al. 2014).

Several studies examine parrot poaching. This research is conducted because parrots are easily poached due to their size, and because parrots are among the most threatened bird species globally for the pet trade (Clarke and Rolf 2013: 336). While habitat loss is an important factor affecting parrot declines, parrots may also be impacted by poaching. Informed by an application of Clarke's situational crime prevention/routine activities theory (called the CRAVED model:

concealable, removable, available, valuable, enjoyable, and disposable), Clarke and Rolf argued that efforts to protect endangered species through creation of wildlife habitats could negatively impact endangered species by promoting their spatial concentration, making them easier to poach if policing in those areas is low. To address this question, Clarke and Rolf created a matched sample of endangered and non-threatened species of birds. Controlling for habitat, they found that areas with reduced enforcement had elevated levels of poaching and more generally, poaching had a far greater effect on population losses for species than habitat loss. Several other conservation criminology studies have found that various environmental crimes involving poaching of wildlife and flora have spatial dimensions (for extended review, see Kurland et al. 2017). For example, using GIS data, Maingi et al. (2012) found that elephant poaching in Kenya was spatially and seasonally clustered; Pires et al. (2016) observed that 80% of parrots were poached in a rather small area, and similar results have been displayed for rhinoceros poaching (Eloff and Lemieux 2014). These spatial findings can have important social control implications by identifying locations that should be targeted by enforcement activities.

Pires and Clarke (2012) examined the role opportunistic poaching played on parrot poaching and populations. They found that poached parrot species are more readily accessible, removable, and abundant than other species of parrots, fitting CRAVED model expectations (and now known as CRAAVED). They found that opportunistic poaching was more widespread among the poor as well (see also Pires and Clarke 2011; Pires and Petrossian 2016 on parrot poaching in Bolivia; Pires 2015 on the illegal parrot trade in seven markets in Peru; Tella and Hiraldo 2014 on Mexico).

Petrossian and Clarke (2014) employed the CRAAVED model to examine the illegal taking of fish. As in Pires and Clarke's parrot study, the researchers created two matched groups to compare findings: fish taken illegally were matched to a sample of control fish. Illegally taken fish were more easily concealed by being sold through a larger number of ports; were more easily removed than the control species; were more abundant and accessible than controls; were more valuable due to their larger size; and were more enjoyable because they are featured in more food dishes than controls. Petrossian and Clarke suggest these results imply that nations need to engage in better targeted control responses related to the assumptions of the CRAVED model to reduce illegal fishing. Similar results were obtained in a study by Petrossian, Weis and Pires (2015) related to illegal crab and lobster fishing. Research has also explored whether the characteristics of port facilities affects the transport of illegal, unreported, and unregulated (IUU) fishing (Petrossian, Marteache and Viollaz 2015). That study indicated that vessels containing IUU fish catches "were more likely to visit a port that facilitates concealability of the vessel and its activities due to higher levels of daily general and fishing vessel traffic and larger harbor size" (p. 45).

Using multiple data sources (public reports, news media, interviews, and court documents), Zabyelina (2014) examined the illegal market in black caviar, changes in that market over time, and evidence of an underground black caviar market. Zabyelina noted that the illegal black caviar market targeted Caspian sturgeon in the 1990s, but due to a severe decline in sturgeon in that area, it shifted to North America. Using various data sources, this article provides an understanding of the illegal global trade in caviar (see also van Uhm and Siegel 2016).

Empirical studies of illegal wildlife markets for other species have also been published. Van Uhm (2016) employed interview data to examine the illegal trade in Barbary macaques in Morocco. Goyes and Sollund (2016) employed interview data with experts in Colombia and Brazil to describe traffickers' modus operandi, and wildlife trafficking and its control in those countries. While the researchers report these countries seize a large number of illegally trafficked animals, they note that expert interview data indicated that the structure of laws in those nations makes it difficult to enforce relevant regulations. Interview data has also been employed by Wong (2017a, 2017b) to examine the trade in illegal wildlife species used as delicacies in China, and the sale of illegal worked ivory in Hong Kong; Silvy et al. (2018) to examine illegal marine resource harvesting in The Bahamas; Moreto and Lemieux (2015) to create poaching typologies from interviews with wildlife conservation officers in Uganda; Rizzolo et al. (2017) to examine how cultural factors and law affected perceptions of risk associated with poaching in Madagascar; Højberg, Nielsen and Jacobsen (2017) to assess attitudes among a rural population in Jutland, Denmark, where the gray wolf had recently returned, to discover how people in that area would respond to the presence of wolves, with 60% of respondents indicating they would employ illegal measures as a response; and by Kahler and Gore (2015; see also Kahler, Roloff and Gore 2013), along with other data, to examine how perceptions of risk from wildlife in the Zambezi region of Namibia can be employed to understand attitudes towards poaching wildlife and management of conservation areas.

There are a number of empirical studies of poaching outside of criminology that endeavor to discover the extent and distribution of poaching, as well as factors influencing poaching (Herrera and Hennessey 2007). While such studies have long been of interest to conservationist, conservation criminologists have contributed to the expansion of this literature, arguing that it is necessary to gather and analyzed data on poaching to better understand its spatiotemporal patterns in order to create better targeted social control responses to poaching (Pires et al. 2016). Employing data on 9,013 poached parrots in the illegal wildlife market in Santa Cruz de la Sierra, Bolivia, Pires et al. found certain factors that could be useful for addressing enforcement strategies that might limit poaching opportunities. For example, they found that 90% of poached parrots originated within 234 km (145 miles) of the marketplace, and that most of the poached parrots came from seven specific locations. They also found that poaching was seasonal, an empirical finding noted in other conservation criminology studies (Kurland and Pires 2017; Moreto and Lemieux 2015; for further review of these issues including non-criminological studies, see Kurland et al. 2017).

Gore, along with several colleagues,[3] has made widespread and impressive use of survey, interview, and focus group data to understand perceptions of and attitudes toward wildlife crimes, providing information necessary for crafting environmental policies (Gore et al. 2016). These studies have focused on several issues, such as perceptions and minimization of human-wildlife conflicts (Gore et al. 2008, 2007a); how perceptions/attitudes toward wildlife impact poaching (Kahler and Gore 2012); how exposure to news stories about human-wildlife conflicts and animal danger affects public attitudes toward wildlife (Gore and Knuth 2009); gender differences in risk perceptions of human-wildlife conflict (Gore and Kahler 2012); and conflicts among stakeholders involved in wildlife management processes (Lute and Gore 2014a; Gore et al. 2006, 2007b).

Jarrell, Ozymy and Sandel (2017) performed a content analysis of 972 US federal environmental cases to assess the depiction of animals as victims. In their earlier study on depictions of human victims (Jarrell and Ozymy 2014), they found that prosecutors made reference to human victimization in only 3% of cases. In the latter study, prosecutors made reference to animal victims 6% of the time. The interesting differences between these results requires further study. This difference may, for example, be the result of the kinds of cases brought to trial (e.g., there are more wildlife crime cases than toxic waste cases). Or, this may result from prosecutor attitudes toward environmental victimization of human and animals (e.g., humans can defend themselves, and animals cannot).

In an extensive study integrating fishing and wildlife data, Petrossian, de By and Clarke (2018) examined the effects of long-line fishing on declines in the albatross population. Long-line fishing employs a string of baited hooks on lines that may be 60 miles long to capture fish. Fish targeted by this method include tuna, the Patagonian toothfish, and swordfish. Other species, however, also attempt to take bait from those hooks and can become ensnared, leading to extensive death among non-targeted marine species (e.g., turtles, dolphins, pilot whales, sea birds). The authors note that 26 of the 61 species of birds that become entangled in long-line fishing gear are threatened with extinction. The widespread death of non-targeted species has lead the Humane Society of the United States to call this fishing method "a mass slaughter at sea."

While green criminologists often discuss anthropogenic threats to wildlife species, these claims are rarely studied empirically. Petrossian, de By and Clarke's study showed that 17 of 22 assessed albatross species are threatened with extinction through human activities, with the greatest threat posed by long-line fishing. They examined the relationship between two measures of fishing and albatross species status, and estimated a weighted exposure measure for each albatross species to long-line fishing in general (which they refer to as "fishing pressure") and also to illegal long-line fishing hook exposure. The relationship between fishing pressure and albatross species status was defined as moderate. They also found that compared to near threatened albatross species, critically endangered and endangered albatross were 12.15 and 3.34 times more likely to be exposed to illegal long-line hooks, respectively, while there was no difference in exposure to legal long-line hooks. These results suggest the need for enhanced methods for controlling illegal long-line fishing to protect endangered species.

Another study examining anthropogenic effects on species endangerment is Stretesky et al.'s (2018) analysis of the Saker falcon trade. Three theories can be employed to explain market threats to falcons: ecological modernization, unequal ecological exchange, and treadmill of production theory. While each argument has been employed to understand how development impacts ecological conservation, they have not been applied to assessing wildlife trade. The ecological modernization/environmental Kuznets curve argument suggests that while increased economic development initially produces expanding environmental destruction, continued economic development allows excess economic resources to accrue, which are spend on ecological conservation. Over time, this process creates an inverted U-shaped relationship between economic development and ecological destruction. In contrast, ToP theory suggests that the expansion of capitalism requires continued consumption of ecological resources, so over time, ecological disorganization expands. Ecological unequal exchange (EUE) theory posits that the structure of the global economy facilitates unequal ecological exchanges between developed and less developed nations that directs the flow of environmental resources away from less developed to more developed nations which, in the present case, would affect where falcons were exported and imported. Fixed-effects regression models of the Saker falcon trade across 24 nations (1973–2015) rejected ecological modernization indicators, but supported both ToP and EUE arguments. These results suggest that efforts to protect Saker falcons through establishing conservation areas have not and will not likely find success since those efforts are essentially erased by trade market pressures exerted by global capitalism as described in ToP and EUE theory.

Few empirical studies examine the known extent of crimes against wildlife. Crow, Shelley and Stretesky (2013) examined this issue using information on 15,657 arrests for wildlife crimes in Florida (see also Cochran et al. 2018). There were eight primary offenses reported: improper permitting; illegal fish taking and methods; illegal hunting methods and taking; illegal possession of fish; illegal game possession; marine conservation offenses; land conservation offenses; and miscellaneous offenses. The majority of offenses involved illegal permits (49.5%). Most offenders were male (81%) and white (95%). Multivariate models, however, indicated that blacks and Hispanics were more likely than whites to be cited for certain violations, including illegal possession of fish. The authors argue that this constitutes an overlooked environmental justice issue. For some populations, subsistence fishing or hunting is an important source of dietary protein, and thus racial/ethnic variations in permit and fish possession incidents may be a consequence of poverty and its distribution in Florida, indicating that social structure plays a role in the variation of offending behavior across racial and ethnic groups. In that view, it is possible that behaviors most likely to be engaged in by racial and ethnic minorities are targeted by laws and enforcement officials, producing racial and ethnic variation in the official data.

Conclusion

The 117 quantitative conservation/green criminological studies reviewed here have not been widely referenced by traditional criminologists, who continue to demonstrate reluctance to address environmental harm and destruction as important research issues. On the latter point, as noted, there is significantly more environmental than street crime victimization. Thus, if criminologists are committed to protecting people and animals from victimization, they should pay greater attention to environmental issues. One can imagine a wide variety of empirical studies that could address green victimization concerns. Criminology lags well behind other disciplines that recognize the importance of addressing environmental/ecological matters. Physical scientists have done much to demonstrate that the most serious issue of our time is environmental destruction, while criminologists have failed to learn this important lesson.

Notes

1 Studies were identified using Google Scholar and other academic search indexes. Search terms included "green criminology," "conservation criminology," "CRAVED," "CRAAVE," "wildlife crime," and "wildlife trafficking." Searchers were also conducted for individual scholars known to contribute to these literatures.
2 Only one study was classified as "other": Lynch and Stretesky's (2012) study of US automobile CO_2 pollution regulations. That study presents an empirical analysis of the additional funds that would be raised for carbon offsetting from users of high-emission vehicles in the US from Lynch/Stretesky's CO_2-car emissions proposal.
3 Given the large number of these studies, several additional studies are listed here: Everett and Gore (2015), Gore et al. (2005, 2011, 2016), Gore, Ratsimbazafy and Lute (2013), Lute and Gore (2014b), Lute et al. (2016), Muter, Gore and Riley (2009), Jager et al. (2016), and Muter et al. (2013).

References

Almer, C., and T. Goeschl. 2010. Environmental crime and punishment: Empirical evidence from the German penal code. *Land Economics* 86 (4): 707–726.

Ash, M., Boyce, J.K., Chang, G., and Scharber, H. 2013. Is environmental justice good for white folks? Industrial air toxics exposure in urban America. *Social Science Quarterly* 94 (3): 616–636.

Barrett, Kimberly L. 2017. Exploring community levels of lead (Pb) and youth violence. *Sociological Spectrum* 37 (4): 205–222.

Barrett, Kimberly L., Michael J. Lynch, Michael A. Long, and Paul B. Stretesky. 2018. Monetary penalties and noncompliance with environmental laws: A mediation analysis. *American Journal of Criminal Justice* 43 (3): 530–550.

Beirne, Piers. 1999. For a nonspeciesist criminology: Animal abuse as an object of study. *Criminology* 37 (1): 117–148.

Billiet, C. M., and S. Rousseau. 2014. How real is the threat of imprisonment for environmental crime? *European Journal of Law and Economics* 37 (2): 183–198.

Bisschop, Lieselot. 2014. Illegal e-waste transports: Exploring their harmfulness, scale, social organization and governance. Pp. 171–184 in T. Spapens, R. White and M. Kluin (eds.), *Environmental Crime and Its Victims.* London: Routledge.

Bullard, Robert. 1983. Solid waste sites and the black Houston community. *Sociological Inquiry* 53 (2–3): 273–288.

Chakraborty, Jayajit, and Donna Green. 2014. Australia's first national level quantitative environmental justice assessment of industrial air pollution. *Environmental Research Letters* 9 (4): 044010.

Chandramouli, K., Colin D. Steer, Matthew Ellis, and Alan M. Emond. 2013. Effects of early childhood lead exposure on academic performance and behaviour of school age children. *Archives of Disease in Childhood* 94 (11): 844–848.

Clarke, Ronald V., and A. Rolf. 2013. Poaching, habitat loss and the decline of neotropical parrots: A comparative spatial analysis. *Journal of Experimental Criminology* 9 (3): 333–353.

Cochran, Joshua C., Michael J. Lynch, Elisa L. Toman, and Ryan T. Shields. 2018. Court sentencing patterns for environmental crimes: Is there a "Green" gap in punishment? *Journal of Quantitative Criminology* 34 (1): 37–66.

Crow, Matthew S., Tara O'Connor Shelley, and Paul B. Stretesky. 2013. Camouflage collar crime: An examination of wildlife crime and characteristics of offenders in Florida. *Deviant Behavior* 34 (8): 635–652.

Cullen, Francis T., John Paul Wright, and Kristie R. Blevins (eds.). 2006. *Taking Stock: The Status of Criminological Theory. Advances in Criminological Theory*, Volume 15. New Brunswick, NJ: Transaction.

Derezinski, Dan D., Michael G. Lacy, and Paul B. Stretesky. 2003. Chemical accidents in the United States, 1990–1996. *Social Science Quarterly* 84 (1): 122–143.

Elliott, Michael R., Yanlin Wang, Robert A. Lowe, and Paul R. Kleindorfer. 2004. Environmental justice: Frequency and severity of US chemical industry accidents and the socioeconomic status of surrounding communities. *Journal of Epidemiology and Community Health* 58 (1): 24–30.

Eloff, Corne, and Andrew M. Lemieux. 2014. Rhino poaching in Kruger National Park, South Africa: Aligning analysis, technology and prevention. Pp. 18–43 in A. Lemieux's (ed.), *Situational Prevention of Poaching*. London: Routledge.

Everett, Michael W., and Meredith L. Gore. 2015. Measuring flow in Michigan youth firearm deer hunters: Implications for measurement and practice. *Society and Leisure* 38 (1): 100–109.

Faulkner, Sally C., Michael C. A. Stevens, Stephanie S. Romañach, Peter A. Lindsey, and Steven C. Comber. 2018. A spatial approach to combatting wildlife crime. *Conservation Biology,* 32 (3): 685–693.

Gilbert, Angela, and Jayajit Chakraborty. 2011. Using geographically weighted regression for environmental justice analysis: Cumulative cancer risks from air toxics in Florida. *Social Science Research* 40 (1): 273–286.

Gore, Meredith L., and Jessica S. Kahler. 2012. Gendered risk perceptions associated with human-wildlife conflict: Implications for participatory conservation. *PLoS ONE,* 7 (3): e32901.

Gore, Meredith L., and Barbara A. Knuth. 2009. Mass media effect on the operating environment of a wildlife-related risk-communication campaign. *Journal of Wildlife Management* 73 (8): 1407–1413.

Gore, Meredith L., Barbara A. Knuth, Paul D. Curtis, and James E. Shanahan. 2007a. Factors influencing risk perception associated with human-black bear conflict. *Human Dimensions of Wildlife* 12 (2): 133–136.

Gore, Meredith L., Barbara A. Knuth, Paul D. Curtis, and James E. Shanahan. 2007b. Campground manager and user perceptions of risk associated with negative human-black bear interactions. *Human Dimensions of Wildlife* 12 (1): 31–43.

Gore, Meredith L., Barbara A. Knuth, Paul D. Curtis, and James E. Shanahan. 2006. Stakeholder perceptions of risk associated with human-black bear conflicts in New York's Adirondack Park campgrounds: Implications for theory and practice. *Wildlife Society Bulletin* 34 (1): 36–43.

Gore, Meredith L., Barbara A. Knuth, Clifford W. Scherer, and Paul D. Curtis. 2008. Evaluating a conservation investment designed to reduce human-wildlife conflict. *Conservation Letters* 1 (3): 136–145.

Gore, Meredith L., Michelle L. Lute, Jonah H. Ratsimbazafy, and Andry Rajaonson. 2016. Local perspectives on environmental insecurity and its influence on illegal biodiversity exploitation. *PloS ONE,* 11 (4): e0150337.

Gore, Meredith L., Michael P. Nelson, John A. Vucetich, Amy M. Smith, and Melissa A. Clark. 2011. Exploring the ethical basis for conservation policy: The case of inbred wolves on Isle Royale, USA. *Conservation Letters* 4 (5): 394–401.

Gore, Meredith L., Jonah Ratsimbazafy, and Michelle L. Lute. 2013. Rethinking corruption in conservation crime: Insights from Madagascar. *Conservation Letters* 6 (6): 430–438.

Gore, Meredith L., Jonah Ratsimbazafy, Andry Rajaonson, Amanda Lewis, and Jessica S. Kahler. 2016. Public perceptions of poaching risks in a biodiversity hotspot: Implications for wildlife trafficking interventions. *Journal of Trafficking, Organized Crime and Security* 2 (1): 1–20.

Gore, Meredith L., William F. Siemer, James E. Shanahan, Dietram Schuefele, and Daniel J. Decker. 2005. Effects on risk perception of media coverage of a black bear-related human fatality. *Wildlife Society Bulletin* 33 (2): 507–516.

Goyes, David R., and Ragnhild Sollund. 2016. Contesting and contextualising cites: Wildlife trafficking in Colombia and Brazil. *International Journal for Crime, Justice and Social Democracy* 5 (4): 87–102.

Greife, Matthew, Paul B. Stretesky, Tara O'Connor Shelley, and Mark Pogrebin. 2015. Corporate environmental crime and environmental justice. *Criminal Justice Policy Review* 28 (4): 327–346.

Herrera, Mauricio and Bennett Hennessey. 2007. Quantifying the illegal parrot trade in Santa Cruz de la Sierra, Bolivia, with emphasis on threatened species. *Bird Conservation International* 17 (4): 295–300.

Højberg, Peter Lyhne, Martin Reinhardt Nielsen, and Jette Bredahl Jacobsen. 2017. Fear, economic consequences, hunting competition, and distrust of authorities determine preferences for illegal lethal actions against gray wolves (Canis lupus): A choice experiment among landowners in Jutland, Denmark. *Crime, Law and Social Change* 67 (4): 461–480.

Huss, Shelia, Paul B. Stretesky, and Michael J. Lynch. 2012. Characteristics of the formalized environmental justice movement: Implications for environmental governance. In D. Gallagher (ed.), *Environmental Leadership: A Reference Handbook.* Thousand Oaks, CA: Sage.

Jager, Corey, Michael Paul Nelson, Lissy Goralnik, and Meredith L. Gore. 2016. Michigan mute swan management: A case study to understand contentious natural resource management issues. *Human Dimensions of Wildlife* 21 (3): 189–202.

Jarrell, Melissa L., Michael J. Lynch, and Paul B. Stretesky. 2013. Green criminology and green victimization. In B. Arrigo and H. Bersot (eds.), *The Routledge Handbook of International Crime and Justice Studies.* London: Routledge.

Jarrell, Melissa L., and Joshua Ozymy. 2014. Few and far between: Understanding the role of the victim in federal environmental crime prosecutions in the United States. *Crime, Law and Social Change* 61 (5): 563–584.

Jarrell, Melissa, Joshua Ozymy, and William L. Sandel. 2017. Where the wild things are: Animal victimization in federal environmental crime cases. *Contemporary Justice Review* 20 (3): 319–335.

Jorgenson, Andrew K. 2012. The sociology of ecologically unequal exchange and carbon dioxide emissions, 1960–2005. *Social Science Research* 41 (2): 242–252.

Jorgenson, Andrew K., and Brett Clark. 2011. Societies consuming nature: A panel study of the ecological footprints of nations, 1960–2003. *Social Science Research* 40 (1): 226–244.

Kahler, Jessica S., and Meredith L. Gore. 2015. Local perceptions of risk associated with poaching of wildlife implicated in human-wildlife conflicts in Namibia. *Biological Conservation* 189: 49–58.

Kahler, Jessica S., and Meredith L. Gore. 2012. Beyond the cooking pot and pocket book: Factors influencing noncompliance with wildlife poaching rules. *International Journal of Comparative and Applied Criminal Justice* 36 (2): 103–120.

Kahler, Jessica S., Gary J. Roloff, and Meredith L. Gore. 2013. Poaching risks in community-based natural resource management. *Conservation Biology* 27 (1): 177–186.

Kosmicki, Sarah, and Michael A. Long. 2016. Exploring environmental inequality within US Communities containing coal and nuclear power plants. Pp. 79–99 in T. Wyatt (ed.), *Hazardous Waste and Pollution.* London: Springer International Publishing.

Kurland, Justin, and Stephen F. Pires. 2017. Assessing US wildlife trafficking patterns: How criminology and conservation science can guide strategies to reduce the illegal wildlife trade. *Deviant Behavior* 38 (4): 375–391.

Kurland, Justin, Stephen F. Pires, Sara C. McFann, and William D. Moreto. 2017. Wildlife crime: A conceptual integration, literature review, and methodological critique. *Crime Science* 6 (1): 4. https://doi.org/10.1186/s40163-017-0066-0

Lee, Sangyun, and Paul Mohai. 2011. Racial and socioeconomic assessments of neighborhoods adjacent to small-scale brownfield sites in the Detroit region. *Environmental Practice* 13 (4): 340–353.

Lemieux, Andrew M., and Ronald V. Clarke. 2009. The international ban on ivory sales and its effects on elephant poaching in Africa. *British Journal of Criminology* 49 (4): 451–471.

Long, Michael A., Michael J. Lynch, and Paul B. Stretesky. 2018. The great recession, the treadmill of production and ecological disorganization: Did the recession decrease toxic releases across US States, 2005–2014? *Ecological Economics* 146: 184–192.

Long, Michael A., Paul B. Stretesky, and Michael J. Lynch. 2017. Foreign direct investment, ecological withdrawals, and natural-resource-dependent economies. *Society & Natural Resources* 30 (10): 1261–1276.

Long, Michael A., Paul B. Stretesky, Michael J. Lynch, and Emily Fenwick. 2012. Crime in the coal industry: Implications for green criminology and treadmill of production theory. *Organization & Environment* 25 (3): 328–346.

Lute, Michelle L., Adam Bump, and Meredith L. Gore. 2014. Identity-driven differences in stakeholder concerns about hunting wolves. *PloS ONE,* 9 (12): e114460.

Lute, Michelle L., and Meredith L. Gore. 2014a. Stewardship as a path to cooperation? Exploring the role of identity in intergroup conflict among Michigan wolf stakeholders. *Human Dimensions of Wildlife* 19 (3): 267–279.

Lute, Michelle L., and Meredith L. Gore. 2014b. Knowledge and power in wildlife management. *The Journal of Wildlife Management* 78 (6): 1060–1068.

Lute, Michelle L., Carlos David Navarrete, Michael Paul Nelson, and Meredith L. Gore. 2016. Moral dimensions of human-wildlife conflict. *Conservation Biology* 30 (6): 1200–1211.

Lynch, Michael J. 2017. The sentencing/punishment of federal environmental/green criminal offenders, 2000–2013. *Deviant Behavior* 38 (9): 991–1008.

Lynch, Michael J. 2013. Reflecting on green criminology and its boundaries: Comparing environmental and criminal victimization and considering crime from an eco-city perspective. In N. South and A. Brisman's (eds.), *The Routledge International Handbook of Green Criminology*. London: Routledge.

Lynch, Michael J., and Kimberly L. Barrett. 2015. Death matters: Victimization by particle matter from coal fired power plants in the US, a green criminological view. *Critical Criminology* 23 (3): 219–234.

Lynch, Michael J., Kimberly L. Barrett, Paul B. Stretesky, and Michael A. Long. 2017. The neglect of quantitative research in green criminology and its consequences. *Critical Criminology* 25 (2): 183–198.

Lynch, Michael J., Kimberly L. Barrett, Paul B. Stretesky, and Michael A. Long. 2016. The weak probability of punishment for environmental offenses and deterrence of environmental offenders: A discussion based on USEPA criminal cases, 1983–2013. *Deviant Behavior* 37 (10): 1095–1109.

Lynch, Michael J., and Paul B. Stretesky. 2014. *Exploring Green Criminology: Toward a Green Revolution in Criminology*. Farnham, UK: Ashgate Publishing.

Lynch, Michael J., and Paul B. Stretesky. 2013. The distribution of water-monitoring organizations across states: Implications for community policing. *Policing: An International Journal of Police Strategies and Management* 36 (1): 6–26.

Lynch, Michael J., and Paul B. Stretesky. 2012. A proposal for a new vehicle based carbon tax: Vehicle based global warming and criminology. In R. White's (ed.), *Climate Change from a Criminological Perspective*. New York: Springer.

Lynch, Michael J., Paul B. Stretesky, and Ronald G. Burns. 2004a. Determinants of environmental law violation fines against oil refineries: Race, ethnicity, income and aggregation effects. *Society and Natural Resources* 17 (4): 333–347.

Lynch, Michael J., Paul B. Stretesky, and Ronald G. Burns. 2004b. Slippery business: Race, class and legal determinants of penalties against petroleum refineries. *Journal of Black Studies* 34 (3): 421–440.

Lynch, Michael J., Paul B. Stretesky and Paul Hammond. 2000. Media coverage of chemical crimes: Hillsborough county, Florida, 1987–1997. *British Journal of Criminology* 40 (1): 112–126.

Lynch, Michael J., Paul B. Stretesky, and Michael A. Long. 2017. State and green crimes related to water pollution and ecological disorganization: Water pollution from publicly owned treatment works (POTW) facilities across US states. *Palgrave Communications* 3: 17070.

Maingi, John K., Joseph M. Mukeka, Daniel M. Kyale, and Robert M. Muasya. 2012. Spatiotemporal patterns of elephant poaching in south-eastern Kenya. *Wildlife Research* 39 (3): 234–249.

Margai, Florence Lansana. 2001. Health risks and environmental inequity: A geographical analysis of accidental releases of hazardous materials. *The Professional Geographer* 53 (3): 422–434.

McKie, Ruth E., Paul B. Stretesky, and Michael A. Long. 2015. Carbon crime in the voluntary market: An exploration of modernization themes among a sample of criminal and non-criminal organizations. *Critical Criminology* 23 (4): 473–486.

Molitor, John, Jason G. Su, Nuoo-Ting Molitor, Virgilio Gómez Rubio, Sylvia Richardson, David Hastie, Rachel Morello-Frosch, and Michael Jerrett. 2011. Identifying vulnerable populations through an examination of the association between multipollutant profiles and poverty. *Environmental Science & Technology* 45 (18): 7754–7760.

Moreto, William D., Rod K. Brunson, and Anthony A. Braga. 2014. "Such misconducts don't make a good ranger": Examining law enforcement ranger wrongdoing in Uganda. *British Journal of Criminology* 55 (2): 359–380.

Moreto, William D., and Andrew M. Lemieux. 2015. Poaching in Uganda: Perspectives of law enforcement rangers. *Deviant Behavior* 36 (11): 853–873.

Moreto, William D., and Matthew C. Matusiak. 2017. "We fight against wrong doers": Law enforcement rangers' roles, responsibilities, and patrol operations in Uganda. *Deviant Behavior* 38 (4): 426–447.

Muter, Bret A., Meredith L. Gore, Katie S. Gledhill, Christopher Lamont, and Charlie Huveneers. 2013. Australian and US news media portrayal of sharks and their conservation. *Conservation Biology* 27 (1): 187–196.

Muter, Bret A., Meredith L. Gore, and Shawn J. Riley. 2009. From victim to perpetrator: Evolution of risk frames related to human-cormorant conflict in the Great Lakes. *Human Dimensions of Wildlife* 14 (5): 366–379.

Needleman, Herbert L., Alan Schell, David Bellinger, Alan Leviton, and Elizabeth N. Allred. 1990. The long-term effects of exposure to low doses of lead in childhood: An 11-year follow-up report. *New England Journal of Medicine* 322 (2): 83–88.

Nelson, Jake R., and Tony H. Grubesic. 2018. Environmental justice: A panoptic overview using scientometrics. *Sustainability* 10 (4): 1022.

Opsal, Tara, and Tara O'Connor Shelley. 2014. Energy crime, harm, and problematic state response in Colorado: A case of the fox guarding the hen house? *Critical Criminology* 22 (4): 561–577.

Ozymy, Joshua, and Melissa Jarrell. 2017. Red state, blue state, green state: Analysing the geography of federal environmental crime prosecutions within and across the US states. *Palgrave Communications* 3: 17063.

Ozymy, Joshua, and Melissa Jarrell. 2016. Why do regulatory agencies punish? The impact of political principals, agency culture, and transaction costs in predicting environmental criminal prosecution outcomes in the United States. *Review of Policy Research* 33 (1): 71–89.

Ozymy, Joshua, and Melissa L. Jarrell. 2015. Wielding the green stick: Criminal enforcement at the EPA under Bush and Obama. *Environmental Politics* 24 (1): 38–56.

Ozymy, Joshua, and Melissa L. Jarrell. 2012. Upset events, regulatory drift, and the regulation of air emissions at industrial facilities in the United States. *Environmental Politics* 21 (3): 451–466.

Ozymy, Joshua, and Melissa L. Jarrell. 2011. Upset over air pollution: Analyzing upset event emissions at petroleum refineries. *Review of Policy Research* 28 (4): 365–382.

Pastor, Manuel, James L. Sadd, and Rachel Morello-Frosch. 2004. Reading, writing, and toxics: Children's health, academic performance, and environmental justice in Los Angeles. *Environment and Planning C* 22 (2): 271–290.

Petrossian, Gohar A., and Ronald V. Clarke. 2014. Explaining and controlling illegal commercial fishing: An application of the CRAVED theft model. *British Journal of Criminology* 54 (1): 73–90.

Petrossian, Gohar A., Rolf A. de By, and Ronald V. Clarke. 2018. Illegal long-line fishing and albatross extinction risk. *Oryx* 52 (2): 336–345.

Petrossian, Gohar A., Nerea Marteache, and Julie Viollaz. 2015. Where do "undocumented" fish land? An empirical study of port characteristics for IUU fishing. *European Journal of Criminal Policy Research* 21 (3): 337–351.

Petrossian, Gohar, Judith S. Weis, and Stephen F. Pires. 2015. Factors affecting Crab and Lobster species subject to IUU fishing. *Ocean & Coastal Management* 106: 29–34.

Pine, John C., Brian D. Marx, and Aruna Lakshmanan. 2002. An examination of accidental-release scenarios from chemical-processing sites: The relation of race to distance. *Social Science Quarterly* 83 (1): 317–331.

Pires, Stephen F. 2015. The heterogeneity of illegal parrot markets: An analysis of seven neo-tropical open air markets. *European Journal on Criminal Policy and Research* 21 (1): 151–166.

Pires, Stephen F., and Ronald V. Clarke. 2012. Are parrots CRAVED? An analysis of parrot poaching in Mexico. *Journal of Research in Crime and Delinquency* 49 (1): 122–146.

Pires, Stephen F., and Ronald V. Clarke. 2011. Sequential foraging, itinerant fences and parrot poaching in Bolivia. *British Journal of Criminology* 51 (2): 314–335.

Pires, Stephen F., and Gohar A. Petrossian. 2016. Understanding parrot trafficking between illicit markets in Bolivia: An application of the CRAVE model. *International Journal of Comparative and Applied Criminal Justice* 40 (1): 63–77.

Pires, Stephen. F., Jacqueline Schneider, Mauricio Herrera, and Jose Tella. 2016. Spatial, temporal and age sources of variation in parrot poaching in Bolivia. *Bird Conservation International* 26 (3): 293–306.

Richardson, Jeanita W. 2002. Poor, powerless and poisoned: The social injustice of childhood lead poisoning. *Journal of Children and Poverty* 8 (2): 141–157.

Rizzolo, Jessica Bell, Meredith L. Gore, Jonah H. Ratsimbazafy, and Andry Rajaonson. 2017. Cultural influences on attitudes about the causes and consequences of wildlife poaching. *Crime, Law and Social Change* 67 (4): 415–437.

Sahramäki, Iina, Lars Korsell, and Terhi Kankaanranta. 2015. Prevention of environmental crime through enforcement: Finland and Sweden compared. *Journal of Scandinavian Studies in Criminology and Crime Prevention* 16 (1): 41–59.

Sampson, Robert J., and Alix S. Winter. 2016. The racial ecology of lead poisoning: Toxic inequality in Chicago neighborhoods, 1995–2013. *Du Bois Review* 13 (2): 261–283.

Silvy, Elizabeth H., M. Nils Peterson, Justa L. Heinen-Kay, and R. Brian Langerhans. 2018. Illegal harvest of marine resources on Andros Island and the legacy of colonial governance. *The British Journal of Criminology* 58 (2): 332–350.

Solomon, Susan, Gian-Kasper Plattner, Reto Knutti, and Pierre Friedlingstein. 2009. Irreversible climate change due to carbon dioxide emissions. *Proceedings of the National Academy of Sciences* 106 (6): 1704–1709.

Stretesky, Paul B. 2006. Corporate self-policing and the environment. *Criminology* 44 (3): 671–708.

Stretesky, Paul B. 2003. Environmental inequity and the distribution of air lead levels across U.S. counties: Implications for the production of racial inequality. *Sociological Spectrum* 23 (1): 91–118.

Stretesky, Paul B., and Jackie Gabriel. 2005. Self-policing and the environment: Predicting self-disclosure of Clean Air Act Violations under the U.S. environmental protection agency's audit policy. *Society and Natural Resources* 18 (10): 871–887.

Stretesky, Paul B., and Michael J. Hogan. 1998. Environmental justice: An analysis of superfund sites in Florida. *Social Problems* 45 (2): 268–287.

Stretesky, Paul, Sheila Huss, and Michael J. Lynch. 2012. Density dependence and specialized environmental justice organizations, 1970–2008. *The Social Science Journal* 49 (3): 343–351.

Stretesky, Paul B., Shelia Huss, Michael J. Lynch, Sammy Zahran, and Bob Childs. 2011. The founding of environmental justice organizations across US counties during the 1990s and 2000s: Civil rights and environmental movement cross effects. *Social Problems* 58 (3): 330–360.

Stretesky, Paul B., Janis Johnston, and Jeremy Arney. 2003. Environmental inequity: An analysis of large-scale hog operations in 17 States, 1982–1997. *Rural Sociology* 68 (2): 231–252.

Stretesky, Paul B., Michael A. Long, and Michael J. Lynch. 2017a. A cross-national study of the association between natural resource rents and homicide rates, 2000–12. *European Journal of Criminology* 14 (4): 393–414.

Stretesky, Paul B., Michael A. Long, and Michael J. Lynch. 2017b. Trends in the formation of environmental enforcement international non-governmental organizations, 1950–2010. *Globalizations* 14 (4): 627–642.

Stretesky, Paul B., Michael A. Long, and Michael J. Lynch. 2013. Does environmental enforcement slow the treadmill of production? The relationship between large monetary penalties, ecological disorganization and toxic releases within offending corporations. *Journal of Crime and Justice* 36 (2): 235–249.

Stretesky, Paul B., Michael A. Long, Ruth E. McKie, and F. Aryee. 2018. Does oil and gas development increase crime within UK local authorities? 2004–2015. *Extractive Industries and Society*. https://doi.org/10.1016/j.exis.2018.03.006

Stretesky, Paul B., and Michael J. Lynch. 2011a. Coal strip mining, mountain top removal and the distribution of environmental violations across the United States, 2002–2008. *Landscape Research* 36 (2): 209–230.

Stretesky, Paul B., and Michael J. Lynch. 2011b. Does self-policing improve environmental compliance? In L. Paddock, D. Qun, L. Kotze, D. L. Markell, J. Markowitz and D. Zaelke (eds.) *Compliance and Enforcement in Environmental Law: Toward More Effective Implementation*. Northhampton, MA: Edgar Elgar Publishing.

Stretesky, Paul B., and Michael J. Lynch. 2009a. Does self-policing reduce chemical emissions? A further test of the EPA self audit policy. *The Social Science Journal* 46 (3): 459–473.

Stretesky, Paul B., and Michael J. Lynch. 2009b. A cross-national study of the association between per capita carbon dioxide emissions and exports to the United States. *Social Science Research* 38: 239–250.

Stretesky, Paul B., and Michael J. Lynch. 2004. The relationship between lead and crime. *Journal of Health and Social Behavior* 45 (2): 214–229.

Stretesky, Paul B., and Michael J. Lynch. 2002. Environmental Hazards and school segregation in Hillsborough, 1987–1999. *The Sociological Quarterly* 43 (4): 553–573.

Stretesky, Paul B., and Michael J. Lynch. 2001. The relationship between lead and homicide. *Archives of Pediatric and Adolescent Medicine* 155 (5): 579–582.

Stretesky, Paul B., and Michael J. Lynch. 1999. Environmental justice and the prediction of distance to accidental chemical releases in Hillsborough County, Florida. *Social Science Quarterly* 80 (4): 830–846.

Stretesky, Paul B., and Michael J. Lynch. 1998. Corporate environmental violence and racism. *Crime, Law and Social Change* 30 (2): 163–184.

Stretesky, Paul B., Michael J. Lynch, Michael A. Long, and Kimberly L. Barrett. 2017. Does the modernization of environmental enforcement reduce toxic releases? An examination of self-policing, criminal prosecutions, and toxic releases in the United States, 1988–2014. *Sociological Spectrum* 37 (1): 48–62.

Stretesky, Paul B., Ruth E. McKie, Michael J. Lynch, Michael A. Long, and Kimberly L. Barrett. 2018. Where have all the falcons gone? Saker falcon (falco cherrug) exports in a global economy. *Global Ecology and Conservation* 13: e00372.

Stretesky, Paul B., Tara O'Connor Shelley, and Matthew S. Crow. 2010. Do conservation organizations influence the social production of natural resource violations? *Organization and Environment* 23 (4): 398–416.

Tella, J. L., and F. Hiraldo. 2014. Illegal and legal parrot trade shows a long-term, cross-cultural preference for the most attractive species increasing their risk of extinction. *PLoS ONE,* 9 (9): e107546.

Telle, K. 2013. Monitoring and enforcement of environmental regulations: Lessons from a natural field experiment in Norway. *Journal of Public Economics* 99: 24–34.

Triezenberg, Heather A., Meredith L. Gore, Shawn J. Riley, and Maria K. Lapinski. 2014. Persuasive communication aimed at achieving wildlife-disease management goals. *Wildlife Society Bulletin* 38 (4): 734–740.

Triezenberg, Heather A., Shawn J. Riley, and Meredith L. Gore. 2016. A test of communication in changing harvest behaviors of deer hunters. *The Journal of Wildlife Management* 80 (5): 941–946.

van Uhm, Daan P. 2016. Monkey business: The illegal trade in Barbary macaques. *Journal of Trafficking, Organized Crime and Security* 2 (1): 36–49.

van Uhm, Daan P., and Dina Siegel. 2016. The illegal trade in black caviar. *Trends in Organized Crime* 19 (1): 67–87.

Winter, Alix S., and Robert J. Sampson. 2017. From lead exposure in early childhood to adolescent health: A Chicago birth cohort. *American Journal of Public Health* 107 (9): 1496–1501.

Wong, Rebecca W. Y. 2017a. The role of reputation in the illegal purchase of protected wildlife in China. *Deviant Behavior* 38 (11): 1290–1302.

Wong, Rebecca W. Y. 2017b. "Do you know where I can buy ivory?": The illegal sale of worked ivory products in Hong Kong. *Australian & New Zealand Journal of Criminology.* 51(2): 204–220. https://doi.org/10.1177/0004865817722186

Zabyelina, Yuliya G. 2014. The "fishy" business: A qualitative analysis of the illicit market in black caviar. *Trends in Organized Crime* 17 (3): 181–198.

4 An agenda for criminological investigation of crimes impacting primates

Lauren Wilson and Justin Kurland

The biological literature documents the devastating effects of human activity on biodiversity and ecosystem function across the planet. Primates are one taxonomic order that is subject to many of the ecological pressures caused by human activities.[1] Common threats to primates include habitat loss or degradation due to agricultural expansion, deforestation, and human settlement; hunting for various uses (food, pets, etc.); and other challenges such as disease (IUCN, 2016).

Ecological assessments have evaluated most primate species and documented their specific threats, often as part of regional assessments. For example, Laurance et al. (2008) conducted ecological surveys of nocturnal mammals (including primates) in Gabon to determine the effects of roads, hunting, and habitat alteration on those populations. Similarly, prior research on wildlife markets have often been geographically specific; for example, Shanee et al. (2017) characterized the basic scale and composition of the illegal primate trade in Peru. A primate-wide empirical analysis to identify the major threats affecting this taxonomic order has not been conducted, most likely because this broad-level analysis is not as useful to the work of conservation, which works to protect or recover species within a specific ecological framework.

However, an agenda for conservation criminology on crimes affecting primates would direct research efforts toward crimes with the largest impact. Additionally, how a target is used has proven relevant to identifying offender selection patterns. For example, thieves who steal cars for joyriding typically select flashier cars with fast acceleration; this pattern differs substantially from that of a thief who steals a car to disassemble it and sell parts (Felson and Clarke, 1999; Wortley and Mazerolle, 2008). Such distinctions may prove useful in understanding how a person illegally hunting for meat differs from one retaliating for a monkey troupe's raid of his crops, or another who is looking for juvenile animals to sell as pets.

These latter examples would be considered "poaching" – the illegal taking of an animal or plant (Crow et al., 2013; Eliason, 1999, 2004; Filteau, 2012; Moreto and Lemieux, 2015). Despite the identification of poaching as a preeminent threat to biodiversity (Bennett and Robinson, 2000; Cronin et al., 2016; Nijman et al., 2011), criminologists have only recently begun to investigate the illegal extraction of natural resources. This study directs such crime- and context-specific investigations by narrowing the research focus to activities that pose a significant threat to wild primate populations.

Theoretical background: conservation criminology and crime science

Criminologists can have little impact on certain biodiversity threats – human population growth or consumer demand for carbon-emitting products, for example. However, the work of criminologists is critical to threats that involve the criminal behavior of persons or groups. Strides have already been made by criminologists interested in understanding and preventing certain wildlife crimes. Marteache et al. (2015) applied Cornish and Clarke's (1987) concept of choice structuring properties to port countries chosen for offloading illegal, unreported, and unregulated (IUU) fishing hauls. Their finding that countries with high-traffic ports, better infrastructure, and weak governance receive more IUU catches provided evidence that offenders prefer ports that increase the concealability and disposability of an illicit haul while reducing the risk of detection. Such a selection pattern also implies that monitoring efforts would be best directed toward ports with high import and export volumes for fish and high levels of infrastructure. Furthermore, evaluative studies are critical to identifying effective policy interventions; for example, Lemieux and Clarke (2009) employed quasi-experimental methods to test the effect of the CITES ivory ban on African elephant populations.

Spatial and temporal patterns along routes can also inform strategies for prevention or detection. Kurland and Pires (2017) examined the circumstances of 40,113 seizures of wildlife products by the US Fish and Wildlife Service (USFWS) between 2003 and 2012 and found significant trends in routes these products took (both countries of origin and US ports of entry), as well as seasonal variation in seizures coinciding with cultural activities. Though enforcement level (a proxy for the likelihood of detection) could not be controlled between ports of entry, their conclusions provide data-derived observations that can be employed by customs and USFWS investigators to maximize their enforcement activities and enhance the detection and confiscation of wildlife products imported illegally into the United States.

Kurland et al. (2017) interrogated the conservation literature to uncover the ways that conservationists' findings on specific wildlife crimes reveal consistency with the principles of crime science. Specifically, they found that wildlife crimes, like "traditional" crimes, are spatially and temporally concentrated, as well as being clustered among products, along routes, and at facilities.

Patterns in animal victimization have supported those predicted by the CRAVED (concealable, removable, available, valuable, enjoyable, and disposable) model, which was originally developed to explain variation in the rates of stolen products using characteristics derived from the rational choice perspective and opportunity theories (Clarke, 1999). Evidence suggests that offenders do not randomly choose targets, particularly for thefts; products that are stolen at higher rates than other products of the same type are assumed to be more attractive to thieves. The CRAVED characteristics capture the overall attractiveness of a particular product to a thief or other criminal. For example, Sidebottom (2013) applied the CRAVED model to livestock thefts in Malawi, finding that highly available (commonly owned) and disposable (commonly sold) livestock species were stolen significantly more frequently than their less available and disposable counterparts.

Not only has the application of this model suggested a rational basis for decision-making in commercial fishing operations (Petrossian and Clarke, 2014; Petrossian et al., 2015), but also its application to non-traditional targets has produced a deeper understanding of relevant illegal market product characteristics. In studying patterns in the poaching of parrots for the pet trade in Mexico, Pires and Clarke (2012) concluded that the CRAVED "A" (*available*) should be separated into two distinct elements – *accessibility* and *abundance*, which is now incorporated into the CRAAVED model. Accessibility refers to the ease or difficulty with which the target is accessed; parrot species whose ranges overlap with human populations would be considered more accessible than those whose ranges are remote. Abundance refers to how commonly the species occurs and would ideally use ecological surveys to quantify population size. Both represent dimensions of availability and reflect rational elements of decision-making by parrot poachers and traders.

The current study

In keeping with the principles of crime science, this study takes a crime-specific approach by considering the purposes of primate hunting rather than lumping all hunting into one category. The analysis presented here identifies determinants of high extinction risk for primates so that future work can be tailored to threats with the highest impacts, thus narrowing studies to the problems whose solutions have the greatest conservation and crime prevention potential.[2]

Distinguishing between legal and illegal activities for each threat and each species is impossible with currently available information. Legality for hunting is species-, site-, and season-specific (i.e., a primate species might be legal to hunt in some areas within one country but not in other areas, or during some times of year but not year-round). Therefore, each threat represents both legal and illegal activities. However, wildlife crime associated with each threat has been documented. The example of the Nigerian-Cameroon chimpanzee (*Pan troglodytes ellioti*) illustrates both the legal complexity and the seriousness of the threats. These chimpanzees are not only of interested because they are listed by IUCN as endangered, but also because their limited geographic range contributes to an increased risk of extinction. Morgan et al. (2011) concluded that legal and illegal logging within chimpanzee habitat, as well as chimpanzee poaching within Nigeria's Gashaka-Gumti National Park, were responsible for reducing the population to an estimated 3,500 to 9,000 remaining individuals.

To contextualize these problems, a 2008 report by the World Wildlife Fund–Germany lists Nigeria as the number 23 source of imported European wood products, identifies Nigeria as a country with known illegal logging problems, and finds that an estimated 36%–56% of wood products exported from African nations into Europe are of illegal or suspicious extraction (Hirschberger, 2008). Globally, INTERPOL estimates the trade value of illegal logging products to be $30 billion to $100 billion annually (Nellemann et al., 2016). These facts serve to underscore the difficulty in separating the effects of legal and illegal activity on wildlife populations and illustrate the widespread role that these criminal activities play, not only in chimpanzee conservation but also in tangentially related illegal global markets.

Furthermore, a United Nations Environment Programme report found documentation of 614 live chimpanzees (of all four sub-species) being trafficked domestically or internationally between 2005 and 2011 (Stiles et al., 2016). In fact, this figure represents thousands of dead chimpanzees, because the capture of a live infant requires the killing of at least one adult and is usually associated with a higher toll (either additional adults killed during the capture or the loss of other captured infants along the journey). Again, to emphasize the criminological relevance of crime affecting primates, the threats to the Cameroon-Nigerian chimpanzee must be situated in the broader context of illegal activities and markets of which it is part.

It is hypothesized that the presence of habitat-related threats and extractive threats will be correlated with higher risk of extinction, and the absence of habitat-related threats and extractive threats will be correlated with a lower extinction risk (Hypothesis 1). Specifically, the threats whose presence are expected to significantly explain higher extinction risk include habitat loss and fragmentation, hunting for food, pets, various cultural uses, and as outcomes of human-wildlife conflict (Hypothesis 2).

Methods

The following analyses evaluate the effects of eight threat types, including six extractive use threats, on primate risk of extinction. Two dependent variables were evaluated as measurements of risk: conservation status (based on ecological, demographic, and genetic data) and population trend (based only on documented demographic patterns). The International Union for the Conservation of Nature (IUCN), an internationally recognized conservation organization, defines five ranked levels of conservation status using evaluation criteria developed by the organization: least concern, near threatened, vulnerable, endangered, and critically endangered.[3] Population trend comprises only three categories (increasing, stable, and decreasing), according to available demographic information (e.g., field surveys). Previous studies have also used the extensive database developed and maintained by IUCN to assess taxonomic order- and class-level patterns in populations and conservation; for example, Luther et al. (2016) investigated correlates of conservation action categories and population trends within at-risk avian species, and Olah et al. (2016) evaluated both ecological and socioeconomic determinants of extinction risk for parrots.

Both variables are helpful in measuring extinction risk. IUCN status reflects the overall state of the population, while population trend reflects the immediate demographic trajectory.

Data

Data on species threats, uses, geography, and population trends came from the IUCN Red List, which identified 433 known primate species at the time of the study. Species profiles that contained insufficient detail for threats or human uses were excluded from the analysis. Sub-species level data existed for 31 species; in these cases, the species-level data were excluded so that a finer resolution of data could be retained. After exclusions, 405 species and 16 sub-species were included, for a total sample size of 421 primates for evaluating IUCN conservation status determinants. Primates with unknown population trends were excluded from analysis on determinants of population trend, reducing this total sample size to 366 (351 species and 15 sub-species). Because closely related species are assumed to be more similar to each other, including in their endangerment and population trends, binary variables were generated for all 15 taxonomic families and five species containing sub-species to control for effects of relatedness.[4]

Eight threats, including six extractive uses, were evaluated for their relative impact on global primate populations: (1) habitat loss, (2) habitat fragmentation, (3) use for food, (4) use as pets, (5) various cultural uses, (6) sport hunting, (7) biomedical research, and (8) human-wildlife conflict (Table 4.1). Threat categories are not mutually exclusive; a particular species may be affected by multiple threats. Correlations between these independent variables were tested and four significant correlations were found. Species that have experienced habitat loss are more likely to experience fragmentation, more likely to be targeted for food, and less likely to be targeted for biomedical research. Species that are hunted for food are also more likely to have various cultural uses. Given concerns about multicollinearity, two approaches were adopted. First, variance inflation factors (VIFs) were calculated to measure the extent to which correlation among the explanatory variables inflates the variance of the estimated regression coefficients in the model. The general rule of thumb is that VIFs greater than 10 indicate excessive multicollinearity requiring correction (Kutner et al., 2004). Results were found to be within an acceptable range for all eight threats, ranging from 1.35 to 1.56. Additionally, low eigenvalues (maximum 0.65) from a factor analysis of all threats supported the determination that collinearity of threats were within acceptable boundaries and not a threat to the validity of the results.

Body weight in grams was used to control for the intrinsically higher risk of extinction for large-bodied species (González-Suárez et al., 2013; Pimm et al., 1988; Pimm et al., 2014). Weights for 78 species were collected from three sources: Milton (1976), the Encyclopedia of Life (2016), and

Table 4.1 Descriptive statistics for independent variables, with definitions for threats to primate species and sub-species

Control Variable	*Mean*	*Standard Deviation*	*Minimum*	*Maximum*
Body Weight (g)	5,081.63	11,108.09	52.74	145,000.00
Threats (binary)	*Number & Percentage of Primate (Sub-) Species Affected in Sample*	*Definition*		
Habitat loss	337 (80.1%)	This occurs when natural spaces used by the species are permanently altered by human activity. Habitat loss can reduce reproductive rates and population size by restricting resources (food and water) and appropriate living spaces.		
Habitat fragmentation	119 (28.3%)	This occurs when land development carves up or "fragments" natural spaces, creating barriers between animal populations, such that gene flow is severely hindered and genetic loss becomes inevitable. Severe genetic loss results in inbreeding, which is associated with reduced reproductive rates and increased health problems.		
Food	256 (60.8%)	Hunting of wildlife ("game") for food includes subsistence hunting, supplementing income through sale of meat, and the culinary commodification of wildlife (e.g., wild game on menus of high-end restaurants in Kinshasa, Democratic Republic of Congo; La Cerva, 2014).		
Pet trade	110 (26.1%)	The pet trade necessitates the taking of live animals and may target in-demand species or be done opportunistically during hunts for other purposes (e.g., taking infants after parents have been killed).		
Cultural uses	88 (20.9%)	Body parts may be used for traditional medicine and other cultural uses (e.g., superstition, customary decoration, accessories).		
Sport/trophy	10 (2.4%)	This serves a recreational purpose and includes trophy hunting.		
Biomedical research	12 (2.8%)	Extraction for this industry targets species that are useful in laboratory experiments.		
Human-wildlife conflict	35 (8.3%)	This occurs when humans kill wildlife either as a precaution or in retaliation for wildlife damages. For example, the sooty mangabey (*Cercocebus atys*) is killed by farmers because it raids crops (Oates et al., 2016).		
N = 421				

Table 4.2 Number and percentage of (sub-)species by population trend and IUCN Red List status

IUCN Current Red List Status						
Population Trend	*Least Concern*	*Near Threatened*	*Vulnerable*	*Endangered*	*Critically Endangered*	*N*
Increasing	4 (1.0%)	0 (0%)	0 (0%)	0 (0%)	0 (0%)	4 (1.0%)
Stable	37 (8.8%)	0 (0%)	1 (0.2%)	1 (0.2%)	1 (0.2%)	40 (9.5%)
Decreasing	41 (9.7%)	21 (5.0%)	80 (19.0%)	121 (28.7%)	59 (14.0%)	322 (76.5%)
Unknown	45 (10.7%)	2 (0.5%)	5 (1.2%)	1 (0.2%)	2 (0.5%)	55 (13.1%)
N	127 (30.2%)	23 (5.5%)	86 (20.4%)	123 (29.2%)	62 (14.7%)	421 (100%)

www.alltheworldsprimates.org (Rowe and Myers, 2016), a primate database that uses peer-reviewed publication data curated by the organization. Because not every species entry contained detail on average body weight, weights were averaged at a higher taxonomic level (either genus or family level).[5]

The majority of primate populations (322) are in decline, 40 are stable, and only 4 are increasing (Table 4.2). All primates with increasing populations are categorized as least concern by the IUCN. On the other end of the spectrum, only one critically endangered primate, the Hainan gibbon (*Nomascus hainanus*), has a stable population, while the other 59 have decreasing populations. Fifty-five primates have unknown population trends and were later excluded from trend-related analysis.

Analysis

Analysis was conducted using Stata v.14.0 (StataCorp, 2015). Body weight was log-transformed to improve normality and reduce heteroskedasticity. Because both response variables – population trend and conservation status – include ordered categories, ordered logistic regression models were employed.

Primate use in medical research and sport hunting, as well as primate victimization from human-wildlife conflict, each threaten less than 10% of the sample, noticeably less than threats related to habitat or victimization by the meat or pet trades and cultural uses (see Table 4.1). In preliminary model investigation, these three variables were found to be non-significant and were then tested for contribution to the model using the Wald and likelihood ratio tests. They were found to have no joint contribution to the models for either response variable and were therefore omitted as regressors.

Ordinality of the response variables was tested using a stereotype logistic regression model. Population trend, with only three categories, was found to exhibit a natural rank order, but conservation status did not. Categories were consolidated into the three groups of endangerment risk: low (least concern and near threatened), medium (vulnerable), and high (endangered and critically endangered). This consolidation achieved ordinality in the response variable, and models with conservation status as the response variable used the collapsed, three-category variable construction.

The parallel regression assumption was tested using a global likelihood ratio-based test, which evaluates whether all regressors in the models have the same impact across thresholds. Taxonomic dummy controls were excluded, as these disallowed the test to reach convergence. All other regressors, including control for body weight, were included and found to be pairwise significant, with no regressor exhibiting disparate impacts across thresholds. In other words, the parallel lines assumption for this form of regression was met.

Results

Here, two sets of models are presented: the first evaluates regressor effects on population trend, and the second on conservation status.

Effects on population trends

Population trend scores were ordered so that a higher value indicates a decreasing population. Habitat loss, habitat fragmentation, and use in the food and pet trades were found to significantly explain a decreasing population trend. Table 4.3 depicts model coefficients, which broadly indicate that habitat-related threats have a larger impact on primate population trends than do extractive uses. Regardless, the positive direction of all threat types indicates that each has a tendency to reduce the robustness of the primate population with all other regressors held constant, though the very large standard errors of the model thresholds prevent confident conclusions. When taxonomic controls are removed, standard errors are acceptably small for significant variables and thresholds, and significance did not change, suggesting that habitat loss and fragmentation, wild game consumption, and hunting for pets do significantly harm primate populations.

A comparison of marginal effects (Table 4.3) suggests more specifically the relative influence of each of the four threat types. Only four variables (habitat loss and fragmentation, food and pet trades) were significant. Every predictor's marginal effect on the likelihood of an increasing or decreasing population moved from negative to positive. In other words, populations are slightly less likely to be increasing and more likely to be decreasing when one of these threats is occurring. More notable is the relatively large effect of habitat loss across outcomes. The probability of a decreasing population trend is 12.4 percentage points (pp) higher for species experiencing habitat loss compared to those with

Table 4.3 Threat effects on population trend

Regressor	*β (SE)*	*Average Marginal Effects on Population Trend*		
		Increasing	*Stable*	*Decreasing*
Body weight (logged)	−0.217 (0.344)	0.002	0.008	-0.010
Habitat loss	2.611*** (0.537)	-0.025	-0.099	0.124
Habitat fragmentation	2.514* (1.088)	-0.024	-0.096	0.120
Food	1.534** (0.591)	-0.015	-0.058	0.073
Pet trade	1.630* (0.785)	-0.015	-0.062	0.078
Cultural use	0.318 (0.616)	-0.003	-0.012	0.015
Thresholds				
Threshold 1	-21.646 (12,975.361)			
Threshold 2	-17.787 (12,975.361)			
N = 366				

Abbreviations: SE = standard error.

Notes: Coefficients for the 20 taxonomic relatedness control variables are not shown; none was statistically significant.

Pseudo R^2 = 0.5293.

*p<0.05, **p<0.01, ***p<0.001.

no documented habitat loss. Extraction for meat and pets appear to have a smaller effect: the probability of a declining population is 7.3 pp and 7.8 pp higher when species are targeted for the food and pet trades, respectively.

Effects on conservation status

The effects on conservation status are roughly consistent with those on population trend. Conservation status was ordered such that a higher score indicates a higher level of endangerment. Four regressors (the two habitat-related threats, meat consumption, and use as pets) significantly and positively influenced the predicted conservation status, indicating that species affected by these threats are significantly more likely to be at greater risk of extinction, as measured by IUCN conservation status, holding all other variables constant (Table 4.4). Cultural use was found to have no significant effect, as in the population trend model, but with a negative direction, which was unexpected. Body weight is significant and in the expected positive direction; comparing two otherwise identical species, a 10% increase in body weight is expected to worsen the predicted endangerment status along the 1 to 5 scale by an additional 0.0887 pp.

For a closer comparison of the relative effects of the five threat categories, marginal effects are also represented in Table 4.4. Habitat loss has the largest impact on predicted IUCN status on either extreme (low- or high-risk categories).

Table 4.4 Threat effects on IUCN conservation status

Regressor	*β (SE)*	*Average Marginal Effects on Conservation Status*		
		Low (LV, NT)	*Medium (V)*	*High (EN, CR)*
Body weight (logged)	0.887** (0.303)	-0.114	-0.011	0.125
Habitat loss	2.143*** (0.397)	-0.275	-0.026	0.301
Habitat fragmentation	2.019*** (0.314)	-0.259	-0.024	0.284
Food	0.587* (0.288)	-0.075	-0.007	0.082
Pet trade	0.887** (0.302)	-0.114	-0.011	0.125
Cultural use	-0.198 (0.305)	0.025	0.002	-0.028
Thresholds				
Threshold 1	6.623*** (1.810)			
Threshold 2	8.100*** (1.828)			
N = 421				

Abbreviations: SE = standard error.

Notes: Coefficients for the 20 taxonomic relatedness control variables are not shown; none was statistically significant.

Pseudo R^2 = 0.3172.

**p*<0.05, ***p*<0.01, ****p*<0.001 (two-tailed significance test).

More specifically, species that have experienced habitat loss are less likely (by 27.5 fewer pp) to be categorized with low endangerment and more likely to be categorized with high endangerment by an additional 30.1 additional pp, compared to species not threatened by habitat loss.

Two extractive categories, the food and pet trades, show a smaller but still significant effect on endangerment status. Species used in either trade are less likely to be categorized with low endangerment and more likely to be categorized with high endangerment, compared to species not traded as food or pets. More specifically, consumed species are 7.5 pp less likely to be categorized with low endangerment and 8.2 pp more likely to be categorized high endangerment, compared to species not hunted for meat. The pet trade exhibits a larger effect with the same pattern; primates used for pets are 11.4 pp less likely to have a low endangerment status and 12.5 pp more likely to have a high endangerment status, compared to primates which remain unattractive as pets to humans.

Summary of findings

The conclusions of this study direct future criminological investigation towards illegal land clearing or disturbance in primate habitat, the poaching of primates for meat and pets, and the illegal trade of primate meat and live primates. Given the role that these activities play in threatening primate populations worldwide, prevention-focused criminological input on these specific crimes has the potential to aid primate conservation and strengthen primate populations (see Future Research section below for examples of potential interventions).

The unexpected finding that four threats (cultural uses, human-wildlife conflict, sport hunting, and medical research) are insignificant was important to the ultimate goal of identifying the most potent primate threats. The determination that the effect of these threats was effectively zero is a strong indication that conservation criminologists should initially focus elsewhere when studying primate-related crime. However, it cannot be assumed that these threats affect no primate species. For example, gorilla populations have been severely impacted by human-wildlife conflict in areas of coltan mining (Redmond, 2001).

Limitations

The study was limited by the fact that predictor variables were binary, providing low impact resolution across threats. There was no differentiation between high and low impacts, only the existence of a particular threat or use. For example, chimpanzees (*Pan troglodytes*) have been widely exploited as pets or tourist attractions and are seriously threatened by poachers and smugglers that seek to meet this demand (Stiles et al., 2016). This use would be expected to have a much larger impact as a threat to the species than in a circumstance in which species are occasionally taken as pets by locals. To adjust for these differences in threat severity, data that would allow finely scaled scoring would improve estimates of threat impacts.

Additionally, data limitations precluded temporal ordering. Causal claims between threats and extinction risk require certainty that the threat preceded the change in extinction risk, which has not been documented for all species and is not included in IUCN species profile. Cultural uses of particular species (meat, pets, and other uses) and developments such as habitat loss typically do precede IUCN endangerment categorization, but the order of threat prior to outcome cannot be verified easily.

Future research

The investigation of the illegal food and pet trades and illegal habitat loss, all of which threaten primate populations globally, represent the best opportunity for conservation criminologists aiming to support primate conservation. Illegal deforestation or land settlement may take the form of cultivation of crops or logging operations within protected areas (e.g., national parks, forest reserves) that ban such activities, and has long vexed conservationists.

However, in areas of extreme poverty and in post-colonial contexts, issues of land tenure and resource access often conflict with conservation priorities of reducing illegal habitat loss and poaching. For example, the Democratic Republic of Congo's Virunga National Park, established in 1919 by King Albert I of Belgium, has a history of both imperialist dispossession and expulsion of residents with valid land tenure claims, as well as a more recent history of illegal settlement, illegal resource extraction (illegal logging and poaching), and armed conflict. Biologists concerned with gorilla conservation have historically advocated for increasing enforcement efforts; yet, the effectiveness of enforcement in reducing crime in the park is unevaluated. In addition, more than 130 park guards have been killed since 1996 (BBC News, 2018), and the increasingly militarized approach to conservation may, in fact, exacerbate local conflict (Verweijen and Marijnen, 2018).

Criminologists, as social scientists, may be better equipped to address these problems by considering the historical, political, and social contexts in which they exist. The social and ecological complexity of these problems requires interdisciplinary research and merits the attention of criminologists interested in both crime prevention and social justice. By investigating the crimes that pose the greatest threats to primates, criminologists can advance the understanding of important social and ecological problems and assist in the development of solutions.

Criminological investigation of these high-impact crimes can be further guided by previous biological research. Responses of mammalian populations, and primate populations specifically, vary according to certain threats, and this variation sheds light on which threats should be more aggressively addressed by criminologists for a given species. Isaac and Cowlishaw (2004) discovered three patterns in primate vulnerability: agricultural pressure significantly reduced the abundance of arboreal leaf-eating primates, logging activity significantly reduced the abundance of habitat specialists, and hunting significantly reduced the abundance of large-bodied primates.[6] These patterns may advise criminological study of primates. Poaching studies should focus on large-bodied species, while criminologists interested in illegal logging should focus on protected areas containing primate habitat specialists.

Given the instrumental nature of crimes affecting primates, the rational choice framework and prevention-focused crime science approaches are clearly relevant (as discussed earlier). For example, quantitative studies on victimization patterns (such as the CRAVED/CRAAVED analysis) could use meat market data to identify the characteristics sought or exploited by poachers. Large-bodied primates would be assumed to be more valuable, and anecdotal evidence does suggest hunter preference for large-bodied mammals (Jerozolimski and Peres, 2003). Other biological characteristics that may impact species vulnerability to hunting may include vocality, as loud groups attract more attention (Oates, 1996); movement pattern, as terrestrial foragers may be more conspicuous to hunters (Linder and Oates, 2011); and activity pattern, as species active during the day (diurnal) are more likely to be seen.

Qualitative field research would be useful to distinguish between species that are targeted for the pet trade specifically or taken opportunistically by poachers after parents have been killed for meat. In cases of meat being trafficked over larger geographies rather than remaining in local markets, social networks analysis may be useful in constructing trafficking patterns.

Place-based approaches to studying and preventing poaching would also be helpful in directing enforcement efforts. In the same way that hot spot policing has reduced local crime (Telep and Weisburd, 2016), strategic policing of poaching hot spots could be helpful in deterring poachers. In areas where park budgets do not allow additional enforcement or where corruption of guards is suspected, situational strategies could be implemented, such as roadblocks that make it more difficult for poachers to gain access to protected areas or signage making the crime less excusable.

These are presented as preliminary ideas for future criminological research, which can continue in a multitude of directions considering the paucity of criminological work on the topic of crime impacting primates. The opportunities for criminological research on these crimes are great, and the priorities identified by this study set an agenda for criminologists interested in primate conservation or areas of the world inhabited by primates.

Notes

1 Living things are categorized according to the following hierarchy (starting at the broadest level and ending at the most basic unit): kingdom, phylum, class, order, family, and species binomial (genus and specific epithet). For example, the human species (*Homo sapiens*) is classified as a member of class Mammalia, within the Primate order and the family Hominidae.

2 Extinction is defined here as the complete loss of a species in the wild.

3 Additional IUCN status categories include Data Deficient, Extinct in the Wild, and Extinct. These categories were not included in this analysis.

4 Families included Aotidae (9 species or sub-species), Atelidae (27), Callitrichidae (33), Cebidae (19), Cercopithecidae (137), Cheirogaleidae (29), Daubentoniidae (18), Hominidae (6), Hylobatidae (16), Indriidae (18), Lemuridae (20), Lepilemuridae (26), Lorisidae (13), Pitheciidae (42), and Tarsiidae (8). Sub-species of the following species were included, with the number of sub-species in parenthesis: *Cacajao calvus* (4), *Ateles fusciceps* (2), *Cercopithecus pogonias* (3), *Macaca radiata* (2), *Rhinopithecus roxellana* (3).

5 Species weights were averaged across genera for 297 species that lacked species-specific data, and genera weights were averaged across families for 123 species that did not have genus-level data. Family provides a sufficiently fine resolution to represent inter-family differences and intra-family similarity in morphology (Clutton-Brock and Harvey, 1980).

6 The term "habitat specialist" describes any species with more restrictive habitat requirements. A species adapted to a specific environment and ill-adapted to other environments is thought to "specialize." "Arboreal" describes species which dwell primarily in the tops of trees, at the mid- and canopy-levels, as opposed to ground-dwelling ("terrestrial") species.

References

BBC News. (2018, April 9). Rangers killed at Congo gorilla park. *BBC News*. Retrieved from www.bbc.com/news/world-africa-43703640

Bennett, Elizabeth L., and John G. Robinson (2000). *Hunting of wildlife in tropical forests: Implications for biodiversity and forest peoples* (No. 21886). The World Bank.

Retrieved from http://documents.worldbank.org/curated/en101611468780290485/Hunting-of-wildlife-in-tropical-forests-implications-for-biodiversity-and-forest-peoples

Clarke, Ronald V. (1999). Hot products: Understanding, anticipating and reducing demand for stolen goods. Police Research Series, Paper 112, Home Office.

Clutton-Brock, Tim H., and Paul H. Harvey (1980). Primates, brains and ecology. *Journal of Zoology 190*(3), 309–323. https://doi.org/10.1111/j.1469-7998.1980.tb01430.x

Cornish, Derek B., and Ronald V. Clarke (1987). Understanding crime displacement: An application of rational choice theory. *Criminology 25*(4), 933–948.

Cronin, Drew T., Cirilo Riaco, Joshua M. Linder, Richard A. Bergle, Mary Katherine Gonder, Michael P. O'Connor, and Gail W. Hearn (2016). Impact of gun-hunting on monkey species and implications for primate conservation on Bioko Island, Equatorial Guinea. *Biological Conservation 197*, 180–189.

Crow, Matthew S., Tara O'Connor Shelley, and Paul B. Stretesky (2013). Camouflage-collar crime: An examination of wildlife crime and characteristics of offenders in Florida. *Deviant Behavior 34*, 635–652.

Eliason, Stephen L. (1999). The illegal taking of wildlife: Toward a theoretical understanding of poaching. *Human Dimensions of Wildlife: An International Journal 4*, 27–39.

——— (2004). Accounts of wildlife Law Violators: Motivations and Rationalizations. *Human Dimensions of Wildlife 9*, 119–131.

Encyclopedia of Life (2016). Retrieved December 19, 2016, from http://eol.org/

Felson, Marcus, and Ronald V. Clarke (1999). *Opportunity makes the thief: Practical theory for crime prevention*. London: Home Office Policing and Reducing Crime Unit, Research, Development and Statistics Directorate.

Filteau, Matthew R. (2012). Deterring defiance: "Don't give a poacher a reason to poach." *International Journal of Rural Criminology 1*, 236–255.

González-Suárez, Manuela, Alicia Gómez, and Eloy Revilla (2013). Which intrinsic traits predict vulnerability to extinction depends on the actual threatening processes. *Ecosphere 4*(6), 1–16.

Hirschberger, P. (2008). *Illegal wood for the European market* (p. 45). Frankfurt, Germany: WWF-Germany. Retrieved from wwf.or.jp/activities/lib/pdf_forest/deforestation/illegal_wood_for_the_european_market_july_2008.pdf

Isaac, Nick J. B., and Guy Cowlishaw (2004). How species respond to multiple extinction threats. *Proceedings of the Royal Society of London, Series B: Biological Sciences 271*(1544), 1135–1141.

IUCN (2016). The IUCN red list of threatened species. *Version 2016–3*. Retrieved November 5, 2016, from www.iucnredlist.org

Jerozolimski, A., and C. A. Peres (2003). Bringing home the biggest bacon: A cross-site analysis of the structure of hunter-kill profiles in Neotropical forests. *Biological Conservation 111*(3), 415–425. https://doi.org/10.1016/S0006-3207(02)00310-5

Kurland, Justin, and Stephen F. Pires (2017). Assessing U.S. wildlife trafficking patterns: How criminology and conservation science can guide strategies to reduce the illegal wildlife trade. *Deviant Behavior 38*(4), 375–391.

Kurland, Justin, Stephen F. Pires, Sara C. McFann, and William D. Moreto (2017). Wildlife crime: A conceptual integration, literature review, and methodological critique. *Crime Science 6*, 4.

Kutner, M., C. Nachtsheim, J. Neter, and W. Li (2004). *Applied linear statistical models* (5th edition). Boston: McGraw-Hill/Irwin.

La Cerva, Gina. (2014). Devouring the Congo. *Tropical Resources: The Bulletin of the Yale Tropical Resources Institute 34*. Retrieved from http://tri.yale.edu/publications/tropical-resources-bulletin/tri-bulletin-archive/tropical-resources-vol-34/devouring

Laurance, William F., Barbara M. Croes, Nicaise Guissouegou, Ralph Buij, Marc Dethier, and Alfonso Alonso (2008). Impacts of roads, hunting, and habitat alteration on nocturnal mammals in African rainforests. *Conservation Biology: The Journal of the Society for Conservation Biology 22*(3), 721–732.

Lemieux, A. M., and R. V. Clarke (2009). The international ban on ivory sales and its effects on elephant poaching in Africa. *British Journal of Criminology 49*(4), 451–471.

Linder, Joshua M., and John F. Oates (2011). Differential impact of bushmeat hunting on monkey species and implications for primate conservation in Korup National Park, Cameroon. *Biological Conservation 144*(2), 738–745.

Luther, David A., Thomas M. Brooks, Stuart H. M. Butchart, Matt W. Hayward, Marieke E. Kester, John Lamoreux, and Amy Upgren (2016). Determinants of bird conservation-action implementation and associated population trends of threatened species. *Conservation Biology 30*(6), 1338–1346.

Marteache, Nerea, Julie Viollaz, and Gohar A. Petrossian (2015). Factors influencing the choice of a safe haven for offloading illegally caught fish: A comparative analysis of developed and developing economies. *Crime Science 4*(1), 32.

Milton, Katharine and Michael L. May (1976). Body weight, diet and home range area in primates. *Nature 259*(5543), 459–462.

Moreto, William D., and Andrew M. Lemieux (2015). Poaching in Uganda: Perspectives of law enforcement rangers. *Deviant Behavior 36*(11), 853–873.

Morgan, B., A. Adeleke, T. Bassey, R. Bergle, A. Dunn, R. Fotso, . . . E. Williamson (2011). *Regional action plan for the conservation of the Nigeria-Cameroon Chimpanzee (Pan troglodytes ellioti)* (p. 52). San Diego: IUCN/SSC Primate Specialist Group and Zoological Society of San Diego.

Nellemann, Christian, Rune Henriksen, Arnold Kreilhuber, Davyth Stewart, Maria Kotsovou, Patricia Raxter, . . . Sam Barrat (Eds.) (2016). *The rise of environmental crime: A growing threat to natural resources, peace, development and security*. Nairobi, Kenya: United Nations Environment Programme.

Nijman, Vincent, K. Anna I. Nekaris, Giuseppe Donati, Mike Bruford, and John Fa (2011). Primate conservation: Measuring and mitigating trade in primates. *Endangered Species Research 13*(2), 159–161.

Oates, John F. (1996). Habitat alteration, hunting and the conservation of folivorous primates in African forests. *Australian Journal of Ecology 21*, 1–9.

Oates, John F., Spartaco Gippoliti, and Colin P. Groves (2016). *Cercocebus atys*. The IUCN Red List of Threatened Species 2016: e.T136933A92247942. Retrieved May 5, 2017, from http://dx.doi.org/10.2305/IUCN.UK.2016-1.RLTS.T136933A92247942.en

Olah, G., Butchart, S.H., Symes, A., Guzmán, I.M., Cunningham, R., Brightsmith, D.J., and Heinsohn, R. (2016). Ecological and socio-economic factors affecting extinction risk in parrots. *Biodiversity and Conservation 25*(2), 205–223.

Petrossian, Gohar A., and Ronald V. Clarke (2014). Explaining and controlling illegal commercial fishing: An application of the CRAVED theft model. *The British Journal of Criminology 54*(1), 73–90.

Petrossian, Gohar A., Judith S. Weis, and Stephen F. Pires (2015). Factors affecting crab and lobster species subject to IUU fishing. *Ocean & Coastal Management 106*, 29–34. https://doi.org/10.1016/j.ocecoaman.2015.01.014

Pimm, Stuart L., Clinton N. Jenkins, Robin Abell, Thomas Brooks, J. L. Gittleman, Lucas N. Joppa, . . . Joseph O. Sexton (2014). The biodiversity of species and their rates of extinction. *Science 344*(6187).

Pimm, Stuart L., H. Lee Jones, and Jared Diamond (1988). On the risk of extinction. *The American Naturalist 132*(6), 757–785.

Pires, Stephen, and Ronald V. Clarke (2012). Are parrots CRAVED? An analysis of parrot poaching in Mexico. *Journal of Research in Crime and Delinquency 49*(1), 122–146.

Redmond, Ian (2001). *Coltan boom, gorilla bust: The impact of coltan mining on gorillas and other wildlife in eastern DR Congo.* Dian Fossey Gorilla Fund Europe. Retrieved from http://archive.niza.nl/docs/200308191256232147.pdf

Rowe, Noel, and Marc Myers (Eds.) (2016). *All the world's primates.* Charlestown, RI: Primate Conservation Inc. Retrieved from www.alltheworldsprimates.org

Shanee, N., A. P. Mendoza, and S. Shanee (2017). Diagnostic overview of the illegal trade in primates and law enforcement in Peru. *American Journal of Primatology 79*(11), e22516. https://doi.org/10.1002/ajp.22516

Sidebottom, A. (2013). On the application of CRAVED to livestock theft in Malawi. *International Journal of Comparative and Applied Criminal Justice 37*(3), 195–212. https://doi.org/10.1080/01924036.2012.734960

StataCorp (2015). *Stata statistical software: Release 14.* College Station, TX: StataCorp LP.

Stiles, Daniel, Ian Redmond, Doug Cress, Christian Nellemann, and Rannveig Knutsdatter Formo (2016). Stolen apes. In Nora Haenn, Richard Walk, and Allison Harnish Harnish (Eds.), *The environment in anthropology (second edition): A reader in ecology, culture, and sustainable living* (pp. 359–361). New York City, NY: NYU Press.

Telep, Cody W., and David Weisburd (2016). Policing. In David Weisburd, David P. Farrington, and Charlotte Gill (Eds.), *What works in crime prevention and rehabilitation: Lessons from systematic reviews.* New York: Springer.

Verweijen, J., and E. Marijnen (2018). The counterinsurgency/conservation nexus: Guerrilla livelihoods and the dynamics of conflict and violence in the Virunga National Park, Democratic Republic of the Congo. *The Journal of Peasant Studies 45*(2), 300–320.

Wortley, Richard K., and Lorraine G. Mazerolle (2008). *Environmental criminology and crime analysis.* Abingdon, UK: Routledge.

5 Using conservation criminology to explore the opportunity structures, obstacles, and deterrence of urban bushmeat trafficking in Lékoumou District, Republic of the Congo

Jessica S. Kahler, Rachel Boratto, Liliana Vanegas, Michelle Wieland, and Meredith Gore

Wildlife has long been used as a source of food for rural people. Today, as Central Africa urbanizes, bushmeat (i.e., wild animal meat) trafficking has become a massive business despite wildlife laws meant to protect species. Traditional strategies of wildlife law enforcement in protected areas such as national parks have not effectively halted this trade, and new strategies are needed. Among these are using a criminology approach to understand the actors and flows of trafficking. This chapter presents findings from in the Lékoumou Department, southern Republic of Congo (hereafter Congo-Brazzaville), and describes a regional bushmeat supply chain from Lékoumou into urban centers (Figure 5.1). The research

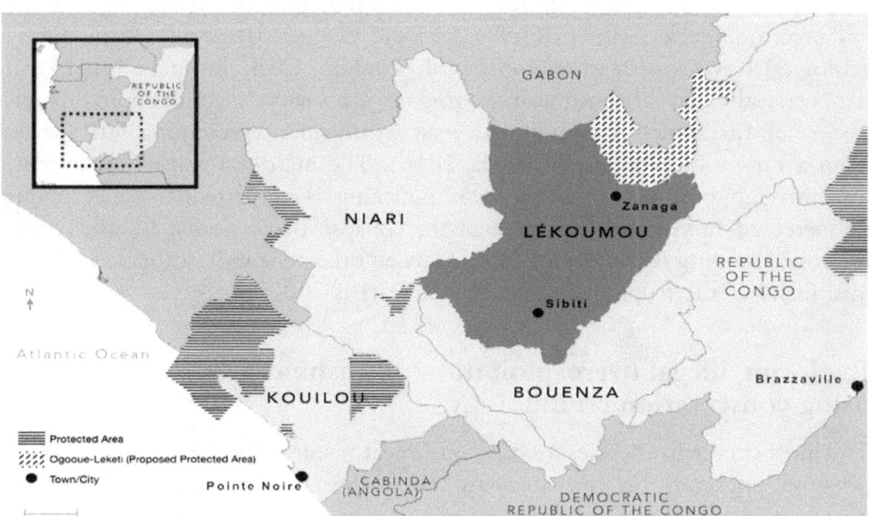

Figure 5.1 Lékoumou Department or Congo-Brazzaville, in the southern Republic of Congo

profiled presented here is, to our knowledge, the first to combine observational studies in transportation hubs and markets (i.e., physical supply chain flows) with face-to-face interviews with the people involved in bushmeat hunting, transport, and sales (i.e., informational supply chain flows). The results support conservation efforts to reduce trafficking and support rural protein security.

For decades, the illegal overharvest of bushmeat has been at the center of a contentious crossroads between human subsistence economies and biodiversity conservation (e.g., Bennett et al., 2006). Since the 1990s, conservationists have acknowledged that the unsustainable bushmeat trade transcends biodiversity concerns and poses risks to human livelihoods, particularly among natural resource–dependent rural forest dwellers (e.g., Wilkie, Curran, Tshombe, & Morelli, 1998). These concerns parallel scientific evidence that declining wildlife populations jeopardize protein sources in subsistence-based economies, which is one of the few sources of income generation with relatively low barriers for participation and opportunity costs for entry (Bowen-Jones, Brown, & Robinson, 2003). Loss or degradation of this resource can threaten food and livelihood security, with the most marginalized peoples disproportionately suffering as they have little or no professional training and few alternative sources of income and protein (Nasi et al., 2008). Additionally, the prevalence of zoonotic diseases which can spread to humans (e.g., Ebola), has been linked with the harvest of bushmeat, with the probability of disease outbreaks increasing as bushmeat is trafficked into large and densely populated urban centers (e.g., van Vliet et al., 2017).

Bushmeat has also been linked to the "biodiversity crisis" surfacing out of a century of unprecedented human population growth, anthropogenic habitat alteration, and resource extraction to fuel the consumer-driven global economy. The overexploitation of bushmeat resources threatens ecosystem function by endangering species with extinction (Ripple et al., 2016) and by disrupting ecological services such as seed dispersal (Poulsen, Clark, & Palmer, 2013). It has been estimated that bushmeat hunting is the primary threat for approximately 26% of all threatened terrestrial mammals worldwide, representing 301 species from a variety of taxa (Ripple et al., 2016). The increased risk of biodiversity loss through bushmeat hunting and trafficking is of particular concern due to increased human population growth, collapse of economic infrastructure, improved hunting technologies, lack of law enforcement and greater accessibility into many of the tropical forests worldwide (Fa, 2007).

Exploring illegal overexploitation of bushmeat using conservation criminology

The most prevalent theories guiding bushmeat research have been the "cooking pot and pocket book" explanations of poacher motivations, where wildlife poaching is seen as a subsistence strategy that provides bushmeat for consumption and income to support impoverished livelihoods (Kahler & Gore, 2012). Beyond long-term strategies to mitigate poverty and provide alternative sources of protein, the most dominant criminological response to illegal overexploitation has been using traditional law enforcement techniques. These include increasing the frequency or efficiency of anti-poaching patrols, which have been found to increase detection rates (e.g., Linkie et al., 2015) and decrease poaching rates in some contexts (e.g., Hilborn et al., 2006). However, the efficacy of these strategies may be undermined by issues of corruption, weak penal systems (Lindsey, Romañach, & Matema, 2011), the paucity of financial and human resources for environmental law enforcement efforts, and the fact that natural resources-related crimes are often not taken as seriously as non-environmental offenses (Wellsmith, 2010). There is a need to move toward wildlife crime prevention. However, a lack of research associated with understanding opportunity structures around poaching hampers this endeavor.

The science of conservation crime or conservation criminology (Gore, 2017), is relevant for exploring the illegal overexploitation of bushmeat by offering an integrative means for addressing both natural and societal dimensions inherent in bushmeat trafficking. Comprising three primary disciplines – natural resources management, risk and decision science, and criminology – conservation criminology seeks to overcome limitations inherent in single-discipline science and provide practical guidance about on-the-ground reforms (Gore, 2017). The current project does not aim to criminalize in any way the individuals who harvest, traffic, and sell bushmeat. Rather, using criminological perspectives enables us to more fully understand characteristics of criminal opportunities and perceptions of deterrence, which create circumstances conducive to crime. This chapter presents empirical research using a conservation criminology approach[1] to understand the perceptions of the actors involved; the bushmeat opportunity structure; the links between rural poaching and the subsequent trade into rural, peri-urban, and urban bushmeat markets; and obstacles to the trade of bushmeat (Kahler & Gore, 2017).

We adapted aspects of opportunity theories of crime (e.g., Huisman & van Erp, 2013) and supply chain management (e.g., Supply Chain Resource Cooperative (SCRC), 2017) to achieve our research goal. Opportunity theories break crime into component stages (e.g., poaching, trafficking, marketing) and illuminate the essential elements required for crime to occur. Understand the underlying architecture and nature of the illegal urban bushmeat supply chain, particularly its physical and informational flows, can be employed to improve the enforcement of and compliance with law. Supply chain management is based on two core ideas: first, that products (e.g., wildlife) reach end users based on the cumulative effort of multiple organizations or actors who collectively comprise the supply chain; second, that understanding the entire chain of activities that delivers products to the final customer, including physical and informational flows that link supply chain organizations, is essential to consider when planning interventions (SCRC, 2017). Together, these theories suggest focusing attention on the logistical parts of the supply chain and the intersection of actors in space and time. Results from this type of exploration can be used to decipher how criminal actors involved in bushmeat trafficking overcome obstacles to physical flows (e.g., transformation, movement, storage of goods) and information flows (e.g., allow supply chain partners to coordinate and control flow of goods and materials up and down) in the supply chain.

Opportunity-based criminological inquires offer several related theories for understanding the bushmeat supply chain and the opportunity structures that enable this illicit activity. First, rational choice theory tells us that offenders weigh the costs against benefits of committing a crime and make a rational decision when choosing whether or not to proceed with criminal behavior (Cornish & Clarke, 1987). Deterrence theory (Beccaria, 1764/1963), a core principle of rational choice theory, is also relevant to the urban bushmeat trade. Deterrence theory postulates that individuals are dissuaded from committing a crime when the punishment is certain, adequately severe, and swift (Beccaria, 1764/1963). In the case of urban bushmeat trafficking, it is reasonable to assume that overall deterrence effects are weak, since bushmeat continues to be openly sold in markets. Interestingly, previous research in Pointe Noire, Congo-Brazzaville, found bushmeat was openly traded in urban markets, yet people would conceal bushmeat during transport or transit into the city (Boratto & Gore, 2017, 2018). It is possible that a deterrent effect exists on the periphery of urban areas and in response traffickers conceal bushmeat. This case study focuses on perceived certainty of being caught and severity of as it relates to urban bushmeat trafficking and omits celerity (i.e., swiftness of punishment), which can be associated with downstream criminal justice activities, such as prosecution and sentencing.

In addition to deterrence theories, normative theories of compliance have been found to be relevant to issues related to common pool or natural resources such as fisheries and wildlife (e.g., Hauck, 2008; Kahler & Gore, 2012). Normative theories of compliance investigate the moral, legitimacy-based, and sociocultural influences on offender decision-making (Hauck, 2008). These types of normative or sociocultural regulations have been found to influence compliance related to wildlife laws. A case study among conservancy (i.e., co-managed wildlife areas) residents in Namibia revealed they believed there was no difference between deterrence and normative models in compelling compliance with wildlife regulations (Kahler & Gore, 2012). Indeed, participants rated the importance of rules being enforced fairly as equally important as the fear that one would get caught (Kahler & Gore, 2012). In contexts where deterrence effects are weak, such as is likely in Congo-Brazzaville, considering normative dimensions, such as the perceived fairness of enforcement, and designing interventions that leverage normative incentives for compliance are likely key.

The goal of this project was to establish a baseline characterization of the *illegal* urban bushmeat supply chain from Lékoumou to Pointe Noire. We set three broad objectives for this project. First, to use a conservation criminology perspective to characterize the regional illegal urban bushmeat supply chain and the route(s) that bushmeat travels from Lékoumou to Pointe Noire. Simply put, we sought to identify the key actors (*who*) and species (*what*) involved, *when* and with what frequency the activities take place, and *where* and *how* the activities take place. The second objective was to describe a suite of obstacles or opportunity-limiting factors within the illegal urban bushmeat trade. This included law enforcement–related obstacles (e.g., enforcement, sanctions) and non-law enforcement–related obstacles (e.g., infrastructure) with the potential to impact trafficking of urban bushmeat. Third, this research explored perceptions of deterrence (i.e., certainty and severity of punishment) and fairness among the hunters, vendors, and transporters operating in Lékoumou District. The sections that follow examine those issues using interview data from actors in a bushmeat supply chain in Congo-Brazzaville.

Case study site: Lékoumou, Republic of the Congo

The country's population of over 4.5 million people is young, with 42% under age 15 (World Health Organization [WHO], 2015). The majority (about 70%) resides in the capital, Brazzaville, the west coast city of Pointe Noire, or along railways that connect these major urban centers (CIA, 2018). Congo-Brazzaville is part of the second-largest contiguous tropical forest in the world, which is home to an estimated 400 mammal, 1,000 bird, and 10,000 plant species, including populations of vulnerable species such as western lowland gorillas, forest elephants, and chimpanzees (United States Fish and Wildlife Service [USFWS], 2014). However, the country's natural resources are under heavy pressure from extractive industries and activities such as oil, industrial fishing, charcoal production, and hunting. In 2003 it was estimated that bushmeat exploitation rates would cause an 80% drop in the Congo Basin's bushmeat protein supply by 2050, and that Congo-Brazzaville would start to see a 10% deficit in bushmeat protein by 2030 (Fa, Currie, & Meeuwig, 2003). Indeed, protein deficiency is already a concern according to data from 2012, and protein-energy malnutrition was responsible for 3% of annual mortality or approximately 1,400 people (WHO, 2015).

Scientific research on bushmeat regulations and use in Congo-Brazzaville

High urbanization levels and limited economic alternatives in rural areas are ripe conditions for lucrative commercial trade in bushmeat. Indeed, urban consumers in Congo-Brazzaville often consume bushmeat as an indicator of social status and due to culturally engrained preferences (USFWS, 2014). The literature has demonstrated that the consumption and trade of bushmeat is and has been common in Congo-Brazzaville (e.g., Mbete et al., 2011; van Vliet et al., 2015). Diverse laws in Congo-Brazzaville regulate legal hunting, and use of bushmeat for subsistence at the village level, such as seasonal restrictions and protected species. Species are regulated by being listed under one of three annexes: (1) fully protected species (Annex I), (2) partially protected species to be hunted with big game license (Annex II-A) or a small game license (Annex II-B), and (3) species without special status (Annex III) (Djombo, 2011). However, although species without protective status can be legally hunted within the context of subsistence-based traditional hunting, any trade, transportation, or trafficking of animals hunted under this annex is strictly prohibited (Djombo, 2011). While it is illegal to sell bushmeat in urban areas, it remains widely available in urban markets in contravention of these laws. For example, in Brazzaville, the country's capital, an urban survey found 88.3% (n = 927) of households consumed bushmeat (Mbete et al., 2011).

Scientific inquiry exploring compliance with bushmeat-related laws primarily focuses on Western and Central African nations (Taylor et al., 2015), and there is little specific information about Congo-Brazzaville. Our study was part of a larger collaborative project designed to understand both the bushmeat supply networks and end consumers to Congo-Brazzaville's economic capital, Pointe Noire (see Boratto & Gore, 2017, 2018). Research from the larger project found that bushmeat was trafficked from 15 districts in four departments (i.e., provinces) across Congo-Brazzaville into Pointe Noire, a city of over one million people. One surprising finding was that bushmeat was coming from Lékoumou, a district nearly equidistant (about 400 km) between the capital Brazzaville and Pointe Noire, and a region where a new national park has been proposed. Lékoumou was selected as a study site because vendors, restaurateurs, and police have previously identified it as a source region for bushmeat into Pointe Noire (Boratto & Gore, 2017). Observations also revealed bushmeat from Sibiti and Zanaga, two large towns in Lékoumou, traded through two ground transportation hubs in Pointe Noire. Additionally, in their research on urban bushmeat consumption in Brazzaville, Mbete et al. (2011) surveyed 27 households where the head of household was native to Lékoumou and 100% of these households reported consuming bushmeat. This chapter presents findings from research efforts in Lékoumou in June and July of 2017 (Figure 5.1).

Research approach[2]

This research used a case study approach with a multiple-method design to achieve its objectives (Yin, 2009). The bushmeat supply chain is commonly divided into discrete stages often depicted by the types of actors involved, the physical location of supply chain activities, and the logistical mechanisms that allow for transfer between these stages. Many supply chain stages remain covert and other stages occur in remote areas, posing barriers to detection. The Department of Lékoumou was the primary research site including the urban centers and 12 known hunting villages. The names and locations of these villages have been excluded to preserve anonymity.

Data collection

Interviews were conducted with multiple bushmeat trade actors (hunters, market vendors, transporters) but intentionally did not focus on bushmeat purchasers. Observations were conducted at key ground transportation hubs and markets to further gather information about the supply chain. A local research assistant with experience and education in local biodiversity conservation and expertise on the hunting community and bushmeat trade was trained according to responsible conduct and collected all data used herein. Participation in our research was voluntary, all respondents were over the age of 18, were surveyed in a language they understood, and completed a consent procedure.

Face-to-face hunter surveys were designed to produce a general estimate of when and with what frequency hunting occurred, how they hunted bushmeat (e.g., tools used, transportation methods), what species were hunted and how much was sold to the urban market, and destination markets for their bushmeat. Further questions queried knowledge of open and closed hunting seasons, perceptions of enforcement sanctions and employment status. Surveys were administered to hunters from villages in the Department of Lékoumou, June 13–25, 2017, and participants were asked to consider the dates between January 1 and June 1, 2017, for their responses. The 12 villages for this study were previously identified as potential source regions for bushmeat by multiple sources (e.g., research team, vendors) (Boratto & Gore, 2017). Although the purposive sampling frame created a non-random sample, thus limiting generalizability, it enhanced construct validity by allowing study efforts to be informed by key informants from villages known to participate in the bushmeat trade. Other considerations from our non-random sample include recruitment bias as hunters were asked to self-identify. In respect of customary protocol, the research assistant consulted the chief of each village to discuss the study prior to any survey participant recruitment and data collection.

Opportunistic sampling (Bernard, 2006) was used along the route between Bambama and Pointe Noire to solicit the participation of transporters (e.g., drivers or conductors along the route). We conducted market surveys to learn more about where vendors bought and sold bushmeat and how it moved through the supply chain. Surveys were conducted orally in person and asked vendors about the species they sold, the frequency with which they sold bushmeat, the types of orders they received and other information about the bushmeat trade and the obstacles they faced.

Surveys were also conducted to determine the individual attributes of markets and transportation hubs where vendors conduct their business. This included the presence of cold storage, access to electricity, the fees and taxes associated with vending, and the presence of parking for unloading goods. All values were recorded during a single visit to each location; results cannot be generalized as the number of tables selling bushmeat is known to vary throughout the time of day and day of the week.

Results

Objective 1: characterization of the supply chain

Who are the actors in the Lékoumou bushmeat chain?

We had a final usable hunter sample of 27 (Table 5.1). Hunters indicated that they sold bushmeat to an average of 14 (min 0, max 120) different people during May 1–31, 2017, meaning there was a wide range of volume between different hunters. A majority of hunters (n = 15, 56%) received

Table 5.1 Demographics of study participants participating in hunter, transporter, and vendor surveys, June 13–25, 2017

Characteristic	*Study participants*		
	Hunters	*Vendors*	*Transporters*
Questionnaires	27[a]	7	1
Observations	0	8	0
Mean age (min, max)	43 (31, 55)[b]	45 (35, 55)	37
Gender	Female = 0 Male = 27	Female = 3 Male = 7	Male (n = 1)
Primary employment	Agriculture (24) Fishing (1) Other (2)	Sell bushmeat (3) Other (4)	Driving (n = 1)
Mean number of children (min, max)[c]	4 (0, 15)	6 (1, 9)	

a The original sample contained 31 hunter surveys, however three hunters surveyed from the Département of Niari and a fourth hunter who no longer hunts were dropped from this analysis, for a final n = 27.
b Three respondents did not answer this question.
c Number of children was quantified as the number of children that respondents pay to feed on a regular basis (this is to include extended family that may be living with the individual, such as grandchildren, nieces or nephews, or other children who may be in their care).

specific bushmeat orders; the majority of orders were placed by people in the hunter's own village (n = 14, 93%) and one (7%) from family members residing in the city.

Multiple bushmeat transporters were solicited to participate in our research, however only one agreed. This was not overly surprising since multiple field assistants attempted, without success, to recruit transporters along other routes into Pointe Noire in 2016. The transporter was male, between 30 and 40 years of age, grew up in Lékoumou, and reported driving as his primary form of employment.

All but one of the seven vendors had regular suppliers from whom they purchased bushmeat and they reported purchasing from between three and five different suppliers during the period between January 1 and June 1, 2017. Four vendors (57%) indicated that they received special orders from family, in the village and city, and restaurants. These orders ranged in size from one to three animals. Most of the vendors indicated that there has been no change in the number of bushmeat buyers since 2009; however, two thought there were more buyers now.

What species are traded?

Multiple species were identified as being part of the illegal urban bushmeat supply chain (Table 5.2). Hunters and vendors also received special orders for six taxon groups, five of which they had in common (Table 5.2).

Table 5.2 Bushmeat observed at transportation hubs in Pointe Noire originating from Sibiti and Zanaga and wildlife hunted, sold by and for which hunters and vendors received special orders

Reported common name	*Scientific classification*	*P.N. hub*	*Hunters*		*Vendor*	
			Sold	*Order*	*Sold*	*Order*
African civet	*Civettictis civetta*	✓	✓	✓	✓	✓
Antelope	Bovidae	✓	✓	✓	✓	✓
Birds[a]	Aves		✓			
Bush pig	*Potamochoerus spp.*		✓		✓	✓
Crocodiles	Crocodylidae				✓	
Forest buffalo	*Syncerus caffur nanus*		✓		✓	
Monkeys[b]	Certopithecidae; Colobidae	✓	✓	✓	✓	✓
Pangolins	*Manis spp.*		✓	✓	✓	
Porcupine	Hystricidae	✓	✓	✓	✓	✓
Rodent (cane rat)[c]	*Thryonomys swinderianus*		✓	✓	✓	✓

a Consists of multiple scientific families reported at order or superorder level.
b Multiple families of monkeys occur in Congo; species belonging to Cercopitheridae and Colobidae are common and protected.
c Multiple species may be present; at least one participant mentioned cane rat.

The list of species or taxa found in Pointe Noire's transportation hub and those sold by hunters and vendors ranged from fully protected under Congolese laws (Annex I species) to those with legal hunting for subsistence use only (Table 5.3). Additionally, the potential size range of species in the taxons observed at transportation hubs or reported in surveys varied widely from cane rats to forest buffalos (Table 5.3).

When are bushmeat trade activities (e.g., hunting, transporting, trade) taking place?

Twenty-six percent of hunters indicated hunting year-round; the rest (74%) did not. There is less hunting via firearms in the dry season as animals can hear hunters approaching due to dry leaves on the forest floor (M. Wieland, personal communication). Seven hunters (33%) indicated that they sold bushmeat every day, 56% (n = 20) sold at least once per week, and 11% sold bushmeat at least once per month. This is most likely due to the fact that hunters often go deep into the forest to hunt for days at a time, which precludes selling bushmeat everyday (Wieland, 2008). All but one of the seven vendors in the study sold bushmeat every day, and the remaining vendor sold bushmeat at least once per week. The transportation driver reported that his cargo included domestic animals, people, food and other products and averaged 12 round-trip journeys

Table 5.3 Taxa of species observed or reported during surveys in Lékoumou according to their respective annex listing under Congolese law (deterrence) and relative measure of the financial reward (kilograms of bushmeat to sell). Representative species in each of the protected annex listings were chosen based on their presence in Congo and literature.

Common name provided	*Species*	*Weight estimates*[a]
Annex I species: Fully protected		
Crocodile (Slender snouted)	*Mecistops cataphractus*	Up to 667 kg[b]
Bush pig (Giant forest hog)	*Hylochoerus meinertzhageni*	130–275 kg[c]
Antelope (Southern reedbuck)	*Redunca arundinum*	50–95 kg
Monkeys (*Colobus* spp.)	*Colobus spp.*	*C. guereza* (7.8–13.5 kg)
Pangolin (Giant ground)	*Smutsia gigantea*	Up to 33 kg[d]
Pangolin (White-bellied tree)	*Phataginus tricuspis*	1.8 kg
Bird (Palm-nut vulture)	*Gyphohierax angolensis*	1.2–1.8 kg
Annex IIA: Species hunted with big game license		
Crocodile (Dwarf)	*Osteolaemus tetraspis*	Up to 317 kg[b]
Forest buffalo	*Syncerus caffer nanus*	Up to 300 kg[c]
Bush pig (Red river hog)	*Potamochoerus porcus*	50–120 kg
Antelope (Bushbuck)	*Tragelaphus scriptus*	25–80 kg[c]
Monkeys (Collared mangabey)	*Cercocebus torquatus*	5–12.5 kg
Bird (Helmeted guineafowl)	*Numida meleagris*	1.3 kg
Annex IIB: Species hunted with small game license		
African civet	*Civettictis civetta*	9.5–20 kg
Antelope (Blue duiker)	*Cephalophus monticola*	3.5–9 kg
Monkeys (Moustached guenon)	*Cercopithecus cephus*	2.9–4.3 kg
Porcupine (African brush-tailed)	*Atherurus africanus*	Up to 2 kg of meat
Rodent (Greater cane rat)	*Thryonomys swinderianus*	Up to 7 kg[c]
Bird (Common snipe)	*Gallinago gallinago*	0.072–0.181 kg

a Weight estimates unless otherwise noted found on ARKive (www.arkive.org/).
b Gross weight estimate calculated by using a simple ratio based on reported length (meters) and weight (kg) of Nile crocodile and provided maximum length as no weight estimates available.
c Weight estimate from *Estes (1991). The Behavior Guide to African Mammals* (University of California Press: Berkeley and Los Angeles).
d Weight found on African Wildlife Foundation website (www.awf.org/wildlife-conservation/pangolin).
e Weight estimate found in *Encyclopaedia Britannica* (www.britannica.com/animal/cane-rat).
f Information found on International Union for the Conservation of Nature (IUCN)'s Red List species account: www.iucnredlist.org/details/2353/0.

per month (between January 1 and June 1, 2017). He estimated that bushmeat was transported on fewer than half of those trips.

Where are bushmeat trade activities taking place?

Delineating the exact trade routes with a high degree of certainty can be challenging. Baseline information suggests there are discrete source regions for bushmeat hunting in Lékoumou as well as bushmeat trade transportation hubs and markets in Dolisie, Sibiti and Zanaga, along with frequently used transportation routes in and out of these urban centers (Figure 5.2). N'Kayi was referred to as a crossroads for the trade in bushmeat, where buyers would come from other regions including the probable source of overland bushmeat from Lékoumou to Brazzaville. Bushmeat also moved along the route from Bambama to Gabon (international), Komono, or Zanaga. The transporter identified his road route as Pointe Noire, Sibiti, Komono, Ngonaka, Bambama, Zanaga, and N'kayi and reported delivering bushmeat to markets and restaurants in Sibiti.

All 27 hunters sold bushmeat to local villages within 5 km of where they hunted. Additionally, five hunters (19%) reported selling to bushmeat buyers: four (15%) to anyone (e.g., individuals along the road), three sold to local markets within a 5 km proximity of where they hunted; and one each to a restaurant and transporter, respectively. Six hunters did not report an end destination for the bushmeat they sold, and the remaining 21 hunters reported at least one market destination, the most common of which was Sibiti. Brazzaville, the country of Gabon, and Pointe Noire were each reported by one hunter as the

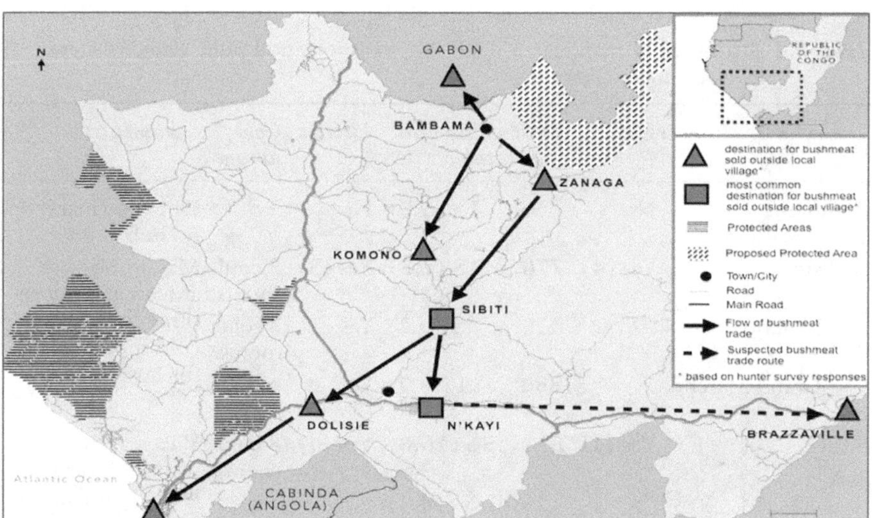

Figure 5.2 Bushmeat trade routes

end destination for their bushmeat. The majority (60%) of hunters reported selling the bulk of their bushmeat outside the village with sales predominately to Sibiti (26%) and N'kayi (15%). One hunter said that the bushmeat went to N'kayi because it is a crossroads with buyers from everywhere. The remaining 40% of hunters indicated that the majority of their bushmeat was sold in the local village.

Attribute surveys were conducted via observation to determine the characteristics of markets (n = 8) and transportation hubs (n = 9). Observations were important to help describe the situational factors that facilitate bushmeat trafficking. This included the presence of cold storage, access to electricity, the fees and taxes associated with vending, and the presence of dedicated parking for unloading goods (Table 5.4). Dolisie (outside of Lékoumou District) and Sibiti were the major cities and transportation hubs for bushmeat. There were four main transportation hubs in Dolisie including the *Gare Routiere Centrale* (the biggest entry point into Dolisie), and routes from these hubs included major population centers including Brazzaville and Pointe Noire (Figure 5.2). Goods were unloaded in these hubs because they are close to markets and villages or they are main points for purchasing goods. Three of these stops had electricity, each with at least one cold storage room, and three hubs had refrigeration dedicated solely to bushmeat (Table 5.4).

Four locations in Sibiti were identified as bushmeat transportation hubs, with routes from these transportation hubs reaching at least eight major cities or towns both inside Lékoumou District (e.g., Sibiti, Zanaga) and outside (e.g., Brazzaville, Pointe Noire) (Table 5.4). Villages close to Sibiti had access

Table 5.4 Attributes of markets (n = 8) and transportation hubs (n = 9) surveyed in Lékoumou District

Towns/cities	*Hub*	*Total tables*	*Bushmeat tables (%)*	*Electric*	*Cold storage*	*Comments*
Bambama	**No**	**6**	**1 (16.7)**	**No**	**No**	Only one market; no hub
Dolisie	**Yes (4)**	**770**	**18 (2.3)**	**Yes (3)**	**3 cold rooms**	Major hub with at least 17 routes; three hubs had cold rooms solely for bushmeat
Mboukou		420	1 (0.2)	Yes	3 cold rooms	
Grand Marché		350	17(4.9)	Yes	4 cold rooms	
Sibiti	**Yes (4)**	**333**	**56 (16.8)**	**Yes (4)**	**3 cold rooms**	Villages have access to motorcycles; at least eight routes from hubs
Moussanda		18	8 (44.4)	No	No	
Marché Central		315	48 (15.2)	No	No	
Zanaga	**Yes (1)**	**40**	**8 (20.0)**	**No**	**No**	Central hub also had small market

to motorcycles, which allowed for easy trade with the city and the delivery of fresh bushmeat. Two markets in Sibiti were sampled and one was a particularly prominent market for the trade in bushmeat with 44% ($n = 8$) of the total tables selling bushmeat (Table 5.4). Neither market had electricity or refrigeration. The central transportation hub in Zanaga also served as a small market with 20% ($n = 8$) of the 40 tables observed to sell bushmeat and routes to markets in Bambama, Brazzaville, Ogoue (village), and Pointe Noire (Table 5.4).

How does the bushmeat trade operate?

Our description of how the illegal urban bushmeat trade operates focused on the supply chain aspects of the movement, storage, flow to market, management of inventory and logistics of flow of bushmeat. All but one hunter used guns, with 69% also using snares or nets; one used nets exclusively. The majority of hunters ($n = 18$, 66.7%) reported they occasionally smoked their bushmeat prior to selling in an effort to manage their inventory; another six (22.2%) reported never smoking their bushmeat; and three (11.1%) reported always smoking their bushmeat prior to trade. With regard to the physical flow of bushmeat into markets, some hunters sold their bushmeat to middlemen, such as local bushmeat buyers ($n = 5$), transporter ($n = 1$), and unspecified others ($n = 4$), to avoid the cost of transportation and the risk of having their inventory confiscated by law enforcement authorities.

All the vendors stated that they had purchased their bushmeat inventory directly from a village ($n = 7$, 100%); two (29%) also had it delivered by a supplier; and one (14%) purchased at the market. An additional vendor stated that they purchased directly from a friend although whether this friend was a hunter from the village, a supplier, or another market vendor remained unclear. Bushmeat was brought into the city by taxi, motorcycle, or 4x4 from a number of different regions including the northern region of Bambama, which is just over 30 km by road to the border crossing into Gabon, and villages around Sibiti and Zanaga. The vendors sold bushmeat in the markets, out of their homes, and out of local restaurants. When asked what they did with bushmeat that did not sell, they all stated that it always sells and some of the vendors also sold other food items. All of the vendors reported selling bushmeat to restaurants and households, while some sold to event planners and other vendors; however, their most prominent clients during the study period were local households.

Objective 2: description of obstacles

Our second objective was to delineate a set of obstacles faced by those involved in the bushmeat supply chain. Earlier research suggested that many obstacles limit the flow of bushmeat into the market, and that these obstacles can be thought of in terms related to situational or enforcement characteristics of the system (Boratto & Gore, 2018). Situational obstacles to trade could include an inability to keep meat fresh, unreliable electricity, lack of reliable transportation, lack of consistent customers, and vendor or parking fees at markets and transportation hubs. Enforcement obstacles included fines, bushmeat confiscations, and road checkpoints. Additionally, we asked vendors if they were concerned about bushmeat resource depletion as a future obstacle to the trade. Lastly, we asked hunters and vendors questions to assess their knowledge about a regulated legal hunting season. This helped us distinguish between those that knowingly illegally harvest bushmeat and for those which the transgression may be incidental.

Situational obstacles

Hunters and vendors discussed situational obstacles to the physical flow of bushmeat inventory from procurement of goods to movement of goods to market and logistics of flow. For example, the majority of hunters (n = 16, 62%) responded that there were some species that were too dangerous to hunt. Hunters also noted that they avoided some species because they are difficult to locate, undesirable, difficult to sell, or that the sale price was not worth the hunting effort. Hunters were asked to outline obstacles they faced when trying to sell bushmeat in the city. Some stated that they had problems getting transportation or that meat would rot before it could be sold. Many hunters (48%) stated that finding buyers for bushmeat was an obstacle, which contrasted with the vendors stating that they always sold their bushmeat stock. Several of these hunters stated they sold bushmeat in the village to avoid the cost of transporting and selling small quantities of bushmeat in the city themselves. However, the majority (63%) reported using motorized vehicles, including 4x4s (n = 1), cars (n = 8), and motorcycles (n = 8) to transport bushmeat. One hunter noted that the distance between market in Bambama and the big cities, as well as the state of the road, did not allow for large-scale bushmeat trade. Therefore, bushmeat from this region was traded at the border with Gabon, which is approximately 35 km away.

Bushmeat vendors noted that they faced numerous situational obstacles, including a lack of suppliers, and bushmeat decomposing (N = 2). To avoid the latter, five of the seven vendors used refrigeration. Most of the vendors said that they would store bushmeat for up to four days, which may have been facilitated by the fact that 78% (n = 21) of hunters said that they sometimes to always smoked bushmeat. Two vendors also stated that limited funds by potential purchasers was an obstacle. When asked if these difficulties have become more or less numerous in the last seven years (since 2009), two said that the number of obstacles had increased, three thought they were about the same, and one stated that there were fewer obstacles.

Enforcement obstacles

The hunters, transporter, and vendors discussed enforcement obstacles to the bushmeat trade, which they felt were less worrisome than the situational obstacles for hunters and vendors. For example, in one village close to Sibiti, a hunter stated that it is easy to move bushmeat by motorcycle and there are no obstacles to this logistical step. While only one hunter mentioned enforcement (by agents from the Ministry of Water and Forestry) as an obstacle to the sale of bushmeat, many hunters stated that selling bushmeat in the village was a strategy to avoid the possibility of having their bushmeat confiscated by authorities. Additionally, the prompt delivery of bushmeat to wholesalers, middlemen, and vendors can reduce confiscation risk. Vendors also mentioned the risk of confiscation of bushmeat inventory by enforcement. Further, when asked if there were species that the hunter chose not to hunt, 48% responded that they did not hunt some species because they were protected.[3] Lastly, in addition to avoiding the risk of confiscation, some hunters stated that they sold bushmeat only in the village to avoid having to pay extra fees or fines to transport their goods.

Forecasting the future of the bushmeat market in Congo-Brazzaville

Vendors were asked about the potential obstacle of facing bushmeat resource depletion when there was no more bushmeat left to sell. They unanimously responded that there is no reason to believe that there would ever be a shortage of bushmeat. They discussed how it was impossible for people to kill all of the animals in the forest. One vendor commented there were still a lot of animals left to hunt due to the rural exodus and migration into cities, and that some places have been fallow for more than ten years. Finally, vendors were asked if they would like their children to grow up and be bushmeat vendors. All of the vendors said no.

Objective 3: perceptions of deterrence and fairness

Awareness of hunting regulations

When asked if there was an open hunting season, and if so, on what dates it occurred, 44.5% of the hunters knew the exact dates of the open and closed seasons; others were uncertain about the dates (44.5%) or did not know them at all (11%). All of the seven vendors knew of the open and closed hunting season, and six were able to correctly give the dates. The transporter, however, expressed that perhaps it was not illegal to trade bushmeat.

Perceptions of enforcement

We asked hunters questions about perceptions of deterrence to gauge the impact of enforcement on trafficking. The transporter and vendor provided thoughts about their perceptions concerning informational flows as well through questions related to obstacles to physical flows of inventory. Since bushmeat brought into Pointe Noire was often hidden or smuggled, it would seem that those transporting bushmeat actively tried to avoid detection during transportation (Boratto & Gore, 2018). Survey questions focused on certainty, the perceived likelihood that an individual will be caught trading bushmeat, the severity of the sanctions if caught, and perceptions of the fairness of those sanctions. Severity questions examined the perceived impact of punishment on the offender. Some hunters refused to respond to these questions; however, we were able to obtain a 70% and 80% response rate, respectively, on questions about certainty and severity and the fairness of such sanctions.

The responses of hunters varied when asked "what is the likelihood that a person selling bushmeat outside of the villages would be caught by the authorities?" When asked about the perceived likelihood of being caught, of the 19 respondents who answered, 47% described it as *very likely* that they would be caught, while 42% perceived it as *somewhat likely*, and 11% deemed it *very unlikely* (Table 5.5). One hunter stated it was *very unlikely* to be caught because the law does not prevent the local sale of bushmeat and therefore he did not see any reason why someone would be caught for something they are allowed to do. Those who perceived the likelihood of being caught with bushmeat as either *somewhat* or *very likely* described possible sanctions as confiscation, fines, or having to pay bribes. Of the 22 respondents who answered the question about the perceived seriousness of sanctions, the majority (68%) believed sanctions were *very serious*,

Table 5.5 Perception of hunters (n = 27) related to the likelihood that a person selling bushmeat outside their village gets caught by authorities, the severity of sanctions if caught, and whether sanctions are fair or unfair

Concept	*Response*	*Total % (n)*	*% who answered (n)*
Likelihood of being caught	Very unlikely	7 (2)	11 (2)
	Somewhat unlikely	0 (0)	0 (0)
	Somewhat likely	30 (8)	42 (8)
	Very likely	33 (9)	47 (9)
	No answer	30 (8)	
	Total	100 (27)	100 (19)
Severity of sanctions[a]	No sanction	4 (1)	5 (1)
	Not serious	0 (0)	0 (0)
	Somewhat serious	22 (6)	27 (6)
	Very serious	56 (15)	68 (15)
	No answer	18 (5)	
	Total	100 (27)	100 (22)
Fairness	Fair	37 (10)	45 (10)
	Unfair	45 (12)	55 (12)
	No answer	18 (5)	
	Total	100 (27)	100 (22)

a Perception of the severity of sanctions if caught measured on a 4-point scale: no sanctions, not serious, somewhat serious, and very serious (refused to answer coded as no answer).

while an additional 27% thought they were somewhat serious (Table 5.5). One hunter stated that if someone is caught with elephant meat they will be sent to prison, which might indicate a difference in perceptions of fines depending upon the species with which an individual is caught. Others described being able to negotiate with those who had seized the bushmeat and merely pay a "tax." Another hunter remarked that the outcome depends on the law enforcement officer's character. Lastly, the transporter saw sanctions as somewhat likely to occur, possibly to include a fine, but did not think that these sanctions would have a serious impact on anyone's decision to transport bushmeat.

Hunters were asked if they thought the sanctions were fair or unfair. A total of 22 (82%) respondents answered the sanction fairness question. Among those who answered, 45% stated that sanctions were fair and 55% saw them as unfair (Table 5.5). Those who saw sanctions as fair felt that the law is the law, as one said: "it's just because no one is above the law [translated, *sic.*]." Some thought that the law was fair, but that sanctions themselves were unfair due to the fact that there is little employment in Republic of the Congo and this lack of employment made sanctions an unjust punishment. For example, the transporter saw sanctions, such as fines, as unfair because trading bushmeat is an income generating activity that is required for improving one's livelihood. Lastly, some hunters expressed that sanctions were not levied fairly, and that those who are considered lower class received unequal punishment.

Implications

The efficacy of traditional enforcement strategies to address the illegal bushmeat trade are often undermined in the conservation context by issues of corruption, weak penal systems (Lindsey et al., 2011), and lack of resources for adequate law enforcement efforts (Wellsmith, 2010). Many of these conditions are likely hampering efforts to reduce illegal bushmeat trafficking and trade in Congo-Brazzaville. For example, Congo-Brazzaville ranks 161 out of 180 countries (1 = least corrupt) on Transparency International's corruption perception index (Transparency International, 2018). Additionally, despite nearly half of surveyed hunters reporting a high likelihood of being caught and one hunter reporting jail time for possession of elephant meat, practitioners on the ground report that a jail sentence is unlikely even for ivory poachers in Lékoumou. However, in this context it is important to remember that punitive deterrence is not limited to prosecution, jail time, and fines but rather being caught, having bushmeat confiscated, or even needing to pay a bribe are the most common deterrence mechanisms associated with local law enforcement.

Situational crime prevention

There is a clear opportunity for integrating diverse and proactive criminological theories to address bushmeat poaching and trafficking in Congo-Brazzaville. We used one such criminological approach, grounded in theories of deterrence and opportunity, to describe the favorable circumstances and obstacles associated with the harvest and trade of bushmeat in a remote district of Congo-Brazzaville. By enhancing clarity about the functional, physical, and information flows of the actors involved in the supply chain and the characteristics of bushmeat system, we can apply and adapt principles from situational crime prevention (SCP). This allows us to consider how to make conditions less desirable for bushmeat trafficking, prevent the activity from occurring in the first place, and expand the suite of tactical responses to include those that reach beyond enforcement. Overreliance on reactive strategies to dissuade environmental crimes (such as increasing randomized enforcement efforts) stands in opposition to evidence from conventional criminological research that these approaches are largely ineffective in terms of achieving significant crime reductions (Weisburd & Eck, 2004; Wellsmith, 2010). After decades of research in urban criminology there remains meager evidence that more police equals less crime. However, current empirical investigations support that crime reductions may be achieved by the implementation of select types of policing (Weisburd, Telep, & Lawton, 2014).

The traditional SCP framework delineates 25 techniques for crime prevention, some of which propose changing the structural environment to increase risks, reduce rewards and provocations, and remove excuses (Clarke, 2008; Lemieux, 2014). The approach is appealing for those that seek to reduce and understand natural resource–based crimes (e.g., Pires & Clarke, 2011; Wellsmith, 2010) because of the immediacy of crime reduction and the proactive, rather than reactive, nature of the techniques used are necessary when criminal activity threatens to irreparably damage the environment and/or cause species extinctions (Wellsmith, 2010). Recent research has investigated the usefulness of SCP in poaching-related crimes (e.g., Kahler, 2018; Kurland, Pires, McFann, and Moreto, 2017) and the illegal trade of endangered species (Wellsmith, 2010). By manipulating characteristics of the built environment, such as parking fees at transportation hubs, the opportunity structure of the bushmeat trade may be shifted to prevent crime from occurring in the first place. Some of these issues are examined below.

Increase effort

Mapping the bushmeat supply chain helps identify SCP interventions that target the physical space used by poachers and traffickers that might reduce these crimes. For example, backfilling logging roads within the department would aid in deflecting poachers away from potential wildlife habitat and increase the effort and expenditures needed to successfully hunt. Further, increasing the use of mobile checkpoints, listed as an obstacle for transportation of bushmeat, and/or sniffer dogs along prominent travel routes out of priority wildlife areas can serve to screen exits. For example, Sibiti was reported to be the most common end destination for bushmeat in the region, in addition to being a trafficking route for destinations such as Pointe Noire and N'Kayi. Setting up 24-hour checkpoints along transportation routes exiting prime habitat for protected species that lead to Sibiti would increase the effort needed by poachers and traffickers to get their illegal bushmeat to markets there. Along the same vein, similar mobile checkpoints could be erected to control access to major markets and hubs such as N'Kayi and Zanaga. These strategies are not new to conservation, although they are hampered by financial and human resources. However, empirical investigation of the bushmeat supply chain allows those on the ground to better prioritize and direct resources to key markets and hubs.

Increase risks

Several techniques can be employed to increase the risk of detection. Reaching out to other agencies, organizations, or civil groups with a stake in commerce, transportation, or wildlife management can extend the number of formal guardians in Lékoumou that intervene along the bushmeat supply chain. For example, representatives and supporting organizations that work with select governmental ministries, such as Transport and Civil Aviation, and Health and Population, could provide additional reporting and monitoring if effectively engaged and incentivized as to how illegal bushmeat trafficking impacts their sectors. Additionally, identifying potential place managers, such as the gatekeepers that control access to market stalls, parking facilities, and restaurant owners, who are willing to comply with wildlife laws and report noncompliance among peers can increase risk to actors along the bushmeat supply chain.

Reduce rewards

It is not feasible to conceal, remove, or translocate wildlife targets as a means to reduce the rewards of the bushmeat trade. However, the current practice of confiscating bushmeat and levying fines were dominant among enforcement-related obstacles reported by poachers and vendors. Conducting randomly timed and unannounced monitoring and enforcement at select cold storage rooms, hubs, and markets can disrupt markets and reduce the rewards of the illegal bushmeat trade. Lastly, unlike neighboring Democratic Republic of Congo, the current wildlife tenure system in Congo-Brazzaville does not engender a sense of proprietorship among communities. Strategies that extend proprietary rights to communities or user groups, such as the formulation of local own-use hunting cooperatives with well-marked boundaries and species harvested, may also reduce the rewards to offenders.

Reduce provocations

There are a number of techniques that can be leveraged to reduce provocations for bushmeat trade. For example, in Cameroon community members asserted that the prosecution of authorities involved in bushmeat trade would aid in avoiding disputes between communities and authorities (Kahler, Viollaz, &

Gore, 2018). Further, although normative approaches are not part of the traditional suite of SCP techniques, practitioners of this regulatory approach have acknowledged that the addition of normative tactics can have a meaningful effect on increasing compliance (Kurland et al., 2017). Indeed, in protected areas where enforcement is either inadequate or absent, normative factors such as trust and legitimacy in authorities were critical components to boost voluntary compliance (Stern, 2008).

Study respondents reported mixed perceptions about the fairness of the law and sanctions associated with the laws. There was a perception among some that sanctions were harsher on those belonging to a lower socioeconomic class. Hunters and vendors in the Congo-Brazzaville would not be alone in identifying that flat fine rates have a more negative effect on the lowest income offenders rather than higher-income offenders. In addition, techniques that increase transparency have the potential to bolster legitimacy and trust in authorities and increase clarity regarding the enforcement system, sanctions, and decision-making in relation to the bushmeat trade (e.g., Kahler & Gore, 2012). One example would be creating regular public meetings or public bulletin boards, which discuss recent enforcement activities, prosecutions, and judicial procedures. Additional research could explore perceptions of trust, procedural fairness, legitimacy, and the fairness of penalties associated with the bushmeat trade as improvements in how the communities perceive these normative factors may increase their compliance.

Remove excuses

There are opportunities to remove excuses associated with the bushmeat trade in the form of alerting public consciousness, providing cooperative extension (i.e., informal training and education directed at rural or vulnerable peoples), and leveraging incentives and alternative benefits. The Wildlife Conservation Society (WCS) is well versed in these strategies having worked to respond to Congo-Brazzaville's bushmeat trade for over a decade. Well-formulated risk communication campaigns, relevant extension, and the provision of alternative benefits focused on vendors and buyers in urban markets may provide a reasonable exit route for participation in the bushmeat trade, particularly when used in conjunction with existing, or if resources allow, increased enforcement efforts as described above. For example, despite the vendors' optimism about the future viability of this market, we saw evidence they may be receptive to cooperative extension, incentives, and alternative benefits programs to divert them away from this problematic and illegal trade: all of the vendors expressed that they did not want their children to follow in their footsteps and participate in the bushmeat trade. Providing trainings, incentives, and alternative benefits to youth that can be identified as high risk for participation in the trade of bushmeat, whether due to a parent's involvement or their own, may reduce participation in this illicit market over time without relying on overly militaristic approaches. Continued collaboration between organizations like WCS and those versed in conservation criminology would allow the continued refinement and addition of strategies to remove excuses while drawing on the unique expertise that both bring to the table.

Concluding thoughts for the future

This study has begun to map out bushmeat supply chains and its actors, and to explore with a small sub-set of these actors how enforcement is perceived as a deterrence measure. The preliminary work delineated in this chapter can benefit from a follow up study with larger samples of participants and observations. As such, results should not be generalized beyond study participants and are not representative of the broader population as a whole. The work presented in this chapter is part of a larger effort that will be continued over the next two years. Future work will include understanding the opportunities, obstacles, and perceptions of bushmeat consumers, and with vendors, may further explore the perceptions of zoonotic disease risks, gender roles along the supply chain, the influence of normative approaches such as perceptions of procedural fairness and trust, and methods to increase transparency. These factors may have significant implications for personal willingness to comply with laws governing bushmeat as well as intervene when witnessing illegal commercial bushmeat activities. Gaps in knowledge related to the opportunity structures at work include but are not limited to information from those who traffic directly into the city (e.g., do not pass through a transportation hub or markets), those who have political, or powerful business ties, and transporters who drive trucks and buses that transport other goods and commodities in to the city.

The "bushmeat crisis" is only likely to expand in scope and scale as some of the obstacles to bushmeat trade, such as poor road infrastructure and reliable access to electricity, are remedied and increasingly larger urban-commodity markets are linked more efficiently to vendors and rural suppliers (Bassett, 2005; Bowen-Jones et al., 2003). Research that answers questions relevant to conservation criminology and crime science, such as understanding the *who, what, when, where*, and *how* of the bushmeat trade, can provide valuable insight into solutions that may provide actionable evidence for resource deployment. Developing tactics that can help delay, disrupt, divert, or destroy the supply chain, inform behavior change strategies, and feed other law enforcement interventions are in demand in Congo-Brazzaville and beyond. Further, tactics that enhance and reinforce normative motivations for compliance and guardianship behaviors among the different actors along the bushmeat supply chain can be aided by insights into the perceptions around contemporary deterrence systems and wildlife hunting laws. One advantage of a criminological approach to understanding bushmeat is that it brings into the conversation a much richer mechanism to understand the fundamentals of human deviance, the opportunities and obstacles, and it provides a much larger suit of strategies to reduce the risks to local people and wildlife associated with the illegal commercial trade of bushmeat.

Notes

1 This research explored questions and implications related to traditional criminology (e.g., deterrence and normative theory) and crime science research (e.g., opportunity theories, situational crime prevention). For the purposes of this chapter we are not distinguishing between these variations, and hereinafter will refer to our approach as conservation criminology (see Kahler & Gore, 2017 for further discussion of distinctions).
2 Much of the information found in the research approach and results sections can be found in Boratto & Gore (2017).
3 There are several shortcomings associated with this research including explicitly discussing the hunters' use of various hunting tools and weapons. For example, nearly half responded they did not hunt certain species because they were protected. However, this assumes the hunters are using firearms rather than snares and traps, which are non-discriminant hunting methods that catch whatever species encounter them.

References

Bassett, T. J. (2005). Card-carrying hunters, rural poverty, and wildlife decline in northern Cote d' Ivoire. *The Geographic Journal*, *171*(1), 24–35.

Beccaria, C. (1764/1963). *On crimes and punishment* (*trans. H. Paolucci*). New York, NY: MacMillan Publishing Company.

Bennett, E. L., Beincowe, E., Brandon, K., Brown, D., Burn, R. W., Cowlishaw, G., . . . Wilkie, D. S. (2006). Hunting for consensus: Reconciling bushmeat harvest, conservation, and development policy in West and Central Africa. *Conservation Biology*, *21*(3), 884–887.

Bernard, H. R. (2006). *Research methods in anthropology: Qualitative and quantitative approaches.* Oxford, UK: AltaMira Press.

Boratto, R., & M. L. Gore. (2017). *Wild meat supply chain and conservation criminology: A case study from Lekoumou, Republic of Congo.* Report prepared for Wildlife Conservation Society. East Lansing, MI: Michigan State University.

Boratto, R., & M.L. Gore. (2018). *The KiBra bushmeat supply chain: A conservation criminology analysis of transport hubs, markets and restaurants.* Report prepared for Wildlife Conservation Society. East Lansing, MI: Michigan State University.

Bowen-Jones, E., Brown, D., & Robinson, E.J.Z. (2003). Economic commodity or environmental crisis? An interdisciplinary approach to analyzing the bushmeat trade in Central and West Africa. *Area*, *35*(4), 390–402.

Central Intelligence Agency. (2018). The World Factbook: Congo, Republic of The. Retrieved from www.cia.gov/library/publications/the-world-factobook/

Clarke, R. V. (2008). Situational crime prevention. In Wortley, R. & Mazerolle, L. (Eds.), *Environmental criminology and crime Analysis, chapter 10* (pp. 178–194). London and New York: Routledge.

Cornish, D. B., & Clarke, R. V. (1987). Understanding crime displacement: An application of rational choice theory. *Criminology*, *25*(4), 933–948.

Djombo, H. (2011). Partie Officielle: A-texte de portee generale: Ministere du Developpement durable, de l'Economie Forestiere et de l' Environnement. [Official Party: A-Generalized text: Ministry of Sustainable Development, Forest Economics and the Environment.]. *Journal official de la Republique du Congo*, 503–505.

Fa, J. E. (2007). Bushmeat markets-white elephants or red herrings? In Davies, G. & Brown, D. (Eds.), *Bushmeat and livelihoods: Wildlife management and poverty reduction* (pp. 47–60). Oxford, UK: Blackwell Publishing Inc.

Fa, J. E., Currie, D., & Meeuwig, J. (2003). Bushmeat and food security in the Congo Basin: Linkages between wildlife and people's future. *Environmental Conservation, 30*(1), 71–78.

Gore, M.L. (Ed). (2017). *Conservation criminology.* West Sussex, UK: John Wiley & Sons.

Hauck, M. (2008). Rethinking small-scale fisheries compliance. *Marine Policy, 32,* 635–642.

Hilborn, R., Arcese, P., Borner, M., Hando, J., Hopcraft, G., Loibooki M., . . . Sinclair, A.R.E. (2006). Effective enforcement in a conservation area. *Science, 314*(5803), 1266.

Huisman, W., & van Erp, J. (2013). Opportunities for environmental crime: A test of situational crime prevention theory. *British Journal of Criminology, 53,* 1178–1200.

Kahler, J. S. (2018). *The situational prevention of wildlife poaching in Bukit Barisan Selatan National Park, Sumatra Indonesia* (Doctoral dissertation). Retrieved from ProQuest Dissertations and Theses database. (UMI No.10815833).

Kahler, J. S., & Gore, M. L. (2012). Beyond the cooking pot and pocket book: Factors influencing noncompliance with wildlife poaching rules. *International Journal of Comparative and Applied Criminal Justice, 36*(2), 103–120.

Kahler, J. S., & Gore, M. L. (2017). Conservation crime science. In Gore, M. L. (Ed.), *Conservation criminology* (pp. 27–43). West Sussex, UK: John Wiley & Sons, Ltd.

Kahler, J, Viollaz, J., & Gore, M. (2018, June). "Beyond the urban crime jungle: Refining the situational crime prevention framework for conservation crime." Presented by J. Viollaz at the International Symposium on Environmental Criminology and Crime Analysis (ECCA). Elche, Spain.

Kurland, J., Pires, S. F., McFann, S., & Moreto, W. D. (2017). Wildlife crime: A conceptual integration, literature review, and methodological critique. *Crime Science, 6*(4), doi:10.1186/s40163-017-0066-0.

Lemieux, A. M. (2014). Introduction. In Lemieux, A. M. (Ed.), *Situational prevention of poaching* (pp. 1–17). New York, NY: Routledge.

Lindsey, P., Romañach, S., & Matema, S. (2011). Dynamics and underlying causes of illegal bushmeat trade in Zimbabwe. *Oryx, 45,* 84–95.

Linkie, M., Martyr, D. J., Harihar, A., Risdianto, D., Nugraha, R. T., Maryati, . . . Wong, W. M. (2015). Safeguarding Sumatran tigers: Evaluating effectiveness of law enforcement patrols and local informant networks. *Journal of Applied Ecology, 52,* 851–860.

Mbete, R. A., Banga-Mboko, H., Racey, P., Mfoukou-Ntsakala, A., Nganga, I., Vermeulen, C., . . . Leroy, P. (2011). Household bushmeat consumption in Brazzaville, the Republic of Congo. *Tropical Conservation Science, 4*(2), 187–202.

Nasi, R., Brown, D., Wilkie, D. Bennet, E. Tutin, C. van Tol, G., . . . Christophersen, T. (2008). *Conservation and use of wildlife-based resources: The bushmeat crisis.* Bogar, Indonesia & Montreal, Canada: Secretariat of the Convention on Biological Diversity and Center for International Forestry.

Pires, S. F., & Clarke, R. V. (2011). Sequential foraging, itinerant fences and parrot poaching in Bolivia. *British Journal of Criminology, 51,* 314–335.

Poulsen, J. R., Clark, C. J., & Palmer, T. M. (2013). Ecological erosion of an Afrotropical forest and potential consequences for tree recruitment and forest biomass. *Biological Conservation, 163,* 122–130.

Ripple, W. J., Abernethy, K., Betts, M. G., Chapron, G., Dirzo, R., Galetti, M., . . . Young, H. (2016). Bushmeat hunting and extinction risk to the world's mammals. *Royal Society Open Science, 3,*160498. Retrieved from http://dx.doi.org/10.1098/rsos.160498

Stern, M. J. (2008). Coercion, voluntary compliance and protest: The role of trust and legitimacy in combating local opposition to protected areas. *Environmental Conservation*, *35*(3), 200–210.

Supply Chain Resource Cooperative. (2017). What is supply chain management (SCM)? *North Carolina State University: Supply Chain Resource Cooperative.* Retrieved from https://scm.ncsu.edu/scm-articles/article/what-is-supply-chain-management-scm

Taylor, G., Scharlemann, J.P.W., Rowcliffe, M., Kümpel, N., Harfoot, M.B.J., Fa, J. E., . . . Coad, L. M. (2015). Synthesizing bushmeat research effort in West and Central Africa: A new regional database. *Biological Conservation*, *181*, 199–205.

Transparency International. (2018). Corruption perception index 2017: Republic of Congo. Retrieved from www.transparency.org/news/feature/corruption_perceptions_index_2017

United States Fish and Wildlife Service. (2014). Republic of Congo. International Affairs, Division of International Conservation. Retrieved from www.fws.gov/international/pdf/factsheet-congo.pdf

van Vliet, N., Moreno, J., Gómez, J., Zhou, W., Fa, J. E., Golden, C., . . . Nasi, R. (2017). Bushmeat and human health: Assessing the evidence in tropical and sub-tropical forests. *Ethnobiology and Conservation*, *6*(3), doi:10.15451/ec2017-04-6.3-1-45.

van Vliet, N., Nebesse, C., Gambalemoke, S., Akaibe, d., & Nasi, R. (2012). The bushmeat market in Kisangani, Democratic Republic of Congo: Implications for conservation and food security. *Oryx*, *46*(2), 196–203.

Vliet, N., Nebesse, C., & Nasi, R. (2015). Bushmeat consumption among rural and urban children from Province Orientale, Democratic Republic of Congo. *Oryx*, *41*(1), 165–174.

Wellsmith, M. (2010). The applicability of crime prevention to problems of environmental harm: A consideration of illicit trade in endangered species. In White, R. (Ed.), *Global Environmental Harm: Ecological Perspectives* (pp. 132–149). Portland, OR: Willan Publishing.

Weisburd, D., & Eck, J. E. (2004). What can police do to reduce crime, disorder, and fear? *The Annals of the American Academy of Political and Social Science*, *593*, 42–65.

Weisburd, D., Telep, C. W., & Lawton, B. A. (2014). Could innovations in policing have contributed to the New York City crime drop even in a period of declining police strength? The case of stop, question and frisk as a hot spot policing strategy. *Justice Quarterly*, *31*(1), 129–153.

Wieland, M. L. (2008). *Wildlife conservation in social, economic, and ecological contexts: Multiple stakeholders and extraordinary resource value in a Congolese National Park* (Doctoral Dissertation). Retrieved from https://conservancy.umn.edu/handle/11299/47857

Wilkie, D. S., Curran, B., Tshombe, R., & Morelli, G. A. (1998). Modeling the sustainability of subsistence farming and hunting in the Ituri Forest of Zaire. *Conservation Biology*, *12*(1), 137–147.

World Health Organization. (2015). Congo: WHO statistical profile. *Global Health Observatory.* Retrieved from http://who.int/gho/mortality_burden_disease/en/

Yin, R. K. (2009). *Case Study Research: Design and Methods.* Thousand Oaks, CA: Sage Publications, Inc.

6 Human-wildlife competition

Exploring human activities, environmental transformation, and mammalian species threat

Kwan-Lamar Blount-Hill and Mangai Natarajan

It is widely accepted that human activities are primary drivers of worldwide species loss, particularly among mammals. For example, the 2017 Convention on International Trade in Endangered Species of Wild Fauna and Flora (CITES) reports poaching as a cause for dramatic losses in elephant communities (UNODC, 2017). Conservation literature suggests that this threat, coupled with that of habitat loss, explains to a large degree species loss and extinction around the world (Bobo et al., 2017; Sukumar, 2006). In the case of habitat loss, among those factors cited as causes are agricultural practices, land conversion for industries or human dwelling, water diversion, pollution, and climate change. In short, the root of wildlife population decline – especially in mammal species – is two-pronged: loss as a direct result of human activity and that which occurs due to human-caused ecological changes.

That activities associated with human development are also associated with wildlife decline presents a conundrum of conflicting interests between humans and other species. This tension is expressed most acutely in the form of acts of aggression between humans and wildlife. A growing body of research has explored human-wildlife conflict (HWC) at a local level and has confirmed increased reporting of incidents of conflict (Anand & Radhakrishna, 2017). Human-wildlife conflict is defined as "any interaction between humans and wildlife that results in negative impacts on human social, economic or cultural life, on the conservation of wildlife populations, or on the environment" (World Wildlife Fund, 2005). This phenomenon can be explained by the principle of competitive exclusion (Pianka, 1974), otherwise known as Gause's law (Gause, 1934), which predicts that competition for the same resource will result in population reduction for at least one competing species.

As resources dwindle, human societies come into competition with other life forms, setting the stage for increasingly detrimental outcomes resulting in species loss. For example, in southern India, expanding urban spaces have pushed the boundaries of subsistence farmers and their small villages farther and farther into forest areas. This development forces farmers to encroach upon lands traditionally used by indigenous peoples for their inhabiting, hunting, and gathering. Moreover, nearly 12,000 elephants, the dominant mammals in this ecology, and a host of other animal species live in the forests of southern

India and must compete with farmers and forest-dwellers for life-sustaining resources (Project Elephant Division, 2017). In this case, development wins over farmers, farmers win over the forest hunter-gatherers, and forest folk win over wildlife, all resulting in drastic declines in the number of elephants. Ecological research identifies several catalytic factors for HWC worldwide, including human population growth; land use transformation; habitat loss, degradation and fragmentation; growing interest in ecotourism and increasing access to nature reserves; increasing livestock populations and competitive exclusion of wild herbivores; reduced abundance and distribution of wild prey; increasing wildlife population as a result of conservation programs; and climatic factors and stochastic events (Distefano, 2005).

One example of a natural resource which might serve as an ignition point for zero-sum competition between species is water. Water is a necessity for all living beings, yet one that is in surprisingly limited supply. Large portions of Earth's hydrosphere are in forms and locales inaccessible for human use, restricting (wo) man to a mere 3%–4% of the Earth's water resources (United States Geological Survey, 2016). According to the United Nations, nearly one-fifth of the world's human population lives with physical water scarcity (where available water supply is below 1,000 m^3 per person) and another quarter of the population faces economic scarcity (where infrastructural and other hurdles make the transport of water to areas of need impossible) (UNDESA, n.d.). By 2025, nearly two billion people may be living in areas of *absolute scarcity*, where water availability averages below 500 m^3 per person.

As with humans, other species must also compete for their share of this important, but scarce, resource. Water scarcity has adverse effects on the survival of wildlife populations. Stommel, Hofer, and East (2016) found that water scarcity displaced hippopotamuses significantly during drier seasons, leading to their concentration in very few locations. Population migrations such as these are a major source of conflict between human and animals, particularly in developing countries, where wildlife travel in search of water into human-occupied territories, such as in nearby villages or agrarian communities, causing damage to livestock and injuries to people. In retaliation, villagers kill the animals (Liu et al., 2011). An increasing human population means greater use of water for irrigation, more water pollution, and increased water diversion for hydropower or drainage for agricultural land. In parallel, rising affluence in some countries means a larger number of people living water-intensive lifestyles, including watering of gardens, cleaning cars, using washing machines and dishwashers, and so on. Rapidly developing economies also result in more industry and, in many cases, this comes without modern technology for water saving and pollution control. All these are compounded by the threat of climate change (Noyes et al., 2009).

In addition to water pollution and scarcity from drought, Elliott (2017) gives an account of a future with numerous environmental challenges, including loss of biodiversity and species, land degradation and deforestation, wildlife smuggling, ozone depletion, atmospheric pollution, and climate change. It is a future rife with factors catalyzing HWC and intensifying overall competition among species for natural resources. It is in the context of this threat that we apply the conflict/competition paradigm arising from HWC literature to a broader, globalized account of the survival of species (in this case, mammal species) in the face of human society.

The present study

In this study, we examine the relationships between measures of direct human activities, ecological/environmental conditions affected by those activities, and the number of species under existential threat across individual countries. In so doing, we offer a perspective viewing HWC as an acute expression of a grander, more diffuse competition between humans and animal species. Those activities associated with human societal development may be directly harmful to animal species, and thus set the stage for competition between human development interests and wildlife survival. Additionally, human activities may harm other species due to competition over finite resources. By studying the drivers of interspecies competition, that also fuel HWC, we hope to shed light on the global issue of HWC and the forces important to micro-level conflicts more traditionally studied by researchers of HWC.

A review of the literature suggests that species loss occurs as a result of (1) natural deaths; (2) extreme ecological conditions, including climate change; (3) ecosystem uses by humans (e.g., for agriculture, industrial development, urbanization) and as pollution sinks; (4) resource scarcity, including water stress and habitat loss; (5) and theriocide (the killing of animals), including poaching and killing animals in retaliation during HWC situations. While studies have been undertaken to examine each of the above factors explaining species loss, there is limited research attempting to integrate these factors into a single model.

We theorize two primary pathways through which human activities might cause a reduction in wild populations (see Figure 6.1). As eluded to, human

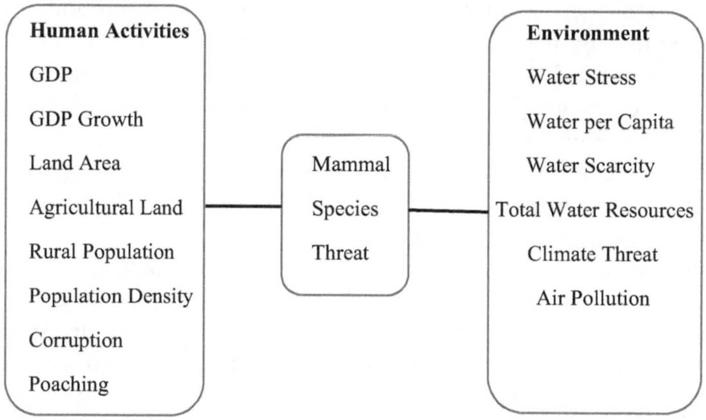

Figure 6.1 Mammal species threat: impact of human species and environment

activities might cause direct damage to other biological life forms. For instance, industries might introduce toxins into water systems that kill downstream fish populations. Alternatively, human activities might cause an alteration in the environment that negatively impacts wild populations. Industries might divert water from streams, changing the nature of water environments downstream. Effective mitigation depends on the nature of the harmful cause: direct harms are more easily identifiable, though they may require cessation or significant change in the nature of the activity in order to reduce species loss. Indirect harms are less readily identifiable but may be corrected, among other ways, by measures offsetting the harm done. Direct harms are also typically acute in their damage but also may be ceased more easily; indirect harms take longer to make an impact but set in motion cascades of events that may be difficult to halt once started.

Identifying significant and primary factors in species loss can assist not only in understanding its macro-level causes, but also in developing more comprehensive and appropriate mitigation measures. This will also assist in linking the determinants of species loss and those of HWC. HWC is, of course, itself a direct cause of species loss as aggression towards wildlife often results in the animal's death – an act referred to as theriocide (Bierne, 2014). Nevertheless, it is also driven by indirect causes of species loss, namely the reduction of available resources for wildlife populations. HWC literature has contributed to theorization about the nature of human-animal interaction by introducing the primacy of competition for resources as a defining feature. Our broad conception of HWC as human-wildlife *competition*, then helps us to reframe discussions about human's destruction of ecological resources from one purely of a lapse in good stewardship to one centralizing creature-class conflict.

Hence our study is an inquiry on direct and indirect causes of species loss. We examine three classes of human activities that may have a direct bearing on this loss. Human population propagation – the mere multiplication of humans – may have a direct destructive impact on species if human presence or the increased chance of contact and conflict are driven by this. Human economic activities may also be directly harmful (e.g., our preceding industrial example). Human governance is a third, slightly different, category. We include data on animal trafficking incidents, incidents that represent, presumably, a direct threat to animal life. However, because such measures likely fall short of a complete estimation of trafficking activity, we also included a measure of government corruption. We assume that poorly governed countries are more likely to have environments compatible with direct threat to wild animals.

We examine three primary ecological changes and compare their respective impact. Much has been written about the destructive impact of global climate change on the continued existence of animal species. We include a measure of climate change exposure within our models predicting the extent of a country's species loss. Air quality has also been named a cause of biotic species loss. We similarly attempt to predict species loss using a measure for this factor. Finally, we suspect that limited access to water – water scarcity – plays a major role in the reduction of wildlife populations. Thus we model the impact of water scarcity using a measure of countries' water stress (levels of water at or below that consumed), total renewable water resources (water availability), water per capita (units of water per person living within a country), and the amount of land covered by water (as a measure of water accessibility).

Mammals are the most studied taxonomic group in the animal kingdom and have been the best documented in terms of distribution and population (Faurby & Svenning, 2015; Keeping & Pelletier, 2014). Previous studies have shown that there is high correlation between the status of species across taxonomic groups (Essl et al., 2013), and mammal species richness – the variety of species found in a place – has been used in previous studies as a proxy for other biotic kingdoms (Ceballos & Ehrlich, 2002). According to Buckley et al. (2012), over 1,000 mammal species are red-listed by the International Union for Conservation of Nature and Natural Resources (IUCN) as critically endangered, endangered, or vulnerable. Despite present conservation efforts, many mammal species are still threatened – even in protected areas – by poaching, subsistence hunting, invasive species, and habitat encroachment by human development. As levels of species threat worsen, eventually threat will lead to extinction (i.e., species loss). Thus measures of species threat help to identify an important point in the process of loss. Accordingly, we use mammalian species threat (MST) as a proxy measure for species loss.

Using cross-national data, the present study explores a series of hypotheses that human activities cause species loss (a) directly and also (b) indirectly, and that (c) some factors may be more significant than others. Our hypotheses are as follows:

H1. Human activities increase MST directly. Across countries, there is

- H1-A: a positive association between human population density and MST.
- H1-B: a positive association between rural human population and MST.
- H1-C: a positive association between GDP and MST.
- H1-D: a positive association between GDP growth and MST.
- H1-E: a positive association between the agricultural land and MST.
- H1-F: a negative association between good governance and MST.
- H1-G: a positive association between incidents of poaching and MST.

H2. Human activities increase MST indirectly through negative impact on the environment and those ecological resources necessary for species survival. Across countries, there is

- H2-A: a negative association between land area and MST.
- H2-B: a negative association between water area and MST.
- H2-C: a positive association between water stress and MST.
- H2-D: a negative association between water per capita and MST.
- H2-E: a negative association between total renewable water resources and MST.

H2-F: a positive association between the threat of climate change and MST.
H2-G: a negative association between air quality and MST.

H3. Direct impacts (population, economic, or governance activity) and indirect impacts (climate change, air quality, and water) have differential import in predicting MST.

To test the above hypotheses, we developed a regression model setting our dependent variable as MST, predicted by independent measures of human activity (human propagation, economic activity, and governance) and anthropogenic changes in natural resources through climate change, air quality, and water stress.

Data analyses and findings

Data

Data for this study were collected for 142 countries (about three-fourths of United Nations membership countries) gleaned from myriad sources (see Table 6.1). Using figures obtained from IUCN's Red List project, we calculated the ratio of the number of mammal species listed as threatened compared with the total number of mammal species, within each country. Hereinafter, we refer to this as MST and use it as our study's dependent variable.

Table 6.1 Study variables, data sources and summary statistics

	Variables	*Data Sources*	*Description of units*	*Summary*
1	Mammalian species threat (MST)	International Union for Conservation of Nature (IUCN) Red List	number of species under threat divided by number of species within a country	Range: 0.014–0.286 Mean: 0.107 *SD*: 0.058
2	Population density	United Nations (UN) Food and Agriculture Organization Aquastat	Average number of persons living within one square kilometer within a country	Range: 1.892–6,468 Mean: 149.3 *SD*: 550.2
3	Rural population	UN Food and Agriculture Organization Aquastat	Multiples of 1,000 persons living within the rural areas of a country	Range: 92.4–891,112 Mean: 23,151 *SD*: 91,030
4	Gross domestic product (GDP)	World Bank	Multiples of one million current US dollars	Range: 964.6–1.86e+07 Mean: 514,626 *SD*: 1,937,681

	Variables	*Data Sources*	*Description of units*	*Summary*
5	GDP growth	World Bank	Percentage increase in a country's 2017 GDP from its 2016 GDP	Range: -9.8–13.4 Mean: 2.810 *SD*: 3.281
6	Proportion of land used for agriculture	World Bank	Quantity of land used for agriculture divided by the total land area of a country	Range: 0.6–82.6 Mean: 42.64 *SD*: 21.92
7	Corruption Perceptions Index (CPI)	Transparency International	Index higher / lower	Range: 9–88 Mean: 41.45 *SD*: 18.65
8	CITES origin or exporting country	UN Convention on International Trade in Endangered Species of Wild Flora and Fauna (CITES)	Is a country listed as an "origin" or "exporting" country within the CITES database (1) or not (0)?	0 = 89, 62.68% 1 = 53, 37.32%
9	Land area	US Central Intelligence Agency (CIA) World Factbook	Square kilometers within a country's borders	Range: 4,770–1.57e+07 Mean: 793,262 *SD*: 1,916,128
10	Water area	UN Food and Agriculture Organization Aquastat	Square kilometers within a country that is covered by water	Range: 0–891,163 Mean: 31,705 *SD*: 116,347
11	Water per capita	UN Food and Agriculture Organization Aquastat	cubic meters of renewable water per annum per person	Range: 1.247–353,279 Mean: 17,898 *SD*: 39,628
12	Total water resources	UN Food and Agriculture Organization Aquastat	10^9 cubic meters per annum	Range: 0.02–8,647 Mean: 366.7 *SD*: 966.9
13	Water stress	World Resources Institute	Index	Range: 0–5 Mean: 1.854 *SD*: 1.584

(Continued)

Table 6.1 (Continued)

	Variables	*Data Sources*	*Description of units*	*Summary*
14	Climate threat exposure	University of Notre Dame Global Adaptation Index – Exposure	Units of 1,000 persons	Range: 0.267–0.633 Mean: 0.426 *SD*: 0.072
15	Air quality	Yale University Center for Environmental Law & Policy/ Columbia University Earth Institute Environmental Performance Index – Air Quality	Index higher/ lower	Range: 13.83–100 Mean: 77.82 *SD*: 17.28

Prior studies have shown that the sheer number of human occupants in an area can predict a dramatic shift in the availability of resources to support wildlife (Dinda, 2004). The Land and Water Division of the UN Food and Agriculture Organization collects national data in its Aquastat dataset. We included two measures of population from the Aquastat data: (1) a country's rural population (measured in thousands, $\bar{x}$ = 23,151, σ = 91,030) and (2) population density. In the Aquastat data, population density is a continuous measure of the number of persons per square kilometer ($\bar{x}$ = 149, σ = 550). Economic activities can also be detrimental to wildlife populations (Stern, 2004). We used three measures of economic activity gleaned from the World Bank: the percentage of land area devoted to agriculture ($\bar{x}$ = 42.64, σ = 21.92); a country's gross domestic product (GDP) measured in millions of current US dollars ($\bar{x}$ = 514,626, σ = 1.9×10^6); and annual percent GDP growth in 2016 ($\bar{x}$ = 2.81, σ = 3.281). There was some concern that the inclusion of GDP and GDP growth would cause issues of multicollinearity; however, correlation analysis demonstrated that the two were very weakly related (r (135) = –.0618, p = .477).

Studies have shown that government policy and other institutional actors are critical to mitigating or aggravating the link between other human activities and environmental impact (Dinda, 2004). As a good governance measure, we included a measure of corruption, often defined as the abuse of public power and authority for private gain (Morse, 2006). We used Transparency International's Corruption Perception Index (CPI), comprising the scaled perception of experts and businesspeople regarding a nation's levels of government corruption (range = 9–88, $\bar{x}$ = 41.5, σ = 18.7). Higher values indicate less perceived government corruption, or rather good governance. Also, we included a dichotomous measure for whether a nation was documented as an exporter or place of origin for wildlife illegally traded in contravention of CITES in 2015 (when most of our data was collected). We should note that the CITES dataset denotes which country is exporter or importer in specific cases, but sometimes lists countries in both categories.

It is near universally accepted that anthropogenic climate change will have dire impacts on the environment. Prior research also connects climate change to declines in biotic species (Chapin et al., 2000; Midgley et al., 2002; Didham et al., 2007). We used the University of Notre Dame Global Adaptation Index, which contains, among others, a measure of ***exposure*** delineating the degree to which food, water, health, ecosystem services, human habitat, and infrastructure will be stressed by future projected climatic changes (range = 0.267–0.633, $\bar{x}$ = 0.426, σ = 0.072) (Chen et al., 2015). To measure of air quality, we used the Environmental Performance Index (EPI) derived by Yale University's Center for Environmental Law and Policy and the Center for International Earth Science Information Network, of Columbia University's Earth Institute, in collaboration with the World Economic Forum. The EPI "ranks 180 countries on 24 performance indicators across ten issue categories covering environmental health and ecosystem vitality" (Yale Center for Environmental Law & Policy, 2018), and its air quality index uses household solid fuels, $PM_{2.5}$ exposure, and $PM_{2.5}$ exceedance as indicators (range = 13.83–1000, $\bar{x}$ = 77.82, σ = 17.28).

Water scarcity includes two types of phenomena: physical water scarcity and social water scarcity (Kummu et al., 2010). As our interest is in wildlife-related outcomes, we choose to emphasize physical water scarcity, that is the lack of adequate water resources. First, we sought a measure of water stress, defined as the point at which water demand exceeds water supply (Clark et al., 2016). We included the Aqueduct Water Stress Projections of water demand and supply countries released in 2015 by the World Resources Institute, which "is defined as the ratio between total water withdrawals and available renewable surface water at the sub-catchment level" (Luo, Young, & Reig, 2015, p. 3). Scores are continuous and range from 0 to 5 ($\bar{x}$ = 1.85, σ = 1.58), with higher scores representing greater levels of water stress. We also included additional measures of water availability. We obtained both total renewable water resources (measured in 10^9 cubic meters per annum, $\bar{x}$ = 367, σ = 967) and total renewable water resources per capita (as cubic meters per person per annum, $\bar{x}$ = 17,898, σ = 36,628) based on 2014 estimates in the Aquastat database. Further, information on countries' total area, measured in square kilometers ($\bar{x}$ = 793,262, σ = 1.9 × 10^6), as well as the total area covered with water ($\bar{x}$ = 31,705, σ = 166,347) were gathered from the US Central Intelligence Agency's (CIA) World Factbook.

A note of caution: the latest species decline data we obtained were from 2008 estimates, representing the state of affairs before the measures we use to predict it. Nevertheless, mammal species become threatened rapidly while reaching extinction over the course of decades (Woinarski et al., 2015) such that our analysis, if anything, likely represents a more positive outlook than what the years between 2008 and 2014–2015 have produced. The probable course is that even *more* species have become threatened and that those previously carrying that designation have retained it, meaning our models may *overstate* current mammalian species richness and *underestimate* mammalian species threat.

Analysis

First, to test each of the hypothesis listed above, we undertook bivariate analyses. We calculated Pearson's r to determine bivariate relationships between our dependent variable, MST, and our various independent variables (see the correlation matrix in Table 6.2). We found that only six variables were significant at $p < 0.05$: Rural population ($r = .2478$, $p = .003$), GDP growth ($r = .1996$, $p = .0203$), CPI ($r = -.1892$, $p = .0246$) (supporting H1: B, D, F), climate threat exposure ($r = .1753$, $p = .0369$), water stress ($r = .2625$, $p = .0016$) and air quality ($r = -.3194$, $p = .0001$) were all weakly to moderately, but significantly, correlated with MST, supporting hypotheses H2, C, F and G. Additionally, the proportion of land used for agriculture ($r = -.1570$, $p = .003$) and total renewable water resources ($r = .2478$, $p = .003$) were significant at $p < 0.1$.

To further test hypothesis H3, we then performed a multivariate regression analysis to predict MST including the six variables that were significant at $p < 0.05$ (see Table 6.3) in our bivariate analysis. Notably, these included both human activities and environment variables including one measure of human propagation (i.e., rural population), one measure of economic activity (GDP growth), and one measure of human governance (CPI) as well as three environmental/ecological variables: climate threat exposure, air quality, and water stress. The model was significant: $R^2 = .2565$, F (6, 127) = 7.30, $p < .001$. When analyzed together with environmental variables, interestingly, none of the three human activity variables with significant bivariate relationships was found to retain its significance in the regression model, rebuffing our hypothesis that human activities had direct harmful effects on MST over and above that caused by ecological changes – so that hypothesis H1 was not supported. However, the three ecological measures which had been significant in bivariate analyses were significant in the regression model as well, supporting our hypothesis that changes in the quality or quantity of natural resources, of the type caused by human activities, increases MST, supporting H2 and subparts C, F, and G. Notably, while climate threat ($\beta = .242$, $p = .009$) and air quality ($\beta = -.263$, $p = .008$) were significant, water stress was more so, reaching a more exacting level of significance and registering a higher beta value ($\beta = .38$, $p < .001$). This supports our hypothesis that some factors – namely, water stress – impact MST more starkly than others. From these findings, it appears that ecological changes are significantly related to MST.

Table 6.2 Bivariate analysis: correlation matrix

	MST	*Land area*	*Area covered by water*	*Pop. density*	*Rural pop.*	*GDP*	*GDP growth*	*Portion land agriculture*	*CPI*	*CITES*	*Climate threat exposure*	*Air quality*	*Water stress*	*Total water resources*
Land area	.05													
Area covered by water	.01	.85***												
Pop. Density	.07	.05	–.02											
Rural pop.	.25**	.32***	.31***	.05										
GDP	.03	.53***	.55***	–.00	.36***									
GDP growth	.20*	–.09	–.02	–.01	.19*	–.01								
Proportion of land used for agriculture	–.16^A	–.10	–.13	.20*	.10	.02	.06							
CPI	–.19*	–.00	.14^A	–.02	–.05	.26**	–.06	–.18*						
CITES	.05	.30***	.26**	.12	.20*	.28***	–.03	–.04	.19*					
Climate threat exposure	.18*	.12	.13	–.07	.24**	.08	.04	–.04	–.27**	.07				
Air quality	–.32***	.05	.04	.02	–.46***	–.03	–.33***	–.10	.30***	–.02	–.30***			
Water stress	.26**	.02	–.00	.14	.11	.13	.01	.04^A	.03	.08	–.40***	.17*		
Total water resources	.14^A	.78***	.62***	–.03	.29	.40***	–.10	–.15	.00	.32***	.24**	.02	–.06	
Water per capita	–.12	.04	.09	–.08	–.08	–.06	–.13	–.36***	.01	–.07	.07	.16^A	–.20*	.14^A

* $p < 0.05$.
** $p < 0.01$.
*** $p < 0.001$.
A $p < 0.1$.

Table 6.3 Multivariate regression analysis

Model 1	*B*	*SE*
Rural population	.004	5.80E-08
GDP growth	.091	.001
CPI	–.051	.000
Air quality	–.263**	.000
Climate threat exposure	.242**	.075
Water stress	.380***	.003
Notes: $R^2 = .2565$ ($p < .001$).		

* $p < 0.05$.
** $p < 0.01$.
*** $p < 0.001$.

Discussion and conclusion

This study demonstrates that human activity is associated with species loss. We argued that this might be seen from the perspective of a ***globalized*** human-wildlife conflict, or rather global ***human-wildlife competition***. We sought to build upon the emphasis on resource competition within human-wildlife conflict literature by refocusing attention from individual incidents of physical violence to macro-level activities tied to human society that may result in the death of individual specimens and the decline of species populations. We found that water stress, air quality, exposure to threat from climate change, corruption, rural population, and GDP growth were all significantly correlated with MST. However, when analyzed collectively, only environmental factors significantly explained variance (25%) in MST across countries.

Living beings, whether animals or humans, depend on their habitat to meet their basic needs including food, water, and air to breathe, and changes in their environment may affect their survival. However, in the course of withdrawing resources, species inevitably change the environment, especially when resource withdrawal outpaces the rate of resource renewal. Overtaxing resources exhausts finite supplies, exacerbating resource scarcity and increasing competition over what remains. Some fauna and flora can adapt to the environmental change, though many others may not, leading to increased vulnerability to endangered status and potentially leading to eventual extinction. While human activities may have some direct responsibility in diminishing wildlife populations, our study suggests that the real detriment is caused through decreased quantity and quality of water and air, along with overall changes in climate. Importantly, then, the rationale used to explain individual-level incidents of human-wildlife conflict – seeing them as competitive clashes between humans and wild animals for limited resources – may also explain the link between development and species threat. Heretofore, many discussions around environmental threat has taken a custodial view, encouraging greater stewardship out of a sense of good neighborliness to our fellow biota. A perspective emphasizing resource ***competition*** reframes our task from one of becoming better caretakers to one of adjusting our goals and interests to make room for other species to compete.

We should also note that the current pace of environmental change foreshadows a potentially dire predicament, where necessary resources become even scarcer and studies such as ours should help encourage measures to mitigate impending effects. Moreover, more analyses must be undertaken to more fully understand the impact of various resource constraints. As we noted, threats to species that come in indirect form have murkier cause-and-effect pathways that need rigorous inquiry in unpacking. Perhaps more positively, though, if the problem is the impact of activities on the environment, and not the activities themselves, it may be possible to devise ways of counteracting damage done, in effect, interrupting the pathway between human actions and species loss. Unfortunately, we may not have much time, for as with many indirect harms, environmental changes have only risen to prominence as they have become more concentrated and acute and we are well down the causal pathway to a range of negative outcomes, including increases in species loss, unless we take a significant turnabout.

While they are interesting statistically, indeed, there are several limitations to our study to consider before generalizing these findings. Most principally, the nature of our study is cross-sectional, not longitudinal, precluding any demonstration of cause-and-effect relationships between changes in our independent variables and resultant changes in the dependent variable. At this stage, and with this dataset, we can only show associations between items. Thus, a first step in future research would be the use of longitudinal data to test the accuracy and time order of the relationships we found. Moreover, we used data gathered by a variety of sources, with different aims prompting their collection, different methods, and varying times. Our sample did not include all countries, only those for which reliable water-related data was found. We surely hope that, in the future, more of our world's countries will be forthcoming with data on various points of interest. In the meantime, sophisticated methods of imputation or computer model simulation will be useful to fill in data gaps and provide more accurate pictures of the full community of nations. Most importantly, our models exclude a host of potential variables impacting the outcomes we sought to explain. One such variable, for instance, would be a measure of habitat loss, the primary cause of species declines (Chapin et al., 2000; Czech, Krausman, & Devers, 2000). It will be necessary for more powerful methods, such as structural equation modeling (McKinney, Kick, & Fulkerson, 2010), to be used in the future to confirm our exploratory findings. Still, each species reacts to human activity in a different way, and aggregate measures such as species under threat may detract from these species-specific stories. There is some debate on whether level of species threat is even the best outcome measure; we might have chosen instead species population decline or range retraction, both more useful in revealing early impacts. However, both require adequate data to measure them.

Our results raise the necessity of further research, particularly using a conceptual frame of global-stage human-wildlife competition. We believe our results contribute to meaningful debates in the fields of conservation biology, human ecology and economics. For example, our expectations that fewer resources would prompt greater competition between humans and animal species was informed by assumptions drawn from conflict theory, a paradigm important within criminology and justice studies but also applied to water conflicts in the past. One tenet of conflict theory suggests that conflict arises in the context of limited resources. Yet, recent studies in natural resource economics have posited the existence of a "curse of natural resources" (Sachs & Warner, 2001). In this view, countries with abundant natural resources tend to develop more slowly and less robustly than nations with fewer natural resources. These "cursed" nations are often associated with corrupt and inefficient governments (Pick & Thein, 2010), and resource abundance can produce incentives that reinforce corruption and inefficiency (Weins, 2014). Some have found evidence that resource abundance causes conflict (Rahman, 2012). Our bivariate analyses finding of no significant correlation between MST and several measures of resource abundance (e.g., total renewable water resources), appear to show a different story with respect to the number of species under threat in a country.

Of interest to criminologists, this study also raises the issue of the role of corruption in explaining MST. While it does not appear to play a direct role on national-level species decline in our analyses when equated to environment factors, it may be a significant predictor of natural resource scarcity (work in progress). For instance, given water's influence on species decline, policies addressing government corruption may be important to protecting threatened species from extinction by improving water management practices. Additionally, poaching investigations under CITES play a seemingly insignificant role in MST. This suggests that the impact illegal trafficking has on animal species may be best explained by its being an indicator of the crime opportunity structures associated with corruption and poor governance. Since we used only mammalian species collectively, it is hard for us to confirm what effect poaching/trafficking has on specific species loss. Notably, studies have confirmed the role of human predators in the extinction of species in the past, for example, passenger pigeons (Roberts et al., 2017). We believe that data on specific mammals and birds would help discern the impact of poaching.

Our hope is that continued research into the ways in which human societies contribute to the decline of other species, through overuse of a bevy of natural resources, will lead not only to scientific conclusions but also to moral ones, including about the awesome blessing of life as seen in all creatures and a duty to respect that life by being responsible stewards of our shared planet.

Acknowledgments

We thank the editors for their helpful comments. We also thank Satish G. Nathan for his support and editorial review. Finally, we thank Mudiayi Ngandu for his work and inspiration in seeking fair, efficient, and effective management of natural resources.

References

Anand, S., & Radhakrishna, S. (2017). Investigating trends in human-wildlife conflict: Is conflict escalation read or imagined? *Journal of Asia-Pacific Biodiversity*, *10*(2), 154–161.

Bierne, P. (2014). Theriocide: Naming animal killing. *International Journal for Crime, Justice and Social Democracy*, *3*(2), 49–66.

Bobo, K. S., Ntumwel, C. B., Aghomo, F. F., & Ayemele, K. A. (2017). The conservation status of two threatened primates in the Korup region, Southwest Cameroon. *Primate Conservation*, *31*, 37–48.

Buckley, R. C., Castley, J. G., de Vasconcellos Pegas, F., Mossaz, A. C., & Steven, R. (2012). A population accounting approach to assess tourism contributions to conservation of IUCN-redlisted mammal species. *PLoS ONE*, *7*(9), e44134.

Ceballos, G., & Ehrlich, P. R. (2002). Mammal population losses and the extinction crisis. *Science*, *296*, 904–907.

Chapin, F. S., III, Zavaleta, E. S., Eviner, V. T., Naylor, R. L., Vitousek, P. M., Reynolds, H. L., Hooper, D. U., Lavorel, S., Sala, O. E., Hobbie, S. E., Mack, M. C., & Diaz, S. (2000). Consequences of changing biodiversity. *Nature*, *405*, 234–242.

Chen, C., Noble, I., Hellmann, J., Coffee, J., Murillo, M., & Chawla, N. (2015). *University of Notre Dame global adaptation index* [technical document]. South Bend: University of Notre Dame.

Clark, B., DeFries, R., & Krishnaswamy, J. (2016). Intra-annual dynamics of water stress in the central Indian Highlands from 2002 to 2012. *Regional Environmental Change*, *16*(1), 83–95.

Czech, B., Krausman, P. R., & Devers, P. K. (2000). Economic associations among causes of species endangerment in the United States. *BioScience*, *50*(7), 593–601.

Didham, R. K., Tylianakis, J. M., Gemmell, N. J., Rand, T. A., & Ewers, R. M. (2007). Interactive effects of habitat modification and species invasion on native species decline. *TRENDS in Ecology and Evolution*, *22*(9), 489–496.

Dinda, S. (2004). Environmental Kuznets curve hypothesis: A survey. *Ecological Economies*, *49*, 431–455.

Distefano, E. (2005). *Human-wildlife conflict worldwide: Collection of case studies, analysis of management strategies and good practices*. Rome: Food and Agricultural Organization of the United Nations, SARD Initiative Report. Available from www.fao.org/sard/common/ecg/1357/en/hwc_final.pdf.

Elliott, L. (2017). Environmental regionalism: Moving in from the policy margins. *The Pacific Review*, *30*(6), 952–965.

Essl, F., Moser, D., Dirnböck, T., Dullinger, S., Milasowszky, N., Winter, M., & Rabitsch, W. (2013). Native, alien, endemic, threatened, and extinct species diversity in European countries. *Biological Conservation*, *164*, 90–97.

Faurby, S., & Svenning, J. C. (2015). A species-level phylogeny of all extant and late Quaternary extinct mammals using a novel heuristic-hierarchical Bayesian approach. *Molecular Phylogenetics and Evolution*, *84*, 14–26.

Gause, G. F. (1934). *The struggle for existence*. Baltimore: Williams & Wilkins.

Keeping, D., & Pelletier, R. (2014). Animal density and track counts: Understanding the nature of observations based on animal movements. *PLoS ONE*, *9*(5), 1–11.

Kummu, M., Ward, P. J., de Moel, H., & Varis, O. (2010). Is physical water scarcity a new phenomenon? Global assessment of water shortage over the last two millennia. *Environmental Research Letters*, *5*, 1–10.

Liu, F., McShea, W. J., Garshelis, D. L., Zhu, X., Wang, D., & Shao, L. (2011). Human-wildlife conflicts influence attitudes but not necessarily behaviors: Factors driving the poaching of bears in China. *Biological Conservation*, *144*(1), 538–547.

Luo, T., Young, R., & Reig, P. (2015). *Aqueduct projected water stress country rankings* [technical note]. Washington, DC: World Resources Institute. Available from www.wri.org/sites/default/files/aqueduct-water-stress-country-rankings-technical-note.pdf.

McKinney, L. A., Kick, E. L., & Fulkerson, G. M. (2010). World system, anthropogenic, and ecological threats to bird and mammal species: A structural equation analysis of biodiversity loss. *Organization & Environment*, *23*(1), 3–31.

Midgley, G. F., Hannah, L., Millar, D., Rutherford, M. C., & Powrie, L. W. (2002). Assessing the vulnerability of species richness to anthropogenic climate change in a biodiversity hotspot. *Global Ecology & Biogeography*, *11*, 445–451.

Morse, S. (2006). Is corruption bad for environmental sustainability? A cross-national analysis. *Ecology and Society*, *11*(1), 22–42.

Noyes, P. D., McElwee, M. K., Miller, H. D., Clark, B. W., Van Tiem, L. A., Walcott, K. C., Ewin, K. N., & Levin, E. D. (2009). The toxicology of climate change: Environmental contaminants in a warming world. *Environment International*, *35*(6), 971–986.

Pianka, E. R. (1974). *Evolutionary ecology*. New York: Harper and Row.

Pick, D., & Thein, H. H. (2010). Development failure and the resource curse: The case of Myanmar. *International Journal of Sociology and Social Policy*, *30*(5/6), 267–279.

Project Elephant Division (2017). *Synchronized elephant population estimation India, 2017*. New Delhi: Ministry of Environment, Forest and Climate Change, Government of India.

Rahman, M. A. (2012). Water security: Ethiopia-Egypt transboundary challenges over the Nile River Basin. *Journal of Asian and African Studies*, *48*(1), 35–46.

Sachs, J. D., & Warner, A. M. (2001). The curse of natural resources. *European Economic Review*, *45*, 827–838.

Stern, D. I. (2004). The rise and fall of the environmental Kuznets curve. *World Development*, *32*(8), 1419–1439.

Stommel, C., Hofer, H., & East, M. L. (2016). The effect of reduced water availability in the Great Ruaha River on the vulnerable common hippopotamus in the Ruaha National Park, Tanzania. *PLoS ONE*, *11*(6), e0157145. Available from https://doi.org/10.1371/journal.pone.0157145.

Sukumar, R. (2006). A brief review of the status, distribution and biology of wild Asian elephants Elephas maximus. *International Zoo Yearbook*, *40*(1), 1–8.

United Nations Department of Economic and Social Affairs. (n.d.). Water scarcity [web page]. Available from www.un.org/waterforlifedecade/scarcity.shtml.

United Nations Office on Drugs and Crime. (2017). *Wildlife crime status update, 2017*. Vienna: United Nations.

United States Geological Survey (2016). How much water is there on, in, and above the Earth? [web page]. Available from https://water.usgs.gov/edu/earthhowmuch.html.

Weins, D. (2014). Natural resources and institutional development. *Journal of Theoretical Politics*, *26*(2), 197–221.

Woinarski, J.C.Z., Burbridge, A. A., & Harrison, P. L. (2015). Ongoing unraveling of a continental fauna: Decline and extinction of Australian mammals since European settlement. *PNAS*, *112*(15), 4531–4540.

World Wildlife Fund. (2005). *Human wildlife conflict manual*. Nairobi: WWF-World Wide Fund for Nature Southern African Regional Programme Office. Available from http://d2ouvy59p0dg6k.cloudfront.net/downloads/human_wildlife_conflict.pdf.

Yale Center for Environmental Law & Policy (2018). *Environmental performance index*: Table. New Haven: Yale University and Center for International Earth Science Information Network, Earth Institute, Columbia University. Available from https://epi.envirocenter.yale.edu/epi-topline?country=&order=field_epi_score_new&sort=asc.

7 A comparison of seizures of illegal wildlife between the US and the EU

Implications for prevention

Daan P. van Uhm, Stephen F. Pires, Monique Sosnowski, and Gohar A. Petrossian

Introduction

The trafficking of wildlife has emerged as a significant threat to plant and animal species worldwide. The illegal trade in wildlife has an estimated annual worth of approximately $20 billion, making it one of the most profitable criminal enterprises alongside the trafficking in narcotics, firearms, and human beings (WWF/Dalberg, 2012; Rosen and Smith, 2010; European Commission, 2016; African Wildlife Foundation, 2015; UNODC, 2016; Nellemann et al., 2014). The United Nations Office on Drugs and Crime (UNODC) has designated the engagement in wildlife trafficking a "global phenomenon" and a "serious crime" punishable by a minimum of four years in prison (UNODC, 2016).

The illegal trade in wildlife involves the illicit procurement, transport, and distribution of animals, animal parts, and derivatives thereof in contravention of foreign or domestic regulations. This often includes the poaching or otherwise taking of protected or managed species, which has escalated into an international crisis (van Uhm, 2016a; USFWS, n.d.; Wyler and Sheikh, 2013). The wildlife trade can involve a diverse range of commodities including live animals sold to private collectors, pet shops, animal brokers, game farms, biomedical labs, circuses, and meat dealers; animal parts such as elephant ivory, rhinoceros horn, tiger bones, or leopard pelts; and plant species often sold to meet consumer demands for holistic medicine or landscape décor (Warchol, 2007; TRAFFIC, n.d.). Among the most lucrative products are caviar, elephant ivory, exotic birds and reptiles, and rhinoceros horn, which sells for an estimated value between $35,000 and $65,000 per kilogram (Mander, 2012).

Given the serious nature of the illicit wildlife trade at the global level, analysis of wildlife trafficking patterns is paramount for understanding the nature of the trade and to inform policies designed to control wildlife trafficking. The present study examines wildlife seizure patterns made in two of the largest demand markets in the world (the US and the EU) to unveil common characteristics and differences in those markets as they relate to products, and places from which wildlife emanates. In doing so, our study can inform how resources can be better allocated to target export countries more effectively and inform customs agents in the EU and the US on patterns of heavily trafficked wildlife products.

The wildlife trade

The international illicit movement of plant and animal species directly affects global biodiversity, as well as hinders the economic and social development of countries via loss of flora and fauna, spread of invasive species, and introduction of health threats (WWF/Dalberg, 2012). The increase in trade of certain wildlife products has caused direct and dramatic population declines. This is explicitly seen in the case of African elephants (*Loxodonta africana*), whose population plummeted from 1.3 million in 1979, to an estimated 600,000 in 1989, due to the trade in ivory (TRAFFIC, n.d.). The pet trade has also pushed many species to the brink of extinction in the past few decades, including Indonesian bird species, such as the scarlet-breasted lorikeet (*Trichoglossus forsteni*) and yellow-crested cockatoo (*Cacatua sulphurea*) (Eaton et al., 2015), as well as many species of the family Psittacidae, commonly known as parrots, in the neotropics (Pires, 2012). This direct removal of flora and fauna, and subsequent potential loss of species, threatens more than biodiversity and animal welfare, as it damages the health of ecosystems that provide the platform upon which food production and economies are ultimately based upon. Ecosystems play a crucial role in providing development opportunities and supporting livelihoods, particularly those which rely heavily on natural resources, such as agriculture, forestry, and fisheries (Nellemann et al., 2014; Duffy, 2010).

The movement of wildlife further creates opportunity for the introduction of harmful, non-native species that may damage existing ecosystems. These invasive species can affect human, animal, and plant health, as well as cause environmental or agricultural damage. The pet trade is a known route for invasive species introduction; many species are banned only after their damaging effects become well-documented in the new environment (Rosen and Smith, 2010; Wyler and Sheikh, 2013; Ferrier, 2009). The import of plant and animal species also opens the doors for the introduction and spread of disease. Similarly to the threats of invasive species, disease can cause social and economic harm, threatening people, wildlife, agriculture, and ecosystems. Several notable disease outbreaks, including zoonoses, have emerged due to the wildlife trade (van Uhm, 2016a; Wyler and Sheikh, 2013; Gomez and Aguirre, 2008; Karesh et al., 2005).

The demand for wildlife products arises from a number of different consumer groups and is often influenced by social and cultural drivers. Demand is fueled by the perceived medicinal value of some products and social status associated with them, as well as opportunistic buying by tourists purchasing souvenirs or pets abroad and the desire to possess exotic pets and hunting trophies (WWF/Dalberg, 2012; Wyler and Sheikh, 2013; van Uhm, 2018). Steady or increasing demand has driven illicit trafficking of wildlife to increase in recent years. The world is currently losing an estimated 30,000 elephants annually for their tusks; rhinoceros poaching reached a record high in 2015, with nearly 1,215 killed in South Africa alone; and Asian range states seized at least 1,425 tiger parts between 2000 and 2012, indicating the overexploitation of wildlife (TRAFFIC, 2015).

Overview of wildlife seizure research

Seizure data can provide valuable information about import and export countries, and has become an accepted method by which to gain insights into wildlife trade practices (UNODC, 2016; Kurland and Pires, 2017; Petrossian, Pires and van Uhm, 2016; van Uhm, 2016b). Although seizures make up only a selective sample of global activity, they are relevant and reliable to understand global confiscation patterns. The majority of seizure studies have examined the trade in specific commodities, such as elephant ivory (Underwood et al., 2013; Martin and Stiles, 2008), marine ornamental species and coral to the US (Rhyne et al., 2012), and amphibians (Schloegel et al., 2009).

Few studies, however, examine national and international seizure records. A 2010 study by Rosen and Smith (Rosen and Smith, 2010) analyzed 12 years of wildlife seizure records (1996–2008) compiled by the wildlife trade monitoring network, TRAFFIC, to reveal international trafficking patterns, namely the origin and destination of illegal wildlife products around the world. They concluded that most products were exported from Southeast Asia, which had been a recently identified hot spot of emerging infectious diseases. The study noted that imports were not evenly distributed across taxa, with mammals and mammal derivatives constituting 51% of all seizures.[1]

At the national level, Petrossian et al. (2016) analyzed seizures made at US ports of entry between 2003 and 2012 using the LEMIS database managed by the US Fish and Wildlife Service (USFWS). Their findings revealed that 94% of species seized across the US belonged to six major groups, namely mammals, mollusks, reptiles, fish, birds, and coral. Further, it was found that the majority of these US seizures were exported from six countries. In a related US study on the concentration of wildlife seizures by place and products, Kurland and Pires (2017) identified that roughly 80% of all seizures made between 2003 and 2012 were exported from approximately 20% of countries, and occurred at about 20% of US entry points. Additionally, this study found that the most seized genera for the US included *Crocodylus, Python, Caiman, Panthera*, and *Strombus* (Kurland and Pires, 2017).

At the regional level, van Uhm (2016b) performed a similar illicit wildlife seizure analysis within the EU. Using the EU-TWIX seizure database, van Uhm examined products confiscated between 2001 and 2010. He discovered that imports were primarily from Africa and Southeast Asia, with top wildlife groups seized being mammals, birds, reptiles, fish, coral, and mollusks. In particular, Thailand, China, and Vietnam, as well as Morocco, Egypt, and Algeria were important source countries, along with Russia and the US (van Uhm, 2016b).

Based on these studies, it is evident that wildlife seizures are concentrated in various ways, and certain wildlife products are more in demand. However, studies focusing on EU patterns differed from US-based studies as it related to patterns analyzed and the time frame of each study. Consequently, it is unclear whether there are common characteristics between each demand market during the same time period with regard to concentrations of wildlife seizures. That is the focus of the present study. The following section will provide a theoretical explanation for why these seizure patterns may exist.

Theoretical framework

In global illegal wildlife markets, numerous endangered species are traded for a variety of reasons (Petrossian et al., 2016; Van Uhm, 2016a). The demand for illegal trade in wildlife is often socially and culturally driven. For example, animal skins and furs are historically used as wearing apparel in Western societies (Kalof, 2007); tiger bones and rhinoceros horn are used in traditional Asian medicine (Ellis, 2005); live tortoises, parrots, and monkeys are driven by fashion trends or the pet industry (D'Cruze et al., 2015; Pires, 2012); specific fish species are traded for consumption as a delicacy (Petrossian and Clarke, 2014); while possession of animal parts, such as elephant ivory or rhinoceros horn, are a status symbol (Martin and Stiles, 2008). Thus, the value placed upon wildlife products is a function of attributions, motivations, and exchanged commodities instead of the forms or functions of trade (Simmel, 1978; Appadurai, 1986; Van Uhm, 2018). For instance, the possession of luxury or scarce objects manifests one's prestige and "offers access to social networks and to other resources that are closed to those lacking prestige" (Renfrew, 1986: 161). Therefore, the patterns of illegal wildlife can be seen as a reflection of social and cultural demand for certain products.

In addition to sociocultural demand patterns, the illegal wildlife trade is influenced by opportunity structures in the environment. Past research has shown that wildlife crime is highly concentrated in time and space, among offenders and species, and these concentrations are highest where the opportunities are greatest (Petrossian et al., 2016). For example, parrot poaching in the neotropics is concentrated among species, space, time, and by methods (Pires et al., 2016; Pires and Clarke, 2011, 2012) and illegal fishing is highest where there are greater concentrations of highly commercial fish (Petrossian, 2015; Petrossian et al., 2015; Marteache et al., 2015; Petrossian et al., 2016). As such, preventive measures designed to reduce opportunities for poaching can, in turn, reduce overall crime (Moreto and Pires, 2018; Kurland et al., 2017).

Consistent with the expectations outlined above and dwelling on the main findings of illegal imports of wildlife into the United States (Petrossian et al., 2016) and the EU (van Uhm, 2016b), we would expect to find significant concentrations of illegal imports by species groups, export countries, and types of products. We would expect these concentrations to reflect overlaps in demand markets in the US and EU, where a large proportion of seizures would involve a significantly small proportion of wildlife groupings, genera, and types of products, along with a few countries accounting for the largest number of illegal exports. Additionally, we would expect to see specific patterns that reflect the sociocultural demand for these products in the US and the EU. To understand the differences between the US and EU markets and the reasons behind these differences, trends and patterns of illegal wildlife imports into these two markets will be discussed in the context of criminogenic aspects of the illegal wildlife markets.

Methodology

To understand the patterns of illegal wildlife trafficking in the context of two major demand markets, the US and the EU, data on confiscations between 2003 and 2010 were obtained. In the US, confiscated wildlife is recorded in the Law Enforcement Management Information System (LEMIS) database. The LEMIS dataset was obtained through the Freedom of Information Act (FOIA) request made on 23 September 2013 to the USFWS-LEMIS division. The EU dataset was obtained from the European Union Trade in Wildlife Information eXchange database (EU-TWIX), a database of information on wildlife seizures in the EU. From these confiscations, *only those incidents that were deemed illegal and seized by authorities were analyzed* (see Kurland and Pires, 2017). Regarding the LEMIS database, 28,201 seized incidents of illicit wildlife were recorded between 2003 and 2010, while 15,295 incidents of animals and animal products were recorded in the EU-TWIX database during the same period.

The variables in both databases overlap regarding seizure incidents by genus, species, sub-species, CITES status, wildlife description (e.g., live animal, leather product), quantity (reported in individuals or products), unit of measurement (e.g., number of specimens, kg, m^3), country of export and origin, date of entry, exporting country, source country, import and export purpose, source (wild, captive bred, ranch raised, and unknown), and transportation mode. Regarding the wildlife description variable, some attributes in both datasets were slightly different from each other as the EU-TWIX database has fewer attributes. To overcome this issue, attributes in the LEMIS dataset were recoded to be consistent with the EU TWIX categorization of wildlife description attributes. For example, the EU-TWIX wildlife description attribute, whole corals, would encompass all whole coral categories in the LEMIS dataset such as COR,[2] CPR,[3] and ROC.[4]

Analytical strategy

Seizure shipments typically include multiple types of species in varying amounts. Each line of data represents one particular species that was confiscated, and therefore this study treated each entry as a unique seizure incident (Petrossian et al., 2016; van Uhm, 2016b; Kurland and Pires, 2016). Descriptive statistics are predominantly used in this paper to demonstrate how illicit wildlife incidents are concentrated in numerous ways in both datasets. In the results section, we:

1 Analyze the groupings of wildlife seized in both the US and the EU
2 Discuss the top ten most seized product types by incidents in the US and the EU
3 Describe the top 25 genera seized in the US and the EU.

Related to the third analysis, the taxonomic rank of genus was the lowest classification that could be successfully analyzed for seizure patterns, as the lowest taxonomic ranks of *species* and *sub-species* had a substantial amount of missing data in both datasets and precluded us from using such data.

Finally, for the last section, we test whether certain genera and export countries disproportionately account for most seizure incidents by creating Lorenz curve plots and their corresponding Gini coefficients (1921). To do this, four lists were created. For the first two lists, the cumulative percentage of seizures across all known genera seized in both the (1) EU and the (2) US were plotted against the cumulative percentage of total genera seized in both the EU and the US. As a result, the distribution of incidents among genera seized in both datasets are displayed in the left panel of the Lorenz plot of Figure 7.1. For the third and fourth lists, the cumulative percentage of seizures across exporting nations seized in both the (3) EU and the (4) US were plotted against the cumulative percentage of total nations. The resulting Lorenz plot is shown on the right panel. To test the equality or inequality of the distribution, the Gini coefficient was calculated as seen below (range 0.0–1.0), whereby 0.0 suggests the distribution is not skewed (i.e., perfect equality) and 1.0 indicates perfect inequality.

$$G = \frac{A}{(A+B)}$$

The reliability of the data from both LEMIS and EU-TWIX is entirely dependent on the accuracy of these data as reported by states and nations (Blundell and Mascia, 2005). As law enforcement experts estimate that no more than 10% of all contraband wildlife is confiscated (e.g., Stiles et al., 2013), the seizures are likely to reflect only a fraction of the illegal trade (Coleman and Moynihan, 1996). This is likely to specific countries' inadequate reporting of their seizures. For example, Greece is a well-known smuggling hub for illegal wildlife entering Europe, and yet it has zero confiscations recorded. While these are serious limitations, this chapter's objective is not to report the exact quantities of seizures but rather to identify possible trends based on the existing data on seizures.

Results

Table 7.1 presents the different animal groupings seized in the US (left) and the EU (right) between 2003 and 2010. Of the ten major identified groupings, more than half of the seizures in both the US (53.1%) and the EU (50.2%) consist of reptile and mammal species. The largest grouping, around one-third of the seizures in both the US (28.1%) and EU (33.5%), consists of reptiles and their derivatives. The mammal category primarily consists of raw material for traditional Asian medicine and corresponds with worldwide demand patterns for illegal wildlife. Bird-related seizures were identified as the third-highest grouping in the US (12.2%) and as the sixth-highest grouping in the EU (5.7%), while coral seizures were identified as much higher in the EU (21.1%) compared to the US (8.4%). Mollusk seizures are noteworthy as the fourth grouping in both the US (11.1%) and the EU (10.8%) and fish seizures – mainly caviar – consist of 7.9% and 8.8% in the US and the EU, respectively. Relatively low percentages of incidents were related to the groupings of marine mammals, arachnids, insects and amphibians that share the bottom four places in both lists.

Table 7.1 Groupings of wildlife seized by *N* of incidents in the US and the EU (2003–2010)

US Seizures				*EU Seizures*			
Rank	*Grouping**	*Incidents*	*%*	*Rank*	*Grouping**	*Incidents*	*%*
1	Reptile	7,925	28.1	1	Reptile	5,127	33.5
2	Mammal	7,043	25.0	2	Coral	3,225	21.1
3	Bird	3,433	12.2	3	Mammal	2,550	16.7
4	Mollusk	3,141	11.1	4	Mollusk	1,654	10.8
5	Coral	2,381	8.4	5	Fish	1,350	8.8
6	Fish	2,219	7.9	6	Bird	871	5.7
7	Marine Mammal	798	2.8	7	Arachnida	101	0.7
8	Insect	499	1.8	8	Marine Mammal	90	0.6
9	Amphibian	191	0.7	9	Insect	75	0.5
10	Arachnida	135	0.5	10	Amphibian	26	0.2

* This list only documents known species that were seized.

Table 7.2 Top ten most seized product types by % of incidents in the US and the EU (2003–2010)

US Seizures			*EU Seizures*		
Rank	*Types of Products**	*%*	*Rank*	*Types of Products*	*%*
1	Small leather product	10.3	1	Whole corals	21.1
2	Garments (including shoes)	10.3	2	Live specimens	14.3
3	Medicinal part/product	9.7	3	Shells	9.7
4	Carvings	8.4	4	Dead animal (whole)	8.4
5	Shells	7.4	5	Small leather product	7.9
6	Meat	6.8	6	Caviar	7.0
7	Dead animal (whole)	6.5	7	Large leather product	5.0
8	Live specimens	6.0	8	Skins	3.9
9	Whole corals	4.7	9	Carvings	3.7
10	Trophy (all parts)	4.6	10	Derivatives	3.5

* The US top ten products (out of 76) account for 64% of all seizures in the LEMIS Dataset and EU top ten products (out of 45) account for 76% in the TWIX-EU dataset.

Table 7.2 shows the top ten most common types of wildlife seized. These ten types account for three-quarters or more of the documented product type seizures in both the US (74.7%) and the EU (84.5%). Most seizures are related to animal products in the US (94.0%) and the EU (85.7%), rather than live animals (6.0% and 14.3%, respectively). Many types of wildlife products are associated with one of the US or EU wildlife groupings. For instance, most leather products were made of reptiles, seizures of medicinal products were predominantly from mammals, while live animals consist mainly of live reptiles and live birds. Seizures of garments, meat, medicinal part/product, and trophies were only identified in the top ten in the US, while caviar, large leather products, skins, and derivatives seem to play a more important role in the EU.[5]

Table 7.3 presents the most seized genera in both the US and the EU. Following upon the prominent presence of reptiles in wildlife seizures, the majority of

Table 7.3 Top 25 genera seized by *N* of incidents in the US and the EU (2003–2010)

US Seizures					*EU Seizures*			
Rank	*Genus*	*Common Name*	*Incident*	*%*	*Genus*	*Common Name*	*Incident*	*%*
1	*Crocodylus*	Crocodile	1170	4.1	*Loxodonta*	Elephant	976	6.4
2	*Caiman*	Caiman	769	2.7	*Strombus*	Sea snail	940	6.1
3	*Panthera*	Big cats	767	2.7	*Testudo*	Tortoise	710	4.6
4	*Python*	Python	751	2.7	*Python*	Python	616	4.0
5	*Varanus*	Large lizard	597	2.1	*Naja*	Snake	503	3.3
6	*Ursus*	Bear	589	2.1	*Varanus*	Large lizard	266	1.7
7	*Alligator*	Alligator	588	2.1	*Crocodylus*	Crocodile	255	1.7
8	*Moschus*	Deer	584	2.1	*Hippocampus*	Seahorse	228	1.5
9	*Struthio*	Ostrich	583	2.1	*Panthera*	Big cats	215	1.4
10	*Loxodonta*	Elephant	524	1.9	*Ursus*	Bear	175	1.1
11	*Hippocampus*	Seahorse	483	1.7	*Moschus*	Deer	172	1.1
12	*Pinctada*	Clam	478	1.7	*Alligator*	Alligator	170	1.1
13	*Strombus*	Sea snail	467	1.7	*Tridacna*	Clam	154	1.0
14	*Odocoileus*	Deer	438	1.6	*Trachemys*	Turtle	137	0.9
15	*Acipenser*	Sturgeon	374	1.3	*Acropora*	Coral	114	0.7
16	*Saiga*	Antelope	304	1.1	*Chamaeleo*	Chamaeleon	113	0.7
17	*Corallium*	Coral	295	1.0	*Pocillopora*	Coral	111	0.7
18	*Huso*	Sturgeon	265	0.9	*Boa*	Boa	103	0.7
19	*Iguana*	Iguana	262	0.9	*Tupinambis*	Lizard	100	0.7
20	*Tridacna*	Giant clam	254	0.9	*Canis*	Canid	90	0.6
21	*Anas*	Duck	209	0.7	*Elephas*	Elephant	88	0.6
22	*Cervus*	Deer	193	0.7	*Acipenser*	Sturgeon	79	0.5
23	*Naja*	Snake	180	0.6	*Pandinus*	Scorpion	76	0.5
24	*Crotalus*	Viper	168	0.6	*Psittacus*	Parrot	72	0.5
25	*Phoca*	Seal	166	0.6	*Amazona*	Parrot	59	0.4

* The top 25 seized genera in the United States, or 2% of all genera, account for 40.6% of all known and unknown genera seizures. In the EU, the top 25 seized genera, or 5.8% of all genera, account for 42.5% of all known and unknown genera seizures.

genera in both top five lists were reptiles. The reptile products consist mainly of crocodile, caiman, lizard and snake species, while big cats (e.g., tigers, leopards), bears (e.g., black bears) and deer (e.g., musk and saiga deer) were mainly related to Asian traditional medicine (ATM). Tortoises and parrots were predominantly related to live animals. In both demand markets, the top ten seized genera included crocodiles, big cats, pythons, large lizards, bears, and elephants.

Regarding the top panel in Figure 7.1, the Lorenz-plot curve reveals the inequality of genera seizures in the EU and the US more comprehensively than Table 7.3. Because the observed lines for both the EU and the US significantly deviate from the line of equality, it can be concluded that a small proportion of genera account for a large share of seizures. In fact, the Gini coefficient for the US is 0.845 and the EU is 0.846, proving that a small proportion of genera in both datasets account for most seizures (see also Table 7.3).

As it relates to exporting country of wildlife contraband, the bottom panel in Figure 7.1 reveals the inequality of seizures from exporting nations across all nations. The Gini coefficient for the US is 0.828 and the EU is 0.716, proving that a few nations account for most wildlife seizures made in both the EU and the

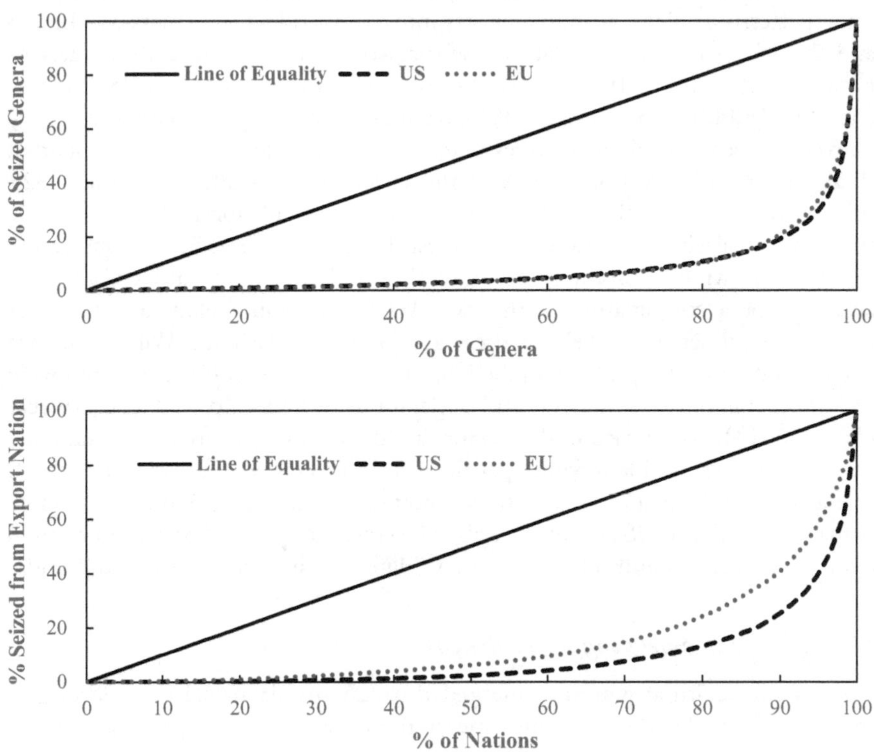

Figure 7.1 Lorenz-plot curve of seizures by genera (top panel) and export country (bottom panel) in the EU and the US

US. In fact, there are some similarities of problematic countries in both demand markets. For example, Southeast Asia and China account for a large share of seizures in both markets. In the US, 30% of all seizures are exported from China, Thailand, the Philippines, Hong Kong, Vietnam, and Indonesia, whereas in the EU, 17.6% of all seizures emanate from China, Indonesia, Vietnam, and Thailand. However, a number of differences between the two major demand markets also exist. In the US, for example, two of the top three problematic exporters are their North American neighbors, Mexico and Canada, accounting for a quarter of all seizures. In the EU, however, Mexico only accounts for 1.5% of seizures, while neighboring regions or countries, such as North Africa (Egypt, Algeria, Morocco, and Tunisia), account for 9.6%. In addition, Russia and Ukraine are responsible for 6.0%, and Switzerland (a non-EU member) is responsible for 1.5% of seizures. Interestingly, the top exporter of seizures into the EU is the US, with 8.8%.

Discussion

Sociocultural demand

In an effort to identify the impact of social and cultural demand in shaping the trade patterns of illegal wildlife imports into the world's major markets, the US and the EU, we examined data on seizures of wildlife entering these markets between 2003 and 2010. Over 28,000 seizures from the US LEMIS database and over 15,000 from the EU-TWIX database were analyzed. The discrepancy between those values alone provides an insight into wildlife demand. In comparing these values with the populations of the EU and US – 508 million and 323 million, respectively – the US has roughly half the population and nearly double the number of seizures. This would suggest that the US has either a larger overall demand for wildlife products or more thorough detection and enforcement activities, or a combination of the two. While we cannot eliminate the latter explanation, it seems unlikely, as there are so few US Fish and Wildlife Service agents tending to this problem in the US. The US only has 330 agents nationwide to inspect millions of shipments and declarations of imported wildlife every year (Fears, 2014). To measure the sociocultural demand patterns, we examined wildlife seizures by identifying specific animal groupings and genera in both markets. By linking these illegal trade findings to existing literature on wildlife demand in both the US and EU, we aimed to reveal embedded social and cultural demand similarities and differences for wildlife that is at the heart of the trade.

Similarities in emerging sociocultural patterns

Various sociocultural patterns emerged through the data analysis. Specifically, the analysis revealed demand similarities in the US and EU for reptiles, mammals, mollusks, and fish. Further examination of the data at the product level indicated that, generally, animal products were preferred over live species in both markets.

Over half of the species illegally imported in both markets were reptiles and mammals, with reptile products and raw mammal products dominating the seizures within these two groups. Reptiles alone, which included snakes, lizards, amphibians, crocodiles, turtles, tortoises, and tuataras (IUCN, 2013), were the largest group in both markets, making up approximately one-third of seizures. At the lower taxonomic level of genus, many of the most seized reptiles were found in the top 25 list in both markets. For example, *Crocodylus, Python, Varanus, Alligator*, and *Naja* disproportionately accounted for most seizures in both markets. Overall, reptile seizures consisted primarily of products, such as skins or by-products for medicinal purposes, as opposed to live specimens. The EU has previously been identified as the world's largest importer by value of reptile skins (Engler and Parry-Jones, 2007), importing a large number of the over ten million reptiles that are killed annually for the largely unregulated leather industry (Liddick, 2011). Substantial and diverse, our data analysis indicates the existence of a large sociocultural demand for reptiles for products in both the US and EU. Frequently seized products of large monitor lizards (*Varanus* spp.) and reticulated python (*Python reticulatus*), for example, are particularly prized for processing into luxury leather goods, such as handbags and shoes (Natusch and Lyons, 2014; Engler and Parry-Jones, 2007). This poses a serious threat to wild populations in the forms of species removal. As of 2013, 1 in 5 reptile species was threatened with extinction (Böhm et al., 2013).

The mammal grouping, which came in second for the US and third for the EU, consisted mainly of raw products for traditional Asian medicine. Although the data reflect that wildlife was imported for numerous reasons, medicinal parts and products made up 9.7% of US seizures and did not appear in the top ten EU categories. However, in the EU, medicine, dominated by ATM, is the largest category across categories in terms of quantity (>47,000 medicines), including mammal products such as big cat, musk deer, bear, saiga antelope, pangolin, and rhinoceros products. Although the effectiveness of traditional Asian medicine treatments is debated (Swan and Conrad, 2014), it is clear that a sociocultural demand has created a sizable market in the Western world (Still, 2003; Jia, 2012; Williamson et al., 2013).

Similar rates of seizures for mollusks and fish in both the US and EU indicate equal demand for these groups, and similar sociocultural preferences. Caviar, included in the fish grouping, was the sixth-most commonly seized EU product but did not appear in the top ten US seizures by product type. This would indicate that although these group seizure rates were similar, the makeup of these groups is likely distinct and varied. However, both Europe and the US are well-known outlets for legitimate and illegitimate caviar (Zabyelina, 2014; Van Uhm and Siegel, 2016).

Diverging sociocultural patterns

Aside from the discrepancy in medicinal product seizures and likely seafood makeup, the findings revealed substantial differences between four categories: corals, birds, the elephant genera, and garments. Overall, less than half of the genera seized in the US coincided with those seized in the EU, most likely reflecting similar cultural demand. Importantly, the Lorenz curve plots demonstrated that a small proportion of genera accounted for a large proportion of seizures in both the US and EU. That said, there were substantial differences. The EU had 1.3 times as many seizures for coral by number of incidents than the US, and 1.9 times as many seizures of the elephant genera. The US, in contrast, had four times as many bird seizures.

Coral was the second most common EU seizure. At the grouping level, corals accounted for 21.1% of all EU imports while accounting for only 8.4% of US imports. Examination at the product level suggests that "whole corals" accounted for the majority of the EU coral seizures. This would imply that corals were imported primarily for jewelry and decorative uses as opposed to marine aquaria purposes. According to Green and Shirley (1999) and Wood et al. (2012), rising demand in Europe for coral has been noticed since the 1990s. The 1.3 time discrepancy in the coral seizures by number of incidents and 2.5 time discrepancy relating to whole coral imports is suggestive of a much stronger sociocultural demand for corals in the EU. This market puts pressure on coral reefs, one-fourth of which are considered damaged beyond repair, and another two-thirds under serious threat (e.g., Carpenter et al., 2008).

Another notable discrepancy between the US and EU was identified for the genus *Loxodonta*. A recent report has identified Spain, the UK, France, and Germany as the four countries that have seized the largest amount of ivory in the EU, all four have seized over one ton and together account for nearly three-quarters of the total EU volume (EIA, 2017). The substantial number of seizures occurring within Europe highlights the significant role the EU has in the global ivory trade (Martin and Stiles, 2008; EIA, 2017).

With regard to birds and garments disproportionately seized in the US as compared to the EU, the differences were striking: bird seizures in the US were four times that of the EU. This discrepancy may be explained by the EU ban on bird imports. As of 2006, wild birds are hardly legally imported to the EU due to protection measures in response to the growing threat of avian influenza (2005/94/E.G.; Cooney and Jepson, 2006). The trade in wild birds has dropped by 90% between 2005 and 2011, translating to a decrease from 1.3 million individuals traded to merely 130,000 (Reino et al., 2017). The existence of this trade ban could explain the comparatively higher levels of US bird imports.

The role of opportunity

The demand in these major markets could be driven by not only sociocultural practices but also opportunity in the form of proximity to the markets that can meet this demand. Some of the genera frequently seized in the United States, such as deer (*Cervus*), caiman, iguana, great horned owl and Canada goose, are specific to the North and South American continents. This could indicate that demand for this wildlife in the US could be a mere reflection of the availability and accessibility of these species in neighboring countries. Easier access to transportation routes from these countries into the United States in addition to US citizens vacationing in neighboring countries more often (and bringing back illicit wildlife souvenirs), could explain the reason why these species appear in the US more often than in the EU. Similarly, in the EU, the demand for tortoises, corals, chameleons, and parrots, some of which originate from Africa, such as the spur-thighed tortoise, the African grey parrot (*Psittacus erithacus*) or the common chameleon (*Chamaeleo chamaeleon*), could be driven by the relative proximity to and accessibility of these species for EU markets. For example, since the late 1990s, Europe is highly involved in the illegal trade in spur-thighed tortoises, where Morocco serves as its main supplier (Interpol, 1996; Bergin and Nijman, 2014). Consequently, certain populations of spur-thighed tortoises have suffered over a 90% decline in Morocco (Van Dijk et al., 2004).

Concentrations were also evident when seizures from exporting countries were examined. The findings revealed that not only did a handful of countries accounted for most exports into both the EU and the US, but also that these markets shared similar exporters, namely Thailand, China, Indonesia, and Vietnam. Importantly, 25% of the seizures made in the US were from its neighboring countries, Mexico and Canada. The relatively large proportion of imports from these two countries could be explained, in part, by busy travel between these countries and the US (Petrossian et al., 2016) or deer hunting patterns from Canada into the US (Ferrier, 2009). This pattern of proximity relating to seizures, however, was not as evident with EU seizures. Only 17% of seizures made in the EU were exported from non-EU states nearby such as North African nations, Switzerland, Russia, and Ukraine.

Policy implications

Comparing patterns of illegal wildlife imports into these two major markets and drawing conclusions about the similarities and differences in these patterns can help devise useful policy recommendations.

Where the US and the EU face similar problems, such as in the case of types of products and the common exporting countries, countries can work closely to devise collaborative prevention strategies. “Illegal markets will thrive as long as there is a public demand for their commodities” (Paoli, 2002: 88). Sociocultural demand patterns reflect the importance of influencing consumer behavior with consumer education campaigns (Ayling, 2015). Identified consumer patterns in the US and the EU can help inform (including education and guilt creation) both the purchasers and the traders about the serious threat of wildlife trade for endangered populations. This has to take into account different kinds of harms, as the illegal wildlife trade may affect humans, local and global environments, and animals (White, 2011). Because sociocultural shifts and trends in demand patterns are often intricate, idiosyncratic, and difficult to tackle – with some noteworthy exceptions[6] – policy changes in the destination countries can be rather easy and may have considerable impact.

At the respective countries' ports of entry, limited inspection resources can be allocated to the specific species groups (and genera), especially if these are imported from the identified countries known to be repeat "offenders." Measures, such as requirements that export documents be provided electronically and approved before the exports are initiated, and inspecting the imports more rigorously that involve these genera and the identified exporters at arrival, are likely to not only deter the exporters from shipping illegally obtained goods but also discourage them from engaging in obtaining such goods in the future. The reduction in the demand at these major markets may lead to the reduction in the supply (Schneider, 2008).

Another option would be in line with the EU-IUU Regulation. The EU-IUU Regulation requires that the EU assess exporting countries based on their efforts to address illegal fishing in their waters. These countries then receive green (good), yellow (warning), and red (failed) cards, where the latter means temporary trade bans on all the imports of fishery products until the country that received a red card demonstrated that it made significant steps to address illegal fishing within its waters (The EU IUU Regulation, 2016). Similarities in the types of products and the top exporters of these products indicate that not only there is similar demand for illegally harvested wildlife, but also this demand is met by a handful of suppliers (i.e., countries). Therefore, creating similar programs in the form of trade sanctions as a way of "strengthening formal surveillance" can be a useful tool in curbing illegal imports from these countries, as well as serve as a deterrent for other likely emerging exporters.

Finally, normative reactions, such as blaming, shaming, and rewarding (e.g., Braithwaite, 1989) may be successful in reducing the illegal wildlife trade. For example, campaigners have supplied scientific evidence regarding stocks and habitats of whales and reported on violations of quotas and hunting restrictions. By blaming countries and companies involved in the hunting, this resulted in norm development, raising awareness, and persuading states to embrace tougher regulations (Eilstrup-Sangiovanni and Bondaroff, 2014). From that perspective, the US and EU as being important wildlife consumers, or identified source states in the illegal wildlife market can be influenced by normative blaming and shaming reactions (e.g., Eilstrup-Sangiovanni and Bondaroff, 2014).

Future research and conclusions

That there is urgent need to stop the overexploitation of natural resources and the killing of wildlife is incontrovertible. This illegal activity has a multitude of harmful consequences not only for the wildlife involved, but also for humans and the world ecosystems. For some species, such as the West African black rhinoceros, illegal hunting has led to extinction. Thousands of other species suffer plummeting populations as a consequence of wildlife overexploitation. And if the current rates of overexploitation remain unchanged, it will soon be impossible for certain species to fully recover. Informing consumers with education campaigns and normative reactions, such as blaming, shaming, and rewarding actions of perpetrators or countries may be successful in reducing the trade in wildlife. More can be done to ascertain risk at ports of entry into major demand markets to increase the difficulty and risk of transporting illicit wildlife, and this paper offers one way of doing so. Unfortunately, we could not obtain reliable seizure data at the port level in both datasets, which precluded us from analyzing variation in seizures at the port level. Data on the number of law enforcement agents and wildlife shipments in each port was also unavailable so that we could calculate a seizure *rate* and determine whether the United States does indeed have a higher demand for protected wildlife or the higher number of seizures experienced in the US is merely a reflection of better enforcement techniques. Future research could attempt to obtain such data to identify patterns of the illegal wildlife trade at the more micro-level and determine the effectiveness of law enforcement efforts to curtail the trade. Alternatively, these patterns could be explained by a political economy approach, by arguing that species demand is driven by the organization of global capitalism (see Stretesky et. al., 2018; Rice, 2007). Empirical assessments of this viewpoint have been made in terms of global fisheries (Clausen and Clark, 2005) and overall species decline (McKinney et al., 2010; Lynch et al., 2015; Shandra et al., 2010), and future analyses that combine this viewpoint to that of the sociocultural demand explanation may reveal interesting results.

Notes

1 This may be due to TRAFFIC's focus on frequently publishing about mammals.
2 COR stands for coral, raw or unworked, excluding live or coral rock.
3 CPR stands for coral products.
4 ROC stands for live rock (e.g., coral rock).
5 Note that animal products may be placed in different categories: an animal skin may be placed in the category garments in the US and in the category skins in the EU.
6 For a long time Japan ranked as the world's largest importer of rhinoceros horn and ivory, but due to domestic awareness campaigns and social pressure, the market for these products declined significantly over the years (Kitade and Toko, 2016).

References

African Wildlife Foundation. (2015). The United States' little known role in wildlife crime. Retrieved February 2019 from https://www.awf.org/blog/united-states-little-known-role-wildlife-crime.

Appadurai, A. (1986). *The social life of things: Commodities in cultural perspective.* Cambridge: Cambridge University Press.

Ayling, J.M. (2015). A regulatory approach to demand reduction in the illegal wildlife market. *RegNet Research Paper No.* 2015/82.

Bergin, D., & Nijman, V. (2014). Open, unregulated trade in wildlife in Morocco's markets. *Traffic Bull*, *26*, 65–70.

Blundell, A. G., & Mascia, M. B. (2005). Discrepancies in reported levels of international wildlife trade. *Conservation Biology*, *19*(6), 2020–2025.

Böhm, M., Collen, B., Baillie, J.E., Bowles, P., Chanson, J., Cox, N., . . . Rhodin, A.G. (2013). The conservation status of the world's reptiles. *Biological Conservation*, *157*, 372–385. https://doi.org/10.1016/j.biocon.2012.07.015

Braithwaite, J. (1989). *Crime, shame and reintegration.* Cambridge: Cambridge University Press.

Carpenter, K. E., Abrar, M., Aeby, G., Aronson, R. B., Banks, S., Bruckner, A., . . . Wood, E. (2008). One-third of reef-building corals face elevated extinction risk from climate change and local impacts. *Science*, *321*, 560–563. doi: 10.1126/science.1159196

CITES. What is CITES? Retrieved from https://cites.org/eng/disc/what.php

Clausen, R., & Clark, B. (2005). The metabolic rift and marine ecology: An analysis of the ocean crisis within capitalist production. *Organization & Environment*, *18*(4), 422–444. https://doi.org/10.1177/1086026605281187

Cooney, R., & Jepson, P. (2006). The international wild bird trade: What's wrong with blanket bans?. *Oryx*, *40*(1), 18–23.

D'Cruze, N., Singh, B., Morrison, T., Schmidt-Burbach, J., Macdonald, D. W., & Mookerjee, A. (2015). A star attraction: The illegal trade in Indian Star Tortoises. *Nature Conservation*, 13, 1–19.

Duffy, R. (2010). *Nature crime: How we're getting conservation wrong.* New Haven, CT: Yale University Press.

Eaton, J. A., Shepherd, C. R., Rheindt, F. E., Harris, J.B.C., van Balen, S. B., Wilcove, D. S., & Collar, N.J. (2015). Trade-driven extinctions and near-extinctions of avian taxa in Sundaic Indonesia. *Forktail*, *31*, 1–12.

EIA (2017). Illegal trade seizures: Elephant ivory in Europe: Mapping the crimes. Retrieved from https://eia-international.org/illegal-trade-seizures-elephant-ivory-europe.

Eilstrup-Sangiovanni, M., & Bondaroff, T.N.P. (2014). From advocacy to confrontation: Direct enforcement by environmental NGOs. *International Studies Quarterly*, *58*(2), 348–361.

Ellis, R. (2005). *Tiger bone & rhino horn: The destruction of wildlife for traditional Chinese medicine.* Washington, DC: Islands Press.

Engler, M., & Parry-Jones, R. (2007). *Opportunity or threat: The role of the European union in global wildlife trade.* Brussels: Traffic Europe.

The EU IUU Regulation (2016). *Building on success; EU progress in the global fight against illegal fishing.* Retrieved from https://wwf.be/assets/RAPPORT-POLICY/OCEANS/ UK/IUU-report-01–02–16-web.pdf

European Commission (2016). Environment: Species. Retrieved from http://ec.europa.eu/environment/cites/species_en.htm

Fears, D. (2014). Overwhelmed US port inspectors unable to keep up with illegal wildlife trade. *The Washington Post*, October 17.

Ferrier, P. (2009). The economics of agricultural and wildlife smuggling. *Economic Research Service, United States Department of Agriculture*, *81*, 1–35.

Gini, C. (1921). Measurement of inequality of incomes. *The Economic Journal*, *31*(121), 124–126.

Gomez, A., & Aguirre, A. A. (2008). Infectious diseases and the illegal wildlife trade. *Animal Biodiversity and Emerging Diseases*, *1149*(1), 16–19. https://doi.org/10.1196/annals.1428.046

Green, E. P., & Shirley, F. (1999). *Global Trade in Coral.* World Conservation Monitoring Centre. World Conservation Press, Cambridge, UK.

Interpol (1996). *Internal Report: Noah.* Lyon: Interpol.

IUCN (2013). Almost one in five reptiles struggling to survive. www.iucn.org/content/almost-one-five-reptiles-struggling-survive

Jia, Q. (2012). *Traditional Chinese medicine could make "Health for One" True.* Washington, DC: WHO. Retrieved from www.who.int/intellectualproperty/studies/Jia.pdf?ua=1

Kalof, L. (2007). *Looking at animals in human history.* London: Reaktion Books.

Karesh, W. B., Cook, R. A., Bennett, E. L., & Newcomb, J. (2005). Wildlife trade and global disease emergence. *Emerging Infectious Diseases, 11*(7), 1000–1002. doi: 10.3201/eid1107.050194

Kitade, T., & Toko, A. (2016). Setting suns: The historical decline of Ivory and Rhino horn markets in Japan. TRAFFIC, Tokyo, Japan.

Kurland, J., & Pires, S. F. (2017). Assessing U.S. wildlife trafficking patterns: How criminology and conservation science can guide strategies to reduce the illegal wildlife trade. *Deviant Behavior, 30*(4), 375–391.

Kurland, J., Pires, S. F., McFann, S. C., & Moreto, W. D. (2017). Wildlife crime: A conceptual integration, literature review, and methodological critique. *Crime Science, 6*(4). https://doi.org/10.1186/s40163-017-0066-0

Liddick, D. R. (2011). *Crimes against nature: Illegal industries and the global environment.* Goleta, CA: ABC-CLIO.

Lynch, M. J., Long, M. A., & Stretesky, P. B. (2015). Anthropogenic development drives species to be endangered: Capitalism and the decline of species. In Sollund, R. A. (Ed.), *Green harms and crimes* (pp. 117–146). London, UK: Palgrave Macmillan.

Mander, Damien. (2012). *Damned if you do and damned if you don't: Legalizing the Rhino Poaching horn trade: My journey to Vietnam.* Victoria, Australia: International Anti-Poaching Foundation.

Marteache, N., Viollaz, J., & Petrossian, G. A. (2015). Factors influencing the choice of a safe haven for offloading illegally caught fish: A comparative analysis of developed and developing economies. *Crime Science, 4*(1), 32.

Martin, E., & Stiles, D. (2008). *Ivory markets in the USA.* Retrieved from http://savetheelephants.org/wp-content/uploads/2016/11/2008IvoryMarketsUSA.pdf

McKinney, L. A., Kick, E. L., & Fulkerson, G. M. (2010). World system, anthropogenic, and ecological threats to bird and mammal species: A structural equation analysis of biodiversity loss. *Organization & Environment, 23*(1), 3–31. https://doi.org/10.1177/1086026609358965

Moreto, W., & Pires, S. F. (2018). *Wildlife crime: An environmental criminology and crime* science perspective. Durham, NC: Carolina Academic Press.

Natusch, D.J., & Lyons, J.A. (2014). *Assessment of python breeding farms supplying the international high-end leather industry.* IUCN.

Nellemann, C., Henriksen, R., Raxter, P., Ash, N., & Mrema, E. (Eds). (2014). The environmental crime crisis: Threats to sustainable development from illegal exploitation and trade in wildlife and forest resources. A UNEP Rapid Response Assessment. United Nations Environment Programme and GRID-Arendal, Nairobi and Arendal. Retrieved from www.grida.no. ISBN: 978-82-7701-132-5.

Paoli, L. (2002). The paradoxes of organized crime. *Crime, Law and Social Change, 37*(1), 51–97.

Petrossian, G. A. (2015). Preventing illegal, unreported and unregulated (IUU) fishing: A situational approach. *Biological Conservation, 189*, 39–48.

Petrossian, G. A., & Clarke, R. V. (2014). Explaining and controlling illegal commercial fishing: An application of the CRAVED theft model. *British Journal of Criminology, 54*(1), 73–90.

Petrossian, Gohar A., Nerea Marteache, and Julie Viollaz. (2015). Where do "undocumented" fish land? An empirical assessment of port characteristics for IUU fishing. *European Journal on Criminal Policy and Research*, *21*(3), 337–351.

Petrossian, G. A., Pires, S. F., & van Uhm, D. (2016). An overview of seized illegal wildlife entering the United States. *Global Crime*, *17*(2), 181–201.

Pires, S. F. (2012). The illegal parrot trade: A literature review. *Global Crime*, *13*(3), 176–190. doi: 10.1080/17440572.2012.700180

Pires, S. F., & Clarke, R.V. (2011). Sequential foraging, itinerant fences and parrot poaching in Bolivia. *The British Journal of Criminology*, *51*(2), 314–335. https://doi.org/10.1093/bjc/azq074

Pires, S. F., & Clarke, R. V. (2012). Are parrots CRAVED? An analysis of parrot poaching in Mexico. *Journal of Research in Crime and Delinquency*, *49*(1), 122–146. doi: 10.1177/0022427810397950

Pires, S. F., Schneider, J. L., Herrera, M., & Tella, J. L. (2016). Spatial, temporal and age sources of variation in parrot poaching in Bolivia. *Bird Conservation International*, *26*(3), 293–306.

Reino, L., Figueira, R., Beja, P., Araujo, M. B., Capinha, C., & Strubbe, D. (2017). Networks of global bird invasion altered by regional trade ban. *Science Advances*, *3*(11). doi: 10.1126/sciadv.1700783

Renfrew, C. (1986). Varna and the emergence of wealth in prehistoric Europe. In Appadurai, A. (Ed.), *The social life of things* (pp. 141–168). Cambridge: Cambridge University Press.

Rhyne, A. L., Tlusty, M. F., & Kaufman, L. (2012). Long-term trends of coral imports into the United States indicate future opportunities for ecosystem and societal benefits. *Conservation Letters*, *5*, 478–485.

Rice, J. (2007). Ecological unequal exchange: Consumption, equity, and unsustainable structural relationships within the global economy. *International Journal of Comparative Sociology*, *48*(1), 43–72.

Rosen, G. E., & Smith, K. F. (2010). Summarizing the evidence on the international trade in illegal wildlife. *EcoHealth*, *7*(1), 24–32. doi: 10.1007/s10393-010-0317-y.

Schloegel, L. M., Picco, A. M., Kilpatrick, A. M., Davies, A. J., Hyatt, A. D., & Daszak, P. (2009). Magnitude of the US trade in amphibians and presence of Batrachochytrium dendrobatidis and ranavirus infection in imported North American bullfrogs (Rana catesbeiana). *Biological Conservation*, *142*, 1420–1426. doi: 10.1016/j.biocon.2009.02.007

Schneider, J. L. (2008). Reducing the illicit trade in endangered wildlife: The market reduction approach. *Journal of Contemporary Criminal Justice*, *24*(3), 274–295.

Shandra, J. M., McKinney, L. A., Leckband, C., & London, B. (2010). Debt, structural adjustment, and biodiversity loss: A cross-national analysis of threatened mammals and birds. *Human Ecology Review*, 18–33.

Simmel, G. (1978). *The philosophy of money*. London: Routledge & Kegan Paul.

Stiles, D., Redmond, I., Cress, D., Nellemann, C., & Formo, R. K. (Eds). (2013). *Stolen apes – The illicit trade in chimpanzees, gorillas, bonobos and orangutans*. A Rapid Response Assessment. United Nations Environment Programme. Norway: Birkland Trykkeri.

Still, J. (2003). Use of animal products in traditional Chinese medicine: Environmental impact and health hazards. *Complementary Therapies in Medicine*, *11*(2), 118–122.

Stretesky, P. B., McKie, R. E., Lynch, M. J., Long, M. A., & Barrett, K. L. (2018). Where have all the falcons gone? Saker falcon (falco cherrug) exports in a

global economy. *Global Ecology and Conservation*, *13*. https://doi.org/10.1016/j.gecco.2017.e00372
Swan, K., & Conrad, K. (2014). The conflict between Chinese cultural and environmental values in wildlife consumption. In *Routledge handbook of environment and society in Asia*. London: Routledge.
TRAFFIC. (n.d.). *Wildlife trade: What is it?* Retrieved from www.traffic.org/trade/
TRAFFIC (2015). *UN adopts resolution on tackling wildlife trafficking*. Retrieved from www.traffic.org/home/2015/7/30/un-adopts-resolution-on-tackling-wildlife-trafficking.html
Underwood, F. M., Burn, R. W., & Milliken, T. (2013) Dissecting the illegal ivory trade: An analysis of ivory seizures data. *PLoS ONE*, *8*(10). https://doi.org/10.1371/journal.pone.0076539
UNODC (2016). World Wildlife Crime Report: Trafficking in protected species. *UNODC Research* (New York). Retrieved from www.unodc.org/documents/data-and-analysis/wildlife/World_Wildlife_Crime_Report_2016_final.pdf
USFWS. (n.d.). *Wildlife trafficking*. Retrieved from www.fws.gov/international/wildlife-trafficking/
van Dijk, P. P., Corti, C., Mellado, V. P., & Cheylan, M. (2004). Testudo graeca. The IUCN Red List of Threatened Species. Version 2014.2.
van Uhm, D. P. (2016a). The illegal wildlife trade: Inside the world of poachers, smugglers, and traders (Doctoral dissertation, University Utrecht). doi: 10.1007/978-3-319-42129-2
van Uhm, D. P. (2016b). Illegal wildlife trade to the EU and harms to the World. In Spapens, T., White, R., and Huisman, W. (Eds.), *Environmental crime in transnational context: Global issues in green enforcement and criminology* London: Routledge.
van Uhm, D. P. (2018). The social construction of the value of wildlife: A green cultural criminological perspective. *Theoretical Criminology*, *22*(3), 384–401.
van Uhm, D. P., & Siegel, D. (2016) The illegal trade in black caviar. *Trends in Organized Crime*, *19*(1): 67–87.
Warchol, G. L. (2007). The transnational illegal wildlife trade. *Criminal Justice Studies*, *17*(1). doi: 10.1080/0888431042000167933
White, R. (2011). *Transnational environmental crime: Toward an eco-global criminology*. London: Routledge.
Williamson, E.M., Lorenc, A., Booker, A., & Robinson, N. (2013). The rise of traditional Chinese medicine and its materia medica: A comparison of the frequency and safety of materials and species used in Europe and China. *Journal of Ethnopharmacology*, *149*(2), 453–462.
Wood, E., Malsch, K., & Miller, J. (2012). International trade in hard corals: Review of management, sustainability and trends. *Proceedings of the 12th International Coral Reef Symposium*, Cairns, Australia, 9–13.
WWF/Dalberg (2012). *Fighting illicit wildlife trafficking: A consultation with governments*. (Gland, Switzerland).
Wyler, L. S., & Sheikh, P. A. (2013). *International illegal trade in wildlife: Threats and U.S. policy*. Washington, DC: Congressional Research Service.
Zabyelina, Y. G. (2014). The "fishy" business: A qualitative analysis of the illicit market in black caviar. *Trends in organized crime*, *17*(3), 181–198. https://doi.org/10.1007/s12117-014-9214-z

8 Examining factors predicting the use of wildlife killing by the US Fish and Wildlife Service across states

Leo Genco

Green and conservation criminologists have examined numerous issues related to the causes and prevention of wildlife crimes. Several studies have attempted to explain why wildlife crimes occur (Eliason, 2012, 2003, 2002; Wellsmith, 2011), while other studies examine how non-government organizations endeavor to control wildlife and other environmental crimes (Nurse, 2013a; Stretesky, Long and Lynch, 2017). Research has also examined animal cruelty enforcement (Wellsmith, 2011; Whiting, 2013), the illegal trade of wildlife across international borders (Bennett, 2011; Green, 1999; Nurse, 2013b; Petrossian, Pires and van Uhm, 2016; Zimmerman, 2003), and methods for preventing wildlife crime (Kurland and Pires, 2017; Petrossian, 2015; Lavorgna, 2014; Nurse, 2011; Pires and Moreto, 2011).

In the majority of those studies, wildlife crime is typically defined as illegal trade or poaching, or as behaviors that cause harm to wildlife by violating the law. However, other forms of wildlife killings also occur that are legal but which still create harms against wildlife. These latter harms/killings have not been widely examined in the green criminological literature (Lynch, 2019). For instance, the US Fish and Wildlife Service (USFWS) employs multiple methods to remove/control an animal that is defined as "in conflict" with humans. One of those methods is taking the life of the animal. As a method of controlling animals, killing seems contradictory to one of the official purposes of the USFWS, which is to protect wildlife from harm (Lynch, 2019).

The USFWS has to fulfill contradictory roles assigned to the agency by law. It must protect wildlife from harm, but at the same time prevent human-animal conflicts and protect the economic interest of humans, especially specific groups, such as farmers. As noted by Chambliss and Seidman (1971), both the construction of law and the behavior of law enforcement organizations is shaped by the interests of powerful economic and political groups and actors. More generally, this observation suggests that economic and political power shapes government actions. To examine this hypothesis the current study examines whether indicators of economic interests across US states are associated with the use of wildlife killings by USFWS from 2007 to 2013. State-level economic variables measuring farming, hunting and animal interest group resources along with political party membership indicators are employed to measure variations in animal killings by

USFWS across states. To establish the relevance of the model and variables, the next sections elaborate on the study's model and explanation of the variables.

Interests, values, and governance

Chambliss and Seidman (1971) suggest that the government is a dynamic entity influenced, for example, by multiple groups in conflicts over the structure, content and enforcement of law. These conflicts occur around different interests, at various organizational levels (e.g., local, state, national, in specific institutions) and involve differentials in and the application of different kinds of power. As Chambliss and Seidman note, these conflicts may involve struggles between different political parties, or groups with different economic or social interests. With that said, and according to these authors, over the long term there is a tendency for those in power to be able to maintain their power, preserving the existing system and leading to little significant change in law or its application and enforcement.

Nevertheless, it is common to assume that in a stratified society, various power differentials exist and multilayered conflicts between groups with assorted interests also exist. This common assumption would suggest that these conflicts would change law and its application over time. That is, in a nation where wealth is stratified widely, law is employed to define, maintain, and reinforce the boundaries of society and its link to the existing power structure within society (Chambliss and Seidman, 1971). As Chambliss and Seidman argue, in this way an existing system of values codified in law imposes those values on members of society in an effort to prohibit behaviors that conflict with the values of the powerful.

Outside of discussions of treadmill of production theory (Stretesky, Long and Lynch, 2013), green/conservation criminology has generally failed to explain the factors that shape environmental law and its content, and has failed to explore explanations for variations in the application of environmental law (Stretesky et al., 2017). Drawing on observations made by Chambliss and Seidman, the current study examines whether variations in different dimensions of power across states affects the behavior of the US Fish and Wildlife Service with respect to the killing of wildlife. Following Chambliss and Seidman, it is hypothesized that differences in the economic and political power of various interest groups (environmental, farming, hunting, etc.) across states may affect USFWS use of animal killings. These issues are described in the section that follows.

Groups related to animal law, protection, and business

Chambliss and Seidman (1971) argue that conflicts between various groups, and the economic and political resources those groups control, can affect which group's interests become represented in law, and can also affect whether and how the law is applied once created. In the context of the present study which examines the use of animal killings by the US Fish and Wildlife Service, it is necessary to identify relevant interest groups and to measure the kinds of power that they might potentially wield that, in turn, could potentially influence USFWS behavior. In order to identify groups that might affect the application of law by the US Fish and Wildlife Service, the theoretical and empirical literature addressing factors that affect the creation and codification of animal legislation was examined. Numerous studies have examined this issue (Upadhya, 2014; Burger, 2013; Boyd and Lamparello, 2013; Whiting, 2013; Nurse, 2013b; Iannacone, 2011; Wilde, 2010; Ascione and Sharpiro, 2009; Britton, 2006; Farve, 2010; Robbins, 2006; Pyc, 2002; Tannenbaum, 1995; Schmahmann and Polacheck, 1995). According to that literature, the following five groups have a significant relationship to or effect on the creation and application of wildlife laws: farm businesses, hunting businesses, pro-animal interest groups, the Republican Party, and the Democratic Party. These groups and measures of their power are described below.

Political parties

Studies have argued that the political left (i.e., liberals) supports animal protection (Allen, 2005; Lutz and Lutz, 2011; Koski, 2007). Kymlicka and Donaldson (2014), however, argued that liberals are hesitant to fully support animal rights, and that their political priority is to obtain equality for minorities. According to Kymlicka and Donaldson (2014), some liberals view promoting animal rights and minority rights as being in conflict, and view efforts to obtain rights for animals as undermining the significance of ensuring rights for minorities (Costello and Hodson, 2009; Kim, 2007). Studies have also found that more conservative political parties tend to reduce the likelihood of pro-animal legislation within a state (Allen, 2005; Lutz and Lutz, 2011), and that when republicans adopt animal protection laws, the scope and strictness of those laws are diminished (Koski, 2007).

In the present study, political party interests are hypothesized to affect the extent of animal killings by USFWS across states. The power of each political party is measured using a revenue measure, or as dollars of revenue donated to each party in each state.

Animal interest groups

There are numerous animal interest groups, and these groups may work in the interest of specific animals, or animals more generally (Allen, 2005; Koski, 2007) in efforts to influence the construction and implementation of animal rights/protection laws. In the current study, animal interest groups (AIG) were defined as groups that advocate for animal protection. Following the extant literature, farm-related interest groups were not included in this category. The effect of animal interest groups on the passage of animal legislation has not been consistent across studies. Some find animal interest group effect passage of animal-related legislation (Allen, 2005; Koski, 2007), while others have not

(Tauber, 2010). In the present study, the influence/power of animal interest groups is measured using an income/donation indicator, as described later in this chapter. It is hypothesized that states where animal interest groups have higher economic power/more donations will have lower levels of USFWS animal killings.

Farms and agricultural businesses

Farm businesses are the most discussed interest groups in the animal legislation literature (Lutz and Lutz, 2011; Whiting, 2013; Iannacone, 2011; Morris, 2013; Allen, 2005; Burger, 2013; Lacy, 2013). Prior studies have found that farm businesses promote different, though not contradictory, interest outcomes. Allen (2005) found that farm business does not affect the adoption of felony animal legislation but does lessen the severity of sanctions and fees associated with animal legislation (for similar results, see Koski, 2007). Lutz and Lutz (2011) found that the number of agricultural employees affected the amount of pro-animal legislation within a state. In additional, farm businesses also promote hunting, and farms also sell access to lands for hunting activities (Montgomery and Blalock, 2010; Mehmood, Zhang and Armstrong, 2003).

The extant literature does not explain the reason for the impact of farms on animal legislation. Lutz and Lutz (2011) argued that states with higher levels of agricultural employment might demonstrate less support for animal rights legislation. Allen (2005), however, has argued that the impact of the economic power of agriculture on animal related legislation might be more visible through indicators measuring land area devoted to agriculture. Allen also argues that in many states, agreements between agricultural land owners and hunters promote hunting and hunting access, perhaps undermining the promotion of animal protection legislation. Reflecting the above and Chambliss and Seidman's power-law argument, in the current study, farm business interests/influence are measured economically (i.e., as agricultural income), and would be expected to increase USFWS wildlife killings.

Hunting businesses

Hunting businesses and animal harm have historically been linked (Anderson and Loomis, 2006; Herman, 2014). Hunting businesses have an economic interest in protecting wildlife (Baen, 1997). According to Herman (2014), hunters lobbied for bag limits to protect a number of game species (Herman, 2014). Consistent with that argument, Mehmood, Zhang, and Armstrong (2003) found that private hunting businesses limit opportunities to hunt, protecting wildlife species from harms such as overhunting. Additionally, hunting businesses and hunters have a history of legislative involvement and have long supported hunting regulation and wildlife conservation (Anderson and Loomis, 2006). For example, in the US, hunters and anglers contributed a total over \$1.8 billion for wildlife funding per year (Association of Fish and Wildlife

Agencies, 2018). Typically, these funds are employed to preserve game wildlife, not non-game wildlife (Anderson and Loomis, 2006). Given that hunting businesses have an interest in preserving wildlife stock, it is hypothesized that hunting industry revenue would be inversely related to USFWS killings of wildlife.

Data

The study examines the potential effect of economic power and conflict on the use of wildlife killings by the US Fish and Wildlife Service. Data on animal killings and group economic assets covered the period from 2006 through 2013. Some of the census and economic data is not available for each of these years, and is reported only every five years. Thus the data for some years used in this study must be interpolated from trends between years for which official data are available. The data were then analyzed across years and states. Table 8.1 displays the descriptive statistics for the variables in the current study.

Data on wildlife killed (ANIMALS) by the USFWS was extracted from the US Department of Agriculture Animal and Plant Health Inspection Service Program Data Report, and is a count of wildlife killed or euthanized per method (traps, snares, firearms, gas, etc.) in each state by year. To ensure that the economic conditions preceded the amount of wildlife killed, reports from 2007 to 2013 were used as the dependent variable.

Independent variables

Economic variables were measured as monetary assets. Farm business revenue (FBR) and hunting businesses revenue (HBR) assets were measured as revenue from business operations. For animal interest groups (AIG), the Republican Party (REP), and the Democratic Party (DEM), assets were measured from annual donations. These data were extracted from a variety of sources, organized by state, and expressed as a ratio per $10,000. Because the data for each state was in time series form, missing data were interpolated.

AIG revenue data were extracted from the Internal Revenue Service (IRS) Exempt Organizations Business Master File, National Center of Charitable Statistics (NCCS) database. The database defines animal interest groups by the IRS National Taxidermy of Exempt Entities codes, specifically code D20. Animal interest groups are non-profit animal protection and welfare organizations that supply human care, protection, and control of animals and also investigate instances of animal cruelty. Revenue was considered the total amount of revenue reported to IRS on 990 forms. The hypothesis for this variable is as follows:

> **Hypothesis 1**: As the revenue for animal interest groups within a state increases, the amount of animals killed by the United States Fish and Wildlife Service (USFWS) is expected to decrease.

Table 8.1 Descriptive statistics

	2007		*2008*		*2009*		*2010*		*2011*		*2012*		*2013*	
	Mean	*SD*	*Mean*	*SD*	*Mean*	*SD*	*Mean*	*SD*	*Mean*	*SD*	*Mean*	*SD*	*Mean*	*SD*
Dependent														
KILLED (1,000)	47.999	104.179	96.938	236.744	81.438	222.407	96.162	226.151	73.703	164.594	66.417	137.227	84.834	186.652
Independent														
FBR	200	222.76	200	226.60	200	227.67	200	229.72	200	232.47	200	235.71	200	239.28
AIGR	200	271.30	200	270.49	200	268.05	200	267.46	200	268.21	200	269.90	200	272.26
HBR	200	178.65	204.08	169.78	204.08	163.17	204.08	159.41	204.08	158.19	204.08	159.10	204.08	180.72
REP	200	375.419	200	310.31	200	315.16	200	159.41	200	300.73	200	281.85	200	360.60
DEM	200	290.34	204.08	315.01	200	249.83	200	332.39	200	310.16	200	309.16	200	313.91
EDU	26.15	4.60	26.74	4.69	27.08	4.72	23.78	4.75	24.37	4.78	28.10	4.81	28.44	4.85
URBAN	2,511,102	2,594,684	2,552,004	2,637,878	2,566,223	2,656,539	2,312,596	2,675,518	2,365,131	2,694,810	2,608,882	2,714,407	2,623,101	2,734,304

FBR data was extracted from the 2002, 2007, and 2012 Census of Agriculture. According the National Agricultural Statistics Service (NASS), farms are bases of operations that produce and sell greater than or equal to $1,000 of agricultural products. FBR includes income from contracts with operators (renters, sharecroppers, etc.). Individual farms can post negative incomes, and these were included in calculating aggregate FBR. The hypothesis related to this variable is as follows:

> **Hypothesis 2**: As the revenue of farm businesses within a state increases, the amount of animals killed by the USFWS is expected to increase.

HBR data were extracted from the National Survey of Fishing, Hunting, and Wildlife Associated Recreation Census from the years 2001, 2006, and 2011. The measure includes total expenditures for fishing and hunting recreation by individuals aged 16 or older. Equipment for fishing and hunting, trip-related expenses (lodging, transportation, and food), and miscellaneous expenses (membership dues, contributions, licenses, land and leasing ownership, magazines, tags, stamps, and permits) were used to create the expenditures. This study hypothesized the following:

> **Hypothesis 3**: As the revenue for hunting businesses within a state increase, the amount of animals killed by the USFWS is expected to decrease.

There are two political party revenue variables, one for the Republican and one for the Democratic party in each state. This variable measures donations and was extracted from the online database provided by the National Institute on Money in State Politics. There are two hypotheses for political parties:

> **Hypothesis 4:** As the revenue of the Republican Party within a state increases, the amount of animals killed by the USFWS is expected to increase.
> **Hypothesis 5**: As the revenue of the Democratic Party within a state increases, the amount of animals killed by the USFWS is expected to decrease.

Control variables

Following the results of prior research and hypotheses, it is important to add a few control variables to account for other factors that might potentially influence animal killings across US states.

EDUCATION

Allen (2005) argued that higher-educated groups have a historically influential effect on animal-related protection legislation; yet education has rarely been controlled in studies examining wildlife/animal regulation. Indeed, the only empirical study to examine the association between education and animal legislation is Lutz and Lutz (2011). Using a cross-state index on animal rights, they found a marginal, positive relationship ($p = .10$) between education and animal rights laws. In the current study, education is measured by the percent of the population in each state over age 25 with a bachelor's degree or higher as found in the American Community Survey. Consistent with prior studies, it is hypothesized that as level of education across states increases, animal killings by the USFWS will decrease.

URBAN LIVING (URBAN)

Tauber (2010) and Allen (2005) found that urbanization had a significant, positive relationship with animal welfare legislation. Based upon those results, it can be suggested that urbanization might also be related to USFWS animal killings. Here, urbanization is measured as the amount of urbanized land area in each state.

Analytic plan

The data were first analyzed using descriptive statistics to determine the characteristics of the data (e.g., trends in data). Second, once characteristics were defined, a bivariate analysis was conducted to determine whether multicollinearity existed among independent variables. Third, the data were analyzed using panel regressions. A series of statistical tests were used to determine the best means to analyze the data. The Hausman test was used to determine if the model should focus on fixed effects. The Breusch-Pagan Lagrange multiplier was used to determine if there were significant differences across states; this test also determines if a pooled regression should be used instead. Then variables were regressed using numerous models. Lastly, incident rate ratios are reported instead of normal regression coefficient. Incident rate ratios (IRR) are ratios that determine the likelihood of the outcome out of the population at risk at a certain time. Ratios are bounded in relation to the value of 1. An IRR value below 1 indicates a negative relation or a reduction in the rate, while a value above 1 indicates a positive relationship.

Results

The first noticeable observation was the consistency in the mean values for each economic variable in the data (Table 8.1); however, the variation is noticeably larger than the mean which indicates overdispersion. Thus, a negative binomial panel regression was used to compensate for any violation of assumption for statistical regressions.

Table 8.2 shows the bivariate pairwise correlations between variables. From the table, there are many significant correlations. Animal interest group revenue (0.138), hunting business revenue (0.210), and farm business revenue (0.158)

Table 8.2 Correlation matrix of variables after variables were logged (N = 50)

	KILLED	*FBR*	*AIGR*	*HBR*	*REP*	*DEM*	*EDU*	*URBAN*
KILLED	1							
FBR	0.158*	1						
AIGR	0.138*	0.315*	1					
HBR	0.210*	0.620*	0.600*	1				
REP	0.129	0.402*	0.696*	0.633*	1			
DEM	0.081	0.353*	0.781*	0.579*	0.786*	1		
EDU	−0.105	−0.215*	0.355*	−0.160*	0.035	0.288*	1	
URBAN	0.196*	0.419*	0.793*	0.687*	0.711*	0.744*	0.105	1

*$p < .01$.

all have significant correlation with animals killed. Notably, there are multiple significant correlations that suggest concerns of multicollinearity among the independent variables. Although the pairwise correlations were modest at best, ordinary least squares (OLS) models were employed to estimate variance inflation factors (VIF) among the variables. VIFs did not exceed recommended values. Therefore, is it assumed there is no threat of multicollinearity.

In addition, the Breusch-Pagan Lagrange multiplier (Breusch and Pagan, 1979) indicated that the data were best suited for a random effect compared to a pooled regression. The Hausman test indicated the data should be examined using random effects compared to fix effects models (see also Long et al. this volume). Lastly, a modified Wald's test for panel data confirmed that there was no homoskedasticity.

In Table 8.3, four models were used to examine the relationships between variables. Model 1 contains only variables that pertain to businesses (FBR, HBR) or organizations (AIGR). From Model 1, two variables were significant, FBR (farm businesses; IRR = 0.85, SE = .04, $p < .001$) and HBR (hunting businesses; IRR = 1.89, SE = .18, $p < .001$). The concentration of HRB is positively related to USFWS animal killings, rejecting Hypothesis 3. For every $10,000 spent on hunting businesses, the number of animals killed by USFWS increased by a factor of 1.89. For FBR, the relationship is negative, rejecting Hypothesis 2, since for every $10,000 in FBR, animal killings decline by a factor of 0.85. Animal interest group economic resources were unrelated to animal killing, rejecting Hypothesis 1.

Model 2 incorporated political organization variables (DEM and REP), measuring economic power into the model along with farm and organizational economic power measures. The results of Model 2 were nearly identical to those found in Model 1, and the additional variables have no statistically significant impact. These results lead to the rejection of both Hypotheses 4 and 5.

The third model incorporated control variables for education and urban. Adding those variables reduced the effect of FBR and HBR, those relationship

Table 8.3 Panel negative binomial: regressing economic variables on wildlife killed

Variables	*Model 1*	*Model 2*	*Model 3*	*Model 4*
	IRR	*IRR*	*IRR*	*IRR*
FBR	0.85***	0.85***	0.87**	0.89**
	(.04)	(.04)	(.05)	(.05)
AIGR	0.91	0.86	0.57**	0.05**
	(.09)	(.10)	(.10)	(.06)
HBR	1.89***	1.85***	1.61***	1.47**
	(.18)	(.18)	(.19)	(.18)
REP	–	1.01	0.99	–
		(.06)	(.05)	
DEM	–	1.06	0.99	–
		(.07)	(.07)	
EDU	–	–	1.04*	1.04
			(.02)	(.02)
URBAN	–	–	1.89***	.87
			(.36)	(.33)
AIGR*URBAN	–	–		1.18**
				(.09)
Constant	.30**	.32**	0.00***	18.78
	(.13)	(.14)	(0.00)	(100.26)
Observations	339	338	338	339
Wald Chi2(5)	56.24	57.39	66.61	73.747
Prob>Chi2	0.00	0.00	0.00	0.00
Log Likelihood	–3,751.7209	–3,738.7083	–3,731.6781	–3,741.9185

Error terms are in parentheses.

*$p < .05$. **$p < .01$. ***$p < .001$.

remained significant. The addition of the control variables also produced a significant effect of AIGR. The effect was in the expected negative direction, and this result now supported Hypothesis 1. Among the control variables, both urban living (IRR = 1.89, SE = .36, p <.001) and education (IRR = 1.04; SE = .02, p < .05) were significant. The more urban area in a state, the higher the number of animals killed by USFWS, suggesting perhaps an increase in human-animal conflicts in highly urbanized states (Lynch forthcoming). At the same time, as education increased, so too did USFWS animal killings, which may reflect an overlap between states with large urban areas, and educational attainment. This outcome suggests a possible suppression effect from urbanization. A fourth model was introduced retaining any variable that was significant in at least in one prior model, and adding an interactive variable between urban living and animal interest group revenue.

In Model 4, the interactive variable was significant, but urban living lost its significance. The loss of significance does not mean that urban living does not have a significant impact on the number of animals killed, but that the effect of urban living is conditioned through an interaction with animal interest groups' economic resources.

It should also be noted that in Model 4, all of the organizational variables were significant. Consistent with the results from prior models, the relationship between FBR and HBR with USFWS animal killings rejects the respected hypotheses, while the results for animal interest groups supported the proposed hypothesis. Overall, the results suggest the volume of wildlife killed by the USFWS is affected by economic factors/economic power at state level.

Discussion

Drawing on prior literature, this study examined whether the economic and political power of business, organizational and political groups was associated with the distribution of animal killings by the US Fish and Wildlife Services across US states. It was hypothesized that the economic resources of hunting businesses, farm businesses, and animal interest groups would influence the volume of animal killings initiated by USFWS across states. The results indicated that (1) as hunting revenue increased, USFWS animal killings increased, contradicting the hypothesis; (2) as farming business revenue increased, USFWS animal killings decreased, also contradicting the hypothesis; and (3) as animal interest group resources increased, USFWS animal killings declined, supporting the hypothesis. What can be made of these results?

First, hunting business had the largest effect on the number of wildlife killed by the USFWS. The specifics of the political stance of hunting lobbyists are roughly known, and hunting lobbyists generally support the protection of wildlife to preserve hunting populations (Anderson and Loomis, 2006). Hunting business should then have a negative relationship with wildlife deaths, but the findings suggest otherwise. There may be more to the relationship. Baen (1997) discussed how farms offer land for hunting recreation, which allow more monetary gains for farms; this also allows farms to protect crops against unwanted invaders. This suggests that farm and hunting businesses may have a relationship. An interactive term between the two groups was created, but when added to the analysis, the term was not significant. Since regressions are derived from linear analyses (Pampel, 2000), the relationship between farm and hunting businesses may not be linear. Unfortunately, the current study had no theoretical or empirical justification to investigate such a relationship; however, the findings and discussion provide some support to warrant future studies.

Second, farming businesses revenue was predicted to have a positive relationship to USFWS animal killings, though the opposite result was discovered in the empirical analysis. It is noteworthy that the effect of farm business is small. Some readers may expect a larger effect in general; however, this study indicted the opposite. It would be intuitive for farms to have a small relation with animal protection or killing. According to Tannenbaum (1995), farms want to protect their animal assets. Farm owners desire enough protection for livestock without impeding the opportunity to earn income from hunting access sales (Montgomery and Blalock, 2010). In other words, farm business, unlike hunting businesses, do not have a single goal, which appears to lessen their relationship to the outcome.

Other explanations that may explain this relationship may be impacted by other dimensions of human and animal conflict within a state, not between them. That is, certain states may have agricultural business where there are animals that threaten the safety of crops and other livestock. This rational would fall in line with Tannenbaum (1995) who argued that animal legislation protected animal investment. In this case, some states may support the killing of wildlife that threatens farm businesses' investments. Since this is more of a case-by-case relationship within a state, the relationship may not appear at the national level. Therefore, the relationship may suggest that farms may have a larger influence on state agencies than federal agencies within states that requires further assessment (e.g., across locations within states).

Third, the second hypothesis concerning the expected negative effect of animal interest groups on USFWS animal killings was not supported until control variables were included within the model. The concern with these findings was that there was a suppression effect between urban living and animal interest groups. After an interaction was added, animal interest groups become the most influential variable; however, this relationship may be an artifact of the analysis. First, the animal interest groups effect may be conditioned by urbanization. As urban living grows, support for animal interest groups expands. Musto, Faraone and Cellini (2014) argued that there is enhanced support for animal welfare in urban citizens due to the difference in how urban and rural citizens obtain food. Rural citizens have a more direct relationship with animals and have different uses for animals. Urban citizens have a disconnection between the products they buy and the animal sources of those products, particularly food (Musto et al., 2014). Thus, urban citizens place a different value on animals than rural inhabitants. Second, urbanization requires natural resources and replaces the physical environment with human development (Lynch et al., 2017; Lynch and Stretesky, 2016). As a result, there is less opportunity for wildlife to exist in a state as urban living expands, wildlife habitat is minimized, and wildlife populations decline, minimizing the quantity of wildlife available (or which "need") to be killed.

Fourth, contrary to expectations, neither political party hypothesis was supported. Prior studies suggest that the relationship between political parties and animal interests and rights may be affected by the level of analysis. At the federal level, prior studies suggest that political parties have little to no impacts on federal animal regulations (Kymlicka and Donaldson, 2014; Costello and Hodson, 2009; Kim, 2007; for exceptions, see Lutz and Lutz, 2011; Koski, 2007). In the current case, the outcome under examination was the behavior of a federal agency. Consistent with prior literature, it appears that local political party resources do not have an impact on the behavior of USFWS with respect to animal killings. This may be the result of how political parties and their lobbying direct the use of party-related economic resources with respect to the kinds of environmental issues they address.

Earlier in this manuscript, Chambliss and Seidman's (1971) argument that economic power and conflicts affects the values which the government promotes, and the behavior of governments was reviewed. Based on Chambliss and Seidman's argument, hypotheses concerning the relationship between of society and the economic power they control and the distribution of animal killings by the US Fish and Wildlife Service were proposed. Overall, while the results indicate an association between economic power and USFWS animal killings, the effects were generally (with the exception of the animal interest group hypothesis) not in the expected direction. Thus, there was some support for the general argument proposed by Chambliss and Seidman, but not for the specific hypotheses derived herein to express those power relationships. In other words, while the finding did not support the specific direction of the hypotheses, they nevertheless supported Chambliss-Seidman assumptions about group economic power affecting government behavior. Those results are consistent with other tests of conflict theory within criminology (Liska, Chamblin and Reed, 1985; Williams and Drake, 1980).

Criminologists have performed few empirical studies related to green crimes and their control. The present study illustrated that Chambliss and Seidman's argument provides a useful mechanism for examining how economic power affects government social control of animal populations. Future research can build on this approach and should explore other operationalizations of power relationships. In addition, one limitation in the present study was the measure of animal interest groups and their economic power. That data is available only in limited forms, and there are problems with missing data over time. Thus caution also needs to be applied when interpreting the results for animal interest groups.

There is also the opportunity for other empirical studies examining the social control of animals, government-wildlife conflict management activities, and the effects of animal advocacy on the construction and application of wildlife and other animal protection laws. For instance, while there is a large body of literature in the medical fields that debates the welfare and treatment of animals in medical research (Ferdowsian, 2011; Latham, 2012; Morrison and Purpura, 1990; Rollin, 2012; Schrengohst, 2011; Westermann-Cicio, 2002), few studies examine how the experimental animal industry affects the construction of and application of animal related laws, or violations of animal protection laws at animal research facilities.

There is a wealth of data on the enforcement of animal protection laws that has yet to be examined by green/conservation criminologists. Examining these various sources of data can reveal new issues for criminologists to explore and new understanding of green crime and justice.

References

Allen, M. D. (2005). Laying Down the Law? Interest Group Influence on State Adoption of Animal Cruelty Felony Laws. *The Policy Studies Journal*, *33*(3), 443–457.

Anderson, L. E. and Loomis, D. K. (2006). Balancing Stakeholders with an Imbalanced Budget: How Continued Inequities in Wildlife Funding Maintains Old Management Styles. *Human Dimensions of Wildlife*, *11*(6), 455–458.

Ascione, F. R. and Sharpiro, K. (2009). People and Animals, Kindness and Cruelty: Research Directions and Policy Implications. *Journal of Social Issues*, *65*(3), 569–587.

Association of Fish and Wildlife Agencies (2018). Hunting in America: An Economic Force for Conservation. From the International Association of Fish and Wildlife Agencies Website: www.fishwildlife.org/afwa-informs/research.

Baen, J. S. (1997). The Growing Importance and Value Implications of Recreational Hunting Leases to Agricultural Land Investors. *Journal of Real Estate Research*, *14*(3), 399–414.

Bennett, E. (2011). Another Inconvenient Truth: The Failure of Enforcement Systems to Save Charismatic Species. *Oryx*, *45*, 476–479.

Boyd, M. E. and Lamparello, A. (2013). Vulnerable Victims: Increasing Animal Cruelty Sentences to Reflect Society's Understanding of the Value of Animal Lives. *Connecticut Law Review*, *45*(5), 31–40.

Breusch, T. S. and Pagan, A. R. (1979). A Simple Test for Heteroscedasticity and Random Coefficient Variation. *Econometrica*, *47*(5), 1287–1294.

Britton, A. H. (2006). Bones of Contention: Custody of Family Pets. *Journal of the American Academy of Matrimonial Lawyers*, *20*(1), 1–38.

Burger, K. A. (2013). Solving the Problem of Puppy Mills: Why the Animal Welfare Movement's Bark Is Stronger Than Its Bite. *Journal of Law and Policy*, *43*(1), 259–284.

Chambliss, W. J. and Seidman, R. B. (1971). *Law, order, and power*. Reading, MA: Addison-Wesley Pub. Co.

Coleman, C. and Moynihan, J. (1996). *Understanding crime data: Haunted by the dark figure* (Vol. 120). Buckingham: Open University Press.

Costello, K. and Hodson, G. (2009). Exploring the Roots of Dehumanization: The Role of Animal-Human Similarity in Promoting Immigrant Humanization. *Group Processes & Intergroup Relations*, *13*(1), 3–22.

Eliason, S. (2002). From the King's Deer to a Capitalist Commodity: A Social Historical Analysis of the Poaching Law. *International Journal of Comparative and Applied Criminal Justice*, *36*(2), 133–148.

Eliason, S. (2003). Illegal Hunting and Angling: The Neutralization of Wildlife Law Violations. *Society & Animals*, 11(3), 225–243.

Eliason, S. (2012). Trophy Poaching: A Routine Activities Perspective. *Deviant Behavior*, *33*(1), 72–87.

Farve, D. (2010). Living Property: A New Status for Animals within the Legal System. *Marquette Law Review*, *93*(3), 1021–1071.

Ferdowsian, H. (2011). Human and Animal Research Guidelines: Aligning Ethical Constructs with New Scientific Developments. *Bioethics*, *25*(8), 472–478.

Green, A. (1999). *Animal underground*. New York: Public Affairs/Perseus Books.

Herman, D. J. (2014). Hunting and American Identity: The Rise, Fall, Rise and Fall of an American Pastime. *The International Journal of the History of Sport*, *31*(1), 55–71.

Iannacone, S. (2011). Felony Animal Cruelty Laws in New York. *Pace Law Review*, *31*(2), 748–770.
Kim, C. J. (2007). Multicultural Goes Imperial. *Du Bois Review: Social Science and Research on Race*, *4*(1), 233–249.
Koski, C. (2007) Regulatory Choices: Analyzing State Policy Design. *Law and Policy*, *29*(4), 407–434.
Kurland, J. and Pires, S. F. (2017). Assessing U.S. Wildlife Trafficking Patterns: How Criminology and Conservation Science Can Guide Strategies to Review the Illegal Wildlife Trade. *Deviant Behavior*, *38*(4), 375–391.
Kymlicka, W. and Donaldson, S. (2014). Animal Rights, Multiculturalism, and the Left. *Journal of Social Philosophy*, *45*(1), 116–135.
Lacy, S. (2013). Hard to Watch: How Ag-Gag Laws Demonstrate the Need for Federal Meat and Poultry Industry Whistleblower Protections. *Administrative Law Review*, *65*(1), 127–154.
Latham, S. R. (2012). U.S. Law and Animal Experimentation: A Critical Primer. *Animal Research Ethics*, *42*(1), S35–S39.
Lavorgna, A. (2014) Wildlife Trafficking in the Internet Age. *Crime Science*, *3*(5), 1–12.
Liska, A. E., Chamblin, M. B. and Reed, M. D. (1985). Testing the Economic Production and Conflict Models of Crime Control. *Social Forces*, *64*(1), 119–136.
Lutz, B. J. and Lutz, J. M. (2011). Interest Groups and Pro-Animal Rights Legislation. *Society & Animals*, *19*(3), 261–277.
Lynch, M. J. (2019). To Protect and Kill: United States Fish and Wildlife Service's Management of Human-Wildlife Conflict, 1996–2011. *Society & Animals*, *27*, 174–196.
Lynch, M. J., Long, M. A., Stretesky, P. B. and Barrett, K. L. (2017). *Green criminology*. Berkeley, CA: University of California.
Lynch, M. J. and Stretesky, P. B. (2016). *Exploring green criminology: Toward a green criminological revolution*. New York, NY: Routledge.
Mehmood, S., Zhang, D. and Armstrong, J. (2003). Factors Associated with Declining Hunting License Sales in Alabama. *Human Dimensions of Wildlife*, *8*(4), 243–262.
Montgomery, R. and Blalock, M. G. (2010). The Impact of Access, Cost, Demographics, and Individual Constraints, on Hunting Frequency and Future Participation. *Academy of Marketing Studies Journal*, *14*(2), 115–131.
Morris, M. C. (2013). Improved Nonhuman Animal Welfare Is Related More to Income Equality Than It Is to Income. *Journal of Applied Animal Welfare Science*, *16*(3), 272–293.
Morrison, A. R. and Purpura, D. P. (1990). Legislative Shift on Animal Research. *BioScience*, *40*(3), 172.
Musto, M., Faraone, D. and Cellini, F. (2014). The Role of Cognitive Styles and Sociodemographic Characteristics in Consumer Perceptions and Attitudes toward Nonhuman Animal Welfare. *Journal of Applied Animal Welfare Science*, *17*(3), 198–215.
Nurse, A. (2011). Policing Wildlife: Perspectives on Criminality in Wildlife Crime. *Papers from the British Criminology Conference*, *11*, 38–53.
Nurse, A. (2013a). Privatising the Green Police: The Role of NGOs in Wildlife Law Enforcement. *Crime, Law and Social Change*, *59*(3), 305–318.
Nurse, A. (2013b). *Animal Harm: Perspectives on Why People Harm and Kill Animals*. New York, NY: Routledge.

Pampel, F. C. (2000). *Logistic Regression: A Primer*. Thousand Oaks, CA: Sage.

Petrossian, G. A. (2015). Preventing Illegal, Unreported and Unregulated (IUU) Fishing: A Situational Approach. *Biological Conservation*, *189*, 39–48.

Petrossian, G. A., Pires, S. F. and van Uhm, D. P. (2016). An Overview of Sized Illegal Wildlife Entering the United States." *Global Crime*, *17*(2), 181–201.

Pires, S. F. and Moreto, W. D. (2011). Preventing Wildlife Crimes: Solutions That Can Overcome the "Tragedy of the Commons." *European Journal on Criminal Policy and Research*, *17*(2), 101–123.

Pyc, J. (2002). Changing the Animal Legal Paradigm Using the United States Tax Code. *Capital University Law Review*, *30*(4), 947–972.

Robbins, J. (2006). Recognizing the Relationship between Domestic Violence and Animal Abuse: Recommendations for Change to the Texas Legislature. *Texas Journal of Women and the Law*, *16*(1), 129–147.

Rollin, B. E. (2012). The Moral Status of Invasive Animal Research. *Animal Research Ethics*, *42*(1), S4–S6.

Schmahmann, D. R. and Polacheck, L. J. (1995). The Case against Animal Rights. *Boston College Environmental Affairs Law Review*, *22*(4), 747–781.

Schrengohst, K. L. (2011). Animal Law: Cultivating Compassionate Law: Unlocking the Laboratory Door and Shining Light on the Inadequacies and Contradictions of the Animal Welfare Act. *Western England Law Review*, *33*(3), 855–900.

Stretesky, P. B., Long, M. A. and Lynch, M. A. (2013). *The Treadmill of Crime: Political Economy and Green Criminology*. London: Routledge.

Stretesky, P. B., Long, M. A. and Lynch, M. A. (2017). Trends in the Formation of Environmental Enforcement International Non-Governmental Organizations, 1950–2010. *Globalizations*, *14*(4), 627–642.

Stretesky, P. B., Lynch, M. A., Long, M. A. and Barrett, K. A. (2017). Does the Modernization of Environmental Enforcement Reduce Toxic Releases? An Examination of Self-Policing, Criminal Prosecutions and Toxic Releases in the United States, 1988–2012. *Sociological Spectrum*, *37*(1), 48–62.

Tannenbaum, J. (1995). Animals and the Law: Property, Cruelty, Rights. *Social Research*, *62*(3), 539–607.

Tauber, S. (2010). The Influence of Animal Advocacy Groups in State Courts of Last Resort. *Society and Animals*, *18*(1), 58–74.

Upadhya V. (2014). The Abuse of Animals as a Method of Domestic Violence: The Need for Criminalization. *Emory Law Journal*, *63*(5), 1163–1209.

Wellsmith, M. (2011). Wildlife Crime: The Problems of Enforcement. *European Journal on Criminal Policy and Research*, *17*(2), 125–148.

Westermann-Cicio, M. L. (2002). Animal Rights and Experimentation: Exploring and Examining the Issue on the Internet. *Internet Reference Services Quarterly*, *7*(4), 41–53.

Whiting, T. L. (2013). Policing Farm Animal Welfare in Federated Nations: The Problem of Dual Federalism in Canada and the USA. *Animals*, *3*(4), 1086–1122.

Wilde, K. (2010). Animal Law in Nevada: All Bark and No Bite. *Nevada Law Journal*, *11*(1), 254–281.

Williams, K. R. and Drake, S. (1980). Social Structure, Crime and Criminalization: An Empirical Examination of the Conflict Perspective. *The Socialogical Quarterly*, *21*, 563–575.

Williamson, E. M., Lorenc, A., Booker, A. and Robinson, N. (2013). The Rise of Traditional Chinese Medicine and Its Materia Medica: A Comparison of the Frequency and Safety of Materials and Species Used in Europe and China. *Journal of Ethnopharmacology*, *149*(2), 453–462.
Zimmerman, M. E. (2003). The Black Market for Wildlife: Combating transnational Organized Crime in the Illegal Wildlife Trade. *Vanderbilt Journal of Transnational Law*, *36*, 1657–1690.

9 The ten-year (1999–2008) trend in hazardous waste violations and punishments in the United States from US EPA Resource Conservation and Recovery Act data

Michael J. Lynch

Despite the rapid growth of green/conservation criminology, environmental crime and its enforcement remains understudied. This is surprising in some contexts. In the US, for example, federal and state agencies maintain a wide range of environmental enforcement data (Lynch, Burns and Stretesky, 2014; Burns and Lynch, 2004). Twenty years ago, criminologists could justify overlooking environmental crime/enforcement issues due to limited data access, but this is no longer true.

Significant research addressing environmental/green issues has emerged. However, empirical studies remain an exception (see studies in this volume). Less attention has been paid to pollution in that literature. It is increasingly important for criminologists to draw attention to environmental crime/enforcement assessments in an era where researchers in other disciplines have drawn attention on environmental problems as among the major concerns facing societies today (McMichael and Butler, 2011; Shah et al., 2013), which require the use of empirical data to address (Jorgenson, 2016; Jorgenson, Schor and Huang, 2017). It is widely recognized in scientific literature that rapid ecological destruction and deficient environmental policy, planning, and enforcement plays a role in producing ecological harms, and that significant planetary boundaries have been or are on the verge of being crossed (Rockstron et al., 2009), threatening global ecological stability. Pollution has become so widespread it is now considered ubiquitous (e.g., Brauer et al., 2006; Renberg, Bindler and Brannvall, 2001). In the US, Gallup polls indicate increased public concern with environmental protection since 2011 (www.gallup.com/poll/1615/environment.aspx). Green/conservation criminologists can play important roles in addressing the concerns noted above.

The present study does so by examining patterns of hazardous waste crime and punishment in the US (1999–2008) from the US Environmental Protection Agency's (EPA) Resource Conservation and Recovery Information System (RCRIS). RCRIS data includes information reported by states under the Resource Conservation and Recovery Act (RCRA) related to the handling of hazardous waste and the enforcement of hazardous waste regulations. Here, we use these data to examine the distribution of pollution, pollution violations, and punishments for environmental offenses.

Background

Few studies on the extent of environmental violations exist in the criminological literature. Extant criminological literature has long examined the theoretical rationale that underlies environmental enforcement practices (e.g., DiMento, 1993), while ignoring the distribution and frequency of environmental crimes and environmental enforcement. RCRIS data provides access to environmental violations officially reported across states related to hazardous waste management, and it is useful for establishing some measure of the extent of the officially recognized volume of toxic waste crime in the US and how those crimes are addressed across states.

Technically, RCRA violations are not crimes from a traditional criminological definition of crime, which requires a violation of ***criminal law*** (Lynch, Stretesky and Long, 2015). Most RCRA violations are ***administrative or regulatory violations***, and few are treated as criminal violations by environmental regulators (Burns and Lynch, 2004). The decision to treat any particular RCRA violation criminally is not made directly in the law, but on a case-by-case basis by regulators. That decision does not necessarily reflect the nature of or harm caused by the offense but likely reflects organizational constrains such as funding, which in turn affects staffing and thus the monitoring and enforcement of these offenses. In the present study, in place of the arbitrary designation of some RCRA violations as criminal, we treat all RCRA violations as environmental crimes as defined within green criminology (Lynch et al., 2017).

Empirical studies examining the scope of environmental crime are limited and often dated. In an early study, Cohen (1992) noted that even though the Refuse Act of 1899 allowed for criminal prosecution of discharges to waterways, there were only 25 criminal prosecutions for environmental crimes in the US by the end of the 1970s. The trend in environmental prosecutions changed significantly in the 1980s, following establishment of the EPA's Office of Criminal Enforcement (OCE). Once OCE was established, criminal prosecutions referred by US EPA to the Department of Justice increased to approximately 100 cases per year by the early 1990s (from 1983 through 1990, $N = 703$, or about 87.9 per year). Criminal cases account for a small percentage of environmental crimes, and are infrequent compared to the opportunity for such crimes at the nation's 3.1 million registered EPA facilities (Lynch, 2017).

Cohen's 25-year-old study is among the few studies addressing the volume of environmental crime from criminal case data. Instead of assessing the volume of environmental offending, extant research has employed environmental data to test theories of crime or responses to environmental crimes (i.e., deterrence; e.g., Karpoff, Lott and Wehrly, 2005); to address the processing of environmental crime cases (Billiet, Blondiau and Rousseau, 2014; Billiet and Rousseau, 2014); or to report on individual environmental offender and firm characteristics (Rousseau, 2009). Studies that provide evidence of the widespread nature of environmental crimes draw on data that extend beyond criminal environmental cases. For example, Ozymy and Jarrell (2012) employed data from the Texas Emission Event Report Database to examine air upset events or accidental chemical releases due to startup, shutdown, and maintenance processes and fugitive air releases (Title 30, Texas Administrative Code, §101.1). Ozymy and Jarrell examined upset events at oil refineries in Corpus Christi, Texas, from 2003 to 2008. They discovered nearly 7,500 individual air emission upset events, or about 1,250 per year (3.42/day) that technically are not counted as environmental crimes. Extrapolating from their findings, one can derive an estimate of the national scope of this problem. The US Energy Information Administration reports that were 142 operating oil refineries in the US, with six of those facilities located in Corpus Christi. Using Ozymy and Jarrell's results, it can be estimated that these 142 oil refineries produce more than 177,000 upset events annually. Exclusion of this type of environmental crime from prior efforts to estimate the volume of environmental crimes in the US dramatically underrepresent the scope of these offenses (for discussions, see Burns and Lynch, 2004; Lynch, Burns and Stretesky, 2014).

The lack of such studies has several consequences for criminology and the study of crime. First, criminologists cannot easily refer to prior studies to ascertain how many environmental crimes exist, because such studies are rare. Second, in the absence of such studies, criminologists must visit primary sources and collect data each time they desire to refer to the extent of environmental crime. In contrast, numerous studies of street crime estimate the volume of those crimes, and the lack of a comparable literature can lead criminologists to overlook including environmental crime estimates in discussions of the "crime problem" in the US. Omitting environmental crimes from crime estimates paints an inaccurate picture of crime, and depicts the crime problem as comprising entirely street crime offenses; perhaps this could be avoided if a sufficient, relevant literature on environmental crime's extent was more readily available.

Although the present study draws attention to environmental crimes, its scope is restricted by referring only to hazardous waste crimes. There are numerous types of environmental crimes, and examining only one of those forms underrepresents the full scope of the problem. Attention is draw to RCRA offenses here because RCRA violations have largely gone unaddressed in the criminological literature.

One advantage of using RCRA data is that they contain information on reported offenses, potential offenders, enforcement actions and fines. As a result, these data can be used to assess assumptions commonly made in the criminological literature about, for example, the lenient punishment of environmental offenders (see Lynch, 2017).

The RCRA data and measures

The RCRIS/RCRA used here are available from the US EPA[1] and cover the years 1999–2008, which at the time the data were collected was the most recent data available. US EPA aggregates these data at the state level and over time, so the data represents a ten-year aggregation by state. Data is not available for individual years.

RCRA data includes information on hazardous waste transactions required to be reported to state agencies, and on state-level responses to hazardous waste violations. State agencies report required information to EPA annually, and EPA aggregates those data. State-level data include information on the following, which are assessed in the remainder of this chapter: (1) hazardous waste handlers (which includes waste generators, transporters, and "treaters, storers and disposers," or TSDs); and (2) information on responses to environmental offenders/offenses, which includes the number of (A) significant acts of non-compliance (SNC), (B) formal environmental violations (#V), (C) correction actions (C-Action), (D) enforcement actions (#E), (E) punishments (#P), and (F) fine amounts. Corrective actions require compliance with RCRA provisions, but are not considered punishments, while enforcement actions, which also correct RCRA noncompliance, are issued as punishments. In the current study, fine data was collapsed into categories found in Table 9.4. These data can only be employed to construct a summary image of officially reported hazardous waste crime, enforcement and punishment.

The US EPA regards RCRA as a compliance and control measure, meaning these data can be used to assess compliance with hazardous waste permits, hazardous waste violations, and hazardous waste clean-up activities. RCRA data have been used to examine questions related to environmental justice (Benn and Gupta, 1997; Spina, 2015), hazardous waste facility siting (Saha, 2005) and compliance with environmental regulations (Stafford, 2002, 2003). Overall, however, few studies employ RCRA data, and there is little mention of RCRA in the criminological literature.

In portions of the analysis, the data are presented as an *offense rate* per 100 handlers to aid in cross-state comparisons to adjust for wide variations in the number of toxic waste handler across states (range = 9–1,846). Variation in toxic waste handlers is likely to affect discovered cases, and thus these data need to be standardized based on the number of hazardous waste handlers to aid in their analysis. The number of handlers is important because it clearly affects the opportunity for hazardous waste crimes across states.

Results

Table 9.1 displays aggregated RCRA data for each category by state for 1999–2008. The results section is divided into three parts: (1) a summary of the aggregate data, (2) a description of state level variability in reported environmental crime, and (3) a discussion of fines for environmental offenses across states.

Table 9.1 Number of RCRIS handlers and violation outcomes, 1999–2008, by state

State	*Number Handlers*	*SNC*	*C- Action*	*#V*	*#E*	*#P*
AK	52	0	10	10	15	0
AL	294	5	67	210	203	23
AR	178	4	37	99	98	27
AZ	295	3	96	146	145	10
CA	1,846	37	152	662	602	113
CO	115	4	38	82	81	23
CT	369	6	97	219	209	39
DE	70	3	12	46	44	4
FL	502	17	57	249	234	112
GA	347	2	66	257	256	72
HA	55	4	5	30	27	7
IA	141	3	42	104	104	8
ID	27	4	7	13	13	6
IL	733	27	141	302	301	32
IN	503	13	104	366	354	85
KS	188	12	24	155	157	39
KY	279	9	56	214	214	38
LA	1,039	14	70	174	185	22
MA	605	6	35	272	262	40
MD	506	5	26	77	50	10
ME	94	0	21	63	60	9
MI	658	10	95	407	406	27
MN	269	2	28	200	184	43
MO	458	23	55	280	221	25
MS	173	4	19	49	44	21
MT	50	3	9	20	21	2
NC	467	4	55	308	306	34
ND	14	0	5	14	13	0
NE	68	5	19	52	52	12
NJ	774	11	90	291	284	108
NH	157	0	6	81	82	27
NM	52	4	17	32	32	8
NV	76	3	7	55	50	16
NY	1,779	13	113	491	492	71
OH	1,652	40	242	839	843	85
OK	145	1	24	106	105	10
OR	183	3	15	111	114	19
PA	1,373	12	129	423	203	70

(Continued)

Table 9.1 (Continued)

State	*Number Handlers*	*SNC*	*C- Action*	*#V*	*#E*	*#P*
RI	92	2	10	73	76	12
SC	289	9	48	226	223	47
SD	17	0	2	2	3	1
TN	558	7	48	328	319	21
TX	1,778	15	246	606	513	98
UT	97	5	21	45	46	21
VA	294	11	76	212	203	33
VT	40	0	8	34	35	1
WA	942	4	35	282	285	11
WI	554	3	45	316	318	8
WV	101	6	26	81	79	21
WY	9	4	6	6	5	2
Total	21,345	382	2,658	9,719	9,232	1,552
Mean*	426.9	7.64	53.2	194.4	184.6	35.04

*Ten-year/state means (divided by 10 = one year/state mean).

Aggregate data across states

Handlers: During the period examined, there were 21,345 RCRA-permitted facilities, which ranged from 9 (Wyoming) to 1,846 (California), with a mean of 427 facilities/state (Table 9.1). As noted, variation in the number of handlers across states affects the number of violations/enforcement actions/punishments that occur across states. Thus, Table 9.2 shows standardized rates of violations, enforcement actions, and so forth per 100 handlers in each state.

Violations: There were 9,719 violations (#V) across states (Table 9.1), or an average of 194.4 violations per state over ten years (19.4 violations per state/year). In the aggregate, the volume of these crimes is rather small.

The aggregate *violation rate* (Table 9.2) for facilities was 43.3 per 100 handlers across states. Unfortunately, due to the nature of this data, repeat offenses/offenders cannot be distinguished and described separately. Repeat offenses are counted as part of the total, and thus the violation rate (43%) does not mean that 43% of all handlers are violators. It has long been recognized that some corporations, just like some street offenders, have extensive criminal records. For example, Sutherland (1949) found that corporations averaged 14 criminal acts apiece. Here, since the number of repeat offenders is unknown, *these data can only be employed to examine violations and not violators.*

Across states over ten years, the number of violations varied from 2 in South Dakota (with 17 facilities, South Dakota's violation rate was 17.7%)

to 839 in Ohio (Ohio's violation rate was 51.0%). Twenty-two states had a greater number of violations than the mean (mean = 194.4), and 11 states had more than 300 violations each. Those states (California, Illinois, Indiana, Michigan, North Carolina, New York, Ohio, Pennsylvania, Tennessee, Texas, and Wisconsin) contained 53.2% of facilities and 52% of violations, indicating a relationship between number of facilities in a state and violations (see further discussion below).

Enforcement actions: For violations, 95% met with some type of enforcement actions (#E), while only 16% of cases (N = 1,552) drew a financial penalty (#P).[2] However, 28.8% of violations also met with a corrective actions (#C = 2,658). Corrective actions begin as administrative orders (RCRA, sections 3008(a) and (h), 3013, and 7003), and involve efforts to clean up hazardous waste contamination. Failure to comply with a corrective action can lead to civil or criminal actions and sanctions. Corrective actions and enforcement actions may overlap in any given case (a handler may receive both responses), and in the present data it is impossible to determine the number of cases in which both corrective actions and an enforcement action co-occur.

Significant noncompliance: There were 382 cases of *significant noncompliance* (SNC), or an average of only 0.764 acts of SNC *per state per year*. As a rate, there were only 0.0047 acts of SNC per 100 handlers.

SNC determinations are made under the Hazardous Waste Civil Enforcement Response Policy (hwww.epa.gov/compliance/resources/ policies/civil/rcra/finalerp1203.pdf). According to EPA (www.epa-echo.gov/echo/ dfr_data_dictionary.html#sumd1), a SNC occurs when:

> the site has been determined to *cause actual exposure* or has *a substantial likelihood of causing exposure* to a hazardous waste or constituent; *is a chronic or recalcitrant violator*; or *deviates substantially* from the terms of a permit, order or agreement, or from RCRA statutory or regulatory requirements. Under the RCRA program, the SNC designation is removed for a given site when the site is in full physical compliance with statutory and/or regulatory requirements.

The policy's wording (emphasized in italics above) gives EPA administrators significant discretion in applying the SNC label. As noted, a SNC designation can be removed, and thus the rather small number of SNC designations may indicate that numerous sites correct conditions that earned an SNC rating.

State level variability

There is significant variability in hazardous waste crimes across states in RCRA data visible in different environmental crime indicators.

Significant noncompliance: Six states reported no SNCs over the ten-year period (Alaska [54 handlers]; Maine [94 handlers]; North Dakota [14 handlers]; New Hampshire [157 handlers]; South Dakota [17 handlers]; and Vermont

[40 handlers]). This outcome seems rather implausible, since across these handlers and years there were 1.372 million potential violation days. Moreover, based on the estimated likelihood of an SNC violation among the remaining states (2/100 facilities), one would expect to discover about 7.5 acts of SNC across the 376 handlers in these ten states.

From these data, it appears that states with a small number of handlers tend to have fewer SNCs. That possibility was assessed by examining the correlation between number of handlers and SNC violations, which yielded a significant, positive correlation ($r = 0.730$; $p = 0.01$). That relationship was explored further by examining grouped SNC data. The 20 states with five or more SNC violations contain 292 (77.7%) of all SNC violations, and the violation rate among these states was 20 times higher than for states that had four or fewer SNC violations, suggesting that this group drives this relationship. This may occur because states with the largest number of handlers devote more resources to the social control of these offenses, and have better control, inspection, and reporting practices – which is an area for future research, since no prior studies have addressed this issue. Nevertheless, this result indicates the possibility of underreporting of SNC violations in some states, and that perhaps SNC designations are an organizational outcome, affected not by behavior of handlers but by the ability or willingness of environmental agencies in different states to employ a SNC designation.

Violations: Because the number of violations across states is likely a product of opportunity (e.g., the number of handlers in each state), the number of violations were transformed into rates per 100 handlers to make them comparable across states in Table 9.2.

Table 9.2 RCRIS violation rates per 100 handlers across US states, 1999–2008

State	*Number Handlers*	*SNC*	*C-Action*	*#V*	*#E*	*#P*
AK	52	0	19.2	19.2	28.9	0
AL	294	1.7	22.8	71.4	69.1	7.8
AR	178	2.2	20.8	55.3	55.1	21.1
AZ	295	1.0	32.5	49.5	49.2	3.4
CA	1,846	2.0	8.2	35.9	32.6	6.1
CO	115	3.5	33.0	71.3	70.4	20.0
CT	369	1.6	26.3	59.4	56.6	10.6
DE	70	4.3	17.1	65.7	62.9	5.7
FL	502	3.4	9.2	49.6	46.6	22.3
GA	347	0.6	19.0	74.1	73.8	20.8
HA	55	7.3	9.1	54.6	49.1	12.2
IA	141	2.1	29.8	73.8	73.8	5.7

State	*Number Handlers*	*SNC*	*C-Action*	*#V*	*#E*	*#P*
ID	27	14.8	25.9	59.1	59.1	22.2
IL	733	3.7	23.3	41.2	41.1	4.4
IN	503	2.6	20.7	72.7	70.4	16.9
KS	188	6.4	12.8	82.5	83.5	20.8
KY	279	3.2	20.1	76.7	76.7	13.6
LA	1,039	1.4	6.3	16.8	17.8	2.1
MA	605	1.0	5.8	45.0	43.3	6.6
MD	506	1.0	5.1	15.2	9.9	2.0
ME	94	0.0	2.2	6.7	6.4	9.6
MI	658	1.5	14.4	61.9	61.7	4.1
MN	269	0.7	10.4	74.4	68.4	16.0
MO	458	8.9	12.0	61.1	48.3	5.5
MS	173	2.0	11.0	28.3	25.4	12.1
MT	50	6.0	19.0	40.0	44	4.0
NC	467	0.9	11.8	66.0	65.5	7.3
ND	14	0.0	35.7	100	92.9	0.0
NE	68	7.4	27.9	76.5	76.5	17.7
NJ	774	1.4	11.6	37.6	36.7	14.0
NH	157	0.0	3.8	51.6	52.2	17.2
NM	52	7.7	32.7	61.5	61.5	15.4
NV	76	4.0	9.2	72.4	65.8	21.1
NY	1,779	0.7	6.4	27.6	27.7	4.0
OH	1,652	6.1	14.7	50.8	51.1	5.2
OK	145	0.7	16.6	7.4	7.2	6.9
OR	183	1.6	8.2	60.6	62.2	1.0
PA	1,373	0.9	9.4	30.8	7.5	5.1
RI	92	2.2	10.2	79.4	82.6	13.0
SC	289	3.1	16.6	78.2	77.2	16.3
SD	17	0.0	11.8	11.8	17.6	5.9
TN	558	1.3	8.6	58.8	57.2	3.8
TX	1,778	0.8	13.9	34.1	28.9	5.5
UT	97	5.2	21.6	46.4	47.4	21.7
VA	294	3.7	25.9	72.1	69.1	11.2
VT	40	0.0	20.0	85.0	87.5	2.5
WA	942	0.4	3.7	29.9	35.3	1.2
WI	554	0.5	8.1	57.0	57.4	1.4
WV	101	5.9	25.7	80.2	78.2	20.8
WY	9	44.4	66.7	66.7	55.6	22.2
Mean*		3.64	17.14	54.08	52.50	10.32

*Ten-year/state mean (divided by 10 = one year/state mean).

As noted, violations vary significantly across states (2 to 839). The violation rate also varies widely, from 6.7/100 in Maryland to 100/100 in North Dakota, with a mean of 45.5/100 across all states. In 28 states, the violations rate was greater than 50/100. At the high end, eight states had violation rates exceeding 75/100 handlers, while at the low end, six states exhibit violation rates below 20/100 handlers. Since there may be multiple violations at the same facility and the RCRAinfo data does not allow those cases to be identified, caution should be used in interpreting the meaning of these results (i.e., as noted earlier, these are *violation data*, and cannot be used to suggest anything about the number of *violators*). These data, however, indicate significant variability in the rate at which violations are discovered, which again, is likely a product of how handlers and the resources states employed to discover those violations are distributed (for discussion, see Opp, 2011). Nevertheless, this result indicates that the 28 states with violation rates above 70%, either spend more effort enforcing RCRA, *or* have handlers that engage in more risky behavior, producing more violations. Further studies are needed to determine how risk-related behaviors (Gibbs et al., 2009), facility characteristic and enforcement practices affect violation rates, and absent such studies, one can only guess which factors might influence these rates.

Enforcement actions: There is significant variability in enforcement actions per 100 handers across states, which range from 6.4/100 handlers in Maryland to 92.9/100 handlers in North Dakota (mean = 43.3). In four states the rate of enforcement could be considered *very* low: fewer than 10/100 handlers. At the other end of the scale, enforcement rates are very high (greater than 75/100 handlers) in eight states. Interestingly, the correlation between the violation rate and the enforcement rate is quite high (r = 0.9757). This is likely the result of the structure of detecting and enforcing environmental regulations. That is, the organizational process that discovers violations and the organizational structure for punishing violations must be highly integrated for this to occur. While criminologists have often examined how crime control budgets or number of police affect the distribution of crime, this issue has not been sufficiently examined in the environmental crime literature, creating the opportunity for such research in the future.

Punishment/fines: These data also indicate significant variability in the rate of punishment/100 handlers (Table 9.2) across states, which varied from 0/100 (Alaska) to 22.3 (Florida), with a mean of 7.3 fines/100 handlers. Since these data do not contain seriousness score measures or comments on the nature of the offense, we cannot address how seriousness affects the rate of punishment, and this is a question future research might address. It would be possible to construct such a study from individual cases file information on RCRA violations.

The correlation between the enforcement and punishment rate is low (r = 0.2672) and nonsignificant (p = 0.061). Thus, while the relationship between discovering hazardous waste crime and enforcement actions may be organizationally driven, a similar result does not hold for the relationship between enforcement and punishment. This result opens up an interesting avenue for research: attempting to explain or discover factors across states that may affect the likelihood of punishing environmental violators.

These data can be employed to assess whether the enforcement and punishment outcomes might be a function of the concentration of handlers within each state. To do so, Pearson's r correlations between number of handlers and the three outcomes described above were calculated: (1) the violation rate; (2) enforcement rate; and (3) punishment rate. For violations/handlers, $r = -0.3636$ ($p = 0.01$). The negative correlation indicates that *the more handlers within a state, the lower the violation rate*. That result again suggests that the discovery of violations may be a function of the organization of environmental enforcement. For the enforcement rate/handlers association, $r = -0.4177$ ($p = 0.01$). This result is not surprising given the strong correlation between violations and enforcement noted early, but *again indicates that states with more toxic waste handlers enforce RCRA less*. For the punishment rate/handlers relationship, $r = -0.1705$ and *is not significant* even when $p = 0.1$. In short, while the violation rate and the enforcement rate are negatively correlated with handlers, the rate of punishment appears unrelated to handlers. In other words, while the concentration of handlers decreases known violations and enforcement action, some other (unknown) factors affect the application of fines. Again, this finding opens up the potential for a wide variety of research studies that attempt to address this issue.

Examining this finding further, Table 9.3 shows differences in violation and enforcement outcomes for states with 500+ handlers compared to states with fewer than 500 handlers in Part A. Part A shows that while the 16 states with 500+ handlers contain about 74% of all hazardous waste handlers, for every measure of environmental crime, the percent of cases in each category is below 74%. In contrast, for the 16 states with fewer than 500 handlers, the percentage of cases in each category is higher than expected. That comparison confirms the results above and indicates that the more handlers a state has, the less rigorously they appear to enforce hazardous waste law. This result may indicate that there is a treadmill of production effect on enforcement (Stretesky, Long and Lynch, 2013), which would explain the co-occurrence of reduced enforcement in states where the treadmill of toxic production is located.

In Table 9.3, Part B, the state handler relationship is disaggregated further. Here we see additional evidence that states with the largest number of handlers discover, enforce and punish violators at levels below any other handler grouping. Part B also shows that compared to other handler groupings, the 11 states with 251 to 499 handlers typically discover, enforce and punishment outcomes *well above* expected levels (i.e., in this case, greater than 15.7%).

This is also generally true for the other handler categories (101–250, and fewer than 100), but the relationship is visibly weaker. These results imply that the relationship between handlers and hazardous waste crimes/enforcement discovered using Pearson's r are not linear, and hides something about that process. Thus, research with data not available for this study are required to make further sense of that relationship.

Table 9.3 RCRIS comparisons. Part A: 16 states with 500 or more handlers versus remaining states. Part B: Grouped by number of hazardous waste handlers (*N* = number of states in each category).

Part A

	16 States	*34 States*
#Handlers	15,802 (74.0%)	5,543 (26.0%)
SNC	222 (58.1%)	160 (41.9%)
C-Action	1,628 (63.3%)	1,030 (38.7%)
#Violations	5,678 (58.4%)	4,041 (41.6%)
#EnforcementActions	4,732 (51.3%)	4,500 (48.7%)
#Penalties	886 (57.1%)	666 (42.9%)
#Fines	1,031 (57.5%)	768 (42.5%)

Part B

#Handlers	*N*	*Handlers*	*SNC*	*C-Action*	*#Violations*	*Enforcement*	*Penalties*	*Fines*
>500	16	15,802	222	1,628	5,678	4,732	886	1,031
%	32	74.0	58.1	61.3	58.4	51.3	57.1	66.7
251–499	11	3,349	86	640	2,678	3,154	350	221
%	22	15.7	22.5	24.1	27.6	34.2	22.7	14.3
101–250	8	1,381	37	231	868	867	215	195
%	16	6.5	9.7	8.7	8.8	9.4	13.9	12.6
<100	15	813	37	159	495	479	101	98
%	30	3.8	9.7	6.0	5.1	5.2	6.6	5.5
Total	50	21,345	382	2,658	9,719	9,232	1,552	1,545

Fine amounts: Fine data is presented in Table 9.4. Before beginning, it should be noted that the number of fines is greater than the number of punishments. This is due to the fact that the number of punishments excludes corrective actions, which are administrative fines and not, technically speaking, punishments. Unfortunately, RCRAinfo does not disaggregate fines by type.

Table 9.4 RCRIS handlers and fine outcomes, 1999–2008, by state

State	*Number Handlers*	*Fine Group in $ Range*							*Total*
		<1k	*<10k*	*<50K*	*<100k*	*<250k*	*<500*	*>500*	
AK	52	0	1	0	0	0	0	0	1
AL	294	1	6	15	2	2	0	0	26
AR	178	1	9	12	3	2	0	0	27
AZ	295	0	2	7	1	3	1	0	14
CA	1,846	1	36	54	12	10	4	3	120
CO	115	0	9	13	0	0	1	0	23
CT	369	0	7	36	5	4	0	2	54
DE	70	1	1	2	2	0	0	0	6
FL	502	8	55	54	4	2	0	0	123
GA	347	6	35	16	1	1	0	0	59
HA	55	0	2	2	2	1	0	1	7
IA	141	0	1	7	2	0	0	0	10
ID	27	0	1	2	0	1	1	0	5
IL	733	0	7	21	8	3	2	1	42
IN	503	0	36	55	5	0	0	1	97
KS	188	0	9	25	6	2	0	0	42
KY	279	14	5	17	4	1	0	0	41
LA	1,039	1	8	16	1	4	1	3	34
MA	605	1	26	16	3	3	0	0	49
MD	506	0	10	3	2	0	0	0	15
ME	94	0	3	8	0	0	0	0	11
MI	658	1	5	13	5	6	1	0	31
MN	269	2	32	11	2	1	0	1	49
MO	458	0	11	18	2	1	1	0	33
MS	173	0	12	10	3	1	0	1	27
MT	50	0	1	2	0	1	0	0	4
NC	467	0	9	20	6	1	0	0	36
ND	14	0	1	0	0	0	0	0	1
NE	68	0	3	7	3	0	0	1	14
NJ	774	8	75	31	4	2	0	0	120
NH	157	1	18	9	0	2	1	0	31

(Continued)

Table 9.4 (Continued)

State	*Number Handlers*	*Fine Group in $ Range*							*Total*
		<1k	*<10k*	*<50K*	*<100k*	*<250k*	*<500*	*>500*	
NM	52	0	0	3	2	3	0	0	8
NV	76	0	15	0	1	0	0	0	16
NY	1,779	0	23	44	5	5	1	0	78
OH	1,652	0	14	62	8	4	2	4	94
OK	145	1	3	7	1	0	0	0	12
OR	183	0	14	7	0	1	0	0	22
PA	1,373	8	40	22	6	1	0	0	77
RI	92	0	2	9	2	0	3	0	16
SC	289	0	18	31	0	0	0	1	50
SD	17	0	1	0	0	0	0	0	1
TN	558	0	15	11	1	1	0	0	28
TX	1,778	6	47	50	10	7	2	3	119
UT	97	0	8	4	2	1	1	0	16
VA	294	0	13	20	1	3	0	0	37
VT	40	0	3	0	0	0	0	0	3
WA	942	0	3	6	2	3	0	0	14
WI	554	0	2	6	3	2	1	1	15
WV	101	0	5	12	2	2	0	0	21
WY	9	0	2	0	0	0	0	0	2
Total	21,345	65	664	796	129	92	23	23	1,792
Mean*	426.9	1.3	13.28	15.9	2.58	1.84	0.46	0.46	35.8

*Ten-year mean (divide by 10 = annual state mean).

There was at least one fine in every state, which ranged from 1 (both Alaska and South Dakota) to 123 (Florida). There was a total of 1,792 fines, or about 179/year or 17.9/state/year. Numerically speaking, the volume of fines is quite low compared to the number of offenses. For example, while there is a mean of 194.4 violations and 184.6 enforcement actions per state, there are only 35.8 punishments and about 18 fines per state. Summarizing that result, 18.4% of violations lead to punishment, while just 9.2% of violations received fines.

Punishments were concentrated in eight states that produced 46% (N = 824) of the punishments: California (120), Florida (123), Indiana (97), New Jersey (120), New York (74), Ohio (94), Pennsylvania (77), and Texas (119). Those eight states were also home to 45.5% of facilities, and thus the distribution of punishment is similar to the distribution of facilities across states.

In terms of fine ranges, the majority of fines (nearly 82%) fell across two categories: fines between $1,001 to $10,000 (37.1%) and between $10,001 and $50,000 (44.4%). Thus, 82% of fine were $50,000 or less. There were only

23 cases (1.28% of penalties) where the fine was "very large" – in excess of $500,000. Four states accounted for 13 (56.5%) very large fines. In most cases ($N = 9$), *those states employed a very large fine on only one occasion across the ten-year time period.* There were only ten fines in excess of $1 million. The largest fines were meted out in three cases: Illinois (a $7.7 million fine to ExxonMobil in 2005); Texas (a $9.9 million fine to Shell Oil in 2001); and Mississippi (a $20 million fine to Morton International, fined in 1996 but paid in 2001). The $37.6 million in fines meted out in these three cases represented *42% of all fines levied* during the entire ten-year period across all states. This finding is consistent with assumptions widely made in the criminological literature about punishments applied to corporations: they are often relatively small, and large fines are rare.

At the other end of the fine scale, a fine of only $1 was applied four times. Overall, these fine data support contentions that corporations are typically fined relatively small amounts (less than $50,000), and that while major fines are an exception rather than the rule, major fines comprise a majority of the total fines meted out.

Rates of punishment: Table 9.5 and Figure 9.1 displays alternative measures of the rate of punishment. Column 1 in Table 9.5 displays the rate of SNC per 100 handlers across states, and is included for comparison. Column 2 shows the rate of punishment for every 100 violations, which in this case is the sum of corrective actions and number of violations.

Table 9.5 RCRIS (1999–2008) violation rates; significant non-compliance per 100 handlers; penalties per 100 corrective actions and violations

State	*Number Handlers*	*SNC/100 Handlers*	*Penalties/100 Corrective + Violations*
AK	52	0	0
AL	294	1.7	8.3
AR	178	2.2	19.9
AZ	295	1.0	6.6
CA	1,846	2.0	13.9
CO	115	3.5	19.2
CT	369	1.6	12.3
DE	70	4.3	6.9
FL	502	3.4	36.6
GA	347	0.6	22.3
HA	55	7.3	20.0
IA	141	2.1	5.1
ID	27	14.8	20.0
IL	733	3.5	7.2

(*Continued*)

Table 9.5 (Continued)

State	*Number Handlers*	*SNC/100 Handlers*	*Penalties/100 Corrective + Violations*
IN	503	2.6	18.1
KS	188	6.4	21.8
KY	279	3.2	14.1
LA	1,039	1.3	9.0
MA	605	1.0	13.0
MD	506	1.0	9.7
ME	94	0	10.8
MI	658	1.5	5.4
MN	269	0.7	18.9
MO	458	5.0	7.5
MS	173	2.3	30.9
MT	50	6.0	6.9
NC	467	0.9	9.4
ND	14	0	0
NE	68	7.4	16.9
NJ	774	1.4	28.4
NH	157	0	31.0
NM	52	7.7	16.3
NV	76	4.0	25.8
NY	1,779	0.7	11.8
OH	1,652	2.4	7.9
OK	145	0.7	7.7
OR	183	1.6	15.1
PA	1,373	0.9	12.7
RI	92	2.2	14.5
SC	289	3.1	17.2
SD	17	0	25.0
TN	558	1.3	5.4
TX	1,778	0.8	11.5
UT	97	5.2	31.8
VA	294	3.7	11.5
VT	40	0	2.4
WA	942	0.4	3.5
WI	554	0.5	2.2
WV	101	5.9	19.6
WY	9	44.4	16.7
Total	21,345		
Mean		1.8	12.53
Above Mean		26	26

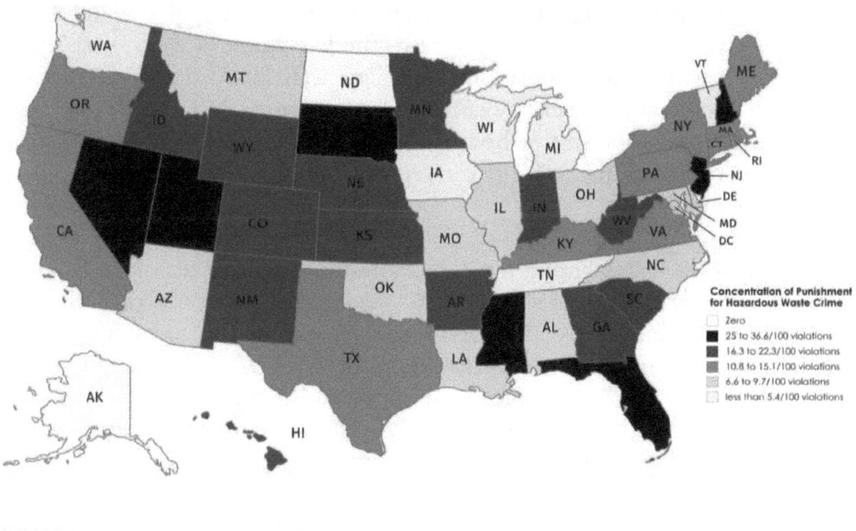

Figure 9.1 Distribution of punishment for hazardous waste crimes, RCRIS, US, 1999–2008

Source: Created using tools from https://mapchart.net/, CC BY-SA

The rate of punishment per 100 violations ranged from 0 (Alaska and North Dakota) to 36.6 (Florida), with a mean of 12.53, and indicates that environmental violations are *unlikely* to be met with a punishment, confirming the general observation in the literature that environmental crime is rarely punished.

Figure 9.1 shows the punishment rate geographically. Mapping these data is useful for assessing whether the punishment rate might be a product of the EPA region in which states are located, and whether EPA region affects punishment. There is little evidence of such a relationship in Figure 9.1.

Discussion and conclusion

The distribution and frequency of environmental crime and punishment has received little criminological attention. The present study examined those issues using RCRA violations data, and is limited in this regard since RCRA only addresses hazardous waste crimes in the US.

The findings can be summarized by five main results. First, there were few (N = 9,719) RCRA violations across states *over ten years*. This low frequency of violations indicates that either hazardous waste violation is rare, or that enforcement of these regulations is lax. Future research can address this issue.

Second, few states have a large number of RCRA violations and, unsurprisingly, the number of violations appears to be a function of the number of toxic waste handlers within a state. Third, the likelihood of a financial penalty was small. Fourth, among violation types, significant noncompliance (the most serious hazardous waste crime) was the rarest violation (0.76/state/year). This outcome may be the result of how RCRA is enforced, the frequency of such violations, or the fact that a facility can remove an SNC designation by following compliance guidelines.

Fifth, fines tend to be relatively small. Most fines are meted out by eight states, and those states have a high concentration of waste handlers. Few fines (1.28%) were large, and only ten (0.56%) fines were in excess of $1 million. If, in theory, large fines are a deterrent, then this evidence corroborates recent findings of a lack of deterrent capacity of large fines (Lynch et al., 2016).

The volume of officially reported environmental crime in RCRAinfo is small, involving fewer than 200 violations across all 50 states each year. The low number of violations may be the result of how environmental laws are enforced. Moreover, it is difficult to imagine that the violation rate discovered here (4.47/100 handlers) measures the real violation likelihood. Based on a random error rate of 1%, one would expect 1,000 violations/100,000 handlers/year, or 223 times the officially reported violation rate. Thus, the official data appears to dramatically underreport hazardous waste offending.

Despite underreporting, these data tell us something about the enforcement of known violations but appear to have little utility for understanding the volume of environmental crime. Consequently, criminologists need to devise alternative measures of environmental crime if they seek to understand the prevalence of that behavior.

Toxic/environmental crimes, as noted, are a significant social problem with global consequences that have been well documented as being related to various disease patterns; greater adverse impacts among the poor and minorities; degradation of ecosystem quality; adverse health impacts for wildlife and waterway systems; and in the scientific literature, to be related to global imbalances in planetary boundaries and to outcomes such as climate change (carbon pollution). Within criminology, while green/conservation criminologists have demonstrated the importance of these observations, more generally criminologists has been slow to recognize these concerns (for exceptions, see Sampson and Winter, 2016; Winter and Sampson, 2017).

This analysis has suggested that much more empirical research is required to understand the distribution and enforcement of pollution regulations – the issues examined here – and numerous questions remain open for further empirical examination.

Notes

1 EPA's new data system generates enforcement data for five-year time periods (beginning 2015). Data used in this study were downloaded prior to that change. RCRA data can also be downloaded via the Right-to-Know Network website (www.rtknet.org/db/rcris) and EPA's Enforcement and Compliance History

Online (ECHO) search engine (www.epa.gov/enviro/index.html), using the "compliance" link. ECHO searches are conducted on a state-by-state basis. To reach RCRA, users must click on each facility link individually, and on each facility page, click the "Enforcement and Compliance" link.

2 Violation can result in more than one enforcement action, and the enforcement actions may be a response to an earlier violation outside the data range. Thus the number of enforcement actions may not necessarily create a completely accurate indicator of the number of violations that were penalized.

References

Benn, Vicki, and Francis Gupta. 1997. Coming to the nuisance or going to the barrios – a longitudinal analysis of environmental justice claims. *Ecology Law Quarterly* 24: 1–56.

Billiet, Carole M., Thomas Blondiau, and Sandra Rousseau. 2014. Punishing environmental crimes: An empirical study from lower courts to the court of appeal. *Regulation & Governance*. doi:10.1111/rego.12044

Billiet, Carole M., and Sandra Rousseau. 2014. How real is the threat of imprisonment for environmental crime? *European Journal of Law and Economics* 37, 2: 183-198.

Brauer, Michael, Ulrike Gehring, Bert Brunekreef, Johan de Jongste, Jorrit Gerritsen, Maroeska Rovers, Heinz-Erich Wichmann, Alet Wijga, and Joachim Heinrich. 2006. Traffic-related air pollution and otitis media. *Environmental Health Perspectives* 114, 9: 1414–1418.

Burns, Ronald G., and Michael J. Lynch. 2004. *Environmental Crime: A Sourcebook*. New York: LFB Scholarly.

Cohen, Mark A. 1992. Environmental crime and punishment: Legal/economic theory and empirical evidence on enforcement of federal environmental statutes. *Journal of Criminal Law and Criminology* 82, 4: 1054–1108.

DiMento, Joseph F. 1993. Criminal enforcement of environmental law. *The Annals of the American Academy of Political and Social Science* 525: 134–146.

Gibbs, Carole, Meredith L. Gore, Edmund F. McGarrell, and Louie Rivers III. 2009. Introducing conservation criminology: Towards interdisciplinary scholarship on environmental crimes and risks. *The British Journal of Criminology* 50, 1: 124–144.

Jorgenson, Andrew K. 2016. Environment, development, and ecologically unequal exchange. *Sustainability* 8, 3. Open Access: www.mdpi.com/2071-1050/8/3/227/htm

Jorgenson, Andrew, Juliet Schor, and Xiaorui Huang. 2017. Income inequality and carbon emissions in the United States: A state-level analysis, 1997–2012. *Ecological Economics* 134: 40–48.

Karpoff, Jonathan M., John R. Lott Jr, and Eric W. Wehrly. 2005. Reputational penalties for environmental violations: Empirical evidence. *Journal of Law and Economics* 48, 2: 653–675.

Lynch, Michael J. 2017. The sentencing/punishment of federal environmental/green offenders, 2000–2013. *Deviant Behavior* 38, 9: 991–1008.

Lynch, Michael J., Kimberly L. Barrett, Paul B. Stretesky, and Michael A. Long. 2016. The weak probability of punishment for environmental offenses and deterrence of environmental offenders: A discussion based on US EPA criminal cases, 1983–2013. *Deviant Behavior* 37, 10: 1095–1109.

Lynch, Michael J., Ronald G. Burns, and Paul B. Stretesky. 2014. *Environmental Law, Crime and Justice, 2nd Edition*. El Paso, TX: LFB Scholarly.

Lynch, Michael J., Michael A. Long, Paul B. Stretesky, and Kimberly L. Barrett. 2017. *Green Criminology: Crime, Justice and the Environment.* Oakland, CA: University of California Press.

Lynch, Michael J., Paul B. Stretesky, and Michale A. Long. 2015. *Defining Crime: A Critique of the Concept and its Implications.* New York, NY: Palgrave-McMillan.

McMichael, A. J., and C. D. Butler. 2011. Promoting global population health while constraining the environmental footprint. *Annual Review of Public Health* 32: 179–197.

Opp, Susan. 2011. Bureaucratic discretion and political control of the Resource Conservation Recovery Act (RCRA). *International Journal of Public Administration* 34, 12: 753–763.

Ozymy, Joshua, and Melissa Jarrell. 2012. Wielding the green stick: Criminal enforcement at the EPA under the Bush and Obama administrations. *Environmental Politics* 21, 3: 451–466.

Renberg, Ingemar, Richard Bindler, and Maja-Lena Brannvall. 2001. Using the historical atmospheric lead-deposition record as a chronological marker in sediment deposits in Europe. *The Holocene* 11, 5: 511–516.

Rockstron, Johan, Will Steffen, Kevin Noone, Asa Perrson, F. Stuart Chapin, Eric Lambin, Timothy M. Lenton, . . . Jonathan Foley. 2009. Planetary boundaries: Exploring the safe operating space for humanity. *Ecology and Society* 14, 2: 32–47.

Rousseau, Sandra. 2009. Empirical analysis of sanctions for environmental offenses. *International Review of Environmental and Resource Economics* 3, 3: 161–194.

Saha, Robin. 2005. Historical context and hazardous waste facility siting: Understanding temporal patterns in Michigan. *Social Problems* 52, 4: 618–648.

Sampson, Robert J., and Alix S. Winter. 2016. The racial ecology of lead poisoning: Toxic inequality in Chicago neighborhoods, 1995–2013. *Du Bois Review: Social Science Research on Race* 13, 2: 261–283.

Shah, Anoop SV, Jeremy P. Langrish, Harish Nair, David A. McAllister, Amanda L. Hunter, Ken Donaldson, David E. Newby, and Nicholas L. Mills. 2013. Global association of air pollution and heart failure: A systematic review and meta-analysis. *The Lancet* 382, 9897: 1039–1048.

Spina, Francesca. 2015. Environmental justice and patterns of state inspections. *Social Science Quarterly* 96, 2: 417–429.

Stafford, Sarah L. 2002. The effect of punishment on firm compliance with hazardous waste regulations. *Journal of Environmental Economics and Management* 44: 290–308.

Stafford, Sarah L. 2003. Assessing the effectiveness of state regulation and enforcement of hazardous waste. *Journal of Regulatory Economics* 23, 1: 27–41.

Stretesky, Paul B., Michael A. Long, and Michael J. Lynch. 2013. Does environmental enforcement slow the treadmill of production? The relationship between large monetary penalties, ecological disorganization and toxic releases within offending corporations. *Journal of Crime and Justice* 36, 2: 233–247.

Sutherland, Edwin H. 1949. *White Collar Crime.* New York: Holt, Rinehart and Winston.

Winter, Alix S., and Robert J. Sampson. 2017. From lead exposure in early childhood to adolescent health: A Chicago birth cohort. *American Journal of Public Health* 107, 9: 1496–1501.

10 Waste crimes in Italy

An empirical exploration of their geographic distribution

Daniela Andreatta

The understanding of green crime and the possibility of organizing efficient policies to hinder it requires expanded use of empirical analyses of relevant data. A growing number of studies by green and conservation criminologists illustrate those contentions, particularly in multiple geographical contexts. Indeed, cross-national studies can provide important insights into factors that impact the scope of environmental crimes in the world and also offer different perspectives about how to deal with them. In light of these considerations, this chapter addresses the need for expanded empirical research by focusing on Italy. Specifically, it investigates the problem of waste crimes by exploring its spatial distribution across the peninsula and the possible underlying reasons for these patterns.

The problem of illegal waste management and the necessity of empirical research

Now nearly 30 years old, green criminology has long advocated that criminologists pay greater attention to environmental issues (Lynch and Stretesky 2014). New research could help to enlarge theoretical and empirical knowledge but also design suitable solutions by organizing efficient policy and enforcement interventions. Answering the call for more empirical knowledge in green criminology, the current chapter draws specific attention to the problem of illegal waste management in Italy and how to explore it.

Illegal waste management can be defined as "any movement of waste which is not in accordance with environmental regulations" (Tompson and Chainey 2011, 180). The violation of law, both through unauthorized acts and omissions, results in crimes, and if they include conduct connected to waste, we can label those behaviors as *waste crimes.*

The problem of legal and illegal waste management gained significant attention over the last 50 years. Demographic growth, industrial development and the associated increase in consumerism produced significant volumes of waste and the necessity of disposing of it properly. On the contrary, the illegal management of that waste can cause several negative consequences. First, improperly disposed waste is likely to pollute the soil, water, and air and to create both environmental and human health hazards (Bisschop 2014). Second, particularly polluted territories are characterized by a lower quality of life and a worse distribution of scarce resources (Wyatt 2016). Third, under an economic perspective, illegal waste management starts a vicious cycle where the availability of illegal services causes a decline in legitimate waste management prices, discouraging legitimate entrepreneurs from continuing their business, leading to growing opportunities for illegal waste management and to expanded hazards associated with illegal disposed waste (Vander Beken and Balcaen 2006).

Illegal waste activities involve both the illicit management and/or trafficking of waste (Calderoni et al. 2014). On the management side, illegalities can occur in order to reduce or avoid the cost of treatment, transportation, and disposal of waste (Germani, Pergolizzi, and Reganati 2015). Indeed, compared to other markets where a producer supplies a commodity in exchange for money, in the waste sector, the "commodity" is a by-product of manufacturing. Such waste is regulated; involves costs to handle, transport, store and treat, which cuts into profit-making; and consequently creates motivations for the emergence of an illegal waste market and management options (Bisschop 2012). Moreover, waste price suffers from inelasticity because specific treatments are required by regulations and they cannot legally be substituted for one another (Dorn, Van Daele, and Vander Beken 2007; Liddick 2010). This form of inelasticity keeps the price of waste treatment stable and opens up opportunities for illegal waste management practices that offer below-market prices. As in other business sectors, entrepreneurs in the waste sector are compelled by economic drivers, and they can decide to turn to the illicit market to protect their profits (Sahramäki et al. 2017). On the trafficking side, waste can be a profitable good for resale on the black market, domestically and internationally, and it should be viewed in the same way as trafficking or smuggling of other types of goods (Meško, Dimitrijević, and Fields 2010). Much of the demand comes from some developing countries (e.g., in Africa and Asia), where waste represents an important source of income, because it can be dismantled and sold as raw materials or as secondhand goods (Liddick 2010; Bisschop 2012).

Despite growing interest in environmental crimes, empirical studies on the topic are limited, particularly within criminology. In recent years, European researchers have increased attention to green crimes, but those studies have primarily been descriptive or qualitative (e.g., Massari and Monzini 2004; Vander Beken and Balcaen 2006; Ruggiero and South 2010; Crofts et al. 2010; Klenovšek and Meško 2011; Bisschop 2012; Huisman and van Erp 2013; Wyatt 2016; Sahramäki et al. 2017). Qualitative studies can provide useful information about the characteristics of the illegal market, the actors involved, and the modus operandi. Nevertheless, quantitative data and methods are also needed to extend statistical knowledge and to produce generalizable results related to the hazards of waste crimes. Moreover, quantitative studies can also help green criminological issues to gain more credibility in the eyes of traditional criminology (Lynch et al. 2017).

It is also fair to say, though, that the absence of a substantial body of quantitative studies on waste reflects scarcity and sometimes poor quality of statistical data about environmental crimes in Europe (EnviCrimeNet 2015).

Causes of the lack of data are various, but mostly depend upon three major limitations: (1) difficulty in directly observing the crime and reporting it to the police; (2) the absence of conscious victims or witnesses who can press charges; and (3) inadequate capacity or inability of detection by law enforcement agencies (Huisman and van Erp 2013). Due to these circumstances, producing quantitative analysis on environmental crimes in Europe is challenging, but not impossible. Focusing on the Italian context, the present chapter explores the availability of statistical data on waste crimes and conducts some descriptive geographical analysis, supported by synthetic measures of concentration and statistical correlation. Such analyses can contribute to identifying new paths for future studies and encouraging further quantitative research.

The next section specifically introduces the problem of waste crimes in Italy and advances some basic hypotheses about factors that may influence the distribution of waste crimes across the peninsula.

Illegal waste management in Italy

Concern regarding waste crimes in Italy began in the 1990s, when local authorities discovered tons of toxic material illegally disposed in some southern regions, mostly Campania and Sicily (Massari and Monzini 2004; Liddick 2010). Here, the problem was also connected to the presence of different Mafia-type groups, and indicate the involvement of traditional organized crime groups (hereinafter OCGs), specifically the Mafia, Camorra and 'Ndrangheta. Anticipating the potential for profit, OCGs in Italy joined the waste sector in the second half of the 20th century (Liddick 2010) and they become central in Italian illegal waste management, leading to the introduction of the neologism "Ecomafia" in 1994 (Massari and Monzini 2004).

OCGs activities within the Italian waste cycle are manifold and can occur both nationally and internationally. Criminal groups can trade waste abroad (mostly Eastern Europe, Africa, and Asia), dump it on the land or at sea, use it as secondary raw material, or mix it with other materials (Massari and Monzini 2004; Liddick 2010). The tactics employed to allow the transfer, illegal dumping, and improper reuse of waste are several, including falsification of waste documents to hide its origins and content. OCGs also channels illegal waste through the takeover of legal companies, employed as shell companies to enter the legal market and win public contracts (Pasotti 2010). These behaviors produce serious damage, not only to the environment and citizens' health but also to the economy, perceptions of corruption, and efficacy of the political and legal systems. In addition, the presence of OCGs in the legal waste sector jeopardizes the development of legal waste management, resulting in poor waste services provision.

However, OCGs are not the only actors in the illegal waste cycle in Italy (Szasz 1986; Liddick 2010; Pasotti 2010; Baird, Curry, and Cruz 2014). On the contrary, they soon encounter a corrupt political situation and a collusive entrepreneurial environment that lead to the diffusion of the phenomenon all over the country. On the one hand, officials of public administrations and controlling regulatory bodies easily accept bribery and other favors to allow waste crime offenders to evade proper waste management (Pasotti 2010; Legambiente 2015, 2016). On the other hand, businessmen and entrepreneurs are incentivized to take advantage of the illegal dynamics, to cut their management and disposal costs (Massari and Monzini 2004). Indeed, waste crime offenders (both OCGs or not) can reduce the price of disposal substantially by (1) declaring a different nature of waste handled (and consequently avoiding the more expensive treatments of, for example, hazardous waste) or (2) dumping it illegally, without any expense (Szasz 1986). For instance, some estimates on the Italian context indicates that the prices of illegal waste disposal market are between one-third and one-fifth of those charged in the legal one (Calderoni et al. 2014), or even up to ten times less (Legambiente 2011).

Nevertheless, the price of disposal can vary according to the type of waste and consequently, the incentive to commit waste crimes can be different across waste market segments. Usually, waste can be divided into (1) domestic, urban, or municipal waste produced by households and (2) special or industrial waste, which results from industrial activity (Pasotti 2010). Both domestic and special waste can be further subdivided into hazardous and non-hazardous categories (Ministero dell'Ambiente 2017). European law defines hazardous or toxic waste "when it contains properties or substances that might make it harmful to human health or the environment" (Vander Beken and Balcaen 2006, 306). Generally speaking, industrial and hazardous waste needs a major effort in management and disposal activities, because they are potentially more polluting (Massari and Monzini 2004). In turn, they are more likely to be treated improperly, in order to spare money and time.

The preceding history described the problem of waste crimes in Italy as a complex phenomenon. It seems to be spread across the whole peninsula and is possibly influenced by different factors. In this regard, the present chapter advances some basic hypotheses. First, the distribution of waste crimes in Italy could be related to the presence of OCG that has been historically involved in the illegal waste market. Second, waste crimes could also be partly a function of where businesses are located, because entrepreneurs are important actors of the illegal market and they can turn to illegal behaviors to decrease their costs. Third, waste production can be positively related to waste crimes, because high amounts of waste need more efforts to be properly disposed, and illegal management can create the opportunity to spare money.

Waste crimes data in Italy

Data availability

Attention toward the problem of illegal waste management in Italy has grown over time. Public opinion, political circles, and researchers in different subjects demonstrate their concern on the issue and raised awareness of the necessity for urgent interventions. In particular, scholars started to undertake interesting qualitative studies that allowed a better understanding of the phenomenon in Italy (Massari and Monzini 2004; Pasotti 2010; Ruggiero and South 2010; Sahramäki et al. 2017). At the same time, some authors in environmental economics began to pay attention to this issue, producing some quantitative studies on both the legal and illegal waste management problem (D'Amato et al. 2014; D'Amato, Mazzanti, and Nicolli 2015; Germani, Pergolizzi, and Reganati 2015; Mazzanti et al., 2008). However, the state of the art of quantitative research on waste crimes is still limited in Italy, and it exists outside of criminology. Indeed, criminologists can make important contributions to the investigation of waste crimes by applying and testing theories of criminal offending. In turn, this would be an important support to public policies that aid in the efficient prevention of illegal waste management.

In Italy, there are two public data sources on environmental crimes and they specifically provide information on waste illegalities as well. The first one is the Italian National Statistical Office (ISTAT), which has published data on the issue since July 2018. The second one is *Legambiente* (Italian League for the Environment), which since the 1990s has released annual reports on environmental crimes. Considering that only Legambiente's data is available for different administrative units (i.e., provinces and regions), they have been considered more suitable for the geographical analysis of the present chapter.

Legambiente reports the number of verified infractions related to waste legislation, mostly according to the Legislative Decree 152/2006 (the "Environmental Code") and, starting in 2015, the Italian Penal Code.[1] Data is accessible year by year for every Italian region and, starting from 2009, also at the province level. Usually, analysis at province level represents a more appropriate choice for robust statistical analysis because it provides more variance between the observations and a good number of cases. Consequently, also this study privileges Italian provinces as units of analysis, which provides for 110 province level observations.[2] In certain cases, the province level data is not available, making necessary analysis at the regional level ($N = 20$).

One relevant limitation of Legambiente's data that should be specified here is that waste-related offenses are presented in aggregate counts, without distinguishing different types of violations from one another. In this chapter, no effort was made to examine variations in the distribution of specific sub-categories of waste crimes, and the goal in this preliminary analysis was to explore what mapping these crimes can tell us about the geographic distribution of waste crimes in Italy and the factors related to such patterns.

Method

In order to verify the advanced hypotheses, the present chapter analyzes the geographical distribution of waste crimes and of the factors possibly related to them. ArcGIS software is employed to visualize and investigate the phenomena across Italian provinces or regions. In order to strengthen the geographical analysis and provide a formal test of the possible statistical correlation between the main phenomenon and the other factors, the present study will also report the value of the Pearson coefficient.

The maps are drawn according to the average of the number of events registered in a province or a region between 2009 and 2015. The average number of the time span is then employed in the maps as absolute values or computed as a rate. Indeed, rate data is usually preferred over count data for purposes of illustrating the distribution of a phenomenon and as a basis for comparing it across locations, since rate data is standardized. In one map, the location quotient has also been employed, which is a measure of relative concentration and shows the concentration of waste crimes in a province as compared to the whole nation.

The values are then expressed in the maps as natural breaks divided in five classes. Natural breaks are often used in crime mapping because they seek the best organization of the classes of data and reflect efforts to group similar values together and minimizing their differences (Chainey and Ratcliffe 2005).

Before starting the geographical analysis, the chapter also provides some descriptive analysis of waste crimes in the last years, as well as two synthetic measures of concentration across the units of observation: Lorenz curve plot and its corresponding Gini coefficient.

The Lorenz curve is a function that shows how evenly distributed the variable is over space. The line of equality is what would be expected if the cumulative percentage of provinces plotted against the cumulative percentage of verified violations were the same (Kurland and Pires 2016). In other words, if the count of waste crimes is evenly distributed across provinces, the line would match perfectly with the line of equality. Thus, the greater the deviation of the Lorenz curve from the line of equality, the greater the inequality.

From the Lorenz plot it is possible to geometrically calculate the Gini coefficient of inequality that helps in quantifying the variation in the concentration of waste across the units of analysis. The Gini coefficient can be computed using the formula , where *A* is the area between the diagonal line of equality and the Lorenz curve and *B* is the proportion of the area of below the Lorenz curve. The outcome ranges from 0 (representing completely even distribution) to 1 (completely uneven distribution) (Kurland and Pires 2016).

The dynamics of waste crimes in Italy: an exploratory analysis

In the last few years, verified waste infractions in Italy followed a quite stable trend, fluctuating between about 4,200 and 7,200 offenses per year with a peak in 2014 and a drop in 2015 (see Figure 10.1). The increased level of discovery in 2014 was influenced by a significantly large increase in reported environmental crimes in the city of Bari, which recorded nearly eight times its usual average number of offenses. Indeed, this high value represents an outlier in the distribution and, in order to be involved in further analysis, it has been substituted with the average value between the other years of the distribution.

Figure 10.2 displays the Lorenz curve to verify the concentration of waste crimes variable across Italian provinces. The graph suggests that 50% of violations occurs in 20% of provinces, and the other 50% of violations occur in the 80% of provinces. On the Gini scale, 0 is perfect inequality, and 1 is perfect inequality.

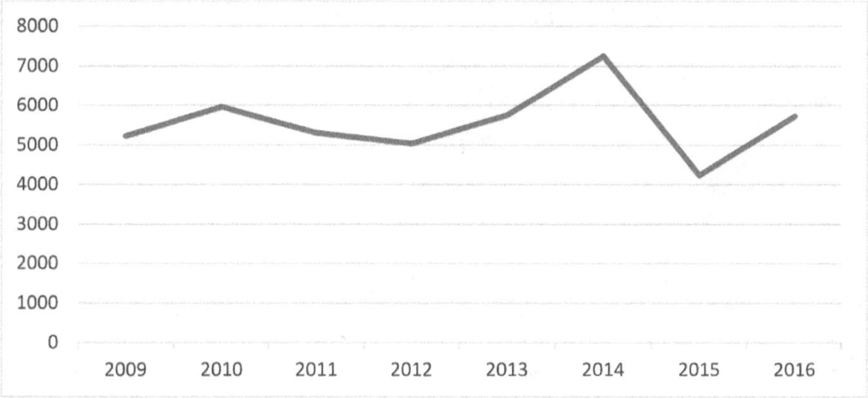

Figure 10.1 Known waste crimes, Italy, 2009–2016

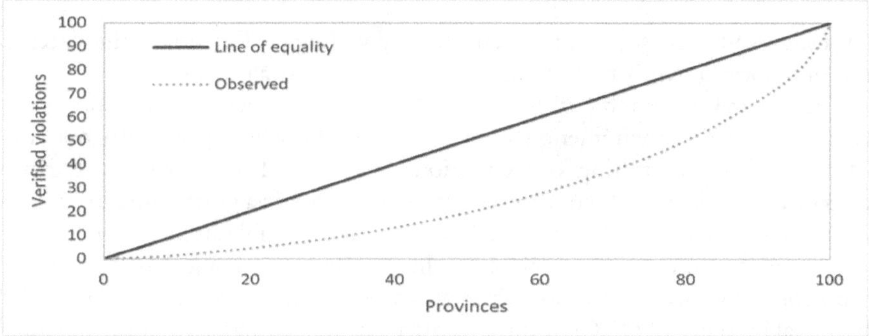

Figure 10.2 Lorenz curve

In Italy, the Gini coefficient for the waste crimes variable was 0.4577, indicating that the distribution of waste crime is somewhat unequal.

Figure 10.3 shows the preliminary depiction of the geographic distribution of waste crimes across the 110 provinces in Italy, and it includes a count, a rate, and a location quotient map. In the count map (A), the highest concentration of violations occurred in several southern and central Italian provinces. In particular, high values are registered in Bari, Naples, Rome, and Reggio Calabria. However, in the rate map (B), the distribution of waste crimes seems more homogenous, although the concentration of offenses in central and southern Italy is still apparent. Indeed, the major concentration is present in Vibo-Valentia province, followed by other cities across the peninsula. A similar image is also displayed in Figure 10.3(C), corresponding to the location quotient map. High waste concentrations are confirmed in Vibo-Valencia, Benevento, Matera,

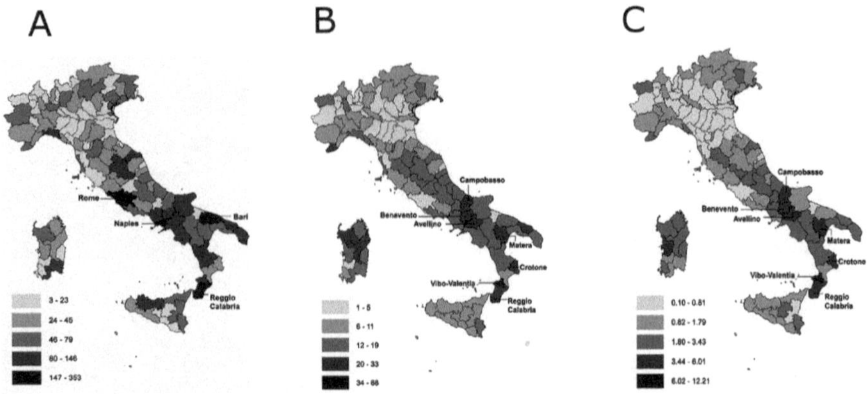

Figure 10.3 Distribution of waste crimes as (A) a count, (B) a rate per 100,000 inhabitants, and (C) location quotient. Provincial level, years 2009–2015.

Crotone, Campobasso, Avellino, and mostly in Reggio Calabria – the latter is the only location with high waste crime values across all maps.

The general geographic distribution of waste crimes across Italian provinces confirms that the phenomenon is spread across the whole peninsula, but that there are some interesting concentrations in the southern provinces. Further empirical analysis of these concentrations can help to gain a greater understanding of the phenomenon and of the factors that could possibly influence it.

One of the hypotheses advanced for the present chapter suggests that part of the geographic pattern of waste crimes can be explained in relationship to the historical presence of OCGs in Italy. In particular, it is supposed that the distribution of waste crimes across the peninsula should reflect the distribution of OCGs within the provinces. This relationship is illustrated in Figure 10.4, where (A) displays again the rate of waste crimes and (B) shows the distribution of organized crime presence, measured according to the number of offenses for Mafia-type associations reported to law enforcement agencies. The value corresponds to the average number of crimes registered in the time span 2009–2015. The two maps illustrate a similar concentration of the two phenomena across provinces, even though waste crimes are more frequent. On the contrary, Mafia groups are historically concentrated in the southern provinces, whereas their presence in the north is less evident (for discussion, see Calderoni 2011). The comparison of the two maps suggest that waste crimes and OCGs concentration are positively, even if scarcely, correlated (Pearson's $r = 0.0961$, significant at 95% confidence level).

The second hypothesis of the study postulates that waste crimes could be associated to the presence of businesses because entrepreneurs are important actors of the illegal market and they can turn to illegal behaviors to decrease their costs. Figure 10.5(B) shows the distribution of the number of businesses,

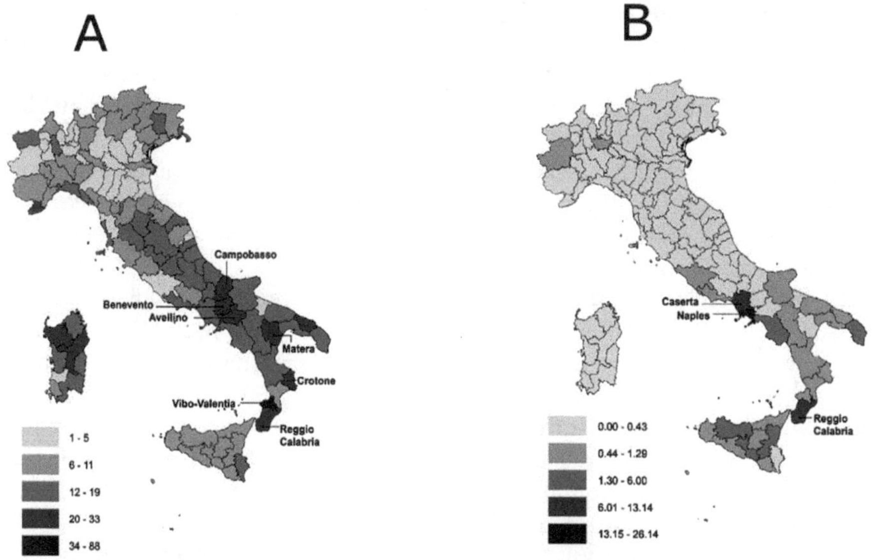

Figure 10.4 Distribution of waste crimes as (A) rate per 100,000 inhabitants and (B) organized crime group presence. Provincial level, years 2009–2015.

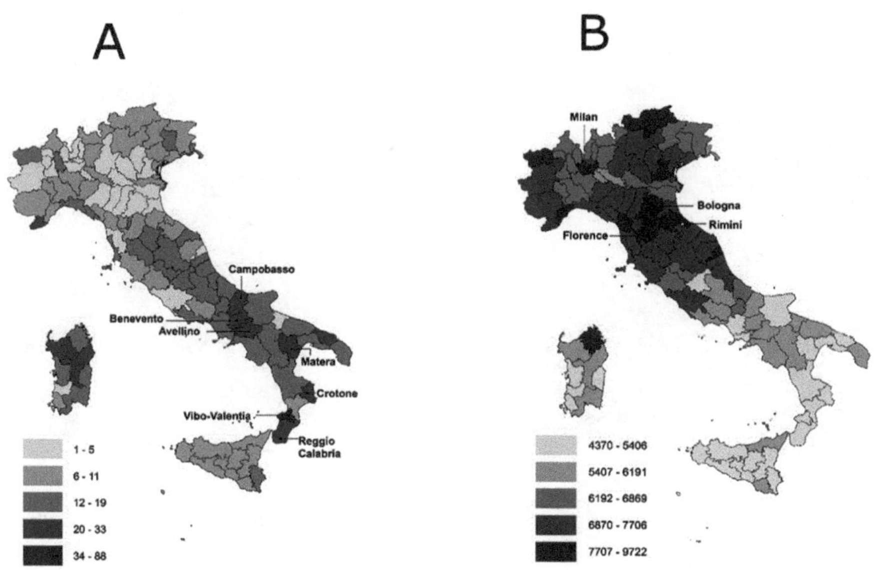

Figure 10.5 Distribution of waste crimes as (A) rate per 100,000 inhabitants and (B) number of businesses per 100,000 inhabitants. Provincial level, years 2009–2015.

computed as rate per 100,000 inhabitants. Northern and central provinces seem to have a more flourishing entrepreneurial environment as there is a higher concentration of businesses. On the contrary, there are no high rates of waste crimes in those territories (Figure 10.5(A)), suggesting instead a negative relation between the two variables (Pearson's $r = -0.3080$, significant at 95% confidence level).

The third hypothesis considers the opportunity of waste crimes related to waste production. High amounts of waste should be properly disposed, but considering the high costs of the legal waste management sector, they could also be an object of illegal conduct.

As mentioned above, the disposal of special waste requires specific treatment that increases the cost of management (Massari and Monzini 2004), and hence the motivation for engaging in waste crimes to save money. Consequently, mapping the production of industrial/special waste could potentially be associated with the distribution of waste crimes in Italy. However, data about waste production in Italy are available at the province level only in regard to urban waste, whereas information about the production of special waste is limited at regional level for the two years 2014–2015.

The geographical analysis here considers the distribution of both factors. Figure 10.6 shows the distribution of urban waste production across provinces, whereas Figure 10.7 the distribution of special waste production across regions. Both figures indicate a concentration of waste production in northern and

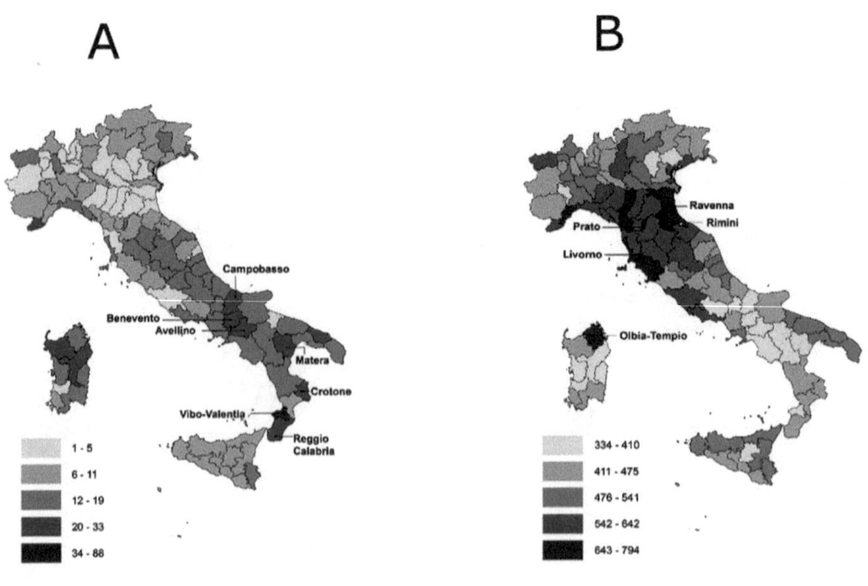

Figure 10.6 Distribution of waste crimes as (A) rate per 100,000 inhabitants and (B) production of urban waste (kg/population). Provincial level, years 2009–2015.

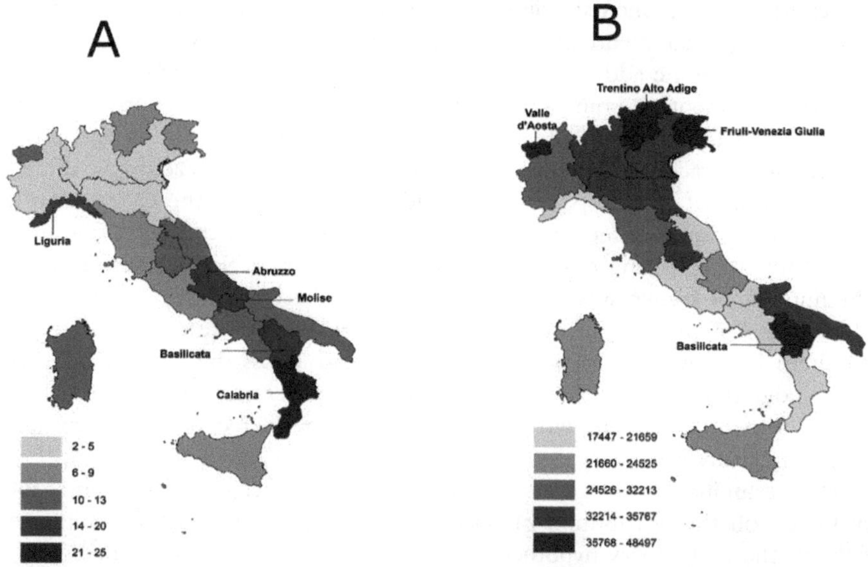

Figure 10.7 Verified waste infraction as (A) rate per 100,000 inhabitants and (B) production of special waste as rate on business population (kg/business pop). Regional level, years 2014–2015.

central areas. Consequently, the relation between illegal waste management and waste production appears to be negative, both for urban (Pearson's $r = -0.2114$, significant at 95% confidence level) and special waste (Pearson's $r = -0.5104$, significant at 95% confidence level).

Conclusions: theoretical interpretation and necessity of further studies

This study examined the geographic distribution of waste crimes in Italy. As noted, green criminology advocates for a better knowledge of green crimes in a variety of geographical contexts to better understand the scope, causes and potential mechanisms for controlling these environmental issues. To facilitate such studies and outcomes, green criminologists need to engage in empirical research, especially by the means of a quantitative approach. This would provide more generalizable results on environmental issues and a better comprehension of the importance of these phenomena as new research topics in criminology (Lynch et al. 2017).

Using data on the geographic distribution of waste crimes, the present chapter showed that there are about 5,550 waste crimes per year in Italy across its 110 provinces. As noted, in the temporal trend of verified infractions there is a peak in 2014 and a drop in 2015. The peak is due to a remarkable increase in reported environmental crimes in the city of Bari, even if the source of information (Legambiente 2015) does not provide a precise explanation for this high number. Some additional information has been obtained from newspaper articles that mention some important judicial investigations coordinated by police forces of Bari in 2014. This could have contributed to the increase of the verified infractions in that province (La Gazzetta del Mezzogiorno 2015). On the contrary, the drop in 2015 could be the result of the change in the laws defining waste crimes in Italy (Penal Code Law 68), causing a transition period for the reporting requirements for these offenses. Nevertheless, in 2016 the number of known waste crimes returns to the average level.

In terms of the rate of offending, the majority of those crimes occurs in southern Italy, even if the phenomenon is spread across the whole peninsula. The geographical analysis tried to explore the potential correlates of waste crimes with other factors, whose role has been considered relevant according to the literature review.

The preliminary results found some very small effect of the concentration of OCGs on the distribution of waste crimes. The results did not completely confirm the preliminary hypothesis, but they do not allow them to be entirely rejected either. Indeed, one limit of the analysis could be the nature of the data employed. Mafia-related crimes usually suffer from underreporting problems (i.e., dark number). These are due to the difficulty of law enforcement to discover this specific form of crime and to the scarce propensity of victims and witnesses to press charges, mostly because of the threat of retaliation by OCGs (Calderoni 2011). This problem results in a very low number of registered crimes per province and a possible high dark figure that jeopardizes the strength of the correlation. Further research is needed to measure Mafia presence with other methods and deepen the analysis about the possible correlation with waste crimes.

The second hypothesis of the study suggested a positive relationship between waste crimes and presence of entrepreneurs, considered as important actors in the illegal waste market. Geographical and correlation analyses do not support this idea and find the opposite pattern – that is, where there are more businesses, less waste crimes occur. With regard to the third hypothesis, this study found no empirical support of a positive relationship between waste production and waste crimes at the provincial or regional level. Also in this case, the relationship was found to be negative. However, these results can find another possible interpretation. The negative relationships can be due to the existence of an internal movement of waste in Italy, that from the northern and central regions is addressed to the southern regions, where it is illegally disposed. This would be consistent with observations in prior studies which suggest the existence in Italy of an extensive domestic illegal market for (mostly) hazardous waste (Massari and Monzini 2004). In the last several decades, a negative synergy came to light, showing flourishing industrial production of the northern and central regions taking advantage of the uncontrolled disposal of waste in the south, in order to cut their management costs (Pasotti 2010; D'Amato,

Mazzanti, and Nicolli 2015). As mentioned above, the traditional presence of OCGs could facilitate the illegal management in the south, because they have greater control of this territory.

In conclusion, the present study is exploratory in nature and it provides some preliminary insights of the factors connected to the distribution of waste crimes in Italy. These ideas should be further and better investigated by employing other relevant data and stronger quantitative methods. Empirical research in green criminology is fundamental to enhance the knowledge about the diffusion of environmental issues, variations in distribution patterns, and how those observations might impact the development of appropriate mechanisms for controlling waste and other green crimes in different nations.

Notes

1 In 2015, Italy witnessed a very important legislative intervention which introduced four environmental felonies (also connected to waste) into the Italian Penal Code, according to the Law 68/2015. The new offenses are pollution, environmental disasters, obstruction of controls and illegal transport, and abandonment of radioactive materials (Legambiente 2015). This intervention marks an important step towards protecting the environment, because it recognizes the criminal relevance and an adequate punishment of environmental offenses.

2 For the realization of this chapter, data was available until 2015 and the number of Italian provinces was 110. Administrative changes in 2016 and following years caused a reduction of the number of provinces.

References

Baird, Jim, Robin Curry, and Paulo Cruz. 2014. An Overview of Waste Crime, Its Characteristics, and the Vulnerability of the EU Waste Sector. *Waste Management & Research* 32 (2): 97–105. DOI: 10.1177/0734242X13517161.

Bisschop, Lieselot. 2012. Is It All Going to Waste? Illegal Transports of e-Waste in a European Trade Hub. *Crime, Law and Social Change* 58 (3): 221–249. DOI: 10.1007/s10611-012-9383-0.

———. 2014. How E-Waste Challenges Environmental Governance. Pp. 27–44 in T. Wyatt (ed), *Hazardous Waste and Pollution*. Cham: Springer. DOI: 10.5204/ijcjsd.v3i2.178.

Calderoni, Francesco. 2011. Where Is the Mafia in Italy? Measuring the Presence of the Mafia across Italian Provinces. *Global Crime* 12 (1): 41–69. DOI: 10.1080/17440572.2011.548962.

Calderoni, Francesco, Serena Favarin, Lorella Garofalo, and Federica Sarno. 2014. Counterfeiting, Illegal Firearms, Gambling and Waste Management: An Exploratory Estimation of Four Criminal Markets. *Global Crime* 15: 108–137. DOI: 10.1080/17440572.2014.883499.

Chainey, Spencer, and Jerry Ratcliffe. 2005. *GIS and Crime Mapping*. Chichester: Wiley.

Crofts, Penny, Tara Morris, Kim Wells, and Alicia Powell. 2010. Illegal Dumping and Crime Prevention: A Case Study of Ash Road, Liverpool Council. *Public Space: The Journal of Law and Social Justice* 5: 23. DOI: 10.5130/psjlsj.v5i0.1904.

D'Amato, Alessio, Massimiliano Mazzanti, and Francesco Nicolli. 2015. Waste and Organized Crime in Regional Environments. *Resource and Energy Economics* 41 (August): 185–201. DOI: 10.1016/j.reseneeco.2015.04.003.

D'Amato, Alessio, Massimiliano Mazzanti, Francesco Nicolli, and Mariangela Zoli. 2014. Illegal Waste Disposal, Territorial Enforcement and Policy: Evidence from Regional Data. *SEEDS Working Paper Series* 3: 1–17.

Dorn, Nicholas, Stijn Van Daele, and Tom Vander Beken. 2007. Reducing Vulnerabilities to Crime of the European Waste Management Industry: The Research Base and the Prospects for Policy. *European Journal of Crime, Criminal Law and Criminal Justice* 23: 23–36. DOI: 10. 1163/092895607X1 93524.

EnviCrimeNet. 2015. *Report on Environmental Crime in Europe*. The Hague: Intelligence Project on Environmental Crime Reporting.

Germani, Anna Rita, Antonio Pergolizzi, and Filippo Reganati. 2015. Illegal Trafficking and Unsustainable Waste Management in Italy: Evidence at Regional Level. *Journal of Security and Sustainability Issues* 4 (4): 369–389. DOI: 10.9770/jssi.2015.4(5).

Huisman, Wim, and Judith van Erp. 2013. Opportunities for Environmental Crime: A Test of Situational Crime Prevention Theory. *British Journal of Criminology* 53 (6): 1178–1200. DOI: 10.1093/bjc/azt036.

Klenovšek, Ana, and Gorazd Meško. 2011. International Waste Trafficking: Preliminary Explorations. Pp. 79–99 in G. Meško, D. Dimitrijević, and C. B. Fields (eds.), *Understanding and Managing Threats to the Environment in South Eastern Europe*. Dordrecht: Springer.

Kurland, Justin, and Stephen F. Pires. 2016. Assessing U.S. Wildlife Trafficking Patterns: How Criminology and Conservation Science Can Guide Strategies to Reduce the Illegal Wildlife Trade. *Deviant Behavior* 38 (4): 375–391. DOI: 10.1080/01639625.2016.119700.

La Gazzetta del Mezzogiorno. 2015. *Legambiente: Puglia "regina" per Smaltimento Illecito Dei Rifiuti*. www.lagazzettadelmezzogiorno.it/news/home/663179/legambiente-puglia-regina-per-smaltimento-illecito-dei-rifiuti.html.

Legambiente. 2011. *Ecomafia 2011 – Le storie e i numeri della criminalità ambientale*. Milano: Edizioni Ambiente.

———. 2015. *Ecomafia 2015 – Corrotti, clan e inquinatori: ladri di futuro all'assalto del belpaese*. Napoli: Marotta & Cafiero.

———. 2016. *Ecomafia 2016 – Le storie e i numeri della criminalità ambientale*. Milano: Edizioni Ambiente.

Liddick, Don. 2010. The Traffic in Garbage and Hazardous Wastes: An Overview. *Trends in Organized Crime* 13 (2–3): 134–146. DOI: 10.1007/s12117-009-9089-6.

Lynch, Michael J., Kimberly L. Barrett, Paul B. Stretesky, and Michael A. Long. 2017. The Neglect of Quantitative Research in Green Criminology and Its Consequences. *Critical Criminology* 25 (2): 183–198. DOI: 10.1007/s10612-017-9359-6.

Lynch, Michael J., and Paul Stretesky. 2014. *Exploring Green Criminology: Toward a Green Criminological Revolution: Green Criminology*. Burlington, VT: Ashgate.

Massari, Monica, and Paola Monzini. 2004. Dirty Businesses in Italy: A Case-Study of Illegal Trafficking in Hazardous Waste. *Global Crime* 6 (3–4): 285–304. DOI: 10.1080/17440570500273416.

Mazzanti, Massimiliano, Anna Montini, and Roberto Zoboli. 2008. Municipal Waste Generation and Socioeconomic Drivers: Evidence from Comparing Northern and

Southern Italy. *The Journal of Environment & Development* 17 (1): 51–69. DOI: 10.1177/1070496507312575.

Meško, Gorazd, Dejana Dimitrijević, and Charles B. Fields. 2010. *Understanding and Managing Threats to the Environment in South Eastern Europe*. New York: Springer.

Ministero dell'Ambiente. 2017. *La Classificazione Dei Rifiuti*. www.minambiente.it/pagina/la-classificazione-dei-rifiuti.

Pasotti, Eleonora. 2010. Sorting through the Trash: The Waste Management Crisis in Southern Italy. *South European Society and Politics* 15 (2): 289–307. DOI: 10.1080/13608740903497733.

Ruggiero, Vincenzo, and Nigel South. 2010. Green Criminology and Dirty Collar Crime. *Critical Criminology* 18 (4): 251–262. DOI: 10.1007/s10612-010-9122-8.

Sahramäki, Iina, Serena Favarin, Shanna Mehlbaum, Ernesto Savona, Toine Spapens, and Terhi Kankaanranta. 2017. Wasting Opportunities-Prevention of Illicit Cross-Border Waste Trafficking. *European Journal of Policing Studies*. www.maklu-online.eu/nl/tijdschrift/ejps/online-first/online-first/wasting-opportunities-prevention-illicit-cross-bor/pdf/.

Szasz, Andrew. 1986. Corporations, Organized Crime, and the Disposal of Hazardous Waste. *Criminology* 24 (1): 1–27. DOI: 10.1111/j.1745-9125.1986.tb00374.x.

Tompson, Lisa, and Spencer Chainey. 2011. Profiling Illegal Waste Activity: Using Crime Scripts as a Data Collection and Analytical Strategy. *European Journal on Criminal Policy and Research* 17 (3): 179–201. DOI: 10.1007/s10610-011-9146-y.

Vander Beken, Tom, and Annelies Balcaen. 2006. Crime Opportunities Provided by Legislation in Market Sectors: Mobile Phones, Waste Disposal, Banking. *European Journal of Criminal Policy and Research* 12: 299–323. DOI: 10.1007/s10610-006-9025-0.

Wyatt, Tanya, ed. 2016. *Hazardous Waste and Pollution: Detecting and Preventing Green Crimes*. London: Springer.

11 Longitudinal methods for analyzing green crime

Michael A. Long, Paul B. Stretesky, and Kimberly L. Barrett

Introduction

In this chapter, we discuss different methods for analyzing green crimes over time, or longitudinally. Along the theme of this edited volume and as argued extensively elsewhere (Lynch et al., 2017), we believe that it is imperative that green criminology employ rigorous statistical analysis of quantitative data to help drive the sub-discipline forward. In particular, the power of longitudinal analyses to predict and explain the social drivers of ecological outcomes is unparalleled. In this chapter, we review several of the most relevant longitudinal statistical methods for panel data for green criminologists. These methods are frequently employed in orthodox criminology (e.g., Martinez et al., 2010; Phillips, 2006) and environmental sociology (e.g., Jorgenson, 2007; Jorgenson & Clark, 2010), but have been only rarely used in green criminology (Long et al., forthcoming; Long et al., 2018, 2017; Stretesky et al., 2013, 2017a, 2017b; Stretesky et al., 2018, 2017, forthcoming).

According to Menard (2002: 3), longitudinal research has two main purposes,

> to describe patterns of change and to establish the direction (positive or negative and from *Y* to *X* or from *X* to *Y*) and magnitude (a relationship of magnitude zero indicating the absence of a causal relationship) of causal relationships.

Alternatively, Fitzmaurice et al. (2011: 19) suggest

> that the major focus of the analysis of longitudinal data is on the assessment of within-individual changes in the response variable over time. That is, longitudinal analysis is concerned with estimating how individuals change throughout the duration of the study and examining factors that influence heterogeneity among individuals in how they change over time.

Longitudinal data has temporal order, meaning the order of the observations matter. Longitudinal data are also usually clustered, as the data are repeated measurements of the same individual or case over time. Repeated measures on the same individual are generally positively correlated, which require methods that can accommodate this. When modeled correctly, results from a longitudinal panel study that examines within-person changes can provide very accurate estimates of the change, due to the person serving as his/her own control, essentially controlling for other extraneous unmeasured factors. Thus, within-person longitudinal designs are able to remove much of the "white noise" from the estimates.

This chapter is a basic, nontechnical discussion of several panel regression models. This chapter draws heavily from numerous excellent sources, which should serve as references and further reading for interested readers. These include Allison (2009), Fitzmaurice et al. (2011), Menard (2002), Pickup (2015), Rabe-Hesketh and Skrondal (2012a), and Singer and Willett (2003). To understand and use this chapter to its fullest, readers should have some familiarity with ordinary least squares (OLS) regression. This chapter will focus on continuous outcomes only. However, the methods overviewed here generally have versions that can be used to model categorical and count dependent variables. The sources listed above and Rabe-Hesketh and Skrondal (2012b) can be used to describe longitudinal models for categorical and count variables. While it is not a requirement, basic knowledge of the computer statistical package Stata (as of this writing, v.15), will be helpful for the reader as the examples are computed with Stata, the Stata syntax is provided and Stata outputs are reviewed. *Italics* are reserved in this chapter for Stata commands. The models described here can also be estimated with other statistical packages such as R and SAS.

In the sections that follow, we review (1) fixed-effects panel models, (2) random-effects panel models, and (3) multilevel models for change. All of these models can be considered regression models for correlated data (Fitzmaurice et al., 2011). To illustrate the models reviewed in this chapter, we use examples from data retrieved from the CITES database (CITES, 2018a), which is a repository of data on the legal international trade in wildlife. The wildlife trade is a subject that has received considerable attention in green criminology. To our knowledge, however, only one longitudinal green criminological study exists using CITES data (Stretesky et al., 2018). Before we turn our attention to the different modeling strategies, we first provide an overview of the different types of longitudinal data, discuss how to properly format your longitudinal data for analysis in Stata, and review some of the major assumptions longitudinal data must adhere to ensure accurate estimates.

Longitudinal data and format

While there are numerous types of longitudinal data, we focus on "panel data" in this chapter. As Finkel (1995: 1) notes, "[p]anel data, which consist of information gathered from the same individual or units at several different points in time, are commonly used in the social sciences to test theories of individual and social change." Panel data are longitudinal data gathered at three or more points in time for the same exact cases (Singer & Willett, 2003). By gathering data on the same cases overtime, making causal arguments about social phenomenon becomes easier than in most other research designs (Finkel, 1995).

For comparison purposes, we review two of the other types of longitudinal data common in the social sciences. First, "time-series data" and methodology refers to data and analysis that follows one case over a relatively long period of time. Time-series data is useful for examining long-term changes within units but is unlike panel data that follows numerous cases over shorter timeframes. Second, "repeated cross-sectional" designs can be considered quasi-longitudinal as the same individuals are not followed over time; rather separate independent random samples are drawn from a population at each time point (Menard, 2002). This type of research design allows for comparisons between time points; however it does not allow for within-subject change to be estimated, decreasing the ability to study change and determine causality. Both time-series and repeated cross-sectional designs have their own set of statistical models. From this point forward, we will be focusing exclusively on panel data and methods for analyzing panel data.

Before analyzing panel data, you need to make sure that the dataset is in the correct format for analyzing longitudinal data. Generally, most statistical packages require longitudinal data to be in what Singer and Willett (2003: 17) refer to as a "person-period data set" rather than a "person-level data set." A person-level dataset has the same number of records as cases and separate columns for each variable at each occurrence. In contrast, a person-period dataset has a separate record for each case at each time point. In Stata parlance, this is referred to as *long* format (as opposed to the *wide* format). Stata needs data to be in the long format to recognize it as longitudinal data. If your data is in wide, or person-level, format, the *reshape* command in Stata allows you to move between long and wide format. Once you have your data in long format, you need to let Stata know that your data is panel data. This is done with the *xtset* command using both a time and a panel variable to specify the data structure. Stata will then report whether the data is balanced or unbalanced. A "balanced" dataset is one where each case has the same number of measurements; in an "unbalanced" dataset there are unequal measurement between cases. Missing data is quite common in panel studies. Fortunately, in most cases the models we review in this chapter can accommodate missing data. However, if missing data are a problem, one way Stata can help (though limitations exist) is through its *mi* suite of commands for multiple imputation, which can help fill in the missing cases and then estimate the models using the imputed data (Royston, 2007).

Assumptions

Now that we have reviewed how to set up the data to be analyzed in Stata, we need to briefly discuss longitudinal model assumptions. Researchers must ensure that their data conform to these assumptions prior to drawing conclusions about their data as it will help to ensure that their statistical results are non-biased.

The following six assumptions have been referred to as the "classical linear model assumptions of time-series regression" (Pickup, 2015: 56–57; Wooldridge, 2010). The assumptions are (1) stationarity, (2) zero conditional mean (exogeneity), (3) no perfect collinearity, (4) homoskedasticity, (5) no serial correlation, and (6) linearity in the parameters. We will briefly review each of these.

The first assumption is stationarity. A longitudinal data series is said to be stationary if the mean, variances, and other statistical properties are constant over time (Pickup, 2015). The Dickey-Fuller test (*dfuller*) can be used to test for nonstationarity. It is a test for whether the variable has a unit root (which is the null hypothesis) or alternatively follows a random walk (Dickey & Fuller, 1979). The presence of a unit root signifies nonstationarity, therefore if you reject the Dickey-Fuller test your data are stationary. Nonstationarity may produce artificially high correlations when variables trend together. Often if there is an existing trend in the data between some of the time-series variables, an option to minimize its impact on the estimates is to de-trend the data by differencing the dependent and independent variables prior to estimating the partial slope coefficients.

Longitudinal data are also expected to be "exogenous." A violation of exogeneity is referred to as endogeneity. Endogeneity results from a correlation between an independent variable and the error term in the statistical model and can occur from omitted variables, measurement error of variables, or simultaneity (Pickup, 2015). Simultaneity, or a simultaneous reciprocal relationship, can be especially problematic in longitudinal data as the causal order or the direction of the relationship between variables is questionable. There are numerous ways to test causal order between two time-series variables. A common method is the Granger causality test (Granger, 1969, 2004), which is a hypothesis used for determining whether one time-series variable predicts a second time-series variable. This can be done using the Stata command *vargranger*.

As in OLS regression, the absence of perfect multicollinearity is an assumption in longitudinal regression models for continuous outcomes. No independent variables can be perfect linear combinations of each other. Longitudinal panel models can be re-estimated using OLS, and then collinearity diagnostics like the variance inflation factor (VIF) can be obtained using the postestimation command *estat vif* in Stata.

Homoskedasticity, or homogeneity of variance, occurs when the standard deviation of the residuals are constant and do not depend on values of the independent variables. When errors are heteroskedastic, standard errors can be incorrect, causing misleading hypothesis tests. Heteroskedasticity can be tested for using the Breusch-Pagan/Cook-Weisberg test (Pickup, 2015), where the null hypothesis is constant error variance. Stata uses the command *estat hettest* to run the Breusch-Pagan/Cook-Weisberg test. The White test can also be used to test for heteroskedasticity, using the Stata postestimation command *imtest, white*, which tests a similar null hypothesis to the Breusch-Pagan/Cook-Weisberg test. If these tests indicate that heteroskedasticity is a problem, using Huber-White robust standard errors often fixes the problem as they take the clustering of observations into account. Robust standard errors can be requested in place of traditional standard errors in Stata using the *vce(robust)* option.

A very important assumption in longitudinal data is serial correlation, also referred to as autocorrelation or serial correlated errors, which occurs when the errors of a time-series variable are correlated over time. Serial correlation may introduce estimation problems in time-series data when it produces inefficient slopes and biased standard errors that distort statistical significance tests. The Durbin-Watson (*estat dwatson*) and Wooldridge (*xtoserial*) tests both test for serial correlation using Stata. If the tests indicate serial correlation is present, first-order autoregressive (AR(1)) standard errors can be used to correct the problem (*xtregar*), or a different estimation method that corrects for serial correlation like Prais-Winsten (*prais*) regression can be used.

Finally, just as in OLS, linearity in the parameters assumption requires that the dependent variable is a linear combination of the independent variables and the residuals. We now turn to a brief discussion of the data we will use in the examples later in the chapter.

CITES and the data

The Convention on International Trade in Endangered Species (CITES) is an agreement between national governments that aims to guarantee that all legal international trade in wildlife does not threaten the long-term survival of the species (CITES, 2018b). CITES began enforcement in July 1975 and offers some level of protection for over 35,000 species of plants and animals, whether they are live animals, animal parts, or derivatives (CITES, 2018b). CITES also keeps a database of all of international trade in wildlife that is available on their website (CITES, 2018a). It contains annual data on international wildlife trade during the period 1975–2017.

For purely illustrative purposes we use a subsample of CITES data to illustrate several different types of regression analyses using longitudinal techniques. Because these data are used for illustrative purposes, the results presented in the following analyses should not be given any substantive meaning.

We downloaded annual export data from 2000–2009 for the family Accipitridae, which contains hawks and eagles. The resulting data was cleaned and aggregated to the country-year level, so we have the annual number of exports (live or parts) of the Accipitridae family, per country, per year. For a country to remain in the dataset, it must have had export data for at least three of the years in the series. The choice of this subset of the CITES data is purely by chance and used for illustration purposes. Once the data were cleaned and in the person-period format, we combined the CITES data with several cross-national demographic and economic variables from the World Bank, World Development Indicators (World Bank, 2018) database to create a panel dataset where time is measured in years (from 2000 to 2009) and the panel is country ($N = 80$; a list of the countries can be found in Appendix A). We also created an indicator of whether or not the exporting country is located in Asia. This is a dichotomous time-invariant variable (Asia = 1, else = 0). At this point, we used the command *xtset* in Stata, to let the program know that our data is panel. We are now ready to do some longitudinal data analysis.

We will follow the same general example using this dataset throughout the rest of the chapter. Suppose we were interested in whether economic growth/decline was somehow related to the international trade in hawks and eagles during the decade of the 2000s. In this example, we use gross domestic product (GDP) per capita to measure the economic welfare of a country, and in the longitudinal models we can model the effects of annual changes (i.e., growth or decline) in economic welfare on hawk and eagle exports. One possible alternative explanation of increases or decreases in hawk and eagle exports could be due to the amount of income that countries make from exports in general. It may be the case that increases in hawk and eagle exports occur because the country is just exporting more total goods. We used the percent of a country's GDP from the exports of goods and services as a control variable in the models. We also control for population density and percent of the population living in urban areas.

To summarize, the dependent variable in our examples is the number of hawks and eagles (or parts) exported from a country in a given year ("birds_ex" in the Stata output). The four time-varying independent variables in the models are GDP per capita ("gdp_pc"), percent of GDP from exports of goods and services in a given year ("exports"), population density ("pop_den"), and percent of the population living in urban areas ("urban"). In models where we are able to estimate the effects of a time-invariant predictor, we use the dichotomous variable that indicates whether an exporting country is located in Asia (coded "1" or elsewhere coded "0"). We report the models in the original Stata v.15.1 output form, rather than placing them into more traditional tables. We do this for pedagogical reasons, as it enables us to discuss the important parts of what Stata provides to the user. We now turn to our discussion of the different panel regression models.

Within and between effects

In longitudinal panel regression, there are two main types of effects that are usually modeled: (1) within the same cases (i.e., at different time-periods) or "within-effects," and (2) between different cases, or "between-effects." "Fixed-effects" regression models focus exclusively on modeling the within-effects. "Random-effects" regression models produce estimates based on both within- and between-effects, while "multilevel models for change" provide separate estimates of the within and between effects. We review each of these models in detail below.

Prior to beginning those analyses, however, we must produce summary statistics of variables that reports the within-subject, between-subject, and total variability. This information can be retrieved using Stata's *xtsum* command. Let's take a look at the different sources of variability for the dependent and main

Table 11.1 Overall, between, and within effects estimates

Variable		Mean	Std. Dev.	Min	Max	Observations
bird_ex	overall	141.5358	962.7615	0	16154	N = 550
	between		443.3776	.6666667	3882.5	n = 80
	within		805.8837	-3,740.964	12,413.04	T-bar = 6.875
gdp_pc	overall	13,357.52	17,084.87	138.9249	97,007.94	N = 800
	between		16,246.29	248.9585	63,057.55	n = 80
	within		5,560.941	-11,553.31	47,307.91	T = 10

independent variable in our hypothetical example. This is done by examining the standard deviation for each variable across the overall, between and within models shown in Table 11.1.

It appears, given the magnitude of the standard deviations, that the majority of variability in bird_ex is *within* countries (805.88 vs. 443.38), while gdp_pc has more *between* country variability (16,246.29 vs. 5,560.94). Under the "observations" columns at the right end of the table is the summary of the observations for each variable where N = total number of valid observations; n = the number of cases (in this case, countries); and *T-bar* = the average number of valid data points per country.

Fixed-effects models

The fixed-effects panel regression model, sometimes also referred to as fixed intercept models, can be specified as:

$$Y_{ct} = X_{ct}B + \alpha_c + e_{ct} \text{ for } t = 1, \ldots, T \text{ and } c = 1, \ldots, N$$

Where Y_{ct} is the dependent variable for the country c at time t, X_{ct} is a $1 \times k$ matrix of predictor variables, α_c is the unobserved time-variant country effect, and e_{ct} is the error term. The error term has mean = 0, a constant variance, and is uncorrelated across time periods and subjects (Rabe-Hesketh & Skrondal, 2012a). We chose to refer to the panel indicator as c for country, because our example analyzes countries over time. Fixed-effects regression models examine within-subject change only; they ignore between-subject differences. This allows the researcher to, as Allison (2009: 1) notes, "control for variables that have not or cannot be measured. The basic idea is very simple: Use each individual (or case) as his or her own control." This enables the fixed-effects models to control for characteristics of the individuals not explicitly included in the models, often referred to as "omitted variable bias." One major downside of fixed-effects models, however, is that only independent variables that vary over time can be included in the models. Fixed-effects panel regression models cannot provide estimates of time-invariant predictors, those variables that do not change over time (e.g., gender, ethnicity, region of the world). This is because time-invariant independent variables are perfectly collinear with α_c from the equation above (Fitzmaurice et al., 2011).

Before moving on, we would like to make a few notes about the example in this section and the ones in the subsequent sections. We are assuming that the data meets the assumptions that were discussed above. In practice, researchers should test for all of the violations of the assumptions using the methods and tests reviewed earlier. Here, we do not review all such tests and focus on those areas that contain the most important information. We recommend consulting Rabe-Hesketh and Skrondal (2012a, 2012b) for further details.

Below we estimated a fixed-effects panel regression model using the *xtreg* command with the *fe* option (Table 11.2). The fixed-effects model provides

Table 11.2 Fixed-effects panel regression estimates

Fixed-effects (within) regression	Number of obs = 541
Group variable: Country_ID	Number of groups = 79
R-sq:	Obs per group:
Within = 0.0048	min = 3
between = 0.0000	avg = 6.8
overall = 0.0004	max = 10
	F(4,458) = 0.55
corr(u_i, Xb) = -0.8461	Prob > F = 0.7016

bird_ex	Coef.	Std. Err.	t	P>|t|	[95% Conf.	Interval]
gdp_pc	.0057641	.0072731	0.79	0.428	-.0085286	.0200569
exports	5.664936	7.491247	0.76	0.450	-9.056543	20.38641
pop_den	-.4029844	2.769476	-0.15	0.884	-5.84544	5.039471
urban	-39.26212	33.23642	-1.18	0.238	-104.5769	26.05266
_cons	2,327.598	2,017.114	1.15	0.249	-1,636.348	6,291.544
sigma_u	1,011.1736					
sigma_e	880.21963					
rho	.56890646	(fraction of variance due to u_i)				

F test that all u_i=0: F(78, 458) = 2.52 Prob > F = 0.0000

estimates of within-country changes in hawk and eagle exports using GDP per capita, total exports, population density, and urban population as the predictors.

In this fixed-effects model, there were 541 cases over time used to estimate the model, coming from 79 of the 80 countries in the dataset. The average number of valid data points per country was 6.8 (range 3 to 10). The overall model is tested with an F test (0.55; p = 0.7016), indicating that the combined effects of the four predictors does not significantly predict annual within-country changes in hawk and eagle exports. The R^2_{within} is very similar to the traditional R^2 in OLS regression. As we would expect from a model that is not significant, it explains less than 1% of the variation in the dependent variable. The "Coef" column contains the partial slope coefficient of each independent variable and the intercept (_cons). These values are interpreted as how annual change in the independent variable affects annual change in the dependent variable. The *t*-tests and probability values ($P>|t|$) demonstrate that none of the independent variables are significant at $\alpha = 0.05$ level. The sigma_u is the estimate of the standard deviation of the level 2 residuals; sigma_e is the estimate of the standard deviation of the level 1 residuals; and rho is the interclass correlation. In sum, this is a very poor fitting model that tells us nothing about what predicts annual within-country changes in hawk and eagle export.

Random-effects models

We now turn to the random-effects panel regression model, sometimes referred to as "linear mixed-effects models." According to Fitzmaurice et al. (2011: 189),

> [t]he underlying premise of linear mixed models is that some subset of the regression parameters vary randomly from one individual to another, thereby accounting for sources of natural heterogeneity in the population . . . The distinctive feature of linear mixed effects models is that the mean response is modeled as a combination of population characteristics, β, that are assumed to be shared by all individuals, and subject-specific effects that are unique to a particular individual.

In other words, random-effects use both within and between differences to create their estimates of population parameters, often yielding standard errors that are much smaller than those from a fixed-effects model. One result of using the between-effects in addition to the within-effects is that random-effects models can include time-invariant predictors in the models.

To estimate a random-effects panel regression model in Stata use the *xtreg* command. Random-effects is the default option for *xtreg* (however, you can also specify it with the *re* option). In Table 11.3 we estimated a random-effect panel regression model using the same dependent variable and predictors as in

Table 11.3 Random-effect panel regression model

```
Random-effects GLS regression                  Number of obs      =     541
Group variable: Country_ID                     Number of groups   =      79

R-sq:                                          Obs per group:
     Within = 0.0007                                        Min =       3
     between = 0.1019                                       Avg =     6.8
     overall = 0.0399                                       max =      10

                                               Wald chi2(5)       =   13.48
corr(u_i, X) = 0 (assumed)                     Prob > chi2        =  0.0193
```

<table>
<tr><th>bird_ex</th><th>Coef.</th><th>Std. Err.</th><th>Z</th><th>P>|z|</th><th>[95% Conf.</th><th>Interval]</th></tr>
<tr><td>gdp_pc</td><td>.0013501</td><td>.0034418</td><td>0.39</td><td>0.695</td><td>-.0053956</td><td>.0080959</td></tr>
<tr><td>exports</td><td>3.525222</td><td>2.784254</td><td>1.27</td><td>0.205</td><td>-1.931815</td><td>8.98226</td></tr>
<tr><td>pop_den</td><td>-.2130645</td><td>.1077511</td><td>-1.98</td><td>0.048</td><td>-.4242528</td><td>-.0018763</td></tr>
<tr><td>Urban</td><td>.0926436</td><td>2.763208</td><td>0.03</td><td>0.973</td><td>-5.323144</td><td>5.508431</td></tr>
<tr><td>Asia</td><td>502.3675</td><td>142.538</td><td>3.52</td><td>0.000</td><td>222.9981</td><td>781.7369</td></tr>
<tr><td>_cons</td><td>-70.78004</td><td>175.1927</td><td>-0.40</td><td>0.686</td><td>-414.1515</td><td>272.5914</td></tr>
<tr><td>sigma_u</td><td>242.18523</td><td></td><td></td><td></td><td></td><td></td></tr>
<tr><td>sigma_e</td><td>881.17989</td><td></td><td></td><td></td><td></td><td></td></tr>
<tr><td>rho</td><td>.07023286</td><td colspan="5">(fraction of variance due to u_i)</td></tr>
</table>

the fixed-effects model above. We have added the time-invariant variable "Asia" as an independent variable, as this is permitted in random-effects models.

At first glance, the random-effects model appears to fit better than the fixed-effects model. Random-effects models use a Wald chi-square to test model significance. In this case the probability value (0.0193) is less than 0.05, so the combined effects of all the independent variables significantly predicts annual changes in hawk and eagle exports. Recall that random-effects models use both the within and between case variability to generate estimates of the slope coefficients. Interestingly, the coefficient of pop_den (–0.213) is significantly related to hawk and eagle exports. Specifically, annual increases in population density lead to significantly fewer hawk and eagle exports. Additionally, the time-invariant predictor, Asia is significant at the $p < 0.001$ level indicating that countries in Asia are exporting more hawks and eagles. However, as the R^2 values indicate, this model does not explain much variability.

Picking between fixed and random effects

The main difference between fixed- and random-effects models is whether the α_c are assumed to be correlated with the covariates. In a fixed-effects model, the α_c are treated as a set of fixed numbers, whereas in random effects the α_c is treated as random with mean = 0, constant variance, and is uncorrelated with the predictor variables (Allison, 2009: 21).

Several factors affect the decision to use either a fixed- or random-effects model. First, if your study requires estimates of time-invariant predictors, you have no choice but to use a random-effects model. Second, you can examine the value of the interclass correlation which provides a measure of how much of the total variation is due to within-effects and how much is due to between-effects. This can be used to decide if it is worth including the between effects and going with a random-effects model over a fixed-effects model. If we return to the random-effects model above (Table 11.3), Stata labels the interclass correlation, rho, which in this case equals 0.07, which is a very low value as the interclass correlation ranges from 0 to 1. A low value means that very little of the variation in the dependent variable is explained by within-effects, suggesting that a random-effects model is preferable to a fixed-effects model. Third, you can conduct a Hausman test, using the *hausman* command in Stata, to determine whether the variation across individuals is uncorrelated with the independent variables, an assumption of the random-effects model. If you fail to reject the null hypothesis of the Hausman test, you should use a random-effects model; if you reject the null, then the assumption of individual level correlation is violated and you should use a fixed-effects model. This is illustrated in Table 11.4. In this case, the Hausman test indicates that the null hypothesis cannot be rejected indicating that a random-effects model should be used.

A final option would be to consider a type of model that can provide estimates of within and between effects separately. Both Allison (2009) and Fitzmaurice

Table 11.4 Hausman test results

bird_ex	----Coefficients ---- (b) fixed	(B) Random	(b-B) Difference	sqrt(diag(V_b-V_B)) S.E.
gdp_pc	.0057641	.0013501	.004414	.0064072
Exports	5.664936	3.525222	2.139713	6.954619
pop_den	-.4029844	-.2130645	-.1899199	2.767379
Urban	-39.26212	.0926436	39.35477	33.12136

```
        b = consistent under Ho and Ha; obtained from xtreg
B = inconsistent under Ha, efficient under Ho; obtained from xtreg

Test: Ho: difference in coefficients not systematic

           chi2(4)  =  (b-B)'[(V_b-V_B)^(-1)](b-B)
                    =  1.63
         Prob>chi2  =  0.8033
```

et al. (2011) discuss the appeal of so-called hybrid models that model fixed and random effects. We now turn to a discussion of one of these types of models, the "multilevel model for change."

Multilevel model for change

As Menard (2002: 77) notes,

> [t]he basic model for multilevel analysis of longitudinal data involves two levels, the individual or case level (level 2), with data that describes characteristics of the case that do not vary over time, and the observation level (level 1), with data on repeated measurements of individual characteristics, including the dependent variable, that do vary over time.

In other words, the level 1 data is used to estimate the within effects, while the level 2 data is used to estimate the between effects. This approach can be quite useful as it is possible to test two different hypotheses (one about the within effects, one about the between effects) at the same time, in the same model.

Singer and Willett (2003) provide a useful framework for writing the multilevel model for change using two sub-models, one for the within-case changes (or how a person/case changes over time) and one for the between-case differences (or how the within-case changes differ between cases). The most basic within-case (level 1) portion of the model consisting of one explanatory variable, "Time" can be written as:

$$Y_{ct} = \pi_{0c} + \pi_{1c}(Time_{ct}) + e_{ct} \text{ for } t = 1, \ldots, T \text{ and } c = 1, \ldots, N$$

The most basic between-case (level 2) portion of the model can be written with the following two equations:

$$\pi_{0c} = \beta_{00} + r_{0c}$$
$$\pi_{1c} = \beta_{10} + r_{1c}$$

where the parameters of interest in the level 1 part of the model (π_{0c} and π_{1c}) are now the outcomes of interest in the level 2 part of the model. Here, β_{00} and β_{10} are the fixed effects (intercepts) for the intercept and slope, and r_{0c} and r_{1c} are the unique effects of the *c*th case on the intercept and the slope (Holden et al., 2008). The command *xtmixed* can be used to estimate multilevel models for change in Stata.

Table 11.5 illustrates a version of the multilevel model of change where the level 1 values are the case's variable values over time, while level two takes the average of the level 1 variables and uses them to examine between effects. In other words, level 1 values will be a country's value at one particular time point and level 2 values will be the average country value over the years 2000–2009. We should note that in this type of multilevel model for change, the level 2 variables do not have to be the average value over the entire period. Through the process of centering (see Singer & Willett, 2003 for an extended discussion on centering), the level 2 variables are often centered around the time-period's midpoint, which turns the level 2 effects into the between effects for the middle year of the time-series. Similarly, endpoint centering is also popular, where the level 2 effects become the between effects for the final year in the time-series. Centering decisions should be made based on what would be most appropriate for the research questions and the hypotheses that you are testing.

In the multilevel model for change below predicting hawk and eagle exports, at level 1 we have the four continuous predictors from our earlier models (GDP per capita, total exports, population density and urban population). We have also included a variable for "Year" to control for the effect of time. In the level 2 portion of the model, we created four new variables that are the average value of the level one variables for each country between 2000 and 2009. These variables are preceded with "L2" in the variable names. The indicator for Asia is also in the level 2 part of the model.

The multilevel model for change uses a Wald test to assess the overall significance of the model, and this model is not significant ($p = 0.1328$). In the within-effects (level 1) portion of the model, urban is significant ($\alpha = 0.05$), indicating that annual increases in the percent of people living in urban areas leads to a decrease in the number of hawks and eagles exported. The *Year* indicator is significant and positive, suggesting that more birds were being exported as the years in the time-series increased – or that over time, these exports increased. Interestingly, L2_urban is significant and positive in the between-effects (level 2) portion of the model. This finding suggests that countries with higher average urban population between 2000 and 2009 exported more hawks and eagles. In some ways, this outcome is contradictory to the finding for the effects of

Table 11.5 Multilevel change model

Random-effects GLS regression	Number of obs = 541
Group variable: Country_ID	Number of groups = 79
	Obs per group:
	Min = 3
	Avg = 6.8
	max = 10
	Wald chi2(5) = 14.98
Log likelihood = -4,454.3323	Prob > chi2 = 0.0193

bird_ex	Coef.	Std. Err.	z	P>|z|	[95% Conf.	Interval]
gdp_pc	-.0052599	.008928	-0.59	0.556	-.0227585	.0122387
exports	4.2341	7.053281	0.60	0.548	-9.590077	18.05828
pop_den	-1.961683	2.692327	-0.73	0.466	-7.238546	3.31518
Urban	-83.47638	39.64425	-2.11	0.035	-161.1777	-5.775084
Year	45.46951	21.95476	2.07	0.038	2.438982	88.50004
L2_gdp_pc	.0056065	.010072	0.56	0.578	-.0141343	.0253473
L2_exports	-.590995	7.762254	-0.08	0.939	-15.80473	14.62274
L2_pop_den	1.696296	2.601348	0.65	0.514	-3.402252	6.794845
L2_urban	84.25191	39.79884	2.12	0.034	6.24762	162.2562
Asia	469.4891	165.8342	2.83	0.005	144.4599	794.5182
_cons	-91,240.74	44,007.53	-2.07	0.038	-177,493.9	-4,987.562

Random-effects Parameters	Estimate	Std. Err.	[95% Conf.	Interval]
Country_ID: Identity				
var(_cons)	129,382.7	34,043.06	77,251.82	216,692.4
var(Residual)	742,105.2	47,808.77	65,4076.2	841,981.5

LR test vs. linear model: chibar2(01) = 40.40 Prob >= chibar2 = 0.0000 urban in the level 1 analysis, and requires further context extracted from the level 2 analysis to interpret. While the effect of urban appears contradictory, at the same time the increased effect of urban on exports is consistent with the level 1 effect for *Year*. Finally, the dichotomous indicator *Asia* was significant, indicating that countries in Asia exported more birds on average compared to countries located elsewhere in the world.

Now that we have estimated all three models, which one should we pick as the most appropriate? As noted earlier, none of the models are very good as they all explain little of the variability in the dependent variable. This is a common problem in criminological studies of factors that are suspected of causing crime, especially at the individual level. In that case, specific hypotheses are being assessed, and the weak outcomes ought to, in those cases, be employed to reject the specific causal hypotheses. In the current example, however, we did not choose this dataset to test any specific hypotheses. Rather we selected the data, including the dependent variables, in order to illustrate the use of a particular empirical method of analysis, and the data used were not selected to test any specific, pre-specified hypotheses. As a result, it should come as no surprise that the empirical results were poor. Nonetheless, the results from the models produce some basic results that illustrate how to determine which model to select. Specifically, given that pop_den and Asia were significant in the random-effects model and the Hausman test was not rejected, the random-effects model is clearly better than the fixed-effects model. We would also argue that the random-effects model is better than the multilevel model for change, as the Wald test for the overall significance of the model was significant in the random-effects model, but not significant for the multilevel model for change.

As noted, the models described above fit the data poorly. This outcome, we suggest, resulted because we did not use theory to guide the specification of our models. One possible perspective that may inform our understanding of the drivers of hawk and eagle exports is ecologically unequal exchange (EUE), which has recently been employed to examine predictors of the global Saker Falcon trade (Stretesky et al., 2018). EUE theory suggests that developed countries externalize a substantial amount of the negative environmental consequences of their consumptive behavior to less developed countries (LDCs). This increases environmental degradation in LDCs, often including natural resource extraction and exports of primary sector commodities (Hornborg, 1998; Jorgenson, 2006). The primary sector of economies generally refers to the natural resources, agriculture, mining, and fishing industries. The export of live animals and animal parts is a primary sector activity. To test the EUE argument with the hawk and eagle export data, we could follow the work of Jorgenson and colleagues (Jorgenson & Rice, 2005; Jorgenson et al., 2009), who have developed a "weighted export flows" measure for primary sector exports, "that quantifies the relative extent to which a nation's exports are sent to more-developed countries" (Jorgenson & Rice, 2005: 433). Creating and using a similar measure to predict hawk and eagle exports may provide stronger results than the ones we found in this chapter.

Similarly, we could test indicators of the "declining-population paradigm" in conservation biology, which attempts to understand the human-drivers of species extinction (Caughley, 1994). In that view, one approach to conservation is to have the government set aside land in the form of parks and wildlife refuges to "protect" it from economic development and other destructive human activities, which in theory would provide protected spaces for species habitats. To assess that argument, researchers could employ the percent of all land in a country that is protected, as recently illustrated by Stretesky et al. (2018). There are numerous other perspectives and hypotheses that could be examined here to further understand what drives hawk and eagle exports including ecological modernization, the treadmill of production, and so forth. Basically, as with all social science, let theory guide your hypotheses, variable choices and model specification.

Conclusion

In this chapter, we have suggested that longitudinal analysis of panel data should play a more prominent role in empirical studies of green crimes. These methodological approaches, which are quite common in orthodox criminology and environmental sociology, have not been widely used within green criminology. It is our hope that we can encourage more green criminologists to analyze panel data. In this chapter, we first described the uniqueness of panel data, followed by a discussion of how to set up your data for analysis and test the numerous assumptions of longitudinal data. We then reviewed fixed-effects regression models, random-effects regression models and multilevel models for change using examples based on CITES data. Throughout the chapter we have focused on how to estimate the models and test and correct for violations of assumption using the statistical package Stata (v.15). Other statistical packages like R and SAS are also able to estimate the models discussed in this chapter. In the end, we believe that longitudinal data analysis can be very beneficial to the development of green criminology because of its ability to model change and examine the causes of ecological destruction. Menard (2002: 80) said it best when he noted in the conclusion to his classic book, *Longitudinal Research*: "[t]he conclusion is inescapable, however, that for the description and analysis of dynamic change processes, longitudinal research is ultimately indispensable."

References

Allison, Paul D. (2009). *Fixed Effects Regression Models*. London: Sage.

Caughley, Graeme. (1994). "Directions in Conservation Biology." *Journal of Animal Ecology* 63 (2): 215–244.

CITES. (2018a). "CITES Trade Database." https://trade.cites.org/ (accessed June 29, 2018).

CITES. (2018b). "What Is CITES?" www.cites.org/eng/disc/what.php (accessed June 29, 2018).

Dickey, David A. and Wayne A. Fuller. (1979). "Distribution of the Estimators for Autoregressive Time Series with a Unit Root." *Journal of the American Statistical Association* 74 (366a): 427–431.

Finkel, Steven E. (1995). *Causal Analysis with Panel Data*. London: Sage.
Fitzmaurice, Garrett M., Nan M. Laird and James H. Ware. (2011). *Applied Longitudinal Analysis*, Second Edition. Hoboken, NJ: John Wiley & Sons.
Granger, C.W.J. (2004). "Time-Series Analysis, Cointegration, and Applications." *American Economic Review* 94 (3): 421–425.
Granger, C.W.J. (1969). "Investigating Causal Relations by Econometric Models and Cross-Spectral Methods." *Econometrica* 37 (3): 424–438.
Holden, Jocelyn, Ken Kelley and Rajiv Agarwal. (2008). "Analyzing Change: A Primer on Multilevel Models with Applications to Nephrology." *American Journal of Nephrology* 28 (5): 792–801.
Hornborg, Alf. (1998). "Towards an Ecological Theory of Unequal Exchange: Articulating World Systems Theory and Ecological Economics." *Ecological Economics* 25: 127–136.
Jorgenson, Andrew K. (2007). "Does Foreign Investment Harm the Air We Breathe and the Water We Drink? A Cross-National Study of Carbon Dioxide Emissions and Organic Water Pollution in Less-Developed Countries, 1975–2000." *Organization & Environment* 20 (2): 137–156.
Jorgenson, Andrew K. (2006). "Unequal Ecological Exchange and Environmental Degradation: A Theoretical Proposition and Cross-National Study of Deforestation, 1990–2000." *Rural Sociology* 71: 685–712.
Jorgenson, Andrew K., Kelly Austin and Christopher Dick. (2009). "Ecologically Unequal Exchange and the Resource Consumption/Environmental Degradation Paradox: A Panel Study of Less-Developed Countries, 1970–2000." *International Journal of Comparative Sociology* 50 (3–4): 263–284.
Jorgenson, Andrew K. and Brett Clark. (2010). "Assessing the Temporal Stability of the Population/Environment Relationship in Comparative Perspective: A Cross-National Panel Study of Carbon Dioxide Emissions, 1960–2005." *Population and Environment* 32 (1): 27–41.
Jorgenson, Andrew K. and James Rice. (2005). "Structural Dynamics of International Trade and Material Consumption: A Cross-National Study of the Ecological Footprint of Less-Developed Countries." *Journal of World-Systems Research* 11: 57–77.
Long, Michael A., Michael J. Lynch and Paul B. Stretesky. (2018). "The Great Recession, the Treadmill of Production and Ecological Disorganization: Did the Recession Decrease Toxic Releases Across US States, 2005–2014?" *Ecological Economics* 146: 184–192.
Long, Michael A., Rebecca Oswald, Paul B. Stretesky and Sarah Soppitt. (forthcoming). "Do Flood Mitigation and Natural Habitat Protection Employment Reduce Youth Offending?" *European Journal on Criminal Policy and Research*. DOI: 10.1007/s10610-017-9365-y
Long, Michael A., Paul B. Stretesky and Michael J. Lynch. (2017). "Foreign Direct Investment, Ecological Withdrawals and Natural Resource Dependent Economies." *Society & Natural Resources* 30 (10): 1261–1276.
Lynch, Michael J., Kimberly L. Barrett, Paul B. Stretesky and Michael A. Long. (2017). "The Neglect of Quantitative Research in Green Criminology and Its Consequences." *Critical Criminology* 25 (2): 183–198.
Martinez, Ramiro, Jr., Jacob I. Stowell and Matthew T. Lee. (2010). "Immigration and Crime in an Era of Transformation: A Longitudinal Analysis of Homicides in San Diego Neighborhoods, 1980–2000." *Criminology* 48 (3): 797–829.
Menard, Scott. (2002). *Longitudinal Research*, Second Edition. London: Sage.

Phillips, Julie A. (2006). "The Relationship between Age Structure and Homicide Rates in the United States, 1970–1999." *Journal of Research in Crime and Delinquency* 43 (3): 230–260.

Pickup, Mark. (2015). *Introduction to Time Series Analysis.* London: Sage.

Rabe-Hesketh, Sophia and Anders Skrondal. (2012a). *Multilevel and Longitudinal Modeling Using Stata, Volume I: Continuous Responses*, Third Edition. College Station, TX: Stata Press.

Rabe-Hesketh, Sophia and Anders Skrondal. (2012b). *Multilevel and Longitudinal Modeling Using Stata, Volume II: Categorical Responses, Counts, and Survival*, Third Edition. College Station, TX: Stata Press.

Royston, Patrick. 2007. "Multiple Imputation of Missing Values: Further Update of Ice, with an Emphasis on Interval Censoring." *Stata Journal* 7: 445–464.

Singer, Judith D. and John B. Willett. (2003). *Applied Longitudinal Data Analysis: Modeling Change and Event Occurrence.* Oxford and New York: Oxford University Press.

Stretesky, Paul B., Michael A. Long and Michael J. Lynch. (2017a). "Trends in the Formation of Environmental Enforcement International Non-Governmental Organizations, 1950–2010." *Globalizations* 14 (4): 627–642.

Stretesky, Paul B., Michael A. Long and Michael J. Lynch. (2017b). "A Cross-National Study of the Association between Natural Resource Rents and Homicide Rates, 2000–12." *European Journal of Criminology* 14 (4): 393–414.

Stretesky, Paul B., Michael A. Long and Michael J. Lynch. (2013). "Does Environmental Enforcement Slow the Treadmill of Production? The Relationship between Large Money Penalties and Toxic Releases within Offending Corporations." *Journal of Crime and Justice* 36 (2): 233–247.

Stretesky, Paul B., Michael A. Long, Ruth E. McKie and Feizel A. Ayree. (forthcoming). "Does Oil and Gas Development Increase Crime within UK Local Authorities?" *The Extractive Industries and Society.* DOI: doi.org/10.1016/j.exis.2018.03.006

Stretesky, Paul B., Michael J. Lynch, Michael A. Long and Kimberly L. Barrett. (2017). "Does the Modernization of Environmental Enforcement Reduce Toxic Releases? An Examination of Self-Policing, Criminal Prosecutions and Toxic Releases in the United States, 1988–2014." *Sociological Spectrum* 37 (1): 48–62.

Stretesky, Paul B., Ruth E. McKie, Michael J. Lynch, Michael A. Long and Kimberly L. Barrett. (2018). "Where Have All the Falcons Gone? Saker Falcon (Falco Cherrug) Exports in a Global Economy." *Global Ecology and Conservation* 13: e00372. DOI: 10.1016/j.gecco.2017.e00372

Wooldridge, Jeffrey M. (2010). *Econometric Analysis of Cross Section and Panel Data*, Second Edition. Cambridge, MA: MIT Press.

World Bank. (2018). "World Bank Data Bank." http://databank.worldbank.org/data/ reports.aspx?source=world-development-indicators (accessed June 30, 2018).

Appendix A

List of countries in the example dataset (N = 80)

Argentina	Ghana	Mongolia	Slovenia
Australia	Greenland	Morocco	South Africa
Austria	Guatemala	Myanmar	Spain
Belgium	Guinea	Namibia	Sudan
Brazil	Guyana	Nepal	Suriname
Cameroon	Hungary	Netherlands	Swaziland
Canada	India	New Zealand	Sweden
Chad	Isle of Man	Nigeria	Switzerland
China	Israel	Norway	Tanzania
Congo, DR	Italy	Pakistan	Togo
Costa Rica	Japan	Panama	Uganda
Côte d'Ivoire	Kazakhstan	Papua New Guinea	Ukraine
Czech Rep.	Korea, S.	Peru	United Arab Emirates
Denmark	Latvia	Philippines	United Kingdom
Ecuador	Lithuania	Poland	United States
El Salvador	Madagascar	Portugal	Uruguay
Estonia	Malawi	Russian Fed.	Uzbekistan
Finland	Mali	Senegal	Venezuela
France	Mexico	Singapore	Yemen
Germany	Moldova	Slovakia	Zimbabwe

12 No longer Victorian children

Understanding green victimization through an analysis of victim impact statements

Joshua Ozymy and Melissa Jarrell

The term "green criminology" was created by Lynch (1990: 1), who suggested the field would examine "environmental destruction as an outcome of the structure of modern industrial capitalist production and consumption patterns." More recently, it has been suggested that the field be formally defined as "the study of those harms against humanity, against the environment, and against non-human animals committed by both powerful institutions and also by ordinary people" (Beirne and South, 2017: xiii). Green criminology is an interdisciplinary sub-field of research interests that has much in common with the related fields of white collar, corporate, and state-corporate crime (Jarrell and Ozymy, 2014; South et al., 2013). Green criminology strives to document the nature and extent of green harm, explore why these harms occur, who is responsible, and propose plans of action and policies to address them (Ruggiero, 2013).

Consistent with the focus of this book, we suggest that during its almost three decades of its existence, green criminology has suffered from a lack of studies employing empirical data. In particular, we would assert that one of the more neglected areas of empirical research relates to victimization, and we suggest that only a handful of studies exist that can help us understand the magnitude of green victimization in general and in specific contexts. More specifically, we draw attention to the fact that green criminologists have done little to use empirical data to depict how green victims perceive their own victimization. The latter problem is magnified by the fact that green victims are rarely recognized by the courts and thus in a legal sense, understanding victimization through the lens of legally identifiable victims is quite difficult and rarely represented in the literature. In short, neither green criminology nor the courts have encouraged understanding how victims of green crime perceive their victimization.

In a rare turn of events in the United States, CITGO Refining was convicted of violations under the US Clean Air Act (CAA) in 2014. At sentencing, the court allowed victims to testify and read victim impact statements regarding their victimization and perceived impact that living in the nearby fenceline community had on their health, their family, and their overall well-being. Fenceline communities are neighborhoods that are adjacent to industrial facilities and related corporate or public hazards that experience detrimental outcome which may, for example, stem from exposure to forms of pollution that impact public health or produce adverse health consequences. The CITGO case was the first time a petroleum refinery had been criminally prosecuted and convicted under the CAA and the first time that green victims were legally recognized and allowed to testify in such a case. The authors engaged in participant observation throughout the investigation, prosecution, and sentencing phases of the CITGO case, which lasted about a decade. In this chapter we provide an overview of the role of victims in the US legal system, a history of the *United States v. CITGO* case and related cases that recognize victims, and then finally an analysis of a sample of the victim impact statements that were read at sentencing. We hope to demonstrate not only the value of this legal case for green victims' rights, but the role academics can play in such a fight and the value of using victim impact statements as a source of data to show how green victims interpret their own victimization.

Green victimization and the regulatory system

Countries generally employ a deterrence approach to controlling environmental crime (Pink, 2013). This approach is steeped in the idea that if environmental criminals know that the state will be willing and able to sufficiently punishment them for wrongdoing their propensity to commit crimes will decrease (Simpson et al., 2013). In practice, corporate environmental offenders are rarely treated as criminals under the standard criminal justice model and victims of these offenders are rarely protected in the criminal justice system or given any voice. While corporate environmental offenders may be prosecuted for environmental crimes or crimes occurring during the commission of said crimes, in practice most of their malfeasance is handled as a regulatory issue (Ozymy and Jarrell, 2016, 2017a). From an enforcement perspective, victims must rely on regulatory agencies to find day-to-day protection from corporate offenders.

The primary problem facing victims in this process if their concerns are heard, the protection of victims must first focus on determining what causes harm and to what degree. Put another way, health effects and exposure limits must be determined before regulatory agencies can begin acting on corporations and other regulated entities (in the United States, sources of pollution can be roughly divided into stationary sources, such as power plants and non-stationary sources, such as cars, chemical spills, etc., or sometimes referred to as point and non-point sources). Then the agency has to create rules, monitor pollution, but they themselves cannot bring criminal charges if malfeasance is discovered.

The Environmental Protection Agency (EPA) was created to address long standing failures of state environmental agencies, but those same agencies often do most of the oversight and enforcement of federal laws today. Many state environmental agencies are openly supportive of industry (McDaniel, 2012). Given the high transactions costs of bringing criminal charges against a corporate polluter particularly in terms of time, money, and potential political pressure, this patchwork approach to environmental federalism means most crimes are handled as civil matters and negotiated through fines and consent decrees rather than lengthy criminal prosecutions, which are quite rare (Brickey, 2001; Daley and Layton, 2004; Ringquist, 1995). Engaging in criminal enforcement efforts can be very time-consuming, expensive from a budgetary and staffing standpoint, and may be unpopular with political principals (Mintz, 2012; Ringquist and Emmert, 1999; Uhlmann, 2009; Yeager, 1987). From this perspective, there is little wonder why environmental regulatory agencies are much quicker to levy administrative fines or negotiate settlements than pursue criminal sanctions against even against the worst offenders. Victims, particularly those in fenceline communities, are lucky to benefit indirectly from such enforcement actions, where they might get exposed to less pollution, due to increased monitoring, technology-forcing solutions that reduce pollution, or fines to deter pollution. Since most pollution has an insidious effect that builds up over time, it is extremely difficult to hold companies liable for their malfeasance towards victims, unless something blows up or causes immediate, direct harm.

Green victimization and the legal system

In the United States, aside from a few salient cases, the criminal prosecution of environmental violations at the federal level is a relatively recent development (Edwards et al., 1996). Prior to 1982, the federal government only prosecuted 25 environmental crimes (Campbell-Mohn et al., 1993). The recognition that environmental crimes necessitated a stronger response resulted in the creation of two key administrative units: the EPA's Office of Environmental Enforcement (1981) and in 1982 the DOJ's Environmental Crimes Section (ECS; Cooney, 2006; Devaney, 1994). The EPA has the power to investigate, but not prosecute environmental crimes. To do so, the agency must rely on federal prosecutors to take up the case and charge offenders. These prosecutors generally work for either the Office of the US Attorneys or the DOJ's Environmental Crime Section, housed within the agency's Environment and Natural Resource Division (ENRD). As Williams (1998: 160) notes, "environmental law has been slow to embrace environmental victimization."

Environmental criminals benefit from this system. Knowing that agencies operate from a transactions cost approach, corporate offenders realize that regulators do not wish to engage in a protracted legal battle. It can be extremely difficult to prosecute environmental offenders, particularly well-funded corporate entities that can file extensive motions, prolong cases, and diffuse authority through their organization to protect high-level employees. In these cases, corporate offenders need not seriously fear prosecution of their key managers and executives and may see litigation with the government as the cost of doing business. In some cases, they simply pay fines and penalties to avoid upgrading costly equipment or complying with environmental laws. Coal-fired power plant operators have engaged in decades-long litigation in the United States to avoid expensive stack-scrubbers that reduce SO_2 from smokestacks, which is not an uncommon practice among large corporations to delay compliance through protracted legal action. In other instances, corporate environmental criminals may simply litigate to wait for an incoming presidential administration that is more sympathetic. There is little doubt that more than a few corporate offenders currently under investigation or involved in active litigation with the US government patiently waited out the Obama administration for the incoming Trump administration, given that Trump has noted its environmental deregulation intent (Lynch et al., 2017).

Legal recognition of victims

In the US legal system victims are often sidelined and act as spectators. While the state investigates and brings charges in a criminal case, victims, if known, are often part of the process, but do not direct the process or outcomes. That point was well summarized in *Kenna v. US District Court*, which stated that victims should be "seen, but not heard."

The idea that victims should have an expanded role in their own defense began to evolve in the United States along the lines of the broader Civil Rights movement in the 1960s. In the United States the victims' rights movement began to bring together an odd pairing of left-leaning civil rights activists, with conservative, law and order proponents in the 1980s and 1990s. The former wanted to expand the concept of civil rights to the rights of crime victims, whereas the latter wanted individuals to be able to play a greater role in the punishment of offenders. Arguably the first very salient case where victims and their legal team pushed for representation was the bombing of the Alfred P. Murrah federal building in Oklahoma City in 1995 and the subsequent criminal trial.

This movement coalesced in legislation passed in 2004, the Crime Victims' Rights Act (CVRA) as part of the broader Justice for All Act (JFAA). The passage of the CVRA represented a broader shift in the idea that victims have rights within the court system and should be able to play a broader role (Beloof, 2006; Cassell and Joffee, 2011). The CVRA maintains eight fundamental or basic rights for victims within the court system (18 USC, 2004):

(1) "to be reasonably protected from the accused"
(2) "to reasonable, accurate, and timely notice of any public court proceeding, or any parole proceeding, involving the crime or of any release or escape of the accused"
(3) "not to be excluded from any such public court proceeding, unless the court, after receiving clear and convincing evidence, determines that testimony by the victim would be materially altered if the victim heard other testimony at that proceeding"
(4) "to be reasonably heard at any public proceeding in the district court involving release, plea, sentencing, or any parole proceeding"
(5) the "reasonable right to confer with the attorney for the Government in the case"
(6) "to full and timely restitution as provided in law"
(7) "to proceedings free from unreasonable delay"

(8) "to be treated with fairness and with respect for the victim's dignity and privacy"

In essence, the CVRA affords a series of procedural rights within the court system, particularly, the rights to be heard and to confer with the prosecuting attorney in the case (Jarrell and Ozymy, 2012). Arguably, the primary intent of the CVRA was to expand rights to victims of street crime and not environmental crime. With environmental crimes, particularly corporate environmental crimes, victims are often sidelined because punishments are negotiated between the state and offenders. A few legal cases have begun opening up space in the US legal system to give green crime victims a role in this process. The courts are beginning to recognize that corporate environmental criminals and the crimes they commit produce widespread victimization.

One of the first legal cases to test the CVRA in the United States was *United States v. BP Products*, where an explosion at the company's refinery in Texas City killed 15 and injured 180 (CSB, 2008). The Occupational Safety and Health Administration charged BP with 17 serious and 301 willful violations. In the case, BP pled guilty to a knowing violation of the CAA and paid a fine ($87 million was levied; BP agreed to pay $50.6 million, and contested $30.7 million of the levied fines). The company was found to have failed to engage in systematic maintenance and upgrades for years at the plant to save money, which put their workers at risk. This was a practice that developed as the company expanded their market presence and wished to save money by deferring expensive maintenance at the facility (Frontline, 2010). The prosecutors and court decided to notify the victims of the case after a plea deal with the offender had been negotiated. About a week prior to the press conference announcing the settlement, victims petitioned the court to be informed of the deal, with some victims arguing against the deal as too lenient (Coon, 2010; Jarrell and Ozymy, 2012). The court did not grant the victims these rights under the CVRA, but felt their ability to enter victim impact statements to the court was sufficient.

In *United States v. W. R. Grace & Co.* the DOJ brought charges against the company for improper disposal and release of asbestos, as well as a series of other charges. In this famous case, the company mined vermiculite near Libby, Montana, for over three decades and exposed much of the city and its residents, causing widespread asbestos-related illnesses. After some 270,000 lawsuits over the health-related consequences of its practices, the company filed for bankruptcy in 2001 (Jarrell and Ozymy, 2012). In this case, the government prosecutors planned to call victims as witnesses in the case, but not until this issue was sent to the Ninth Circuit Court of Appeals for review where the appeal sought to allow residents to be recognized as environmental victims under the CVRA.

In 2006 in Corpus Christi, Texas, CITGO Petroleum and CITGO Refining and Chemicals Co. (the former is the parent company) were charged under the CAA and Migratory Bird Treaty for knowingly using open tanks as oil-water separators, which released volatile organic compounds, including benzene, into neighboring communities. In the case, the prosecution had victims in the nearby communities fill out victim impact statements and petition the court to be considered victims under the CVRA. After a lengthy trial and sentencing that was delayed for almost a decade, the court declared some of these individuals that had been exposed to these harmful air emissions were victims under the CVRA.

All three of these cases involve victims of corporate-environmental crimes. All three begin to show the evolution, at least in the United States, of how a nascent body of case law is beginning to recognize victims of these crimes, as well as an interest in the academic and legal literatures (Atkins, 2010; Baldas, 2009; Cassell and Joffee, 2011; Levine, 2010; Starr, Flack and Foley, 2009; Uhlmann, 2009). They also illustrate the difficulty of prosecuting green victims in the legal system (Ozymy and Jarrell, 2017b). These cases demonstrate the difficulty of victims having some standing to be recognized as victims by the court, as well as the extreme difficulties of stating the obvious – that even when the courts find corporations guilty or the government prosecutes them for their offenses (even this is hard, as the CITGO conviction in the case was overturned on appeal), the courts are generally unwilling to recognize individuals living near heavy industry who are being systematically victimized by corporations in criminal cases. In the Grace case, for example, the EPA (2009) declared the area a public health emergency, and over a quarter of a million civil lawsuits were filed, but the company and its officers were able to escape criminal prosecution. While this is an extreme example, especially given the extent of the victimization and media attention paid to the case, it is not an uncommon exemplar of how green victims are systematically victimized by corporate offenders and, even in the best of cases, how corporate environmental criminals and their officers are able to escape serious criminal punishment.

The CITGO conviction created an important legal precedent when it recognized that an illegal emission from a refinery victimized the fenceline community next door. Generally recognizing green victims is difficult, because drawing connections between the offense and the outcome is scientifically and practically difficult, if not impossible in many cases. For example, in the case of air pollution, the prosecution must be able to prove that the harmful emissions measured in a neighborhood and which are affecting individuals are being released by a particular facility. The CITGO case is notable because the judge, after significant pressure, allowed the prosecution to enter into evidence at sentencing, the content of victim impact statements. This came after an uncommonly long period of about seven years from conviction to sentencing. During this time petitions were issued to declare individuals victims under the CVRA. The judge granted the motion and allowed the prosecution to collect these statements and victims to enter testimony at sentencing.

Analysis and findings

What follows in this section is an analysis of 19 victim impact statements presented at sentencing. In this analysis, we use the content of the statements to allow the victims' testimony to illustrate how they perceive their own victimization in this context. The data for this analysis came from two sources. One of the authors was present during the proceedings and took notes related to each victims' impact statement. In addition, following the trial, copies of the court transcript containing the testimony of each victim was purchased to use in more specific analysis.

Victim testimony was recorded on their victim impact statements. Testimony was given beginning at 9:00 a.m. (CST) on October 13, 2013. Mechanical stenography and computer-assisted transcription were used in the courtroom. The docket was C-06–563, *United States v. CITGO Petroleum.* This represents the final sentencing hearing with Howard Stewart representing the Environmental Crime Section of the Department of Justice. Also in attendance were Special Agent De'Montra Rainey (US EPA), Criminal Investigator Roger Potts (Texas Commission on Environmental Quality), Dan Smith (FBI), two victim-witness specialists from the US Attorney's Office, and the EPA's assistant director of the Office of Environmental Justice and Tribal Affairs. CITGO was represented by Dick DeGuerin, Catherine Baen, in-house counsel, and the plant manager was also present. Nineteen community victims were in attendance and were represented by Paula Pierce, Texas Legal Services Center. The victims were invoking their right to address the court under the CVRA.

The testimony from these 19 victims tells a sad story of chronic illness, fear, and hopelessness living next to heavy industry. These statements also provide a strong narrative of anger towards the refineries and assign responsibility for CITGO's negligence. In Table 12.1, we summarize the primary themes that emerged from these victim impact statements and participant observation in the courtroom in descending order of magnitude expressed in their testimony. We then provide examples of sub-themes that emerged. After the table we provide a narrative description of each victim. Direct quotes from their testimony are given as needed to allow the victims' voices to come through.

In Table 12.1, we collapsed subject areas described by victims into responses: negative health effects, fear, loss, injustice, lack of safety, anger, and mental

Table 12.1 Common themes that emerged in the victims' testimony

General theme	*Sub-theme/examples*
Negative health effects	Respiratory illness/asthma/cancer
Fear	Unable to escape/can't work
	Not living a normal life anymore
Loss	Family members died of cancer
	Children are still getting sick
Injustice compensation	CITGO is negligent and should pay
	People should be relocated
Lack of safety property	Flares and explosions common/debris on
	Chemical smells are chronic/must protect house
Anger warnings	CITGO is responsible/they don't care/no
Mental health problems	Anxiety/depression/suicidal thoughts

health problems. These seven major areas incorporated 19 sub-themes expressed by victims. Given that these are qualitative categories derived from victims' statements, it is possible that the categories presented here are not definitive, that other categories could be extracted, and that the names of the categories might be altered to depict different groupings or to alter how these categories describe the summaries of the victim's statements. Thus, some caution should be taken when interpreting the results in Table 12.1.

The content of victim's individual statements

The first victim lived in the Hillcrest neighborhood since 1996 (about 18 years at the time of giving testimony). She has a son and daughter that lived there, as well as parents that have since passed away; she lives four blocks from CITGO. She reports upper respiratory infections, chronic obstructive pulmonary disease (COPD), Boeck's sarcoid, and sinus infections, and also that bronchial washes are common. She is afraid and wants to get out. We find in her testimony that she feels she has lost her sense of security, ability to protect her children and herself from harm, experiences chronic illness, and has lost her job in the past as a result of her recurring and protracted illnesses. She expresses poignantly the horror she experiences living here and how she sees the large companies next door at fault:

> Your Honor, we were probably the first ones to smell them, experience them, feel them. The burning on your skin, the inability to breathe correctly. Your eyes – you couldn't see. Your eyes would water. It has been pure torture . . . All you did was wake up one day, and these monster companies that could have done better, wanted to skim the money – I don't know whose pockets it went into – but they didn't pay for our safety. We were there. They knew there were there. And they knew that there were children there.

The second victim is disabled and has lived in the area for "many years," and has also worked near CITGO. Her poor health prevents her from working and she experiences chronic respiratory problems, nosebleeds, headaches, and other breathing problems. She wants compensation for her illnesses and inability to work that stems from her health problems she feels were caused by CITGO.

The third victim is 61 years old and grew up and lived in Hillcrest roughly her whole life (51 years). She also has breathing problems and felt this was a good neighborhood before CITGO moved in; she feels she did not have health problems at first, but these have developed over time. She complains CITGO never warns them of what is happening at the plant or if they are in any danger.

The fourth victim to testify has lived in the area 38 years. His father passed away from lung cancer even though he never drank or smoked cigarettes. He himself reports chronic breathing problems and takes medication and his mother had chronic bronchitis and asthma and lived with portable oxygen until she died – he blames CITGO for these outcomes. He feels his life is not normal because of his chronic dependence on medication and doctors. He also has suicidal thoughts and anxiety. His nieces and nephews that live here have breathing problems. He explains the pain of losing his mother:

> It was hard watching my mother, you know, suffer you know, month in and month out, year in and year out, going to the ER, emergency room and convalescent home for breathing problems, memory loss, she was losing weight, vomiting and nose bleeds.

The fifth victim has lived in the area since 1959, only three blocks from CITGO. She is 84 years old. Her children grew up here, but they have myriad health problems and she makes the connection between living near industry and their ailments. Both she, her daughter, and son have cancer, and her youngest son died in 2003 from kidney, liver, and heart problems. Her grandchildren experience burning nose and eye problems. She has lived here prior to much of the refinery development and explains what it is like to live one's life and raise a family in this polluted environment:

> It hasn't been easy living in Hillcrest. I got there in '59, before a lot of the refineries were built, I guess, or those big tanks weren't there, now they're there. So that's the life in the Hillcrest. Everybody you talk to goes through the same problems, same problem, burning nose, burning throat and that's not a healthy place to be, but if you're stuck there, you're stuck there. What can you do, sir? . . . It has never been easy, not for me, not for the rest of the people that live there.

The sixth victim has a similar story of long-term residence (38 years), cancer killed her husband, and like others, she has experienced financial loss from medical problems in the community. She gives a heartfelt description of her love and loss due to brain cancer:

> He was an excellent provider, he was a father, he was a grandfather, he was a son. He was a brother and most of all, my husband of 41 years and my partner. He was a veteran in the Korean War, a Purple Heart recipient, and totally disabled at the time of his death. For nine years prior to his death. I watched his health fade away. The last years of his life the doctors told me he had approximately two to 12 months to live. I literally watched him die day-by-day, one day at a time. The love and pain I feel will never go away and I still feel and miss him every day. He had COPD that required daily medication and treatment, as well as oxygen. Our medical and other related costs took all our life savings, my inheritance as well as refinancing my home.

Victims 7–10 are all long-time residents of Hillcrest. Victims 9 and 10 are mother and daughter. All experience fear from explosions and have respiratory problems and other ailments. Victim 10 grew up in Hillcrest and is in poor health. She explains her health and that history briefly:

> I have breathing problems, even voice change at times. When I wake up in the morning I sometimes have a problem catching my breath. I have breathing problems from the fumes of the refinery. I also have shortness of breath. Sometimes I strain to talk. And my plants, my trees, flowers, have all turned black, have all turned black and will die out. I feel I suffer psychologically and emotionally injuries and problems. I lost my mother, sister and brother to cancer, unexplained cancer for my mother and sister. They lived in Hillcrest for years. I believe the plant is responsible for the cancer because of the chemicals they let out into the air.

Victims 11–16 all reported health problems. They claim watery eyes, asthma, and other breathing problems, which are common ailments for those living in Hillcrest. Explosions and strange smells are common. For one victim, a medical doctor told her the chemical contamination was to blame for her health problems.

The 17th victim is represented by Paula Pierce and former federal district court judge Paul Cassell. She was a cross-country runner and would often run past CITGO when training. She lived across the freeway with her sister and two nieces from 1993–1999. She has enlarged lymph nodes on the back of her throat, chronic laryngitis, and since smelling a "sweet smell" (often attributed to benzene) one day after running nearby has been struck with chronic asthma and migraines. She lived with her sister who also had respiratory problems. She explains what it is like living with these ailments and feels CITGO is negligent and responsible:

> Right now I have a job that only gives me 12 hours a week because I'm afraid to find a full-time job and get fired again. Between the migraines, the chronic laryngitis, throat infections, anxiety and depression, it's beyond difficult to live a normal life. It angers me that a company would knowingly put so many people's lives and also at risk this for profit. . . . I don't know what other ailments that I may have in the future because of what I was exposed to. I would like for Citgo to be find for its negligence and for running people's lives and also at risk. I would also like restitution for myself for what I have suffered, if not what they have done myself, my sister, my family members and my neighbors would all be able to live normal lives.

Victim 18 has lived across the freeway from CITGO since 1990. She reported that she cannot sleep, and that she exposed to "horrible" smells in and around her home and property. Documents also note that she suffers from cancer of the nose. When she has called the police about the smells, they tell her it is from the refineries. One time she heard a large explosion and her house cracked. She received a voucher for a free car wash afterward, due to the fallout from the refinery.

The final victim is 45 years old. She lived in the D. N. Leathers Housing Project from 1993–2003 and grew up in the area. She experiences chronic itchy eyes, breathing problems, and body rashes. She feels that living here is a dangerous place, and notes that she sees the sky lit up with the orange flame (likely an oil flare being burnt at night). She would like to be relocated, but does not have the funds. She explains what it is like being trapped in such a place:

> We had nowhere to run, we had nowhere to go. We couldn't jump up and move because we didn't have the money to move. So, we suffered right along with the rest of the people who lived around there. . . . And, Your Honor, it was just a bad ordeal. It was a nightmare to live down there. Like I said, we had nowhere else to go. Nobody offered us no kind of help and we suffered, and we suffered, and we suffered. As school kids going to school every morning, standing at the bus-stop inhaling all daily gas, it was just horrible. And I feel like nobody should ever have to go [through] something like that ever again. Ever. It's just a nightmare. And still to this day, I still suffer from that. I still suffer from the headaches, the irritating throat, the watery eyes, especially when I go on that side of town to visit family members, and I try not to go over there that much, but I have family that live over there, and I have to go see about my family. And every time I go over there, it's the same result over and over and over and over. It's a bad place to be. It is a horrible place to live. It's a nightmare and nobody deserves that at all, Your Honor. After I moved away from there, I started feeling a little bit better, but then when I go see my momma, she was living down there at times, there it goes again; same thing, irritating throat, stomach ache, diarrhea, throwing up.

She concludes with advice to the judge that nicely summarizes how he and others could appreciate what it is like to live like her:

> It's just horrible. Your nose starts burning. It's just horrible, Your Honor. My mom moved to get away from that. She moved to another state. And she's doing a lot better now since she moved to Oklahoma, a whole lot better, Your Honor, but she won't come to Corpus Christi for nothing because of refineries. That's where my family lives, and there's still family still down there who you are still suffering, Your Honor. . . . But like I said, you get up and go down there one Monday morning and just sit there for a while. You'll start smelling that gas and you'll understand what I'm saying. You'll say Mr. Beasley is right. This needs to be a put a stop to. So these refineries are responsible for this. And they need to compensate us and they need to take care of us.

These narratives demonstrate the primary themes that emerged in the analysis. The most common problem is negative health effects from living near the refinery, particularly breathing and respiratory problems. Many victims report having cancer or having lost family members to it.

It is common for victims to experience feelings of fear and helplessness both by living near a dangerous industrial complex and the flares, smells, debris, and explosions that shake their homes and for their inability to afford to leave. They demonstrate a profound sense of hopelessness or as one victims states they are "not living a normal life anymore." There is a profound sense of loss for family members that have passed on these same diseases and children, friends, or young relatives that live in the community that will likely experience the same ailments if they live here long enough. This loss appears to be magnified by the sense of fear that is pervasive concerning their health and inability to leave that has left some with mental health problems, such as depression, anxiety, or thoughts of suicide.

While fearful and sick, many residents acknowledge a great sense of injustice imposed on them by CITGO and living in a fenceline community. Many feel the company does not care about them, does not issue sufficient warnings to them concerning their safety, and has been negligent. Many residents hold them responsible for their poor health and feel they should be paid compensation and/or relocated.

Conclusion

The relationship between the state and corporations helps to create and reproduce environmental crime victims. A lack of resources, combined with political pressure and diffuse responsibilities creates an overburdened legal-regulatory complex that is ill-equipped to sufficiently protect the public victims of environmental crime (Ozymy and Jarrell, 2015a, 2015b). The first step forward in helping victims is to acknowledge green crimes and associated state-corporate environmental crimes as real crimes with real victims. According to Anthony Pemberton "transformation of the crime frame" is essential if we want to draw attention to green victimization. Understanding the visual nature of green crimes and the victims they produce should become more of a focus for not only green criminology, but the field of criminology in general (Natali, 2016). Corporations and the state have resources to challenge, deflect, deny and avoid responsibility (Pemberton, 2014). "Apart from making the victims more visible, it is important to engage them and see them as local stakeholders with a potential role to play in environmental governance" (Bisschop, 2014: 180).

Human victims of green crime are rarely asked what they want and what they need as a result of their victimization (Hall, 2012, 2013). Empirical research that involves asking victims about their victimization is necessary within the field of green criminology to help fill this gap and provide empirical data about victims' perceptions of their victimization. Not only will we gain a better understanding of green victimization, we will gain a better appreciation of how to respond to such victimization. For example, some victims may simply want "respectful treatment, information, understanding and an apology as opposed to retributive outcomes" (Hall, 2013: 98). Victims who have suffered from a range of health and economic consequences are likely to want monetary compensation and restitution, while other victims desire to be relocated away from the source of the harm. In order for human victims of environmental crimes to have a better role in the court system, the courts should recognize them as victims under the law and accord them the rights they deserve. The courts should build on the legal precedent recognizing green victims described here. This will helps court actors understand how and why victims are produced by living in proximity to industrial sites, and more generally when an environmental criminal is known to violate the law. This will help the courts provide better compensate for the victims of green crimes.

The fact that victims in a fenceline community were recognized in the CITGO case creates a strong legal precedent to recognize similar cases in the future under the CVRA. The primary benefit here for EJ communities is that we are creating case law behind the idea of fenceline communities as victims. This creates a precedent for other victims to speak and their voices to be acknowledged in their community and on the public record. That Act does not guarantee recognized victims the right to restitution, but it does give them the right to be heard and reasonably informed at trial. Acknowledging them as victims sets the stage for potential civil litigation, where enterprising trial lawyers may find it in their self-interest to represent such communities. There is already a small cottage industry dedicated to filling civil rights lawsuits (lawyers contacted us on numerous occasions to see if there was a financial interest in building such civil rights cases) and trying to collect damages, but legal recognition of victims in criminal cases is arguably an equal, if not stronger precedent, that victims may deserve civil restitution.

The victims in the CITGO case report myriad health problems they associate with living in the area, particularly chronic respiratory problems. Many live within a short walk to the refinery complex. While they fear this is not a safe place to live, they experience hopelessness over their inability to afford to move. Flaring, explosions, debris, and chemical smells are common. A pattern of illness that runs through families, such as respiratory disease and cancer are prevalent. Many of the victims hold CITGO responsible and feel they are negligent in releasing emissions that have poisoned their community and that they should pay compensation or relocate them away from harm. Such powerful narratives provide a rather cohesive account of the negative emotions and health effects one can experience living in a fenceline community.

References

Atkins, A. 2010. A Complicated Environment: The Problem with Extending Victims' Rights to Victims of Environmental Crimes. *Washington and Lee Law Review*, 67(4), 1623–1658.

Baldas, T. 2009. Is Crime Victims' Rights Law being Misused in Environmental Cases? *National Law Journal*, April 28.

Beirne, P. and South, N., eds. 2007. *Issues in Green Criminology: Confronting Harms against Environments, Humanity, and Other Animals*. Portland, OR: Willan Publishing.

Beloof, D. E. 2006. Judicial Leadership at Sentencing under the Crime Victims' Rights Act: Judge Kozinski in Kennaand Judge Cassell in Degenhardt. *Federal Sentencing Reporter*, 19(1), 36–43.

Bisschop, L. 2014. Illegal E-Waste Transport: Exploring Their Harmfulness, Scale Social Organization and Governance. In T. Spapens, R. White, and M. Kluin (eds.). *Environmental Crime and Its Victims: Perspectives within Green Criminology*. Surrey, England: Ashgate.

Brickey, K. F. 2001. Charging Practices in *Hazardous Waste* Crime Prosecutions. *Ohio State Law Journal*, 62, 1077–1124.

Campbell-Mohn, C., Breen, B., and Futrell, J. W. 1993. *Sustainable Environmental Law*. St. Paul, MN: West.

Cassell, P. G. and Joffee, S. 2011. The Crime Victims' Expanding Role in a System of Public Prosecution: A Response to the Critics of the Crime Victims' Rights Act. *Northwestern University Law Review Colloquy*, 105, 164–183.

Coon, B. W. 2010. Letter to Judge Rosenthal on Behalf of Victims in United States v. BP, May 6, 2010.

Cooney, J. F. 2006. Multi-Jurisdictional and Successive Prosecution of Environmental Crimes: The Case for a Consistent Approach. *Journal of Criminal Law and Criminology*, 96, 435–464.

Daley, D. M. and Layton, D. F. 2004. Policy Implementation and the Environmental Protection Agency: What Factors Influence Remediation at Superfund Sites? *Policy Studies Journal*, 32, 375–392.

Devaney, E. E. 1994. *The Evolution of Environmental Crimes Enforcement at the United States Environmental Protection Agency*. Paper Presented at the Third International Conference of Environmental Enforcement. Oaxaca, Mexico.

Edwards, S. M., Edwards, T. D., and Fields, C. B. 1996. *Environmental Crime and Criminality: Theoretical and Practical Issues*. New York: Garland Publishing, Inc.

Environmental Protection Agency. 2009. *EPA Announces a Public Health Asbestos Superfund Site*. Retrieved from www.epa.gov/region8/superfund/libby/phe.html. Last Accessed: June 13, 2018.

Frontline. 2010. *The Spill?* Retrieved from www.pbs.org/wgbh/pages/frontline/the-spill/ Last Accessed: June 13, 2018.

Jarrell, M. L. and Ozymy, J. 2012. Real Crime, Real Victims: Environmental Crime Victims and the Crime Victim's Rights Act (CVRA). *Crime, Law, and Social Change*, 58, 373–389.

Jarrell, M. L. and Ozymy, J. 2014. Few and Far between: Understanding the Role of the Victim in Federal Environmental Crime Cases. *Crime, Law, and Social Change*, 61, 563–584.

Hall, M. 2012. Environmental Victims: Challenges for Criminology and Victimology in the 21st Century. *Journal of Criminal Justice and Security*, 13(4), 371–391.

Hall, M. 2013. *Victims of Environmental Harm: Rights, Recognition and Redress under National and International Law*. London and New York: Routledge.

Levine, D. 2010. Public Wrongs and Private Rights: Limiting the Victim's Role in a System of Public Prosecution. *Northwestern University Law Review*, 104, 335–361.

Lynch, M. J. 1990. The Greening of Criminology: A Perspective on the 1990s. *The Critical Criminologist*, 2(3), 1–4 and 11–12.

Lynch, M. J., Stretesky, P. B., Long, M. A., and Barrett, K. L. 2017. Concerns with Social and Environmental Justice, Environmental Pollution and Destruction, and the Trump Presidency: A Criminological View. *Social Justice: A Journal of*

Crime, Conflict & World Order Online. Retrieved from www.socialjusticejournal.org/social-justice-environmental-destruction-and-the-trump-presidency-a-criminological-view/

McDaniel, J. 2012. The 2012 Election is a Critical One for Keeping Environmental Protections in Place. *EMagazine*, July/August: 18–26.

Mintz, J. A. 2012. EPA Enforcement of CERCLA: Historical Overview and Recent Trends. *Southwestern Law Review*, 41, 645–659.

Natali, L. 2016. *A Visual Approach to Green Criminology*. London: Palgrave.

Ozymy, J. and Jarrell, M. L. 2015a. Wielding the Green Stick: An Examination of Criminal Enforcement at the EPA under the Bush and Obama Administrations. *Environmental Politics*, 24, 38–56.

Ozymy, J. and Jarrell, M. L. 2015b. Corporate Environmental Crime and Environmental Victimization: Exploring New Legal Precedents for Securing Recognition and Restitution for Environmental Justice Communities. *Environmental Justice*, 8, 47–50.

Ozymy, J. and Jarrell, M. L. 2016. Why Do Regulatory Agencies Punish? The Impact of Political Principals, Agency Culture, and Transaction Costs in Predicting Environmental Criminal Prosecution Outcomes in the United States. *Review of Policy Research*, 33, 71–89.

Ozymy, J. and Jarrell, M. L. 2017a. Red State, Blue State, Green State: Analyzing the Geography of Federal Environmental Crime Prosecutions within and across the U.S. States. *Palgrave Communications*, 3, 1–11.

Ozymy, J. and Jarrell, M. L. 2017b. Implementing a Partial Buyout of an Environmental Justice Community. *Environmental Justice*, 10, 43–50.

Pink, G. 2013. *Law Enforcement Responses to Transnational Environmental Crime: Choices, Challenges, and Culture*. Transnational Environmental Crime Project Working Paper 4. Canberra, Australia: Australian National University.

Ringquist, E. J. 1995. Political Control and Policy Impact in EPA's Office of Water Quality. *American Journal of Political Science*, 39, 336–363.

Ringquist, E. J. and Emmert, C. E. 1999. Judicial Policymaking in Published and Unpublished Decisions: The Case of Environmental Civil Litigation. *Political Research Quarterly*, 52, 7–37.

Ruggiero, V. 2013. The Environment and Crimes of the Economy. In N. South and A. Brisman (eds.). *Routledge International Handbook of Green Criminology*. London and New York: Routledge.

Simpson, S., Gibbs, C., Rorie, M., and Slocum, L. A. 2013. Empirical Assessment of Corporate Environmental Crime: Control Strategies. *Journal of Criminal Law and Criminology*, 103(1), 231–278.

South, N., Brisman, A., and Beirne, P. 2013. A Guide to a Green Criminology. In N. South and A. Brisman (eds.). *Routledge International Handbook of Green Criminology*. London and New York: Routledge.

Starr, Judson W., Brian L. Flack, and Allison D. Foley. 2009. A new intersection: Environmental crimes and victims' rights. *Natural Resources & Environment*, 23(3), 41–49.

Uhlmann, D. M. 2009. Environmental Crime Comes of Age: The Evolution of Criminal Enforcement in the Environmental Regulatory Scheme. *Utah Law Review*, 4, 1223–1252.

U.S. Chemical Safety Board (CSB). 2008. *Anatomy of a Disaster*. Retrieved from www.csb.gov/videos/anatomy-of-a-disaster Last Accessed: June 13, 2018.

Williams, C. 1998. *Environmental Victims: New Risks: New Injustice*. London: Earthscan.

Yeager, P. C. 1987. Structural Bias in Regulatory Law Enforcement: The Case of the U.S. Environmental Protection Agency. *Social Problems*, 34, 330–344.

Index

FSC
www.fsc.org
MIX
Papier | Fördert
gute Waldnutzung
FSC® C083411

Kolibri 360 GmbH
Ferdinand-Jühlke-Straße 7
99095 Erfurt, Deutschland
produktsicherheit@kolibri360.de